The Contested Murder of
Latasha Harlins

The Contested Murder of Latasha Harlins

Justice, Gender, and the Origins of the LA Riots

BRENDA E. STEVENSON

OXFORD
UNIVERSITY PRESS

OXFORD
UNIVERSITY PRESS

Oxford University Press is a department of the University of Oxford.
It furthers the University's objective of excellence in research, scholarship,
and education by publishing worldwide.

Oxford   New York
Auckland   Cape Town   Dar es Salaam   Hong Kong   Karachi
Kuala Lumpur   Madrid   Melbourne   Mexico City   Nairobi
New Delhi   Shanghai   Taipei   Toronto

With offices in
Argentina   Austria   Brazil   Chile   Czech Republic   France   Greece
Guatemala   Hungary   Italy   Japan   Poland   Portugal   Singapore
South Korea   Switzerland   Thailand   Turkey   Ukraine   Vietnam

Oxford is a registered trade mark of Oxford University Press
in the UK and certain other countries.

Published in the United States of America by
Oxford University Press
198 Madison Avenue, New York, NY 10016

© Brenda E. Stevenson 2013

First issued as an Oxford University Press paperback, 2015.

Library of Congress Cataloging-in-Publication Data
Stevenson, Brenda E.
The contested murder of Latasha Harlins : justice, gender, and the origins
of the LA riots / Brenda E. Stevenson.
    pages   cm
ISBN 978-0-19-994457-6 (hardback : alk. paper); 978-0-19-023101-9 (paperback : alk. paper)
1. Du, Soon Ja—Trials, litigation, etc. 2. Harlins, Latasha—Trials, litigation, etc.
3. Trials (Murder)—California. I. Title.
KF224.D8S74   2013
345.794'025230979494—dc23   2012051021

9 8 7 6 5 4 3 2 1

Printed in the United States of America
on acid-free paper

Thank you God!

Contents

List of Illustrations

List of Tables

Preface

On the unseasonably cool, damp Saturday of March 16, 1991, at approximately 9:35 a.m., 15-year-old Latasha Harlins walked into the Empire Liquor Market located at 9172 South Figueroa Street in South Central LA. Within the course of five short minutes, she lay dying in front of the store's counter, bleeding from a single, close-range gunshot wound to the back of her head. Two neighborhood children ran away from the store in horror. The shop owner's wife, Soon Ja Du, sat crouched on top of the counter, trying to see where Harlins had fallen. The middle-aged woman's face already was beginning to swell and discolor from the brief, but violent, struggle between the two that began when the storekeeper accused her young customer of trying to steal a $1.79 bottle of orange juice. Two useless dollars meant to pay for the juice sat crumpled in the still girl's left hand.[1]

Latasha Harlins was shot and killed two weeks after the LAPD pulled Rodney King out of his car and patrolmen mercilessly whipped him.[2] The videotape of King's senseless beating riveted the world, casting Los Angeles in a stark, but typical, black and white racial, male construct. As painful as it was to watch, the racial dynamic behind the King beating, no matter how disturbing, has been such a fixture in American history that these types of events are almost predictable.

The black community was still digesting this latest version of the white lynch mob turned against black masculinity when another videotape, that of Soon Ja Du shooting Latasha Harlins in the back of the head as she turned to leave Du's store, hit the airwaves. The shooting was devastating; but it also was profoundly different from the usual violent scenarios across racial lines that typically garner public outrage. The people involved, Soon Ja Du and Latasha Harlins, were female, not male. Du was Korean, not white. She was a mother, wife, and shopkeeper, not a policeman, deputy sheriff, security guard, or domestic terrorist with a white sheet over his head. Latasha was killed midmorning with witnesses present, not in some isolated field or highway in the dark of the night. Her murder was not another challenge of black masculinity, that constant theme in the history of race in America. It underscored, instead, the vulnerability of the most defenseless in the nation's socially constructed hierarchy—women and children of the racially, culturally, economically, and politically marginalized.

Eight months after Latasha's death, Soon Ja Du, who had been convicted of voluntary manslaughter, sat quietly in a small, packed courtroom in downtown Los Angeles with her husband at her side. The change of venue for the case from Compton to downtown LA purportedly gave the advantage of a secure courtroom: bulletproof glass shielded the defendant, judge, and lawyers—physically and perhaps emotionally— from anguished and angry spectators alike, all who had come demanding justice.[3] That last eight months had written a telling tale of interracial misunderstanding in South Central Los Angeles, characterized by boycotts, heated public debates, private bitterness, Molotov cocktails, and convenience store murders. Despite the intervention of major civic, religious, and economic leaders from the black and Korean communities, it was clear that the situation between the two groups had continued to deteriorate. Everyone knew that the most immediate answer to this question of justice lay in the hands of the sentencing judge. Many believed that if Judge Joyce Karlin could render a sentence that left most feeling that justice had been served then, perhaps, the hostility and violence that had escalated with little abatement since Latasha's death would begin to dissipate.

Judge Karlin heard defense and prosecution statements as she waited to deliver the first sentence that she would render in a jury trial since she had taken the bench only a few months earlier.[4] Roxanne Carvajal, assistant district attorney, argued passionately for the convicted felon to receive the maximum prison sentence allowed—16 years. "Any other sentence, your honor, would create a perception in the mind of the community that young black children do not receive the full protection of the law."[5] Patricia Dwyer, the appointed representative of Probation Services, who interviewed Soon Ja Du before making a recommendation to the court, agreed that Du should receive the maximum sentence. Charles Lloyd, Du's veteran black attorney with a long and deep connection to LA Mayor Tom Bradley, argued, cajoled, reasoned, and preached, however, for his client to receive only probation. "It's a difficult call, but it would not be difficult if litigants were all black . . . all Korean or [all] white],"[6] he assured the judge. The courtroom was packed and tense as Judge Karlin began to read her sentencing statement.

It was soon apparent to those in court that day that Judge Joyce Karlin was not swayed by the prosecution's arguments that Soon Ja Du should receive the maximum sentence for killing Latasha Harlins. Karlin was not persuaded that Du should receive any jail time. Instead, the judge rendered a sentence that was one of the most lenient imposed on a felon convicted of voluntary manslaughter with the use of a gun in California that year: no jail time beyond what Du had served prior to her release on bail, payment of Latasha's funeral expenses, 300 hours of community service, and five years probation. What kind of "justice" was this, many, and not just in the black community, asked.

Contested Murder recaptures the details of Soon Ja Du's shooting of Latasha Harlins, her trial, Judge Karlin's sentencing logic, and the responses of various factions of the public to it. The *People v. Du* has both historic and contemporary significance. It was, after all, one of two legal cases whose outcomes led to the Los Angeles riots/uprising of 1992, the most deadly and costly race riot in United States history.

In late April 1992, the nation and the world turned its attention to a city on the brink of chaos. For the next five days, they watched in horror as thousands of Angelenos took to the streets to burn and loot, sometimes to assault and kill. "No justice, no peace!" was the anthem of the day as local blacks, Latinos/as, and even a sprinkling of Asian

Americans and whites joined in the five-day "rebellion" that purportedly erupted in response to the injustice of the Simi Valley verdict in
the Rodney King police brutality trial. But for many who actively participated in the protest, as well as in the looting and destruction, and
for the thousands who stayed at home but understood all too well why
others had gone, Rodney King was not the symbol of injustice that
catalyzed the protest—Latasha Harlins was.[7] Indeed, the uprising's slo-
gan, "No justice, no peace," was chanted by protestors at the Empire
Liquor Market immediately after Latasha was killed, a full year before
it became the catchphrase of the Los Angeles riots of 1992. And while
the Rodney King case has been immortalized in popular culture
through song and rap, so too has the death of Latasha Harlins. Ice
Cube's controversial "Black Korea" was a direct retort. Tupac, one of
the most important rappers of his generation, dedicated two songs to
the slain teen: "Hellrazor," and a moving ballad supporting poor black
women and their families, "Keep Ya Head Up." His words in "Hellrazor" captured the feelings of many who wondered at the tragic death of
"little" Latasha:

> Dear Lord if ya hear me, tell me why
> Little girl like LaTasha, had to die.[8]

Tupac also mentions Latasha in three other songs, including "That the
Way It Is" in which he links Rodney King and Latasha Harlins:

> Tell me what's a black life worth
> A bottle of juice is no excuse, the truth hurts . . .
> Ask Rodney, Latasha, and many more.[9]

Consider the consequences of the riots: 54 deaths, 2,300-plus injuries, 3,600 fires, 1,100 buildings destroyed, 4,500 businesses looted,
more than 12,000 persons arrested, and one billion dollars in total
damage. More than 2,300 Korean-owned shops were looted, damaged,
or destroyed because of this case.[10] It was an event so devastating that
Korean Americans have commemorated it with the simple phrase
"Sai-I-Gu"—April 29.

The cases involving Rodney King and Latasha Harlins, and their
attendant judicial processes, have tremendously different characteristics. King, a convicted felon, was driving drunk and eluding the police

in a full-on chase. Harlins was shopping in a neighborhood store. The LAPD badly beat King, but he recovered from most of his injuries. Du shot Latasha in the back of the head, killing her. The Simi Valley jury in the King case found the defendants not guilty. The downtown Los Angeles jury in the Du case found her guilty of voluntary manslaughter with special circumstances. Still the result of each trial was the same—none of the defendants were sentenced to jail time—"No justice, no peace."

An analysis of the *People v. Du* also has great significance because it sheds a unique light on the complicated places of women, historically and currently, in American society. It serves remarkably well as a case study that exposes the complexity of the female in the United States as part of distinct groups, but also in relationship to one another.[11] The gendered, racialized, classist, cultural, and generational aspects of this case are quite unique—unique enough to lend themselves to an examination of the sometimes overlapping, sometimes complementary, sometimes oppositional realities of late twentieth-century female life in urban America. All the case's leading actors, for example—the victim, the defendant, and the judge—were female. They were all from a different race or ethnicity: Du is Korean; Harlins was African American; and Karlin is Jewish. Each represented a somewhat different generation, and all three were from a different socioeconomic class—Du, a shopkeeper, was 49 when she was arrested; Latasha was a 15-year-old girl from the working class; and Karlin was a wealthy, 40-year-old judge whose father was a leading Hollywood insider.

What effects, indeed, did race/ethnicity, culture, class, age, gender, or a combination of some or all these variables have on any, or all, aspects of the case of the *People v. Du* and the questions of justice that emerged from it? Would Latasha Harlins have cursed at or struck a white or black shopkeeper? Would she have behaved this way if Mr. Du had been behind the counter that Saturday morning instead of his wife? Would Soon Ja Du have assumed that Latasha was stealing if the teen were white or Asian, or male, or adult? Would she have pulled a gun on an Asian or white adolescent, whether male or female? Or a black male? Would Latasha have turned and walked away if a white or black woman, or man, had pointed a gun at her? Would the Los Angeles District Attorney's Office have charged Soon Ja Du with first-degree murder with special circumstances—a potential death penalty felony—if she had not been an Asian woman? And her victim not a black girl? If Soon Ja had been male? If the beating of Rodney King had not exposed the LAPD's racist legacy to the world just two weeks before?

What about Judge Joyce Karlin, perhaps the most controversial of the three females. Would she have given Du a harsher punishment had the shopkeeper been of a different race? Or had she been male? Or younger? Or had a different occupation? If Latasha had not been black? If Karlin had not been Jewish? Were her actions, as judge, mere mimicry of what white male judges do when women of color come to their court-rooms, or did her gender or ethnicity have some influence on her decisions? Would she have been assigned this controversial case had she not been young, female, and inexperienced?

"Cultural" difference, a concept at the various intersections of race, class, gender, generation, and even geography, is also important to con-sider.[12] Embedded as culture is within the layered constructs of other socially significant variables and characteristics investigated here, it is sometimes especially difficult to assign what impact it has and/or had on the ways in which women interact with each other formally or infor-mally. It is clear, for example, that the US judiciary system has a cultural foundation rooted in Western ideals, philosophies, and conventions, in-cluding gender conventions. As such, one might imagine that a person's "place" and "treatment" in this system would depend, in part, on one's gendered and racial relationships to Western (European, US) patriar-chal cultures. Were the actions of these three females, singularly, or in relationship to one another, affected by their cultural backgrounds?

Questioning justice, of course, is a right many in American society exercise. It is a well-used, popular, and popularized freedom that is based, not only on the First Amendment to the Constitution that guar-antees everyone a right to express his or her opinions, but also on the principal of equal treatment under the law codified in the Fourteenth Amendment. Indeed, questioning justice has evolved into something of a fine art in the black community. Given the circumstances of this case in which a black child was harmed, it is not surprising that the African American community was the most vocal in their challenges to various decisions made in almost every phase of the case's development, presen-tation, and conclusion. Many believed that the judicial outcome of the criminal case against Soon Ja Du was predictable. That faction of the

African American community, having a general sense of a group history of legal and judicial injustices fueled by events during their lifetimes and those orally passed down through the generations, anticipated that there would be little justice had. Still, others in the community invested mightily in the legal avenues that they hoped would lead to an equitable ending. Were they naïve to do so?

A venerable coalition of politicians, activists, religious leaders, Harlins's family members, and grassroots organizers came together to advocate for justice for Latasha soon after her death. They remained active as the months passed between her shooting and Du's trial. They were still there on the day that Soon Ja Du left the courtroom, virtually a free woman, and they vowed to fight on for justice for Latasha. Traditional political black organizations, like the NAACP and the Urban League, lent assistance to the Harlins family and protested the sentencing. The family and their supporters formed their own activist organization—the Latasha Harlins Justice Committee (LHJC)—before the trial took place and made great strides in keeping the case in the public eye afterward. They helped persuade District Attorney Ira Reiner, for example, to appeal Karlin's sentencing of Du, held candlelight vigils, mounted protest rallies outside of Karlin's courtroom, petitioned the Justice Department to file a civil rights violation case against Soon Ja Du, and organized two petition campaigns to remove Karlin from the bench. But to what end?

Justice, it seems, was as slippery as wet stone when larger political or personal agendas were at stake. Grassroots political organizations like Danny Bakewell's Brotherhood Crusade (BC) and Mothers in Action (MIA), for example, quickly seized upon the tragedy and broadened its implications. They took a black nationalist, self-determination stance that included holding community business owners to a respectful protocol with their black customers on threat of losing their businesses. Black politicians like California Representative Patricia Moore, US Representative Maxine Waters, Compton Mayor Walter R. Tucker III, and Mark Ridley-Thomas (elected to the Los Angeles City Council shortly after the trial) protested the murder and the sentencing. Mayor Tom Bradley attempted to stay neutral, frustrating both the Harlins family and the Korean business lobby. Black church leadership acted not so much as individual entities, but as partners with other activist black groups. Some also became partners with Korean American churches to help ameliorate fears of a black upheaval. Latasha's family continued to worry, with little wonder, that justice for Latasha would get lost in it all—that once the cameras stopped rolling, the elections were won or lost, and businesses had exchanged hands, that no one would be left to pursue the long fight of justice for their loved one.

The black community, however, was not the only voice that doubted justice would be served. The Korean community also questioned the fairness of many aspects of the case, the media coverage, and public perception of what had occurred. They questioned whether Soon Ja Du was arrested and charged with first-degree murder as a scapegoat for the LAPD beating of Rodney King. Didn't Soon Ja, they argued, have a right to protect herself and her store if she felt violently threatened? They wondered whether Du could receive a fair trial in Compton, a predominantly black community that had a history of poor relations between black consumers and Korean shopkeepers.[13] They also wanted to know if the political cachet of black Americans in a city with a five-term black mayor would bend the blade of justice away from them.

Judge Joyce Karlin, who shared responsibility with the jury for delivering justice in *People* v. *Du*, seemed, to many observers, not only to question, but also to nullify the decision of the jury as well as the advice of the court-appointed probation officer. Why? The Jewish community, and other whites as well, remained relatively quiet about the case, but it assisted in her subsequent bid for reelection and supported her later career as a successful politician in Manhattan Beach. Did European American or Jewish communities have any stake in the verdict or sentencing? Ira Reiner, for example, the Jewish district attorney for Los Angeles at the time, fought desperately against Karlin's sentence of Du; he tried to have it overturned and threatened her career status as a judge. In the end, it was Reiner who lost his job. And what of the Bradley coalition that included a large contingent of Westside Jewish residents? Did Judge Karlin represent these interests in this case?

Contested Murder maintains that much about the outcome of this case can be understood when one examines closely the personal biographies and group histories of Latasha Harlins, Soon Ja Du, and Joyce Karlin. Their individual life stories, and those of their ancestors, are windows into their personal socializations and perspectives that must have affected the ways in which they regarded and responded to one other.

These histories illuminate the legal, social, economic, and cultural trajectories that eventually led Harlins, Du, and Karlin to encounter one another and laid the foundations for the terms of those encounters and their outcomes.

Even with history, however, the questions this case evokes are fraught with complexity and difficult methodological choices, particularly the ones related to women in the law. All women, with rare exception, are less likely to appear in legal documents, especially legal documents from earlier eras, than men, because the patriarchal bedrock of our society traditionally limited women's access to legal structures as victims, perpetrators, advocates, or assessors. Moreover, discussions of comparative experiences of females in the legal system across race, class, generation, and time are deeply hampered by disparities in available documentation. Consider, for example, some of the obstacles for studying the ancestors of Latasha Harlins and Soon Ja Du in the American legal system.

Since the large majority (more than 90%) of black females during the colonial and antebellum eras were enslaved—as were Harlins's family members in North Carolina, Alabama, and Mississippi—legal and judicial concerns of theirs, during 250 years of US history, were largely assumed and exercised by their owners, principally European American men of means. As African Americans, they were not citizens until 1868 and, as such, had no inherent right to protection under the law. Southern slave women could not testify against whites in a court of law. Nor did southern free black women have this right, even in cases that affected their children. Moreover, as women, their testimony against other blacks was considered less valid than that of black men. They were particularly vulnerable to sexual abuse by men of any race, partly because black women were considered debased and naturally promiscuous. No southern court, and few outside the South, for example, was willing to hear a case in which a white male was accused of raping a black woman, slave or free. Few, as well, took seriously a black woman's accusation of rape against a black man. Men, boys, and other women whipped, bludgeoned, burned, mutilated, and psychologically terrorized black women without fear of reproach, much less legal consequences, for much of their history. Even when rare cases reached the courts and were proven against perpetrators, justice was awarded to the slave's owner, not the slave woman, or girl, or her family. As crime victims, slave women's owners represented them because of their status as property. The courts' judgments in these cases, therefore, were based on the proven property harm to their masters, not on any personal harm done to the enslaved. Unfortunately, even the passing of the Fourteenth Amendment did little more than to establish Latasha Harlins's ancestors in the Deep South, and later in the Midwest, as quasi-equals before the law.[14]

The study of Asian American females within the context of the history of American law and legal traditions, on the other hand, is immediately hampered by their small numbers, due to legal and customary exclusion during much of the nation's history. It was not until 1965, with the passing of the Immigration and Naturalization Act, for example, that women from most areas of Asia, including Soon Ja Du's native Korea, were able to migrate in moderate numbers. Even so, the diversity of their actual populations; varied dates of arrival; places of concentration; labor experiences; and the native cultures of the Japanese, Korean, Chinese, Laotian, South Asian, Vietnamese, Cambodian, Filipino, and other Pacific Islander groups confound any attempt to speak generally of their experiences. What we do know about shared experiences, however, is that many of these women were located in households and communities where the reliance on Confucian traditions also minimized their relationships to legal systems and courts. Elders and males represented females and the young. Moreover, like black women, Asian women were doubly bound in the criminalization of their "exotic otherness." Few cases made it to court when these women were raped, beaten, or murdered. They were more likely to appear in court as defendants, accused of prostitution. Thus, as women of color, Asian and African American females had, like other American women, limited access to political, legal, economic, and educational resources. They also had other marginalizing factors to overcome, for example, social and cultural ones.

Jewish women, like Joyce Karlin, have been considered both white and nonwhite in US history and, therefore, their paths within the legal arenas have been less linear. Early in their history in the United States, these women, like Asian women, were confined to patriarchies that limited their presence in public institutions, including courts. Those who were criminalized, particularly among the first generations of immigrants from Eastern Europe at the turn of the twentieth century, whom Karlin's ancestors were a part of, too were accused largely of sex crimes. Still, more rapidly than Asian or black women, Jewish women were able to move to the other side of the bar to become a substantial portion of the early generations of female legal professionals and administrators after access to law school became less discriminatory against women. By the late twentieth century, Jewish and Asian women were much more likely to appear in a court as a legal professional or as a victim of crime. Black women, on the other hand, were much more likely to appear as a defendant accused of a crime, rather than as a victim, like Latasha.

While some women of color (blacks, Native Americans, and Latinas in particular) have not had access to protective legal systems, these systems have been successful in controlling their status and roles within society. An examination of the records of adults and youth incarcerated in the states and the nation, historically or presently, for example, fully documents that nonwhite women have been, and still are, disproportionately represented in female prison populations. The lopsided number of blacks and Latinas incarcerated is not just a regional phenomenon, but also a national one. African American females make up the majority of female prison populations in all but 11 of the 50 states. In 15 states, the population of black women in prison outnumbers whites from 10 to 35 times. Statistical analysis of incarceration rates indicates that in California, where the imprisonment rate of black women (18–64 years old) is only moderately high compared with some states, black females are almost seven times more likely to be incarcerated than white women. Latinas are a smaller portion of the prison population than black females, but still much higher than the proportion of white women incarcerated.[15] Could a person like Latasha Harlins—young, poor, female, and black—expect to be treated as a victim in the criminal justice system? Could we expect Soon Ja Du or Judge Karlin to envision her vulnerability, or her innocence, when their society, in general, did not?

This trend of incarceration, after all, is not only one that began early in the nation's history, but one that also begins early in the lives of minorities. Nationally, black youth are 2.1 times more likely to be incarcerated than white youth. Most persons doubtless would believe that the highest rates of minority population incarceration are in the South. In the past, they were. This was a result not only of the region's notoriously racist criminal justice system, but also because the majority of African Americans lived in the South. Decades of migration, however, shifted the axis of the black population both north and west, and the legal trends that had characterized their lives in the South followed them. While there still is some truth to the assumption that black incarceration rates are especially high in the South—Mississippi, Alabama, and Maryland do have particularly high rates of minority (especially black) incarceration—northern seaboard states actually have a larger percentage. In 2000, for example, the states with the highest percentage of their incarcerated identified as either black or Latino were New York and New Jersey (81% and 80% respectively).[16] Women were as much a part of this trend as men.

What one realizes here, however, is that the group histories of females in different races/ethnicities in the United States are both distinct and similar. Today, for example, people often speak of Asian Americans, including those of Korean descent, as the "model minority." A century ago, Asian immigrants were considered one of the racial banes of American society, so much so that they were excluded from migrating to the nation except under very particular circumstances. Jewish immigrants from Eastern Europe received the same xenophobic reception in the 1890s and early 1900s. A decade after World War II, however, Jewish Americans carried the mantle of the "model," although they still had to endure a great amount of suspicion and hesitation regarding their presence in economic, educational, and social arenas traditionally dominated by middle- and upper-class European American Christians—in country clubs and in leading universities, for example. African Americans, too, were not always viewed by everyone as the minority least likely to succeed. Whether it was DuBois's portrayal of an elite, educated Talented Tenth in the early twentieth century, rife with popularized images of hard work, success against the odds, good citizenship, and moral communalism or Booker T. Washington's insistence on a skilled proletariat who were law abiding, hardworking, family focused, and certain to abide by the racial etiquette of the day, African Americans emerged in some corners, at least a generation after the Civil War had ended, as able to contribute positively to American society. Of course, the tenth that

DuBois spoke of and to was hardly the large majority associated with other, "lighter" races and ethnicities considered "model minorities." Blacks always found themselves at the bottom in the public imagination when it came to hierarchies of achievement and influence. This generalized scenario, of course, is just that—generalized.

While it is not the first work on the subjects of women in the law, the comparative histories of American women, or the Los Angeles riots, what *Contested Murder* does do is to speak to the individualized experiences of the three primary females (Harlins, Du and Karlin), while placing their lives and experiences in a broader, historically driven discourse on race, gender, and other socially salient characteristics. It is only then that the question of justice, in this case at least—but hopefully with much broader applicability—can begin to be answered and understood in relationship to the Los Angeles riots of 1992.

Contested Murder is composed of seven chapters. Chapters 1, 2, and 5 recount the lives and group histories of the three main subjects: Latasha Harlins, Soon Ja Du, and Joyce Karlin respectively. Each of these chapters places the personal biographies and family histories of its principal subject within the historical context of their racial or ethnic group(s). This gendered historical analysis includes discussions of immigration and migration status, work trajectories, religious beliefs and practices, place(s) within the law, status within the racial hierarchy in the United States over time, and their relationships with other racialized groups. Chapters 2 and 5 also are somewhat comparative in nature. Chapter 2 includes, for example, comparative discussions on immigrant experiences in the US economy. There are as well sections on the historic relations between blacks and Asians generally, and Koreans more specifically. Chapter 5 comparatively examines the roles of women in education, the economy, and in the legal profession. It has a detailed analysis of the relationships among blacks, Asians, and Jews over time, realistically and in popular discourse. Chapter 3 details the encounter between Soon Ja Du and Latasha Harlins that led to Harlins's death and the varied responses of the black and Korean/Korean-American communities and the media and city government to Harlins's shooting. Chapter 6 focuses on Judge Karlin's sentencing of Du and her judicial reasoning. It also surveys the reactions to the sentencing within various racialized and legal communities, and the mounting, sometimes violent, protests against it. Chapter 7 examines the connections among Harlins's murder, Karlin's sentencing of Du, and the Los Angeles uprising/rebellion/riots of April and May 1992. An epilogue follows.

> The outcome of Latasha's case set in people's minds the concept that there was a different standard of justice in different communities, based on either race or class.
>
> —Joe Hicks, Executive Director, Los Angeles Southern
> Christian Leadership Conference, June 1992[17]

Acknowledgments

Thank you, God, for my many blessings!

Thank you, ancestors, for surviving the struggles!

I moved to Los Angeles in January 1991, to begin my career as a new assistant professor in the Department of History at UCLA. Three months after I arrived, Latasha Harlins was killed. I started thinking about this work almost immediately. It has taken a long time to get to this point, and I would not have been able to do so without tremendous support from all quarters of my personal and professional lives.

Research funding for this project has come from the University of California at Berkeley Chancellor's Office that extended to me a two-year postdoctoral fellowship when I was in the early stages of developing this work. UCLA has generously supported my research through the years with two Career Development Awards and funding through the Center for the Study of Women, the Academic Senate, and the Institute of American Cultures. The Division of the Social Sciences provided me with support for research assistants, travel, equipment, document and book purchases, and course releases while I served as the Chairs of History and Afro-American Studies. I also received other research support specifically from the Division of the Social Sciences during the deanship of Scott Waugh. I am enormously grateful to all.

As always, I would like to honor and thank my parents, the late James W. Stevenson and the late Emma Gerald Stevenson, who valued, nurtured, and supported my curiosity and intellect from the time that I was a small child. The memory of their boundless love sustains me. My sisters, Beverly (and her husband Carlton) and Iris, have always been loving, kind, and generous in spirit, time, and patience. We have our own private sisterhood that is so precious. My husband, James Cones, is wonderful in so many ways. He has stood by me and for me when I was sick and strong, right and wrong. He always has allowed me to just be me, even when it has meant he had to be a little less of himself. Thank you as well to his wonderful East Coast family—Cones and Shields—for supporting my West Coast family. Thank you, Aunt Sarah, for being a Stevenson in LA. My beautiful, brilliant daughter Emma is the delight of my life. She is magnificent and all of my best work always will be dedicated to her.

I have been blessed with great mentors, colleagues, and friends. Paul Gaston, Joseph Miller, and Barry Gaspar wetted my appetite for history when I was a young student at the University of Virginia. The late John Blassingame and Nancy Cott guided my development into a historian when I was a graduate student in African American Studies and then History at Yale. Vincent P. Franklin always has supported my work and has been a wonderful mentor through the years. Lille Ruth Wilson directed my first attempts at writing in the segregated public schools of Portsmouth, Virginia—thank you! Sandy Dijkstra has been an excellent literary agent. Thank you, David McBride at Oxford University Press, for taking on this project. Stephen Aron, Ellen DuBois, and Ronald Mellor in the History Department at UCLA are the best colleagues anyone could ever want. They have given me friendship, love, and opportunities to grow and excel in academia. John Laslett, Lois Banner, Joan Waugh, Peter Reill, Jeff Decker, Jenny Sharpe, Sharla Fett, Lisa Sousa, Kevin Terraciano, Jose Moya, Richard von Glahn, Bobby Hill, Claudia Rapp, Margaret Jacobs, Lynn Hunt, Robin Derby, Leon Litwack, Mary Ryan, Andrew Apter, Ghislaine Lydon, David Myers, Eric Avila, Wilma King, Amy Greene, Hitomi Kawamoto, Gary Nash, Frank Pontillo, Ama Mazama, Sharon Harley, Rita Roberts, Roy Ritchie, Herman Ooms, the late Eric Monkkonen, Jim Gelvin, the late Victor Wolfenstein, Marion Olivas, Irma Munoz, Teo Ruiz, Ivan Berend, Saul Friedlander, Jan

Freeman, Eboni Shaw, Jessica Millward, Lisbeth Gant-Britton, Massamba Mboup, Pam Reid, Floyd and Unjoo Byars, John Barstis, Helena Chang, Martin Quan, Marta Vago, Sandra Castaneda, Darlene Clark Hine, Judy Garber, Reynaldo Macias, Gordon Thompson, Elise Woodson, and Tiffani Chin all have offered me words of support, friendship, and care over the years, or when I especially needed it, and I cherish them for being in the right places at the right times. Nancy Dennis, who was my "sistah" in the UCLA History Department for so many years, has been incredibly supportive, funny, and helped keep me grounded with good, old-fashioned common sense. Nancy assisted me through the trenches of department chairmanship and "recovery," and I will always be thankful for that feat. Hubert Ho has offered invaluable technical support, and I am very thankful for his constant assistance. Paula Moya will forever be my sister by Cuban parents—thank you so much for your love and friendship. My fellow parishioners at St. Timothy's Catholic Church have inspired and prayed for me—thank you! I offer special thanks as well to Jamaica, Mr. Sonny, Mr. KoKo, Blue, and Berry who have given me so much delight.

UCLA undergraduate and graduate students have been a great inspiration to me over the years. I want to thank, in particular, those who have served as research assistants to this project: Daina Ramey Berry, Marne Lynn Campbell, Janira Teague, Danielle Purcell, Jessica Harris, Kaitlin Boyd, Tess Lerner Byars (she was not really my student, but I always wished that she had been), Michelle Jun, Jack Agamba, Leah Goodridge, Selah Johnson, and Erin Randolph. Daina helped me to start the project and Kaitlin helped me to end it, so I would like to especially underscore their assistance and offer my profound thanks. Kaitlin in particular was vitally important to me as I struggled to finally conclude this project. Marne has been a great friend to my family—thank you so much. It takes a village of special people and institutions, and I have truly been blessed with them.

"LaTasha Harlins, Soon Ja Du, and Joyce Karlin: A Case Study of Multicultural Female Violence and Justice on the Urban Frontier," *The Journal of African American History* (Spring 2004): 152–176.

The Contested Murder of Latasha Harlins

FIGURE 1.1 "Latasha Harlins," *Facebook*.

1

'Tasha

The Girl with the Wonderful Smile

The Decedent

The autopsy report was devastatingly clear: "The decedent, Latasha Harlins, died as a result of having sustained a gunshot wound . . . to the back of the head. . . . The entry wound was 2¾ inches below the top of the head. . . . The exit wound . . . is 1½ inch from the mid line of the back of the head."[1]

Latasha Harlins was 15 years old when Soon Ja Du shot her. She died shortly thereafter, face down on the floor of her local convenience store, the Empire Liquor Market located at 9172 South Figueroa Street in South Central Los Angeles. On that day, Latasha became part of a gruesome national statistic: 23.5% of homicide victims are female. Still, Latasha's murder was unusual—only about 10 African American girls her age, out of every 100,000, were killed that year.[2]

The police investigators found two one-dollar bills crumpled in Latasha's hand. The elastic band of the UCLA Bruins cap she wore that morning broke when the bullet passed through it. Paramedics ripped open the front of her multicolored blouse, searching for a heart beat. Blood seeping from her head stained the back of her shirt and jacket, eventually reaching her blue pants. Blouse, pants, cap—seemingly ordinary, casual clothing for a teenaged girl to wear on a Saturday morning. But on that day—March 16, 1991—the ordinary became extraordinary. Store owner Soon Ja Du testified that her son Joseph had told her about people who wore clothes like Latasha's: they were, according to him, gang members and dangerous. Latasha's clothes, her age, and the color of her skin made her, in Du's estimation, an "other" who was not to be trusted, but who was to be feared. Du's perception of Harlins as a racial and/or ethnic stranger as it were, also resonates with national homicide statistics. Three out of ten homicides are interracial when the victim is a "stranger." Most "stranger homicides" also involve a gun.[3]

Latasha Lavon Harlins was born on January 1, 1976, at the Christian Welfare Hospital in East St. Louis, Illinois, the first daughter of 16-year-old Crystal Harlins. The Harlins family, led by Crystal's mother Ruth, had been in East St. Louis since the late 1940s. They were an extended family, with at least three, sometimes four, generations living together. Latasha, her mother, her two younger siblings named Vester, Jr. and Christina,[4] along with Sylvester Acoff, father of Latasha's siblings, joined Ruth Harlins in Los Angeles in 1982.[5] Denise and Shinese, Latasha's maternal aunt and first cousin moved from Atlanta to join the family in 1983. Richard Brown (a.k.a. Harlins), her maternal uncle, also lived in the home.

This is the story of Latasha Harlins. It explores her tragic life in Los Angeles, her family, her community, and the forces—historical, political, economic, cultural, legal, and criminal—which shaped who she was, how she behaved, what she thought, and what happened to her on that morning in the late winter of 1991 that ended her life.

The homicide detectives on the scene seized Latasha's backpack, along with its contents—a jar of cream, a pair of female underpants, a toothbrush, some other toiletry items, and a few other articles—as evidence. The police took photos of her dead body and then walked from house to house in the working-class neighborhood near the site of the shooting, trying to get a positive identification of the murdered youth. Neighbors kept pointing them toward one apartment building, then to one apartment in particular leased by Ruth Harlins. Denise Harlins, Ruth's daughter, opened the door and spoke to the policemen. As his description of what happened to Latasha wafted backward and filled the room with unexpected dread, grandmother Ruth collapsed. Shinese went screaming through their home. The dead girl was not only her cousin, but also her best friend and roommate; Latasha had borrowed Shinese's lime-green backpack with a clock on the front when she left home the previous evening. Soon Ja Du later testified that she was certain Latasha had a weapon in that clock-faced backpack. She was certain Latasha had a weapon that she was going to use to kill her. The police recovered no such weapon.[6]

Fifteen is a difficult age for most girls, particularly for one growing up without her mother or father and coming of age in South Central in the early 1990s. Certainly Latasha, or 'Tasha as friends and family called her, had a family that loved her. Her grandmother Ruth had risked a lot to take in Latasha and her two siblings when their mother Crystal was killed and their father disappeared. Her aunt Denise also was in the home with her. Latasha had the support, comradeship, and affection of her cousin Shinese and the rest of the Harlins clan in Los Angeles as well. Still, her short life had been hard and painful. The toll it took showed—Latasha seemed something of a loner and often was very quiet. But no one expected her untimely death or the alleged reasons Du gave for it. The Harlins family has never been able to understand why Du thought Latasha had a weapon in her backpack with which she intended to kill the shopkeeper.

"'Tasha was just very quiet and very shy. She didn't hang with many people. And she was hard, you could tell. You didn't mess with her. She was like in her own world," a friend from her middle school recalled. JonSandy Campbell also remembered that she, 'Tasha, and two other girls, Tunisia and Sandra, would spend their lunch time at Bret Harte Preparatory Middle School talking about clothes, boys, and especially music. "She was a good dancer. Her favorite group was BBD [Bell Biv Devoe]. . . . We were all kind of outsiders, you know. I came to the school new that year so I didn't know anyone; but she had been there. We got together because we were both alone and very quiet."[7] JonSandy realized that Latasha too was an outsider, but she never really understood why. She had no idea that Latasha's mother had been killed a few years earlier, and that she had never emotionally recovered from the loss.

'Tasha never talked about her family or any of her problems—none of that. We were just silly girls, sitting around talking about music, gossiping about people at the school, you know how girls talk. She didn't think she was pretty, but I thought she was cute. She was dark complexioned. She always wore her hair the same way—bangs in the front, two braids up the side, bangs in the back. She would always look up at you through her bangs. I used to tell her that I liked her cut [slanted] eyes. She wore the same kind of clothes every day—blue dickies, a white T-shirt and a black hoodie, always the black hoodie, and black LA Gear. That was the thing. Gang bangers wore clothes like that, but she wasn't in a gang. She just hung out with us.[8]

Bret Harte, located on South Hoover between 93rd and 94th Streets, just a couple of blocks from where Latasha died, included grades sixth through eighth. The school could not boast of high academic standards or even moderate standardized test scores, but Latasha was successful there as both a student and athlete, running track and placing on the honor roll. She also had friends and success outside of middle school. At the local Algin Sutton Recreational Center, Latasha was a member of the drill team. She also worked as a junior camp counselor during the summer of 1990.[9] After their two years together at Bret Harte, JonSandy and the other girls went to ninth grade at Washington Preparatory High. 'Tasha went to Westchester High located in a middle-class enclave, some distance from the Harlins's home. As an honor student at Bret Harte, she had the choice to attend a high school other than the one closest to her residence. Her family chose Westchester for Latasha and her cousin Shinese because it was a better school academically and they hoped to prepare the girls for college.

The transition between middle school and high school for Latasha could not have been an easy one; she lost most of her middle school friends when she did not follow them to Washington Prep. Moreover, Westchester was a much more rigorous academic environment than Bret Harte. But perhaps more important, in terms of her outlook on life, behavior, and relationship to her family and other members of her social world, Latasha soon would be 15. Like many girls her age, 'Tasha was struggling to find herself, to test life's waters, to push against its personal and institutional boundaries. A girl at heart, with the body of a young woman and an edgy attitude, she was a complex blend of naiveté and maturity, strength and vulnerability, celebration, anger, and heartbreak all wrapped up in a facade of quiet street savvy. The heartbreak came when her mother Crystal was shot and killed six years earlier. The anger was part of the trauma of her loss, but probably began earlier when Latasha lived in her parents' home, a home menaced by domestic violence, drug use, and petty criminality. It certainly was not a life anyone who knew and loved Latasha, or anyone who was an ancestor, would have wanted for her.

Migratory Paths: Leaving Violence and Injustice Behind?

The Harlins family's migration from the Deep South to East St. Louis and then on to Los Angeles was part of a migratory trend of African Americans that extended generations back, at least to Latasha's maternal great-grandparents. Like the vast majority of blacks who lived in the Black Belt of Alabama and Mississippi, Ruth Harlins's ancestors had been enslaved. Ruth's great grandfather, Squire, also known as Sammy, was born around 1867 in Mississippi, but according to census data, Squire's father, A. Hollands, had been born a slave in North Carolina in 1830. As a free farmer during the Reconstruction era, A. had married Millie, who also was from Mississippi and whose slave father had been born in South Carolina. During the antebellum period, Millie and A.'s fathers had, no doubt, like so many others, been sold or transferred from the upper South where tobacco, cotton, and rice was the slaveholder's mainstay to the lower South where "cotton was king." By 1880, A. and Millie resided in Horn Lake, Mississippi, and worked as either tenant famers or sharecroppers. Their son Squire lived and worked with them. When Squire later married Cora, the two had several children, including Ruth Harlins's grandmother, Luella.[10]

By 1920, the family's name had changed a few times—from Hollins to Hollans to Hallins. Many enslaved blacks chose new surnames upon emancipation in 1865. Ruth's family's name changed much later, probably as part of a typical evolution that reflects both developing literacy skills and accents. Luella, who was literate, and her family lived and worked as farmers in Sunflower, Mississippi.[11] Fondly called Lula, Luella later married Ed Thomas. She had a son before marrying— Emmett (a.k.a. Ernest). Emmett was Ruth's father and Latasha's great-grandfather. Ten years later, Lula and Ed Thomas, still farmworkers, moved to Bethany in Pickens County, Alabama, with their two sons Ed and Ben as well as Emmett, who was then 18.[12]

A lot can happen in a young man's life over the course of a decade. By 1940, Emmett Harlins had married and was expecting his first daughter. Ruth Harlins was born in Tuscaloosa, Alabama, in 1941, and spent the first eight years of her life there and in nearby Aliceville with her grandparents, Lula and Ed Thomas.

Unlike Tuscaloosa, which had been the state's capital at one time and was the home of the University of Alabama, Aliceville was a sleepy, small town in Pickens County on the eastern border of Mississippi. It was not quite distinguishable from other Black Belt, cotton-growing locales where most residents were black and most blacks were either sharecroppers or tenant farmers. It was a desperately poor, oppressive life in which blacks labored constantly, but few managed to outwork or outlive their debt. It was part of the Deep South where blacks grew up and grew old in run-down, ragged cabins—often the same cabins slaves had abandoned when they gained their freedom—and the white planters or bosses were the only law that mattered.

Aliceville was quiet and "dry," but residents found ways to enjoy themselves. With places like Bettie's Juke Joint that showcased Delta blues men like Willie King, comedians and entertainers, locals easily found sources of underground pleasure. Baptist churches were their spiritual homes. Aliceville came onto the map in 1943, however, when the US government decided to house 3,000 German prisoners of war there. Many of the local residents, white and black, worked at the camp.[13] Ruth Harlins's family probably was not part of this World War II experience since census data indicates that everyone who lived in her grandparent's home in Aliceville were farmers (most likely sharecroppers).[14] It is certain, however, that the war still brought other opportunities to a restless, oppressed southern workforce that migrated to take advantage of it.[15]

Ruth Harlins, like every generation of blacks after Reconstruction, witnessed and, eventually, was part of this exodus that took southerners, not only to nearby urban centers, but further away as well, to new places and opportunities northeast, northwest, and west. Young black women left poor, agricultural counties where the work was only seasonal and they could make only pennies a day picking cotton—again in the same manner and with the same kind of supervision as had slaves—to live in cities where they could find work as domestics or in mills and factories earning a few dollars a week. They left a repressive southern society

FIGURE 1.2 "Negroes Jitterbugging in a Juke Joint on Saturday Afternoon, Clarksdale, Mississippi Delta," Photograph by Marion Post Alcott, 1939. Courtesy of the Library of Congress.

where educational facilities, particularly those that went beyond the primary level, were mostly nonexistent; where men and women were caught in a never-ending cycle of political exclusion, sharecropping, debt peonage, and high incarceration rates; and where adults and children had to withstand the brutal tyranny of lawlessness in the form of white terrorist groups, or "night riders," such as the Ku Klux Klan and the Knights of the White Camellia. Slavery had ended, but not its racialized marginality that tainted every aspect of a black southerner's life. With the marginality came the terror; the terror for women meant physical violence, rampant sexual harassment and abuse, as well as harm to their children. Segregation had taken the place of slavery; its architects perpetuating a race-based hierarchy where blacks were, and remained, on the bottom.[16]

The Law Was Not on Their Side

Not only were Alabamian blacks, like Ruth Harlins's family, usually on the bottom of the socioeconomic strata, any attempt to move from that position could mean risking one's meager resources and, at times, one's life.

Even after the violent turmoil that led to the Democratic Party's "redemption" of the state in 1874, the following decades were witness to a reign of terror that kept black citizens away from the polls, unable to own land or to compete for jobs, living in the poorest of housing and attending some of the worst public schools in the nation. By the end of the nineteenth century, for example, the number of black men registered to vote in Ruth Harlins's home state of Alabama had declined from 181,000 to 3,000. The numbers for her father's home state of Mississippi were no better. Emmett Harlins and his father's inability to participate in the electorate meant that they, and all Harlins family members, were vulnerable to a high tide of discrimination and abuse. It also meant that the legal justice system was largely unavailable to them. Indeed, the notion of a black victim due legal redress was an anomaly. It was not a question of justice—there was no justice, and there was no greater symbol of their legal vulnerability than the spectacle of public lynchings.[17]

From the late nineteenth century through the era of World War II, hundreds of blacks lost their lives through violent, extralegal means. The Klan, which had diminished in membership from its Reconstruction heyday, began to grow and become active again during World War I. Indeed, some historians believe that the KKK was "the most powerful political force in Alabama during the 1920s."[18] While the early twentieth-century Alabamian Klan seemed to target anyone who was "different," including Catholics, Jews, Asians, southern and eastern Europeans, as well as social "deviants"—divorced persons and alcoholics, for example—African Americans were their central focus. Between 1889 and 1940, whites, many of whom were Klan members or sympathizers, lynched 303 blacks in the state. Between 1888 and 1918, 237 of a total of 271 lynched Alabamian citizens were black. Three were lynched in Ruth's home county of Pickens.[19] No black citizen was safe, male or female, adult or child. Several of the blacks lynched during this period were female.[20] The oral stories, eyewitness accounts, and newspaper articles detailing the cruel brutalities that circulated through every community instilled the desired fear in a "free" black populace, but also made them, people like Ruth Harlins's parents, determined not to raise another generation of children in the South.

Hundreds more Alabamian blacks were killed whose murders constituted "legal lynching," that is they were processed through a court system that was so biased against a black defendant that justice was never certain. One such case involved a young black woman named Pauline McCoy, who was hanged on October 12, 1888, at Union Springs in Bullock County. McCoy, who was 19 or 22 at the time, was accused of murdering a mentally impaired 14-year-old white girl, Annie Jordan, of Montgomery. According to newspaper accounts, Annie was found a few days after she disappeared from home, strangled to death and nude in a pine thicket. Authorities reported that they found Pauline McCoy wearing Annie's dress. McCoy stated that her father had given her the clothing, indicating his possible involvement in Miss Jordan's murder. No one seemed to care, however, that Pauline probably was as much a victim as Annie, tricked into wearing the one piece of evidence that could tie the murderer to the crime. Someone had to pay. A white girl was dead, and it looked like a black girl had killed her. Pauline was found guilty and hanged in the "colored cemetery." She was made to travel to the hanging sitting atop her coffin.[21] Amelia Robinson, of Tuskegee, Alabama, recalled the ritual of lynching blacks in her community. "Some white man might feel that I don't like the way that Negro looks at my wife or that white woman. And string him up to a tree," she noted. "And when they would get ready to lynch him, they'd have a picnic. They'd have told the people, we're gonna have a lynching. And hundreds of people would come. The wives would bring a picnic basket, and bring her little children, and they would have the lynching." One newspaper account indicated that 500 people attended Pauline McCoy's lynching.[22]

Nationally, Pauline McCoy was only one of dozens of lynched women, most of whom were African American. In the period between 1889 and 1923, for example, 83 females (66 of whom were black) were lynched. Mississippi led in number with 14 occurrences, followed by Alabama, Texas, and Georgia with eight documented lynchings each. Lynching black women as a form of justice not only meant murder, it could also mean rape. Laura Nelson, for example, was raped and then hanged, along with her 13-year-old son in 1911, for allegedly killing a local deputy sheriff in Okemah, Oklahoma. Lynching women could also mean murdering their unborn children. One of the white male mob participants in Lowndes County, Georgia, who lynched Mary Turner in 1918 for threatening to have her husband's lynching investigated, sliced her open as she hung from her rope causing her eight-month-old fetus to fall to the ground and begin to cry. The mob stomped the baby to death while some riddled Mary's body with bullets.[23]

Women often were lynched, not because, like Nelson or McCoy, they were accused of a crime, but because males associated with them, or defending them, were. In 1914, for example, another Oklahoma mob lynched 17-year-old Marie Scott because her brother purportedly had killed a white man she accused of rape. Her brother escaped the mob, so they killed Marie instead. Likewise, a Mississippi mob killed two teen-aged girls and a young man in 1918 because the man had supposedly killed a local plantation owner who was accused of impregnating both black female victims, one of whom was the black man's intended wife.[24] The southern legal system, indeed, was no place of solace or justice for many black women at the turn of the century. Others were lynched, but their deaths were never recorded. Rape was more prevalent than lynching.

Indeed, if lynching was the great terror of black men, then rape was the essential fear of any black woman living in the Jim Crow South. It was, as Ida B. Wells aptly coined it, the "southern horror" that was most invisible.[25] Historian Leon Litwack echoed Wells's conclusion that white southerners believed that "Black women were naturally licentious, making rape redundant."[26]

Black female rape was a rarely recorded crime and even more rarely prosecuted.[27] Indeed, the idea of black female sexual victimization had been considered a virtual oxymoron in the southern criminal justice system since the slave era. The story of 22-year-old Recy Taylor, a mother and wife of a sharecropper in Abbeville, Alabama, only some 245 miles from Ruth Harlins's childhood home in Aliceville, is exemplary of what many experienced. Six white men kidnapped, blindfolded, and raped Recy on her way home from the Rockhill Holiness Church about midnight on September 3, 1944. The men later confessed to the crime, but two grand juries refused to try them. Rosa Parks, whose father lived in Abbeville, took on Taylor's case, bringing along the Alabama NAACP. The case became an international cause célèbre.[28] The rapists eventually offered Recy's husband $600 for their crimes so that he would not pursue justice.[29] When the New York *Worker* reported the story, they described Alabama's justice system as "blind, deaf and mute."[30]

FIGURE 1.3 "The Barefoot Corpse of Laura Nelson," photo postcard, Photograph of George H. Furman, May 25, 1911. Okemah, Oklahoma. Courtesy of James Allen.

Lynching was an especially vicious form of judicial repression mostly reserved for African Americans. But prisons were particularly brutal as well, and black males and females dominated prison populations in the South. Incarceration, of course, was another way of controlling the black population and particularly their labor, via the chain gang. Between the 1870s and 1940, the decade Ruth was born, African Americans made up 70% to 95% of the southern prison population.

Lynching, rape, false imprisonment, and execution were reasonable fears for blacks living in the Jim Crow South. Sometimes these violent acts were limited in scope; sometimes they involved large swaths of black and white communities. Race riots in the South, for example, were plentiful and typically resulted in the destruction of black property and other white-on-black crimes including robbery, murder, and rape. Congressional investigative records indicate, for example, that in the Memphis race riot of 1866, five black women were raped; 46 men and women murdered; more than 100 persons robbed; and four churches, eight schools, and 91 homes burned. No one was arrested or prosecuted for these crimes. At least nine other race riots, including an election riot of 1874 in which seven blacks were killed and many of those trying to vote were captured and sold as "slaves" in Ruth's home state of Alabama, occurred in the South before 1900, with similar results for blacks living in those locales.[31] Several other race riots occurred in the region before 1940, including one in Littleton, Alabama, in 1902;[32] another in Ruth's home county of Pickens in 1907;[33] and again in nearby Emelle, Alabama, in 1930.[34] The Harlins family could not expect legal protection under the law, a guarantee of the Fourteenth Amendment, as long as they lived in Alabama or anywhere in the South, and they knew it.

Poor Schools, Poor-Paying Jobs

Ruth Harlins had been raised to revere education, a sermon she often preached to her own children. But education, the resource that blacks believed was most important to their future success, exemplified the enormous gap between the races that southern segregation imposed. The lack of it, along with a dearth of job prospects, as with minimal protection under the law, were powerful factors that led the Harlins family, and so many others, to leave the South. Even by 1940, for

example, expenditure for black primary school education in the region
was on average 212% less than expenditures for whites. In Ruth Harlins's state of Alabama, expenditure on white education exceeded that
of blacks by 225%.[35] The one-room school overflowing with students of
all ages was the Jim Crow South norm. Few educational opportunities,
regionally and nationally, mirrored few black job opportunities. Most
in the South in the early twentieth century either were agricultural
workers or domestics. The first African American woman earning a
law degree in 1880 offered some symbolic change in labor status, but
not much more than symbolism. Still, national census records from
1900 indicate some progress for the most fortunate: 160 black female
medical doctors; seven dentists; ten lawyers; 13,525 school teachers;
164 ministers; and almost 1,200 musicians and music instructors.
Other professionals made up only 1% of black working women, and
few held clerical, sales, or industrial positions. At the turn of the century, 44% of working black women still were domestics.[36]

Since occupational, educational, and social repression were most
extreme in the South, black men and women who lived in that region,
like those in the Harlins family, migrated to find a place where they
could be a little less marginalized and a little less victimized—where
they could hope for a better life. Black women, in particular, left for educational and occupational prospects, and to escape white-on-black violence and sexual abuse. Population records vividly tell the story of
migration—450,000 men, women, and children left their southern
homes between 1870 and 1910. By the 1940s, blacks were leaving the
South at a rate of 1.5 million per decade.[37] In Ruth Harlins's home state
of Alabama, African Americans were 42% of the population in 1910, but
by 1950, only 33%.[38] In 1940, 77% of the nation's African American community lived in southern states, but by 1970, only 54% did. The Harlins
matriarch spoke eloquently of her vision of what life would be like once
she left the South: "When you go someplace else, you're always expecting things to be better. You always have dreams."[39]

Black Urban Life: Female Self-Help or No Help

The twentieth-century black urban success stories of the nation's largest
cities like New York, Detroit, Boston, Los Angeles, Chicago, Cleveland,
and Philadelphia benefited from a slowly growing black middle class,

not the large numbers of working-class southern migrants, like Ruth Harlins's mother, whose lack of education, skilled training, and black rural cultural background narrowed, to barely a crack, their access to a world beyond social stigma and economic marginality. Certainly their lives were better off than they had been in the South. Educational indices for the children of black migrants increased, as did the chances for secondary and even higher education. Black participation in the political arena also soared compared with the discriminative voting practices of the South. Remarkably, black cultural enclaves that showcased African American music, dance, literature, and folk art emerged in many urban arenas.

Every city of substantial size also could boast of black self-help organizations, a legacy that began in the late eighteenth-century urban North, but reshaped itself to accommodate the needs of large numbers of southern migrants after the Civil War.[40] Many of these clubs were, as they had been since the early nineteenth century, predominantly female. In 1895, for example, the National Association of Colored Women became the umbrella organization for efforts centered on women and children—socially, culturally, economically, and politically. In 1921, black women created the Negro Women's Club Home Association to aid single, working women and to make child care available for working mothers. Phyllis Wheatley Clubs also provided important services for young, black female migrants. In 1913, the black women who had formed the Working Girls' Home Association (later called the Phillis Wheatley Association) in Cleveland, for example, opened a 23-room establishment for single, working women in their community. Eventually, their efforts produced a 135-bedroom residence, with six clubrooms, a dining hall, four sitting rooms, and an employment agency.[41]

Black women of means in Los Angeles, the eventual home of Latasha and her family, created by 1904 the Sojourner Truth Industrial Club to "establish a . . . safe refuge" for young, migrant, working women. By 1912, they had raised the funds to create a working girls' home. About the same time, black female Angelenos formed the Women's Day Nursery to provide child care for employed women, the Progressive Women's Club, the Helping Hand Society, and the Stickney Women's Christian Temperance Union. It was, as Darlene Clark Hine, Deborah White, Stephanie Shaw, and other scholars of the

black female experience have noted, a "Lifting-As-We-Climb" philosophy—the motto of the National Association of Colored Women.[42]

Not only did women's clubs come to the assistance of black working
women in developing urban America, but so too did religious organizations. The black church, historically, has been an urban institution. It
also was one that lived off of female membership, labor, commitment,
and financial support. While it was certain that, in most of these institutions, women could not make the defining decisions, they still could
serve vital and visible roles as deaconesses, ushers, choir members, missionaries, Sunday school teachers, and faithful parishioners through
which their voices were heard and their ideas implemented. Biddy
Mason actually founded the first black church in Los Angeles—First
AME—in 1872. In 1910, the city's black female residents were promi-
nently represented in the 11 other black institutions of worship.[43] The
black church was the first institution that people, like Ruth Harlins—
black southern female migrants who wanted to have a "respectable"
social identity in their new place of residence—embraced and were
embraced by. For working-poor women, like those in the Harlins family,
it was a place of welcome and even admiration for their Christian demeanor and commitment to the church's work. It was a place where they
could find comfort from a difficult life; a place where hope lived; a place
where they could find peace when there was no justice. "At times like
these and places like this you really need the Lord," Ruth Harlins admitted when looking back on the many tragedies of her life in East
St. Louis and Los Angeles.[44]

Just as the African American church served as a training ground for
black male leadership, it also did for black women. Churches and clubs
helped hundreds of thousands of twentieth-century black women survive life in the city. Yet, the two institutions could only ameliorate some
of the difficulties of poor black urban life, and only for some of the
people who suffered from these difficulties. For many, there was no
visible institution—secular, sacred, or legal—that could fully erase the
physical and emotional debilitations of living in impoverished, segregated communities characterized by crime, poor education, family instability, political impotence, crowded housing, and limited medical
resources. Life was swift and cheap, and there seemed to be little that
one could do about it. Many refused to turn to the police or the courts,

fearing the history of abuse and neglect these institutions often represented in their poor neighborhoods.[45] The communities in which the Harlins family came to live in East St. Louis and Los Angeles were no different; their lives within them deeply scarred by these realities.[46]

First Stop North and West: East St. Louis

Ruth Harlins's move from the Deep South came in 1949, when she was eight years old. Her parents separated when Ruth was young, and her father moved to Cleveland, leaving Ruth with his parents. Ruth's mother later decided on East St. Louis, taking her child with her.[47] Both cities, like Chicago, Detroit, and Pittsburgh had become prime midwestern migration sites for Deep southern blacks.[48] East St. Louis, located on the Mississippi River, usually was the first major city blacks from Mississippi and Alabama reached when they moved north.

Founded in 1818 as Illinoistown, East St. Louis's history has been one characterized by waves of working-poor migrants, periodic Mississippi River flooding, racial unrest, and industrial boom and bust. The Mississippi, early railroad development, and local natural resources, like oil, made the city ripe for commercial and industrial development.

FIGURE 1.4 "Black Migrants in East St. Louis, Early Twentieth Century." Courtesy of the Department of Special Collections and University Archives, W.E.B. DuBois Library, University of Massachusetts, Amherst.

By 1850, workers from the local and regional agricultural sectors were moving there to take advantage of job opportunities on the railroad, in factories, and in support industries.[49] The decade after the Civil War meant especially rapid growth in infrastructure—railroad lines and the Eads Bridge across the Mississippi, for example. The National Stockyards, the city's first large industry, opened in 1871.

This beginning was followed quickly in the next few decades by factories that produced everything from brass, iron, coal, aluminum, cigars, zinc, steel, paint, shoes, and glass to flour, beer, soap, and syrup and industries that processed wood, tobacco, meat, and a variety of other goods. By the 1890s, East St. Louis was one of the fastest-growing cities in the nation with a population that seemed to double every decade. It had gained a reputation, rightfully so, for swift economic growth and attendant job opportunities, but also for crime and corruption. It already was known as the "dumping ground where the moral filth of St. Louis could . . . plan their deeds of crime."[50] With the dawn of Prohibition, corruption and crime grew even more, spawning organized crime families like the Shelton brothers gang who controlled much of the illegal activity in the southern region of Illinois and were headquartered in East St. Louis.[51] In all things racial, including justice, the city had a decidedly southern attitude. Jim Crow was nearly as palpable there as it was in the Deep South. Apartheid was the order of the day, and whites did not hesitate to employ the threat and reality of violence, including lynching, to maintain the racial status quo. Again, blacks could not rely on the local police or courts for redress.[52]

East St. Louis was a stopping off place for many on their way to more "storied" locations of urban opportunity, such as Chicago and Cleveland. But for those moving up from the Deep South with few economic resources like Ruth's mother, the rapidly developing industrial center became home.[53] African Americans found some openings in nonunionized shops, but, of course, at lesser wages, benefits, and status than their white working peers. The labor force, like every other sector of East St. Louis society, was segregated. Blacks worked in separate shops, ate in separate areas of dining rooms, used separate bathrooms, and then went home to separate neighborhoods, churches, shops, schools, dance halls, and beer gardens. Even in death, their bodies rested in separate graveyards.[54]

East St. Louis was not just a stopping place for poor southern blacks—working-class whites also came in record numbers. Irish and Eastern Europeans immigrants began arriving during the third quarter of the nineteenth century, preceding large blocks of black migrants who began to settle in more significant numbers right at the turn of the twentieth century. While the overall population in East St. Louis was doubling, the number of black residents was tripling. As the migrant black population grew, so too did white fear of job competition. This panic grew tremendously when it became apparent that local companies were actively trying to thwart white unionization by importing black southern workers whom they believed would feel too intimidated to agitate for better working conditions, larger salaries, or the right to organize. The Aluminum Ore Company, for one, hired 470 blacks to replace striking white workers in February 1917.[55]

Racial strife spread from the economic sector to the political. Local Democrats feared the impact that southern black Republicans would have on municipal elections. During a heated, local election campaign in 1917, for example, Democrats charged that Republicans had paid southern migrant blacks to come to the city just to vote. It was a Deep South political scenario all over again—one that blacks had hoped to escape when they moved north. After one such Democratic meeting that May, rumor of a black-on-white robbery circulated, and a gang gathered to strike back. Angry whites beat any blacks they met and pulled them from trolleys and streetcars. The city's mayor had to ask the National Guard to restore peace. That was only the beginning.[56]

"I Saw a Negro Woman Begging for Mercy!" The East St. Louis Race Riot of 1917

City newspapers, politicians, and the police, therefore, further inflamed racial hostility that spring and early summer by blaming rampant crime, such as the incident of robbery noted above, on black residents, even going so far as to prohibit the sale of handguns to them. The handgun, it was rumored, was to be the weapon of choice for a planned black massacre of whites on July 4, 1917.[57] African American migrants who believed that they were escaping the violent repression and injustices of the Jim Crow South soon discovered that it had followed them north. This was apparent as local whites reacted to the fear of potential violence by

oppressed black workers—just as white southerners had reacted in previous generations to fears of slave revolt—they armed themselves and
prepared for a preemptive strike on the black community.

Malicious gossip and white racism fed on each other. Mob beatings
of blacks in East St. Louis began on July 1 and the next day armed whites
began "shooting every Negro they encountered with little regard to age
or sex." African American men, many of whom also were armed and
organized, fought back. During the fray, they killed two white policemen—an act which led to an all out war against black residents.[58]
Local whites set fire to black neighborhoods while onlookers chanted:
"Burn them out!" As black residents fled, the throng shot at them. White
gangs destroyed over 200 black homes. At least one lynched black man
was hung from a telephone pole, and other lynchings were threatened.
The official count of those killed was 39 blacks and three whites, although
a number of additional mutilated black bodies were reported floating in
the Mississippi River during the next few days. Approximately 700
blacks left St. Louis that hot July "holiday," never to return.[59]

FIGURE 1.5 "East St. Louis (Illinois) Riot, 1917." Courtesy of the Department of Special
Collections and University Archives, W.E.B. DuBois Library, University of Massachusetts, Amherst.

The racial tension that led to the riot, and then the riot itself, had a decidedly gendered character. Local whites not only feared the potential political power of the black male vote, but they resented what they believed were black male attempts at white female seduction, both of which had fueled a growing antiblack hostility. So too had the fear of black male criminality and the perception of white victimhood. It all led to a sense of the growing erosion of white privilege, manifest in local racial etiquette. White city workers and dwellers believed that segregation, located in black geophysical, social, economic, and political isolation, was being challenged and perhaps even undermined.[60] While most attributed this erosion to black male social, political, and economic aggression, black women and their children were the easiest victims of white violence since they, unlike local black men, were not armed. Evidence demonstrates that during the riot, white men shot black women and children indiscriminately, and white women felt free to beat and pummel them. Even white prostitutes, whose workplace and residences were close to the black community, became part of the attack mob. These women seemed to resent the "domesticity" of the black women, no doubt jealous that, in comparison, these ladies of the night fell even more short of acceptable female gender conventions than their black neighbors.

Several eyewitness accounts document white female assaults on black women and children. "I saw Negro women begging for mercy and pleading that they had harmed no one," a local reporter wrote, "set upon by white women of the baser sort, who laughed and answered the coarse sallies of men as they beat the Negresses' face and breasts with fists, stones and sticks."[61] One woman was beaten in the face with the heel of a shoe. In another reported incident, three white prostitutes surrounded an elderly black woman and "beat her with the tap of a bar beer pump," which they used like a club.[62] Black female victims were made to strip on the street and were then beaten. "Throughout the whole evening" of July 2, it was reported, white women "beat them and tore off every stitch of clothes they had on."[63] Others reported that they witnessed white prostitutes taking black babies from their mothers and throwing the babies in the fire. The city coroner later testified that he had seen the bodies of these murdered children.[64] None of these women were prosecuted for these assaults. East St. Louis clearly was no haven for black women. This was a lesson the Harlins women would come to learn after arriving. The East St. Louis race riot of 1917 was one of the deadliest in United States, succeeded only by the Detroit riot of 1967 and the Los Angeles riot of 1992.[65]

A City of Poor Black Women

Although blacks who remained in the riot-torn city were able to gain some political, social, and economic concessions—in the way of plans for better housing, a social welfare program, structural changes in the mayor's office, and the creation of a local Urban League—as a result of this massacre and the congressional investigation which followed— white hostility to a growing black presence remained. Indeed, by 1922, the neighboring town of Bellville had become the center of regional Ku Klux Klan activity. Segregation in East St. Louis meant the same for blacks as it had in the South: that is, economic and political marginalization, few and inferior educational and medical resources, sporadic and state-sanctioned violence in retaliation for any purported breach of racial etiquette, and little, if any, recourse to local law officials.[66]

Conditions were worsened by impoverished city coffers that resulted from inexplicably low taxes levied on businesses and industries. The city government's practice of allowing wealthy corporations to establish company towns—small municipalities created, financed, and controlled by these corporations, instead of supporting East St. Louis through an equitable municipal tax—literally bankrupted the city year after year, decade after decade. Not surprisingly, the quality of life for East St. Louis residents worsened. Segregation became more entrenched as white workers moved to company towns, blacks remained in East St. Louis, and the middle and upper classes stayed in St. Louis. Ironically, East St. Louis blacks lived on the margins of a town that was itself merely the margin of a city—St. Louis. In the midst of tremendous economic development and population expansion, East St. Louis had become a metaphor of black urban blight. By 1920, it was the second-poorest city in the nation.[67]

Violence, government corruption, and black second-class citizenship still characterized the locale when Ruth Harlins and her mother moved north. African Americans comprised 22% of East St.Louis's population in the early 1940s. By 1950, the black presence had more than doubled. In 1970, African Americans were 70% of the city's residents.[68] Despite the ugly realities of life there, it was still better and offered greater opportunities than the South, particularly the Deep South.

The black migrant experience was not the same for women as it was for men. National statistics, for example, document that usually more men migrated in a single year than women. East St. Louis, which soon developed a black population that was more female than male, was not typical. Women outnumbered men more and more each year. In 1930, for example, 50 more black women, than men, resided there. By 1950, after the black population had more than doubled during the previous decade, there were almost 1,000 more women than men. By 1960, women outnumbered men by almost 3,500.[69] Since black women's place in the economy always was tentative, even more marginalized than that of black men, East St. Louis was especially poor.

There were a few who found work in factories or as seamstresses, midwives, and sometimes teachers. Some managed to own and operate laundresses, hotels, beauty shops, and catering or eating establishments. Less respectable work came in the form of bar service and prostitution. National occupational statistics suggest the difficulty that black women, like those in the Harlins family, had finding work in the urban areas of the Midwest and West. In 1930, almost 71% of working, black women were in some kind of service (primarily household); one-quarter was in agriculture, and 8% in manufacturing.[70] Progress was very slow until the World War II era. In 1939, black women's weekly income, nationally, was only 41 percent of that of white women and 57% of black men. At mid-century, they were earning, on average, $13 per week—about one-third less than black men. The difference between white and black women's earnings was greatest in the South. African American females also were more likely to be jobless—with unemployment rates three to four times higher, for example, than those of foreign-born, urban white women.[71] Still, the urban arena, regardless of the region, held more chance of black work than rural locales. As the years wore on, most women, even black women, benefited from jobs in the clerical/sales niche. By the 1960s, 1970s, and 1980s, some black women had moved into professional occupations. Even so, their earnings still lagged behind those of white men and women, as well as black men, prompting two prominent scholars to conclude that in years between 1939 and 1984, "black women began and ended this forty-five-year period with the lowest earnings among whites and blacks, male and female."[72]

Arriving in East St. Louis in 1949, Ruth Harlins's mother did not follow the usual black female occupational route that would have ended with work as a domestic. A woman with a child to support on her own sometimes had to be a little creative. Transportation around the city was a problem for blacks. Buses were available, but few ran at night. It also was difficult to get a taxi to their segregated communities. Perhaps this was a way, Harlins must have reasoned, to earn more money while maintaining more control over her labor, working hours, and body. She became a taxicab driver.

While her mother worked, Ruth attended school. Even though a child when her mother moved north, Ruth Harlins had her own ambitions. She dreamed of going to high school and college—two goals virtually impossible to fulfill in Alabama at the time.

Good educational resources for blacks in East St. Louis were limited, but there were some that were close. The neighboring metropolis of St. Louis, for example, could boast that their Charles Sumner High School was the first black secondary school west of the Mississippi River.[73] A historically black college, Lincoln, founded from donations from the 62nd and 65th U.S. Colored Infantries, also was located in nearby Jefferson, Missouri. Unlike Ruth's peers in Alabama, black children in East St. Louis did not have to miss school because they had to work in the fields or because there were no schools. They missed school instead because often they were just too poor—with little food, ragged clothing, and no money for books or transportation (her mother had to use her taxi to make money)—to attend school or to attend consistently. Recalling her school days, Ruth admitted: "'When I was in school, I sometimes only had a quarter. It cost a quarter to take the bus to school and back. I had to decide which way I was going to ride and which way I was going to walk.'"[74]

Like Latasha, by the time Ruth Harlins had reached her midteens, she was ready for a change. At fifteen, she boarded a Greyhound bus headed for Cleveland in search of her father. Less than two years later, she was back in East St. Louis, single, living on her own, and pregnant with her eldest child.[75]

Life, in the form of teenage pregnancy, interfered with Ruth's ambitious plans to graduate from college. She admitted how difficult it was trying to juggle paying bills, buying food for her children and having enough left over for tuition and books. Despite her financial and time management challenges, Ruth Harlins did manage to gain an impressive amount of education for a black, single mother in the 1950s. She completed Lincoln Adult Evening School and received her high school diploma, and then completed enough college classes to gain two years credit. She also invested in self-education, reading widely and watching educational television. Intellectual development remained important to her, a value that Ruth tried to instill in her children and grandchildren. Years later, she recalled a game she played with her offspring when they wanted money to buy ice cream and other snacks—they had to find a dictionary and learn new words to earn the coins.[76]

Ruth's children had started to come when she was very young, just slightly older than Latasha was when she was killed.[77] Other romantic relationships and three additional children would follow. Ruth Harlins made a life for herself and her family, but it was not an easy one. The financial and social success that most migrants sought remained elusive. Certainly they were getting along better in St. Louis than her kin in Tuscaloosa or Aliceville in Alabama. Still, the Harlins clan hardly believed that they had found their American Dream in East St. Louis. Young girls with dreams of a decent life and a stable home, young girls like Ruth and her two daughters—Crystal who gave birth to Latasha when she was 16; Denise who gave birth to her daughter Shinese that same year at age 13—fell victim to a sexualized social world in which they had little control. Like Latasha, the men in Ruth's adolescent social world were much older. The results were single teenage parenthood instead of a big church wedding with the man of their dreams; night school and a high school equivalency test instead of graduation parties and college; and sometimes violence and abuse instead of love, respect, and support.[78]

Fathers were particularly tragic men who often brought difficulty to the lives of the women around them. Ruth Harlins proudly acknowledges that she loved Emmett Harlins, her "daddy," a man who also clearly loved her. Still, Emmett was a hard drinker and was absent most of her life.[79]

Just as Ruth had left her mother to find her father, her daughter Denise recalled the great desire she had for her father, a desire that prompted a paternal aunt to arrange secret meetings between them in Chicago. He was a man much older than her mother Ruth and who had some unfortunate connection to the Chicago mob. Denise's father died violently—shot multiple times in the back. The kind of searing violence that pushed many blacks out of the South found them again in urban streets, back alleys, and bars of the Midwest and West. The Harlins family has been particularly plagued with violence. Not only did Denise's father die violently, so did two of her mother's brothers—R. L. was killed in a bar in East St. Louis in April 1968, and Curtis was killed in a bar in East St. Louis on Thanksgiving Day, 1985. It was the same day that Latasha's mother, Crystal, was shot and killed in a bar in South Central Los Angeles. Hard drinking, hot tempers, untamed mouths, raucous violence, and a justice system that cared little about preventing black-on-black crime claimed the lives of Harlins men and women across the generations.[80]

The absence of black male parents has meant not only the lack of black male visibility, but sometimes also accountability. Consider, for example, that in 1940, 76% of all black families had a nuclear core, with both mothers and fathers living together with their children during most of their offspring's childhood and adolescence. During the 1940s and 1950s, the generation Latasha's grandmother was raised in, about 80% of all black families were nuclear. By 1960, 78% of these families still could be described in this way. By 1985, however, during the era of Latasha's childhood, only 56% of those families were nuclear, a statistic which not only meant that many children were growing up without resident fathers, but also that many more children were growing up impoverished, since female-headed households traditionally have less income and financial resources than male-headed households. Urban families, like the Harlins, demonstrated an even higher incidence of female-headed households.[81]

The result has been devastating—financially, psychologically, and socially for those families with absent fathers. The larger society, of course, has offered little empathy. Instead, black women have been dubbed "Jezebel" and "welfare queens." The problem, in other words, has been deemed personal and cultural, not a result of political exclusion or economic repression. The charge of black sexual disobedience has a long history, one that aspiring middle-class African Americans, in particular, have tried to eliminate. They have felt the great necessity to demonstrate their sexual propriety, privately stressing a strict code of sexual conduct for their families and publicly insisting that the larger community do so as well. Poor African Americans have not been as easily convinced that sexual abstinence, outside the sanctity of marriage, is a prerequisite for social acceptance. One can well imagine why this doubt remained over the generations, when the argument to do so has been anchored on social acceptance by the country's mainstream. Most blacks have understood that their profound social marginality does not hinge on this one behavioral prerequisite. Those who chose to walk the sexual straight and narrow did so because of their religious and/or moral beliefs, and because they believed that families created out of married couples had a better chance of surviving than others. Still, this ideal sometimes was a difficult one to maintain for many families intergenerationally, including the Harlins family.

The research of renowned sociologist Lee Rainwater is instructive here, particularly because his lauded study, *Behind Ghetto Walls*, is drawn from observing the lives of thousands of poor African Americans, many of them migrants (or the children of first-generation migrants) from the Deep South to St. Louis, just a short distance from Ruth Harlins's East St. Louis home. With research conducted in the 1960s, when Ruth was raising Latasha's mother and her other children, he was able to draw several pertinent conclusions regarding family life among Ruth's, and her children's, cohorts. Rainwater notes, for example, that the majority of the persons included in his study believed in the nuclear family ideal, but had come to realize that it was tremendously difficult for them to obtain "in the face of their limited resources," particularly outside of the rural South.[82]

Life in the urban repositories of southern black migrants, therefore, presented new challenges to family life and structure. It also assaulted black ideals regarding premarital sex. Results from Rainwater's 1965 survey in St. Louis indicated that "all but a small minority" of respondents frowned on premarital sex and thought it a "serious" problem in their community. Even so, they also noted that the average age of first sexual relations for both males and females was about 14 years old, with boys usually a few months earlier. A host of conditions, including sustained economic marginality, which discouraged early marriage and/or the creation of male-headed households, along with peer pressure, especially male pressure, resulted in growing numbers of teenage pregnancies and unwed mothers, even though about 40% of those interviewed thought it was "disgraceful" to have a baby before marriage. Rainwater offers, for example, the story of one 14-year-old girl who was planning to have sexual relations with her "steady boyfriend," a "natural" event after dating exclusively for several months. An older sister and cousin had advised her to choose a "decent" boy to commit to, one who would support a baby if she got pregnant; one who would "come and see you and if you have a baby by him[;] he'll buy clothes and baby food and stuff like that . . . [and] not talk bad language." The young interviewee went on to explain that in her community, there were some "decent" boys and some who were not and that others who had dated these boys were willing to tell her "how he act and if he's nasty and how he dress and everything."[83] Ruth's daughters, including Latasha's mother, certainly came into contact with these same kinds of ideas about courtship, premarital sex, and family formation as those in Rainwater's study.

Despite the disappointments and difficulties, Ruth Harlins stayed in East St. Louis with her growing family. Their lives, like others, were touched by the tumultuous Civil Rights era of the 1950s and 1960s. Organizations such as the NAACP, the Urban League, and the Black Panthers were on the scene, utilizing various outreach and protest strategies. So too were homegrown associations, many of them culturally and politically nationalistic in orientation, such as the Black Egyptians, Black Culture, Inc., the Black Economic Union, the Black Liberators, the Black Nationalists, and the Black Imperial War Lords. They protested political corruption, police brutality, joblessness, labor union exclusion, and economic exploitation while advocating black self-determination, political and economic control of black communities, economic self-sufficiency, and black pride.[84] Unfortunately, little sustained improvement in the East St. Louis black condition occurred. If the Civil Rights era had taught Ruth and her family nothing else, however, they had learned that they had a right to expect a better life for themselves and their children than they had. By the 1970s, many were giving up on East St. Louis and its 33% black unemployment rate. They were choosing to move again, this time further north or west.[85] Ruth Harlins moved west to South Central Los Angeles in 1980, hoping to escape the hard luck that she and her family had experienced in East St. Louis.

The West: A Black Utopian Dream Deferred

The Harlins family did not believe that California was an ideal place, but they did think that it would be a better place to situate their family than the other places they had resided: Alabama, East St. Louis, or even Atlanta from where Denise and her daughter Shinese had migrated. A hundred or so years before their arrival, other blacks moving west also had dreamed of racial tranquility and unfettered access to decent, even prosperous, lives. There was even the rare occurrence of utopian communities that blacks created doting the western landscape from Kansas to the Pacific. In the all-black town of Allensworth, California, founded in 1908, for example, black men *and women*, usually elite men's wives, controlled the town's infrastructure, including its political, educational, and economic sectors. Josephine Allensworth was director of the town's school board, founder of its library, and was prominent in a local self-help organization. Dorothy Wells helped to create the town's government.[86] In the end, however, Allensworth, despite its educational and limited economic and political successes, proved not to be the hoped for black utopia, prompting many of its residents to eventually move on, some to the City of Angels.

Unfortunately, early twentieth-century Los Angeles, some 150 miles to the south, was hardly the land of limitless "opportunities" and "possibilities" for blacks that W. E. B. DuBois had reported in the *Crisis* magazine after his visit in 1913.[87] In Los Angeles, like the state in general, 85% of employed black women were either domestics or performed some kind of personal service in 1910, thus offering few avenues for success for most African American women. Ten years later, almost half were still servants and domestics.[88] Nonetheless, the black Angeleno community grew over time and eventually became one that would include the Harlins family.

Few people seem to know that California purportedly was named for a mythical black woman, "Calafia," although, Disney incorporated the story in its film tribute to California history shown at its theme park California Adventure, with the celebrated actress, comedian, and talk-show host Whoopi Goldberg playing the role. Calafia, the name that appears on early sixteenth-century Spanish maps of Baja, California, also is the name of a character in the even earlier sixteenth-century Spanish novel, *Las sergas de Esplandian* (1508), in which the author, Garcia Ordonez de Montalvo, describes an island inhabited only by black Amazonian women, ruled by their queen "Calafia." While the Spanish cartographers and explorers soon discovered that the land designated as "Calafia" was not an island, the name remained and evolved into "California."[89]

Similarly, few people realize that the Spanish settlers who helped found the pueblo of Nuestra Senora la Reina de Los Angeles de Poriuncula, or Los Angeles, in 1781 were predominantly (26 out of 46) "African or part-African." They were, without a doubt, as diverse a group of settlers as one might imagine. Other than those of African descent, there was one Chinese, two European Spaniards, and the remaining were Indian or part-Indian.[90] This dominance of people of color was short-lived. Ten years later, few, if any of the original settlers of African descent claimed their black ancestry in official census records. They had acted quickly to "whiten" or further "hybridize" their "racial classification" in documented population rolls and through marriage. Many who had designated a "mulatto" (African and Caucasian) ancestry in 1781, for example, later indicated a "mestizo" (Indian) or "coyote" (three-quarters) Indian racial designation. Those who had been "African" became mulatto. Although their numbers declined, African-descended families in Los Angeles in 1792 were 39% of the population.[91]

Flexibility in racial categorization, in part, allowed persons of African descent to take on significant social, political, and economic roles within Los Angeles and throughout Spanish California. These opportunities, however, dwindled after the Treaty of Guadalupe Hidalgo in 1848, when California became the possession of the United States. The racial etiquette and discrimination which characterized every section of the mid-nineteenth-century United States, even those regions that were not wedded to chattel slavery, soon infested black life in the West.[92]

In 1860, when the country was on the brink of an internal war precisely over the issue of its black presence, African Americans constituted only 1.1% of California's population and 1.5% of Los Angeles residents. Women began as a small fraction, only 9% of the total number of blacks in the new state in 1850, but their presence within the group grew tremendously over the latter half of the nineteenth century so that by the turn of the new century, they comprised almost half of the total number of African Americans.[93]

While the Civil War did not have grave implications for those living so far west and in a state where the 1850 constitution forbade slavery, there was something of a race war occurring in Los Angeles at about the same time. The two major forces, however, were not white and black. Instead, they were white Americans and Mexican Americans.[94] Whites had the upper hand, at least politically and judicially, which was vividly demonstrated, even this early in the city's history, in a biased criminal justice system. As historian William Deverell notes, a local Los Angeles journalist during the 1850s shed light on the racially differentiated crime rates and punishments when he commented, "punishment seems to be graduated by the color of the skin, and not the color of the crime."[95] While whites and Latinos committed approximately the same rates of violent crimes, for example, Latinos were much more likely to be arrested, found guilty, and given heftier sentences.[96] This tradition of lopsided justice widened to embrace blacks as their numbers increased over time.[97]

By 1900, the overall black presence in Los Angeles had moved upward just slightly, but their numbers had increased tremendously—from 102 to 2,131. By 1910, the boom in black migration to the city was apparent—there were about 7,600 blacks in Los Angeles, the largest black urban concentration in the state, followed by Oakland and San Francisco.[98] Indeed the black population in Los Angeles doubled between 1900 and 1903 because of a single incident—the recruitment of black male labor by the Southern Pacific Railroad to break the strike of Mexican American construction workers. (Not surprisingly, it was not long before African American migrants to Los Angeles were reeling from the stigma of being strikebreakers.) The city continued the distinction of having the state's largest number of black residents, while the number of African Americans in Los Angeles remained at least four times that of Oakland, San Diego, and San Francisco through 1960.[99]

Although relatively few black women migrated as far as California before World War I, thousands still found homes and opportunity in the western states by the end of the nineteenth century. Black women were prominent residents, for example, in the 30 or so black towns in Oklahoma during the 1890s and early 1900s. In Langston, Oklahoma, the eventual site of historically black Langston University, female residents worked hard to have public schools created. Their achievement was astounding—72% of their community could read and 70% could write. This success was rarely replicated elsewhere, but there were other important examples of female advancement, mostly through entrepreneurship, in the early west. Elvira Copley, for example, owned a laundry business in Sheridan, Kansas; Mary Fields opened one in Cascade, Montana; Annie Neal was the proprietress of a hotel in Oracle, Arizona; and Mary Lewis owned an eating establishment in Tucson.[100]

Biddy Mason is the example of black female financial success and civic commitment that most often comes to mind in the discussion of late nineteenth- and early twentieth-century Los Angeles. Arriving as a slave, Mason was one of a handful of early California blacks who sued for her freedom and won. She had a penchant for land speculation and, through a few shrewd deals, was able to garner substantial financial security for her family and to help build important institutions within the fledgling African American community. Charlotta Spears Bass is equally well-known. Not only was she editor of the *California Eagle*, the state's largest, early twentieth-century black newspaper, but she also was the "lady president" of the local United Negro Improvement Association (the UNIA, Marcus Garvey's organization), a member of the National Association for for the Advancement of Colored People (NAACP), and co-founder of the Pacific Coast Negro Improvement Association.[101] The experiences of Josephine Allensworth, Charlotta Bass, Biddy Mason and others, however, occurred under exceptional circumstances—either in all black towns where a racially isolated African American populace had the resources to create opportunities for themselves and then could channel the rewards back to their towns and their inhabitants, or in locales where, if one or two black women managed to excel in some vacated arena of the economy, they hardly were a threat to the majority of white residents.[102] This certainly was not the case for most of the women, including those in the Harlins family, who arrived later in the twentieth century.

The Family Moves to Los Angeles

Regardless of where she lived, Ruth Harlins remained true to who she was and who she had been since her childhood in Alabama and as a teen in East St. Louis. Ruth was a southern woman who loved to see her family eat the collards and cabbage, ham, potato salad, and cornbread that she prepared for them. She was a loving woman who wanted to provide the best for her children and their children. She was the grandmother to Latasha who came to think of the teen as her daughter.[103]

Los Angeles, with a total population of slightly less than three million the year that Ruth arrived, was a giant metropolis compared to East St. Louis and its population of 55,000.[104] Still, LA's black and black female representation in the population was, by East St. Louis standards, minimal. East St. Louis was a city that had been predominantly black and female for decades. Black females have never come close to being a majority in the City of Angels.[105]

Blacks migrating to Los Angeles in the twentieth century had almost always settled along its central corridor and south. Watts, Compton, and Willowbrook were communities of African American migrants who arrived in record numbers from the 1940s onward. Even before then, black life had bristled up and down Central Avenue, producing the West Coast version of the Harlem Renaissance. Indeed, Central Avenue produced, and helped sustain, some of the most important jazz musicians of the twentieth century, including Charles Mingus, Art Pepper, Benny Carter, Dexter Gordon, and Buddy Collette. Along with the music was the community, filled with working families, many of them middle class, churches, shops, and businesses owned by blacks and other ethnic/racial minorities, and relatively good public schools. Yet, by the time of the first Los Angeles riots in 1965, the vibrancy of the Central Avenue community was waning. Nonetheless, Los Angeles still held many possible occupational and educational opportunities for the Harlins family that East St. Louis did not when they arrived fifteen years later.

LA's reputation for black success—it had in 1980, after all, a black mayor—along with its nationally prominent educational resources, and job opportunities—must have been strong pull factors. Ruth and her daughters really wanted their children to be able to earn college degrees. The University of California, the California State University, and the community college systems comprised the best, and most affordable, post-secondary public school system in the nation at the time. And black women had not done badly, relatively speaking, in the city. From the late nineteenth century onward, they had managed to move up the socioeconomic ladder, to create important and effective self-help and self-improvement organizations, to participate in politics, and to even make some advances in Hollywood. By 1919, for example, Los Angeles had its first black female physician: Ruth Temple, who graduated from USC. Bessie Bruington, a Berkeley graduate, was the city's first black teacher in 1922; and Vada Watson-Sommerville became its first black female dentist in 1918.[106] The trend continued in both the city and the state. By 1950, half the employed black women in California had moved out of domestic and personal service to jobs in the industrial, professional, and white-collar economic sectors, a substantial improvement over black women's performance in the labor market nationally.[107]

By the time the Harlins migrated in the early 1980s, California's state economy was booming. It was clear to many that local black women really had managed to excel, not only economically but also politically. In 1952, for example, Charlotta Bass ran as a vice presidential candidate for the Progressive Party. Bass also ran for Congress a decade earlier as part of the Independent Party. California's first black female elected to the state legislature and to the House of Representatives, Yvonne Braithwaite Burke, resided in Los Angeles. So too did the first black woman elected to the state Senate, Diane Watson, as well as Maxine Waters, who served in the State Assembly and still serves in the US House of Representatives. Locally, the 1973 election of Doris Davis, as mayor of Compton, marked the first time a black woman held this position in a metropolitan city.[108]

These women and others managed to craft rewarding, comfortable lives for themselves in a city that, despite its many resources and successes, was still incredibly segregated and overwhelmingly white. Los Angeles Unified Schools did not start to desegregate until 1962, and then only under intense pressure from the NAACP, the ACLU, and the United Civil Rights Committee. Even Martin Luther King Jr., in his 1963 visit to the city, was struck by certain similarities in race relations between Los Angeles and Birmingham.[109] Indeed, Los Angeles County still was 80% white in 1960. Even when immigrants from Asia and Central America dramatically shifted demographic patterns, so much so that non-Hispanic whites no longer were the majority, the overall black representation in the population did not change upward. With the Latino/Latina population increasing from 11% to 36%, the Asian/South Asian/Pacific Islander population growing from 2% to 11%, and the number of Middle Easterners increasing six times between 1960 and 1990, the Los Angeles that Ruth Harlins and her family moved to in the 1980s certainly was different, in profound ways, from the small Alabama hamlet of her childhood or the sprawling East St. Louis of her early adulthood, both of which had predominantly black populations.[110] But if Los Angeles's growing, dynamic mix of peoples had prompted some to christen it the "capital of the Third World," that was only one slice of the pie.[111] Los Angeles also was, and is, for some, a first-class city known as a hub of ostentatious wealth and celebrity as well as a center of economic innovation and popular culture that is eagerly followed around the world.

Los Angeles's profile in the 1980s, under the leadership of Tom Bradley, had reached unprecedented heights nationally and internationally. Still, not all parts of the city were thriving. South Central, a collection of communities that encompassed parts of the city's southwestern district and Inglewood, Compton, Watts, Maywood, and Lynnwood, had declined in many substantial ways. Indeed, one of that area's few attributes that had not shifted substantially downward during the past two decades was its black population—47% in 1990; although that number too was waning since most persons moving into South Central in the 1980s were Latino/a, and most of those moving out were black.[112]

Left Behind—Again

The Harlins family, in other words, had moved into an area of Los Angeles that was in decline. South Central was being hit hard by a deindustrialization trend that was leading to all-time-high unemployment rates. Not surprisingly, poverty also was on the rise. Los Angeles residents went from a 3% poverty rate in 1969 to 15% twenty years later. Both per capita and family income had fallen during those decades.[113] South Central residents were smack in the middle of what sociologists have termed Los Angeles's "poverty core," and 31% blacks residing in that corridor lived below the poverty line.[114] These economic declines occurred as Los

Angeles's population shifted from majority white to majority nonwhite. The shrinking number and kinds of jobs available for immigrants and migrants of color, like the Harlins clan and many others who lived in the surrounding communities, meant most would take low-paying, often temporary, positions with correspondingly poor benefits. Migrant blacks, especially employed black women like Ruth and Denise Harlins, fared better in the job market than many immigrants who initially struggled with English, but their ability to continue to do so certainly was not guaranteed.[115] Ruth Harlins, for example, worked as a clerk in the Department of Social Services in 1991 with a take-home pay of approximately $1,600 per month,[116] and Denise worked for the Department of Insurance.[117] Moreover, while the touted California college systems were thriving, the public K-12 schools that Latasha, her siblings, and her cousins were to attend were sinking under the weight of a dysfunctional bureaucracy, a dwindling tax base, system-wide confusion over how to handle bilingual education, and an embarrassingly high dropout rate. Climbing economic and educational problems signaled mounting social difficulties. Premarital pregnancies, for example, were on a steady rise. It must not have taken long for Latasha's family to realize that South Central was not so different from East St. Louis after all.

Problems, in other words, were everywhere to be found in the Harlins's new home. As the hometown of gansta rap, some areas of South Central lived up to its new image, popularized by local rap pioneers, such as Ice-T and NWA (*Straight Out of Compton*), of urban blight, social dysfunction, police brutality, gang violence, and a seductive and deadly new menace—*crack*. It snowed crack in South Central in the 1980s. Crack cocaine was cheaper, and supposedly more addictive, than the refined white powder cocaine popular among yuppies and the glitz and glamour set—and it claimed victims in epidemic proportions. Literally tons of cocaine from Colombian drug cartels, funneled through Texas, Miami, and especially San Francisco, ended up on the streets of Compton, Watts, and other nearby predominantly black neighborhoods. The Harlins family was hardly immune to its sadistic seduction.

Crack use and addiction were so characteristic of poor black Angelenos in the 1980s that Los Angeles was known as the "crack capital of the world." They produced it, sold it, became addicted to it, killed for it, and were killed by it. Crack was literally created in black Los Angeles when a functionally illiterate Dorsey High School dropout, Rick Ross, made a lasting, and lucrative, connection with a local Nicaraguan FDN supporter.[118] Ross's Nicaraguan associates were able to deliver kilos of cocaine for rock bottom prices. Oscar Danilo Blandon and Norwin Meneses, two Nicaraguan nationals, used the profits they earned from selling cocaine to Ross to support the Contras. This direct pipeline of cocaine grown in Colombia, Nicaragua, and Costa Rica, shipped via El Salvador to San Francisco and Los Angeles, was maintained for several years, principally through the protection of the CIA, who employed some of the major wholesalers as informants.[119]

Usually, powder cocaine was so expensive—with a street value that could be as high as $5,200 an ounce—that only the rich could afford it. But Ricky Ross and a few others soon learned how to take a little bit of powder cocaine and turn it into a lot of "rock" cocaine, or "crack," with a street value of only $20 an ounce. In his heyday, Ross had five cookhouses—sites for the manufacture of crack—in South Central. "It was not uncommon," Ross testified at his trial, "to move $2 million or $3 million worth of crack in one day." It was not just that crack was cheaper, the high that smokers experienced was more powerful and lasted longer than expensive powder cocaine. "Crack turned the cocaine world on its head," one investigative journalist noted.[120] "'Cocaine smokers got an explosive high unmatched by 10 times as much snorted powder. And since only a tiny amount was needed for that rush, cocaine no longer had to be sold in large, expensive quantities . . . It was a substance that is tailor-made to addict people,'" Robert Byck, a Yale expert testifying before a congressional investigation in 1986, asserted.[121]

Thousands in Los Angeles became crack addicts during the 1980s. Many, who did not ingest the drug, sold it. Crack profits made Ricky Ross a multimillionaire, providing him with money that he invested in a staggering amount of local real estate and business interests. Money from crack also swelled the ranks of local black gangs, especially the Crips and the Bloods, who were its primary retailers. Their profits paid for the high-powered weapons that dominated street violence. It was not unusual, after the advent of crack, for example, to read headlines in the local black newspaper like "7 Die, 9 Hurt in Eight Day Gang Spree," an actual story that appeared in the *Los Angeles Sentinel* on April 10, 1986. According to this article, "All of the victims were assaulted in areas known to police as active gang locations. And all of the assaults, without exception, can be traced directly to narcotics or gang activity." Hundreds of thousands, who did not use or sell crack, were related to someone who did. The impact on South Central families and communities, like those of the Harlins family, was devastating, not just because of the highly addictive quality of the drug, but also because those found guilty of selling it received disproportionately high prison sentences, when compared with those found guilty of selling powder cocaine. Addiction, theft, murder, and imprisonment, all linked to crack cocaine, ravaged local black life.

Drugs, Misery, Murder

Ruth Harlins's family followed her to Los Angeles in waves. Crystal came on a Greyhound bus with Latasha, who was then six; Latasha's little brother, two-year-old Vester Montrell Acoff; and an infant daughter, Christina Acoff, in 1981.[122] Denise and her daughter Shinese followed in 1983. Richard, a son of Ruth Harlins, also came during the early 1980s.[123] The family settled in South Central. Crystal and her children lived with Sylvester "Vester" Acoff, father to Crystal's youngest two. Vester also claimed that he was Latasha's father, but her birth certificate, which lists no father, and designates her last name as Harlins rather than Acoff, suggests otherwise. The two young parents found work; Vester in a steel foundry and Crystal as a waitress, but their relationship was stormy and unstable at best.[124]

Vester was known to be physically and psychologically abusive to Crystal, attacking her on many occasions, sometimes in front of Latasha and her siblings. Both parents drank, heavily at times, and there is some evidence that they used drugs, perhaps smoked crack.[125] Their lives seemed always on the verge of spinning out of control, but they managed to maintain some semblance of family life. There were still birthday parties and some family dinners. Latasha and her siblings had their grandmother Ruth, aunt Denise, and uncle Richard, and they had each other. Crystal had decided not to have any more children and had a tubal ligation sometime after Christiana was born.[126] Vester's beatings eventually got so bad that she left him in December 1983. In her petition for a restraining order, obtained after a particularly brutal beating in

1984, Crystal briefly described a history of her relationship with the one man who had been constant in Latasha's life since birth.[127]

She and Vester had been together, Latasha's mother noted, for 12 years by 1984, suggesting that they were childhood sweethearts (she would have been 12 when they started dating). "Lately he has changed and becomes mean and violent, especially when he drinks, which is often," she told the police. "The defendant [Vester Acoff] has harassed me terribly ever since" the breakup. According to Crystal, Vester constantly stalked and beat her, attacking her at home, "on the street or anywhere he sees me." The presence of Latasha and her siblings did not seem to deter Vester's physical, psychological, or verbal abuse.[128]

On a warm summer night, for example, the night of the incident which led to Crystal filing for a restraining order, Vester followed Crystal, and a man she was dating, from her home to Redondo Beach. There, he accosted Crystal and started beating her. When he was finished, Latasha's five-foot-six, 115-pound mother had suffered a split lip, black eye, and scarred ankle, knee, and elbow.[129] One can only imagine the horror Latasha, only eight years old at the time, felt when she saw her mother's swollen, bruised, and humiliated face the next morning. Even though the court granted Crystal the restraining order, which included a mandate for Vester to stay away not only from Crystal, but also Latasha and her sister and brother, Vester ignored it. He continued to stalk, harass, and beat Crystal.

It is certain that Latasha was increasingly aware of Acoff's abuse. Her aunt Denise described an incident where Latasha witnessed Vester publicly beating her mother. "'Tasha wanted to have a party for Joshua at Chuck E. Cheese's,'" Denise explained. "And after they came home, they all went up to the liquor store and then a gang of them went up to the house. On the way, he [Vester] really did Crystal wrong in public. And they saw all that.'"[130] Latasha could no more escape Vester's abuse of her mother, and perhaps threatened abuse to her and her siblings, than Crystal could. She had Vester arrested, *again*. This time, he was charged with battery. It was the second time that Crystal had had Vester arrested for violation of his restraining order.

There is no clear evidence how Latasha's witnessing her mother being abused affected her. Experts writing on the impact of domestic violence on children living in the home, however, note a number of emotional, behavioral, social, and physical consequences that Latasha could have experienced. Psychologists explain that a young child, such as Latasha, when witnessing the abuse, might experience a bevy of debilitating feelings, including depression, helplessness, powerlessness, guilt, anger, shame, grief, embarrassment, and fear. These feelings, in turn, could cause a child to act out or withdraw, seek additional attention, feel like they should behave as a parental substitute, lie to avoid confrontations, and be overly aggressive or passive. The social consequences of domestic violence on children include having stormy relationships; feeling isolated from relatives and friends; an inability to trust those around them, particularly adults; and avoiding home. Finally, physical outcomes range from anxiety and attention-span shortages, to headaches and stomachaches, as well as feeling tired and lethargic.[131]

Any, or most, of these consequences could have been ameliorated in Latasha's life if she had a caring adult who helped her understand what was happening and provided an emotionally safe place.[132] Certainly, grandmother Ruth and aunt Denise were available to help her through these difficult times. Latasha's mother also tried to protect her children from their father by barring his contact with them. Unfortunately, Vester's abuse of Crystal only escalated over time, diminishing the chance that Latasha went unscathed.

Crystal suffered tremendously—that was clear to everyone around her, even her small children. Indeed, many mothers in this situation are filled with so much anger, dread, and depression that it becomes increasingly hard for them to act as an effective parent.[133] Because Crystal lived in constant fear of Vester and what he might do to her, she often complained of "being very nervous" and suffering from "headaches and backaches." She was afraid that Vester was going to literally kill her. Her fears were frighteningly rational. Black women are three times more likely to be killed than white women[134] and more likely than women of any race or ethnicity within this country to be killed by a boyfriend or husband.[135]

While female battery occurs in almost every race, ethnicity, class, and generation, many experts believe that "marital conflicts," even those resulting in spousal abuse, "are shaped by the specific experiences and outlooks of class and ethnicity."[136] Within the black community, some scholars suggest, domestic abuse may be more pervasive than in other communities for several reasons. Nathan Hare, a famed black clinical psychologist and sociologist whose research is centered on black men and families, indicates that some African American male batterers are "jealous, insecure and are attempting to imitate the classic 'street pimp,' playing a 'mind game' with the women by showing a loving and warm side to sustain interest—then inflicting pain."[137] Others, he notes, are imitating behavior they have seen their fathers or other male role models exhibit, rationalizing that women expect abuse. They envision their manhood, Hare goes on to explain, as in part centered on their ability to "control" women who are, in their estimation, "out of control." Any attempt by the women to resist measures of control are deemed an assault on the batterer's "manhood," eliciting even more abuse. "Others," are sociopaths, with "no sense of right and wrong."[138] Psychiatrist Carl Bell writing in *The State of Black America*, a study commissioned by the National Urban League, confirmed Hare's findings. Bell added that alcoholism, frustration, and low self-esteem derived, in part, from being unable to support their families and a lack of ethnic pride, have meant a relative preponderance of spousal abuse by black males.[139] Others explain that the inability to take care of one's family, resulting from unemployment, underemployment, poor vocational skills and training, combined with the lack of affordable housing, particularly in urban environments, leads to anger and frustration, exacerbated by drug and alcohol abuse. The result is a pernicious formula that often results in domestic violence.[140]

Abused black women, on the other hand, are more likely to stay with these men than females of other race and ethnic groups because of their lack of options and resources—shelters, familial support, economic independence, and other men as potential partners. Some women are socialized to be passive in response to male aggression or in response to men in general.[141] Others do not want to report their abuser to the police because they fear a racist response that might have an unexpected negative impact on their family. Likewise, extended families sometimes are reticent to become involved because they believe that what happens between a wife and her husband is "their business," or they too fear victimization.[142] Of course, Crystal did not accept the abuse—she left Vester and went to the police numerous times to try to end it. All the women in her family, even Latasha, detested the way Vester treated her. Still

Western society, including black Americans, sometimes, historically, "allowed" wife beating "within limits." Consider, for example, that it was only in the nineteenth century that men in the United States and Europe began to lose the "legal right" to "chastise" their spouses.[143]

Even afterward, law enforcement officials maintained a well-deserved reputation for not aggressively protecting women from spouses, boyfriends, and partners identified as abusive. Police have sometimes refused to answer domestic disturbance calls, to arrest the alleged batterer, to inform battered women of their rights, or to give them vital information about available shelters.[144] It is not clear how the LAPD responded to Crystal Harlins's accusations of abuse, but the court certainly was willing to issue a restraining order to keep Vester Acoff away from her, Latasha, Vester, Jr., and Christina—unfortunately with little implemental success.

Experts know that domestic abuse is exacerbated by the use of alcohol or drugs, and Vester and Crystal may have used both. It is certain, for example, that Crystal's drinking and acting out in public accelerated over time. She might have drank to calm herself—trying to raise three children on little money with the constant threat of a violent bully who beat her on sight is enough to unnerve anyone. Crystal was also a young (in her midtwenties), vibrant woman who, like most of her peers, liked to have a good time when she could manage it. Her use of alcohol was apparent to those who knew her well or saw her out at a club or social event. It is not certain when or how often Crystal used cocaine, or if Latasha was aware of her mother's drug use—she was only seven or eight at the time—but traces of the drug were in her Crystal's body when she died.[145]

Households where parental drug abuse takes place are not stable ones. Experts note that they often are characterized by the same kind of emotional and physical chaos associated with domestic violence homes, certainly increasing the likelihood that any child, like Latasha, living in a home where both domestic violence and parental drug abuse occurs, will suffer in a number of ways. Children of parents who abuse drugs, for example, usually have to cope with parental mood swings, unpredictability, periods of neglect and/or alienation, and a weakened household structure. Not only do incidences of domestic violence multiply, but also the frequency of unemployment, divorce, mental illness, and legal problems, sometimes dramatically, in these homes. Children do not understand the impact of alcohol or other drugs on their homelife and, as a result, are left feeling responsible for their parent's dysfunctional behavior. They often respond by trying to control the situation themselves or performing some "heroic" act to make their parents feel or act better. Some strive to make good grades, to keep the house clean, or to keep their younger siblings quiet. They do not feel comfortable inviting their peers to their home, fearing that their friends will witness their family's problems. Likewise, parents of their friends might not let them visit a home where they suspect drug abuse occurs.[146]

Family life, therefore, must have been extremely stressful for Latasha. Indeed, specialists explain that children of drug users are more likely to suffer from physical abuse, anxiety, low self-esteem, depression, poor school performance, school truancy, drug addiction themselves, as well as eating disorders. They also are more likely to attempt suicide.[147] Stories of children with addict parents abound from this era, shedding some light on what Latasha's life could have been like. One such story comes from a girl named Savannah, who grew up in Philadelphia and New York in the 1980s and 1990s. She recalls that she was seven when she finally realized that her mother was "doing drugs." The discovery was devastating. Savannah spent much of her late childhood and preadolescence obsessed with her addict mother; always fearing harm would come to her parent. In the end, she confessed, she had to stop. She finally realized that "It'll kill me if I worry as much as it takes."[148] Latasha, of course, never had the opportunity to run this cathartic course with her mother.

Crystal Harlins became a regular at an after-hours establishment in South Central, the B and B Social Club, located on the corner of South Main Street and Florence Avenue. Crystal was no introvert, and she had a temper. She was known to have loud, public arguments with some of the club's other clientele. One of the managers had even barred her from the B and B on occasion. As for Vester, his criminal activity and involvement with drugs expanded over time. He was arrested three times in as many months during that fateful summer and fall—on July 24, 1985, for possession of drugs with the intent to sale; again in August 1985 on the same count; and on Halloween 1985 for burglary.[149] Vester's rage against Crystal also was reaching a crescendo.

The night that Latasha and her siblings witnessed Vester Acoff beat their mother was September 30, 1985, the occasion of Latasha's little brother's fifth birthday. Latasha was nine. Most of the Harlins family was present for the celebration. Vester brought Cora Mae Anderson, a woman he was romantically involved with, to the party. It is not certain how the fight between Vester and Crystal began, but it soon got physical. Crystal got the worst of it. She accused Cora of helping Vester, of holding her down while he beat her. Cora countered that she was just trying to help Crystal, trying to calm her so that Vester's beating would be swift and perhaps not so vicious. Crystal did not buy it. She threatened to get Cora back. Cora and Crystal kept their distance, but a couple of months later, on Thanksgiving night 1985, the two women ran into each other.[150]

The forces that precipitate tragedies like Crystal's death on Thanksgiving night are well known to crime statisticians. African Americans, for example, are seven times more likely to be the victims of homicides. Most homicides are the result of an argument. Most women are killed in a domestic dispute. Most African Americans are killed by another African American. Alcohol use, by the victim, the perpetrator, or both, often has taken place before the fateful event. Cocaine use can increase the rate of female victimization tremendously, especially among black women in their twenties and thirties. Given all this, Crystal's murder largely went by the numbers.[151]

It was about two in the morning, and Crystal Harlins was sitting alone, painting her fingernails at the bar of the B and B Club when Cora Anderson came in with some friends. Crystal ignored Cora and stayed at the bar. About 30 minutes had lapsed when Cora came up to Crystal. She sat down at the bar beside Crystal, and the two talked for about a half hour before a heated argument broke out. Crystal's and Cora's angry voices filled the club and attracted the attention of other customers as well as the club's enforcer, Willie Winston. Soon the two women stood up and seemed to be preparing to fight. Winston stepped between them to prevent any further trouble. He did not know that Cora had a gun in her hand. Without warning, Cora reached across Winston's shoulder and shot Crystal. Latasha's mother grabbed her chest as she fell to the floor uttering, "I've been shot." They were her last words.[152]

Denise Harlins painfully remembered the death of her older sister. She was so shocked and hurt—the entire family was—that they let

Crystal's best friend identify her body. They could not stomach going to see their loved one in the morgue.[153] The official autopsy report documents that Crystal Harlins, age 26, died on November 27, 1985, of a gunshot wound to the thorax. Cora Mae Anderson was arrested on suspicion of murder and released two months later after having raised her $35,000 bail. Anderson's trial did not begin for almost another two years.[154]

Cora Anderson eventually was found guilty of voluntary manslaughter. At Anderson's sentencing hearing, Ruth Harlins spoke on behalf of Crystal: "My daughter," she began emotionally, "was a kind, loving and ambitious person who loved all peoples. She is sadly missed by her mother, her three children, of which she has left behind, which I have got to raise, relatives and friends. As a result of my daughter's death, it has brought agony, pain and hurt to me and my family. My daughter did not deserve to die a cruel and malicious death the way she did."[155] On November 12, 1987, the court sentenced Anderson to five years in prison. The family was horrified—they believed that Anderson should have been charged with first-degree murder, found guilty, and given the maximum sentence. For them, Anderson's sentence was an unthinkable miscarriage of justice. Latasha was nine years old.

Latasha's Pain

"'Tasha was just very quiet, and very shy. She didn't hang with many people. And she was hard, you could tell. You didn't mess with her. She was like in her own world."

Crystal Harlins's violent and unexpected death devastated Latasha. She grieved her loss quietly, but those family members closest to her knew what great pain and loneliness she suffered. Her cousin Shinese remembered that every time Latasha passed a local cemetery, she would cry. "I guess it made her think of her mom. She's not even buried there." Her aunt Denise believed that "She wanted to be with her mother . . . she had this empty feeling inside her."[156] Although only a child when her mother died, Latasha felt keenly that she was responsible for her little sister and brother. She leaned heavily on her grandmother, but even Denise had to admit that Latasha soon became "kind of the leader of the family. She was very protective of her brother and sister."[157] November

27, 1985, was the last day of what was left of Latasha's innocence, of her tattered childhood. Like many children who had lived through the difficulties Latasha faced—growing up in a home witnessing her mother being battered, living with parents who sometimes drank too much and used drugs—Latasha kept her private pain, private. She did not talk about her life at home, and she did not let her friends visit. "I didn't even know she didn't have a mother," a middle school friend admitted. "She never told me anything about her mother getting killed. But then I never went to her house. She came to my house a couple of times," the friend recalled.[158]

Crystal's murder changed the entire family. Denise, for example, explained that she felt particularly forlorn when Crystal died because she had never told her sister that she loved her. She had never told her mother as well. Crystal's death changed that. Denise became more demonstrative to her family. Ruth had to find a way to move on without her oldest daughter. She also had to find a way to grieve for her brother Curtis, who, in a brutal coincidence, had been killed in a fight in an East St. Louis bar on the same day as Crystal. He was the second brother who had been shot and killed in East St. Louis.[159] As usual, Ruth turned to God for comfort and hope.[160]

Ruth Harlins took in Latasha, Vester Jr., and Christina. Grandmothers rescuing grandchildren was not a new experience for her. Ruth had lived with her grandparents Lula and Ed Thomas when her parents first divorced. Grandparents filled the void created by missing parents; the children they took in filled the void of their own sons and daughters who had gone away or had been taken away too soon. Latasha and her siblings were not the only ones who lost a dearly beloved that Thanksgiving.

The Harlins household in Los Angeles, as it had been in East St. Louis before, and Alabama and Mississippi long before that, was one filled with extended kin that spanned across generations. Ruth was brought up to understand that family did not turn their back on family when things got rough. They moved on, readjusted their lives, and did what they had to do to keep the family intact. Ruth brought her strong family values to bear on the children—stressing religion, education, and respect. Everyone agreed that Latasha was very close to her maternal grandmother. Ruth freely admitted that Latasha really was like her own daughter. And Latasha loved to spend time alone with Ruth. A few weeks before her death, her grandmother tearfully recalled, the two had gone shopping. Money was always tight in the Harlins home, so when Ruth offered to buy Latasha two dresses that day—she wanted her to look nice when they went to church—Latasha refused one of them. They ended the day by sitting in a photo booth in Woolworth's, taking pictures.[161]

Vester Acoff did little or nothing to support the children, although Ruth still allowed him to see them, and he even lived in her house with them for a while. After all, she must have reasoned, they had only one parent left. It probably was very painful, however, for Latasha to see Vester. She must have known that he beat her mother routinely. She also must have known, intuitively at least, that he had been instrumental in her mother's death. Without her own words to describe her feelings, it is useful to listen to the words of others with similar experiences. Latisha from Portland, for example, was an African American girl about Latasha's age, who also witnessed her father abuse her mother. The hatred she had for her father, Latisha wrote, endured. "When I was younger," she noted, "he beat on my mom all the time. He beat her with a hammer and a gun and left her for dead. Us kids had to see all that, see her bleeding and rushed to the hospital. It hurt so much to see her like that. Now we just consider our father dead, 'cause we don't got no love or respect for him."[162]

Vester Acoff also continued to run afoul of the law after Crystal's murder—he was arrested just three months after Crystal's death for trespassing and injury of property. Denise Harlins remembered ruefully the last time she saw him—Vester was desperately trying to escape gangsters.[163] He moved back to Illinois, only to continue to break the law and move in and out of prison.[164]

Latasha passed from elementary to middle school three years after her mother died. As a preteen, she was quiet and shy, but Bret Harte Middle School was good for her. Her cousin Shinese was with her and Latasha managed to develop a coterie of friends—JonSandy, Tunisia, and Sandra. Latasha excelled academically, placing on the school's honor roll in both the sixth and seventh grades.[165] She and her friends lived in a world of fashion, boy crushes, pop music, teachers, and grades.

With her mother deceased, and the only man she identified as a father gone, however, Latasha was forced into a world of adult concerns. Although her friends, and even her adult kin, thought of Latasha as mature and knowledgeable beyond her years, she could not have been able to understand and accept her profound personal losses, the meaningless violence that punctuated her life and destroyed her dreams, or the general uncertainty of her life. She went to school and hoped for a better future. Those who knew her well spoke of her desire to become an attorney—to become part of that judicial system which was, from the perspective of her family's history, on the one hand so threatening and on the other, so ineffectual.[166]

Life for Latasha was difficult. The memoirs of girls her age, commenting about various aspects of their lives that mirror Latasha's, reverberate with pain, rage, and isolation. Latasha's anger and frustration sometimes bubbled to the surface. There was the time, for example, that she became irritated with her little sister and threw a fork at her from across the kitchen table. It struck the girl in the right eye, causing permanent loss of sight.[167] Yet, Latasha's life also reverberated with hope and resilience. She was a fighter. Everything she had endured had taught her to survive. "Everyday," one of her contemporaries wrote, "I try and listen to what I know I got inside of me, my personal strength, so I don't become a victim of society."[168]

Latasha struggled not to be a victim; but by the time she entered high school, she had endured many heart-wrenching difficulties, and it showed. Someone at Westchester High School described her as a "teacher's worst nightmare."[169] When asked about this description, Minnie Crews, who was the dean of students during Latasha's brief tenure, recalled that Latasha had visited her office more than the average student and that "she did cut her classes, her academic record was poor, and she was maybe a little bit of a smart-mouth—she was disruptive."[170] A kinder and perhaps more accurate assessment would have been that Latasha was an adolescent challenged by a tragic family life in a new school environment that caused her to sometimes act out and to do poorly academically her first semester. At least one of her teachers at Westchester, Terry Mernin, went on record with a different view than Crews: "Yeah, she was a tough kid," he noted. "Really rough around the edges. But she was intelligent. She could do good work. But she was absent a lot. I thought she might have problems at home . . . She also lived a long way from school. She had to take a lot of buses to get here; maybe it was too much. But I really liked 'Tasha."[171]

A few kids from Bret Harte also attended Westchester, and Latasha did have a social life her freshman year. Her inner circle described her as the girl who was always smiling that "beautiful smile." Mernin recalled, "In many ways, she was just a naïve little girl. And she had this smile, this wonderful smile."[172] "Latasha was real attractive. . . . with a really nice figure. [She] was really cute and she had a lot of boyfriends," one of her close friends noted. Everyone seemed to know her for her big smile, "Chinese eyes," and "school-girl bangs."[173] They nicknamed her "Lil' Gizmo."[174] Gizmo, of course is the furry, loveable Mogwai from the popular 1980s *Gremlins* movie franchise. "I didn't see that side of her," a friend responded, when asked about Latasha's discipline problems at Westchester, but added, "I knew Latasha could be tough, and she would speak up if she didn't feel she was being respected."[175]

Westchester High was some distance, 13 miles, from the Harlins home. Latasha traveled by bus, transferring twice every morning and evening to make her away across town in the busy LA traffic. The ride must have taken at least an hour each way—if she had traffic luck on her side. All the adults in her home were employed—her grandmother, her aunt, and uncle—so it would have been difficult for them to monitor her behavior once they left for work, believing that she had gone to school. Her cousin Shinese traveled with her to school, but she probably would not have reported Latasha's absences to her family. Latasha skipped school more than a few times that freshmen year, hanging out with friends and with boyfriends. "All of us skipped school," a friend noted. "It wasn't that hard to do. Our mothers didn't watch us as much in high school as in middle school."[176] Latasha's family did watch her. Her older female kin, her aunt Denise and her grandmother Ruth in particular, were aware of the problems that Latasha was having with school authorities and often counseled her to attend school regularly, to try hard to arrive on time, and to behave properly once she got there. They reminded her of how well she had done in middle school and encouraged her to pull up her grades so that she could attend college.

The source of growing tension in the Harlins home vis-à-vis Latasha, however, was not just about her average grades but also about her social life. Latasha's girlfriends retrospectively commented on the conflict. "It was always just simple stuff, like staying out after dark. It wasn't big like getting a hole in her nose or a tattoo. 'Tasha wasn't like that," a female friend recalled.[177] Yet, the family's rifts and misunderstandings with the quiet, but determined, teenager sometimes escalated into heated disputes, occasionally ending in Latasha leaving home for a few days to cool off. Her aunt Denise recalled that Ruth, Latasha's grandmother, sometimes let her spend the night with girlfriends if Latasha wanted to do so. The family's matriarch hoped that it would help keep the peace between the teen and her aunt.

Older Men and Young Girls in Latasha's World

One source of particular angst between Latasha and aunt Denise was the relationship that the teen purportedly was having with two adult men: Jerry Foster, a counselor at the local recreational center; and a neighborhood man, known only as Ron. Aunt Denise knew only too well the shattering consequences of early sexual involvement between adult men and vulnerable teenage girls out to prove that they were "grown." Latasha's mother Crystal had given birth to her when she was only 16. Denise, who was younger than Crystal, had bore her only child the same year. Their mother Ruth had become pregnant when she was 16. These premature sexual relationships all had come at a high cost for these two generations of Harlins women, and Denise was trying to make certain that the same thing did not happen to her daughter Shinese or to Latasha. It was not just that Latasha was too young to be sexually active; Foster was too old. His sexual involvement with Latasha, if, indeed, that is what it was, was illegal—statutory rape.[178]

When interviewed after Latasha's death, Jerry Foster reported that he was 29 when he knew Latasha. Other records, however, suggest that he was 32—that he had been born the same year as Latasha's mother.[179] 'Tasha was only 14 that summer after middle school when she became so active at the recreation center where Foster worked as a counselor. A graduate of USC with a Bachelor of Science in Recreation and Physical Education, Jerry Foster had played varsity football in college and then had gone on to have a short career in the Canadian Football League. A single man with a college degree, who had played ball at "SC" and professionally, was an anomaly in Latasha's neighborhood. He would have attracted the attention and admiration of many teenaged girls and young women. Foster may have realized this, for, according to one of Latasha's closest friends, he may have used his social, educational, and financial cachet to seduce many underage girls who frequented the local Algin Sutton Recreation Center.

Sexual predatorship within the black community has not been an issue that many have been willing to publicly acknowledge. Some venerated informational and cultural institutions, like *Ebony* magazine, have tried to warn parents like the Harlins that "child predators don't creep around in dark alleys, choosing instead to operate in the open and have chosen professions (or perhaps volunteer in areas) that give them access to their prey" and that "one of the more common mistakes parents make is giving the assailant unsupervised access to their children."[180] Yet, there has been no significant campaign within the black community against the kind of predatorship that plagued Latasha and her friends, or that plagued her mother, grandmother, and aunts when they were her age.[181]

Like most ethnic communities, African Americans have been reticent to reveal what the majority view as shameful, perverse behavior, made even more so because it embodies crimes perpetrated against black children. To explore sexual predatorship, much like a discussion of incest and very much like a discussion of pedophilia (both of which are present in every community), indicts fundamental community institutions and ideals. Nonetheless, the problem exists, and it existed for Latasha. The problem of older men stalking young girls and sexually harassing them was rampant in Latasha's neighborhood, as it is in many poor black neighborhoods. A friend from middle school remembered that she and Latasha spent a lot of time talking about how much they hated their neighborhood.

> Why? Because of the men on the street. Men who would, you know, try to get with us. Everyday. They would even stand right outside the entrance of the school and around the gate. They were always there when we walked to school and when we went home. I never told my mother. What could she do? I just figured that was the way it was. I would just walk fast with my books and sometimes . . . cross the street, but they would cross the

street too. Sometimes I would tell them I had to go home and do my homework. You know, to let them know that I was a child. Clearly they were older."[182]

This friend, JonSandy Campbell, had recently moved to South Central from a suburb of Memphis, Tennessee, and she found it difficult to understand why no one, an adult authority figure, a member of law enforcement, or a school official, tried to stop these men from harassing them at their middle school. After all, they were only 12, 13, or 14 years old. "In the South, we didn't get bothered," she recalled. "Police patrolled the school yard. If older men are found near the schoolyard, they are given a ticket for trespassing. It was trespassing for older men to talk to young girls at or near the school." At Bret Harte, however, she had no sense of a police presence that could help them with this problem.[183]

Older men took advantage of naïve girls who were looking for fun and a few nice gifts, and who respected those men who had made it, relatively speaking. Most of the boys their age had little to offer in their estimation. African American girls in the 1990s, from working poor black communities like Latasha's in Los Angeles, echoed this sentiment. Fourteen-year-old Latisha, writing from Portland, Oregon, for example, complained bitterly about the kinds of boys she and her friends knew and their treatment of girls their ages. According to her, the boys were all "gang-affiliated" and only interested in having sex with them, not in having a friendly, respectful relationship. "Most dudes are all in gangs, or already dedicated to a female, or just plain messed up." Latisha spoke candidly of her young friends who got pregnant at an early age, and who since had lost all contact with their children's fathers. Both her brothers were gang members—one belonged to the Crips; the other, the Bloods. The older brother, who had been in and out of prison, had a girlfriend who had a baby, but, Latisha added, "He don't help take care of it 'cause he always out gangin' . . . My brother says he loves his girlfriend, but I think the only reason he stays with her is cause of her baby check—you know, the money she gets from welfare . . . So he's stealing his baby's money." Latisha's brother even denied that the child was his, "but the baby looks just like him." She also had a cousin, 13, who already had two children. "Yeah, she was pregnant with the first one when she was eleven, had it when she was twelve."[184]

For girls like Latasha, therefore, Jerry Foster, a college graduate with a steady paycheck, seemed like quite a catch, even if he was their parents' age. Some reasoned that at least older men had the resources to add some comfort, romance, and adventure to their lives, even if for a very short while. Few were mature enough to understand the long-term consequences of these kinds of relationships—the exploitation that led to pregnancies, illness, and fewer future opportunities to improve their lives.

Marcolette Wideman, one of Latasha's friends and a track teammate who spoke openly about her and Latasha's purported sexual relationship with Jerry Foster, offered many details of how both were seduced by a man twice their age. Marcolette was one year older than Latasha, and the two teens sometimes provided cover stories for each other when they were doing something that they knew their family would not allow. Marcolette had borne a child she claimed was Foster's, a son named Christopher, when she was 16. Foster denied paternity, "but everybody on the block knows it's his kid," she asserted.[185]

Jerry Foster vehemently denied that he was sexually involved with the 15-year-old Latasha. He described the relationship instead as extremely close, noting how very bright and mature Latasha was for her age. Latasha, he remembered, was extremely smart and the two enjoyed talking to each other about all sorts of things. Foster insisted that he was not romantically involved with Latasha, pointing his finger instead to another older man purportedly named Ron who lived in her neighborhood. "Ron" was supposedly 22 or 23 years old. Despite Foster's denials, Latasha's friend Marcolette and her aunt Denise were convinced that the two were sexually involved; an "improper relationship," as Denise discretely described it. Marcolette recounted Foster's alleged relationships with her and with Latasha, noting that they had sex at the recreation center, in his car, at motels, and at his mother's house. "The day after the funeral, he told me," she said, "I'm the one who dropped her [Latasha] at the store. She wanted to get some juice."[186] Latasha had told her family that she was going to spend the night with Marcolette.

Denise Harlins confronted Foster with her suspicions weeks before Latasha was killed. Concerned and angry, Denise went to the Algin Sutton Center where she demanded that the counselor stop trying to seduce her niece. Foster probably was nervous when confronted with the out-raged woman, but he managed to turn the table on Denise. She had had something to drink before meeting him, and Foster smelled the alcohol on her. He told curious onlookers that Denise's accusations were just the mistaken ranting of a drunken woman. Foster stood his ground, denied all allegations, and, purportedly, kept seeing Latasha. Denise also fought with Latasha about Foster, to little avail. They supposedly argued about him the night before Latasha's death.[187]

There is no indication that any of Latasha's adult kin or, for that matter, any of the adult kin of Marcolette's, or any of the other local girls Foster was supposed to have abused, reported their suspicions to au-thorities at the Los Angeles Department of Parks and Recreations or to the LAPD. When Marcolette was asked about her mother's response to her serial relationships with older men, she answered that her mother always told her that the men were too old for her.[188] Still, parents and guardians of Latasha and her friends had some legal recourse in this matter. California Penal Code Section 261 stipulates that any person over the age of 21 (Foster was at least in his late 20s) who has sexual re-lations with a minor under the age of 16 (Latasha was 15) is guilty of a felony and can face up to three years in prison and civil penalties that could amount to $25,000.[189]

There were perhaps many reasons why family members of these girls did not seek legal assistance. Many of these relationships, histori-cally, have gone undetected and, therefore, unreported because both the man and the girl, sometimes coerced, sometimes not, agreed to hide it.[190] Aunt Denise suspected that Foster was having an inappropriate relation-ship with Latasha but had no certain evidence. She also might not have shared her suspicions with her mother, the head of the Harlins clan, because she did not want to worry her. Since Latasha was the same age as Denise's daughter, the protective aunt took on much of the responsi-bility of raising her. But Denise may have had other reasons as well for not alerting the police or park authorities.

Many black residents of urban poor communities do not trust the police to protect their interests or to offer help when they request it. The history of statutory rape legislation enforcement in the black com-munity underscores the class and race biases of the larger judicial system. Once accused, black men and women tended to be more readily convicted and received harsher punishments than their white counterparts.[191] Given the failures of the court system to adequately address the past criminal victimization of Latasha's family, the Harlins certainly had little or no reason to believe that it would be helpful in this matter.[192] Moreover, Latasha's maternal kin may have feared that to file a report of sexual abuse might mean that Latasha, and maybe even her siblings, would be removed from Ruth Harlins's home and placed in foster care—a typical fear made even more potent because the grandmother was not the legal guardian of Latasha, Sylvester Acoff was. Ruth had taken care of Latasha and her little sister and brother since her daughter Crystal's death but had never legalized her role as their guardian. Family honor also might have kept them, and other affected families, from admitting that a sexual predator had infiltrated their community and their home. Likewise, Ruth's inability to stop Latasha from seeing these men might have been experienced as an embarrassing loss of parental control. It must have been difficult to know where to turn for help. They certainly would not have considered asking Latasha's male "guardian."[193]

The Scene Is Set

If Marcolette Wideman was correct, on the morning of March 16, 1991, Jerry Foster and Latasha pulled in front of the Empire Liquor Market. Latasha wanted to get some orange juice to take home—perhaps as a peace offering to her aunt or perhaps just as a treat for the family. Since the store was only a couple of blocks from her house, and Foster was not welcome there, the two said their goodbyes and Foster drove off.

Latasha entered the store and walked purposefully to the refrigerated cases located at the back. Scouring the contents, she opened the door and chose a bottle that was priced $1.79. Perhaps unthinkingly, she stuck the bottle of juice into her backpack. The top of the bottle protruded out. Teenagers often act impulsively and provocatively, hardly anticipating the precarious results of their behavior. Latasha turned and approached the counter with two dollars in her hand—the cost of the juice including tax. Soon Ja Du, the store owner's wife, eyed the high school student suspiciously as she approached. "Hostile Korean shopkeeper," Latasha probably thought. Her uncle, a former employee at the store, had told her all about how rudely the Dus treated their customers—how they believed everyone was stealing from them, even their black employees. Latasha may have believed that Du suspected her of stealing, but she had no cause to believe that Du would physically assault her, actually grab her, drag her across the counter, and try to pull her backpack off.

Latasha probably never anticipated that Du would put hands on her in the way that she did. In the street, everyone knows not to touch without permission, especially not to touch aggressively unless you are looking for a fight. Latasha must have been shocked and angered. Du could have hurt her or damaged her cousin Shinese's backpack. She had promised to return it in good shape. A private girl, Latasha would not have wanted Du to look inside the bag.

Her immediate response was to fight back, and fight back forcefully. That was one lesson she had learned over and over again. People in her family were fighters. Sure, they paid a heavy price sometimes for the fight, but they fought nonetheless. And Latasha was known for her street savvy. To be grabbed in her neighborhood meant disrespect and a physical threat. One could not survive letting that go. To do so, set one up to be pushed around again and again. Just a few days before, a group of girls had beaten Latasha because she had refused to join their gang. She was outnumbered but stood her ground. Latasha had learned how to take care of herself the hard way. She was not going to let Soon Ja Du get away with pushing her around.

FIGURE 2.1 "Korean Grocer Soon Ja Du," Photograph of Ken Lubas. Courtesy of the *Los Angeles Times*.

2

Soon Ja Du

"She had a good life in Korea"

The Empire Liquor Market was virtually empty that Saturday morning except for the Korean shop owner's wife, Soon Ja Du, who was alternately sitting and standing behind the counter. "We opened the store around 8:00, almost around 8:00 because the night before my husband had closed the store and he was so tired that we couldn't get there on time," Soon Ja Du began her testimony about the fateful events of March 16, 1991.[1] Only a few customers had come in during the first couple of hours that they were open for business. As the time approached 10 a.m., two customers, a sister and a brother—nine-year-old Ismali Ali and 13-year-old Lakeshia Combs—who had gone to the store to buy their mother some hair gel—came up to the counter to pay for their items. All of the activity in the store was captured on a security video camera. Soon Ja Du had learned to watch her customers carefully through mounted mirrors for signs of stealing. She may have been particularly vigilant this morning as the fear and anger evoked by local gang members' recent threats rested uneasily on her.[2]

By the time the police arrived on the scene some twenty minutes later, Soon Ja Du's life had changed forever. She appeared to have collapsed, physically and emotionally, on top of the check-out counter. On the floor beneath her, lying in a growing pool of blood, was 15-year-old Latasha Harlins, dead from Du's gunshot wound to the back of her head. Beaten on the scene, first by Latasha and then later by her husband, Soon Ja Du continued to move in and out of consciousness for some time. She continued to exhibit intermittent bouts of unconsciousness during her ten-day jail stay.[3]

Du's first two appearances in criminal court were distinguished only by her incoherent state. Any good criminal defense attorney will tell you that half the battle is managing the defendant's image. Du's case was no exception. Her family members had fiery tempers, a strong sense of victimhood, and were not particularly apologetic for Du's part in the death of young Harlins. They were doing little to win the public's sympathy. Her eldest son Joseph, who was especially angry at the vulnerable position he and his family had been placed in by local residents, spoke to the press on Soon Ja's behalf, but only briefly. His father, more diplomatic in tone, publicly admonished Joseph for speaking his mind and told him more than once to be quiet. Soon Ja Du's daughter Sandy, then a theological student at Biola University, a private Christian institution in La Mirada, refused to give interviews but stayed close to her mother's side. "I'm not going to talk with any reporters," she decided. "They came over to our house in the middle of the night and scared the hell out of us."[4] Mrs. Du's lawyers presented her case in the preliminary court hearings. Even during her trial, almost everything she said was publicly articulated (spoken in English) and entered into the formal court record by one of her translators, either Wongsup Kin or Paul H. Yi.

Who, then, was Soon Ja Du on March 16, 1991, the day that she shot and killed 15-year-old Latasha Harlins? According to the biographical accounts newspaper reporters compiled, Du was a wife, mother, and shopkeeper—not unusual roles for some of the women in her Korean immigrant community. And, like many of her peers, she had not always had the dual identity of a traditional homemaker and store clerk. Immigration had changed Soon Ja Du's lifestyle, and her life, forever.

Early Life in Korea

Soon Ja Du was born on December 27, 1941,[5] the eldest daughter of the only doctor and a nurse in her Korean farming village in North Chungcheong Province in the center of what is now the Republic of Korea.

Korea is known as the Land of the Morning Calm and Soon Ja's home province at the time of her birth was beautifully green with notable mountain ranges. Local farmers grew ginseng, tobacco, rice, and barley and there was some mining and silk weaving. Korea was still one country then. Du's home has become a popular tourist spot now, but in the 1940s and 1950s, it was anything but serene or calm. Instead, it was a site of two wars and multiple colonization efforts. During the early 1950s, in particular, when Soon Ja was just entering adolescence, her country was devastated by the Korean War that left millions dead and the nation divided into two hostile countries. Soon Ja's home province, like all the others, was touched by great loss and destruction. North Chungcheong also was the site of a brutal massacre of tens of thousands of political prisoners, as well as civilian men, women, and children, by the Rhee government—the Bodo League Massacre—in 1950.[6] War, colonial oppression, political upheaval, economic depression, and uncertainty characterized the Korea of Soon Ja Du's youth.

Still, Du's professional-class parents managed to raise her as part of the local elite—a class status that Soon Ja never completely relinquished. Her sense that she was of a different class, of a higher class, than most of the people she met in Korea or Los Angeles, colored the way in which she saw the world, particularly after she moved to the United States. As a teen, Soon Ja left home to attend and graduate from a university in Seoul where she studied literature. There, she met Heung Ki (Billy) Du who was six years older. Du was the son of a construction company owner and, unlike the rural raised Soon Ja, had lived his entire life in Seoul. The two were married on September 18, 1958, a few months before she turned 18. Soon Ja's life in Korea moved quickly from that of a schoolgirl to wife to mother.

Mr. Du served in the Korean Army, rising to the rank of major. He also was a martial arts expert, and his work as a teacher of Tae Kwon Do helped support his family. Despite these occupations, however, Billy primarily was a key figure in his father's construction business. The couple eventually had three children—Joseph, Sandy, and Michael—and, when they lived in Korea, Mrs. Du stayed home and cared for them. "She had a good life in Korea," her daughter Sandy recalled. "She never had to work outside the house."[7] Still, the Republic of Korea was not a place

FIGURE 2.2 "Downtown Seoul Korea, 1961," Image courtesy of Bruce Richards.

where she and her husband thought their family, especially their children, could benefit from the limited opportunities this society offered. The nation, after all, was still struggling politically. It also was very much considered a developing nation, even though Korea's economy was growing rapidly, and had been doing so since the early 1960s.[8] Many were leaving for the United States where prospects seemed much more reliable. Like Ruth Harlins, the Dus came to California in search of better educational and career opportunities for their children. What comfort and security the Dus experienced as part of the middle class in Seoul, however, diminshed tremendously when they left Korea.

The Move to Los Angeles

Soon Ja Du and her family came to Los Angeles the year that Latasha Harlins was born, arriving on December 28, 1976. Soon Ja was 35.[9] The move meant drastic changes, not only in her lifestyle, but also in her personal identity. No longer the well-to-do daughter of a doctor, or the educated wife of an army officer, Soon Ja was forced to work outside her home, first as a couch assembler, and then as a crotcheter at St. John's Knits (a garment factory in the San Fernando Valley). The family initially lived in a small apartment in Inglewood, one of the small, incorporated cities adjacent to southwest Los Angeles.

Mr. Du faced just as profound adjustments in status and occupation. He was well educated and had a lot of business experience, but Billy Du did not speak English well. Like many immigrants, his limited English language skills barred him from the kind of work and compensation he desired. Du eventually found work as a repairman at a Radio Shack store. The children enrolled in local schools—certainly not the best in the area, but they helped them become culturally adapted. Soon Ja Du's new work status was a great adjustment. The Korean National Bureau of Statistics, for example, documents that only 29% of women worked in the public sphere in 1984. By 1980, however, 54% of Korean immigrant women in the United States, like Du, did.[10] According to friends, the Du family, like so many other Korean immigrants of their generation, endured great emotional and physical stress during this period of acculturation. Chan Ock Kim, one of Soon Ja's co-workers at St. John's Knits remembered: "She had a lot of stress after she got here. She was only a housewife in Korea. Here she had to work to survive."[11] Anthropologist Kyeyoung Park would agree with this analysis. In her work on Korean entrepreneurs in New York, Park notes that for many Korean immigrant women, their gendered lifestyles changed tremendously when they left their home country. In Korea, women typically did not work outside the home after marriage. Once they arrived in the United States, they stopped working only after having children. Even childbearing, however, did not keep them out of the labor force for long in urban America, because they soon returned to work in family-owned businesses. Moreover, this kind of work provided them with little "positive self-esteem."[12]

All of the Dus, including Soon Ja, no doubt also had to become accustomed to the racial, linguistic, and ethnic diversity of Los Angeles. Korea of the 1950s, 1960s, and 1970s largely was a homogenous society. Ordinary life did not bring one into close contact with people who were racially different. The Dus not only had to adjust to this difference, but they also had to manage the prejudice and racism of other people toward them. Asian immigrants, as well as native-born Asian Americans, attest to the daily racist taunts and race-based exclusion they endure.

Making a New Life with Old Traditions

Still, Soon Ja Du did survive. The Dus worked hard and meticulously saved their money. In 1981, five years after their arrival in the United States, and the same year that the Harlins family moved to Los Angeles, Soon Ja Du and her husband were able to purchase a convenience store in the San Fernando Valley. "It was his," Sandy Du explained of her father's triumph in acquiring their first store. "That was important."[13] None of them had experience in this kind of business, but Billy Du understood some of the basic principles of entrepreneurship from his business experience in Korea. The family worked tirelessly to succeed, and eventually they could see some of the reward for their efforts. Their American dream of financial success was coming true: ownership of two liquor-convenience stores; college education for their children; a home in a middle-class neighborhood; and the creation of a community of friends and extended kin through marriage.

Mrs. Du, like her husband and children, began to build a social group for herself. The family mixed with other Koreans and Korean Americans and joined the Valley Korean Central Presbyterian Church in North Hills. She and her husband even became deacon and deaconess there. Soon Ja Du must have felt more comfortable with her life in Los Angeles, but she retained close ties with Korea. Sons Joseph and Mike both returned to South Korea to marry Korean women, and Soon Ja went with them to participate in their traditional marriage rituals. She also decorated her house with Korean-style furnishings—made of black lacquer and mother-of-pearl; and helped support a leper colony in the Yellow Sea.[14]

Soon Ja Du aspired, in many ways, to be a "traditional" Korean woman. Korean culture has many roots—Shamanism, Buddhism, Taoism, and Confucianism, for example. Buddhism taught its followers the ability to withstand hardship through self-discipline. Taoism emphasized ideals of patience, harmony, and contentment. These were all qualities that Korean immigrants like the Dus needed to successfully build a life for themselves in the United States. The teachings of Confucianism, however, were most influential in Korean culture.[15] In Confucianism, there are many hierarchies in one's social world that must be respected: father and son; older sibling and younger; the elderly and the young;

master and servant; and, for the purpose of this discussion in particular, husband and wife. Drawn to the old traditions, Soon Ja Du, as an adult female, would have defined herself as a wife, mother, and caregiver.[16]

In traditional Korean society, such as the village where Soon Ja Du was raised, a woman did not choose her marriage partner—her father and future spouse made that decision. Moreover, once married, a woman had to behave "appropriately," or risk the shame of being rejected and sent back to her father's house. A wife could not, for example, commit or exhibit one of the "seven evils": jealousy; disobedience of mother- or father-in-law; dishonesty; infertility; an incurable illness; a bad temper; or adultery. A folk saying summarized best what conventional Korean brides were counseled: "to become dumb for the first three years, deaf another three years, and blind still for three years to survive particularly in their early marriage."[17] A mother taught a daughter to think not of herself as an individual, but instead to be submissive to her husband and to her husband's family. A Korean wife was supposed to work in her home and sacrifice her personal happiness for the good of her husband and family. She was not to act out of a sense of individual worth, ambition, or accomplishment.[18] "Silence was disciplined into us," writer Lisa Parks explained.[19]

Some Korean women who migrated to the United States did so to escape the prescribed gender roles of their homeland. An immigrant woman of Soon Ja Du's generation, for example, explained that one of the reasons she wanted to leave Korea was so that she could leave behind restrictive gender roles for women. "Everything is for men," she recalled of her life in mid-twentieth-century Korea. "Cater. King Kong . . . women just cooked . . . they lived in the kitchen. I didn't like [those kinds of] customs." These gender prescribed duties, this woman (Ms. Cho) explained, were part of the overall oppressive and old-fashioned life everyone was subject to in Korea.[20]

Late twentieth-century US society would view such Confucian-driven gender dictates as oppressive to women. Nonetheless, these ideals and internal hierarchies were the basis for much of Korean patriarchal practice and undergird most of the familial dynamics in traditional Korean families. The members of the Du family, therefore, understood that they had to place their families's needs before their own individual ones, and that their own status was wholly dependent on the status of the entire family. Following this order of society and behavior established over centuries, along with the veneration of ancestors, were important principles for the Dus.[21]

While Soon Ja Du's children no doubt exhibited social characteristics drawn from both their traditional Korean culture and the culture of their new country, Soon Ja Du was committed to maintaining, as much as possible, a conventional Korean role within her marriage and family. In the United States, however, Du's feminine, elite Korean traditions clashed with her urban, immigrant reality. What did it mean to be a Korean woman while living, working, and raising a family in America?[22] The answer was varied shades of the same reality—difficulties and compromises.

To be forced into the work world out of economic necessity was one thing, but to work selling liquor was another. She knew that her family needed her to work to support the success of their businesses, but Soon Ja also knew that her new Korean/Korean-American community did not uniformly support her work in a liquor store, even one her family owned. Some of her fellow church members also disapproved of her work. According to one: "A lot of conservative church people feel it's not right . . . like working in a nightclub or massage parlor," despite that a significant slice of the Korean immigrant economy was based on just such labor.[23]

For Soon Ja Du, the work she performed was not only difficult to reconcile with her sense of Korean middle-class respectability and a woman's "place," but it also was physically and psychologically demanding. Working behind the counter of a liquor store also could prove to be dangerous. Nineteen Korean American grocers in Los Angeles, for example, died working behind their store counters in the 1980s.[24] The work too was hard—so many hours a day, almost every day of the week. As sociologist Edna Bonacich explains, many Korean shopkeepers of the Du generation had working conditions similar to those of day workers rather than "petit bourgeoisie," because of their long work hours, lack of benefits, and low earnings.[25] Yet it was Soon Ja's duty as a wife to respect her husband's wishes and dreams, and Billy insisted that the family's opportunity for financial advancement lay in convenience store ownership.[26] He was not alone. Koreans and Korean Americans owned more than 30% of independent liquor stores in Southern California in the early 1990s.[27]

Despite the difficulties, the family prospered. They lived in the middle-class enclave of Mission Hills, where the per capita income was twice that of Latasha Harlins's South Central neighborhood and the population density was only half. Like many of Los Angeles's suburbs, Mission Hills was not a particularly diverse community. There were, for example, only 32 African Americans residing there in 1990. The few black people who did live in Mission Hills were solidly middle class, quite unlike those the Dus served as customers in their South Central store. The per capita income of African Americans living in the Du's community in 1990, for example, was almost $37,000, the highest among all its residents, regardless of race. In contrast, Asian and/or Asian American per capita income in that community that year was $20,557.[28]

Even in the midst of modest success, however, it was clear that Soon Ja Du's life in southern California was not an easy or secure one. It is certain that many Korean Americans successfully invested in convenience and liquor store ownership; yet, it was at sustained financial risk. The owners who flourished did so through a tremendous amount of hard work, perseverance, good luck, and good relations with their customer base. Soon Ja Du typically worked behind the counter with her husband most days and for very long hours. Fatigue, worry, and lack of control, within her family and outside of it, led to bouts of depression and chronic migraine headaches. She once was hospitalized for several weeks after falling into a comatose state. There is some evidence that her marriage may have been difficult, at least at times. Her husband sometimes slapped or punched her. (The police, for example, had to stop him from slapping Soon Ja when they arrived on the scene after Latasha had been shot.)[29] Experts, writing on the occurrence of domestic abuse in Korean American families, note that it is not a rare occurrence. At the base of the abuse, they explain, is a frustrated immigrant patriarchy, threatened by the lack of access to economic success and recognition in the nation's capitalist-driven economy, combined with and a keen sense of their wives's dependence.[30]

Moving the Business to Compton

Mr. Du later sold his first store and bought another: the Bouquet Canyon Liquor store in Valencia. In March 1989, Billy also purchased the Empire Liquor Market in South Central for $388,000. Soon Ja Du opposed buying the new store. She had hoped that he would use the money instead to move the family to a home close to the beach "where they could spend quiet days fishing."[31] In the patriarchal world in which Soon Ja Du lived, however, she essentially had little influence in such decisions. She might have been angry or upset at her husband's decision to buy the Empire Liquor Market, but gendered family traditions hardly would have let her demand that he act otherwise. She had to be his dutiful helpmate in his endeavors. As experts on Korean familial culture note: "An individual learns to suppress disruptive feelings such as hostility, especially towards superiors, in order to maintain family harmony. As a result, many of the repressed feelings may turn into guilt feelings or into depression."[32] Mr. Du insisted that the Compton store would be a good family investment and eventually would give them and their children greater financial security. That was, after all, one of the main reasons they had left Korea—to ensure a better future for Sandy, Mike, and Joseph. "My father said our family should buy the market," Sandy Du recalled. "As a parent, he always wanted to earn enough to leave something behind for us."[33]

But was there was more to the story of Billy Du's financial ambition than the desire to help his children? One Korean businessman named Kim who knew Mr. Du spoke openly of his desire to flaunt his economic success. Even before they purchased the Empire Liquor Market, he noted, "Mr. Du used to be in full feather, and always went to the bank and took part in other activities in the Korean community," leaving Mrs. Du to do much of the work at their store. It was too much for her, Mr. Kim noted. "Mr. Du relied upon family labor, especially his wife, Du Soon Ja. I find it problematic to rely on family labor heavily. You might save some money on wages, but you do not realize that family members force themselves to work beyond their capability."[34]

The new store meant more work for everyone. Billy planned to work at the Empire Liquor store from 7 a.m. to 10 p.m. everyday. "It was so difficult for me, very tiresome for me to open the store, close the store," he noted.[35] Their oldest son Joseph sometimes assisted them from 11 a.m. to 10 p.m. Soon Ja Du worked primarily at their Bouquet Canyon Liquor store, some 52 miles away, from 7 a.m. to 2 p.m. But with her husband and son now mostly on-site at the Compton store, more responsibility fell into her lap at the Valencia business. Before March 16, the date of Latasha's death, Soon Ja had worked in South Central only a few times, usually on the weekends.

By 1989, the Dus had gained some experience in the liquor store industry, but they had never before owned a store in a predominantly poor, black neighborhood. Their store in Valencia was in a solidly middle-class white community—blacks were less than 2% of the new city's population, schools were good, and unemployment rates were beneath state levels. South Central was the polar opposite. The Dus soon began to understand that race, class, and location made a tremendous difference in small-business management and profit.[36]

Things never went smoothly for them as shopkeepers in South Central. Shoplifting was a significant daily problem, as were other crimes, and there were three robberies within the first two years of operation. Mr. Du brought in guns for protection: a M1 carbine rifle and a handgun, a .38 caliber Smith and Wesson. He kept both loaded under the counter.[37] The handgun was stolen during one of the robberies, but later recovered.[38] The alleged crimes committed at the Empire Liquor Market were part of a general trend in the neighborhood. Crime statistics for 1990 indicate that there were 936 reported felonies, including 184 robberies, 254 assaults, nine rapes, and five murders. The neighborhood also was principal residence of an active serial rapist and murderer— Chester Dewayne Turner—who killed at least ten women between 1987 and 1998, most of them on South Figueroa, in the vicinity of the Du's store.[39] Turner was one of three serial murderers who preyed on the area at the time, all targeting young black women. The most prolific was Lonnie David Franklin, known as the "Grim Sleeper," who too murdered at least ten women and one man in the area beginning in 1985.[40] The neighborhood that the Dus worked in and that the Harlins family lived in was, by any standard, a very dangerous place.[41]

The Empire Liquor Market also did not turn a significant profit for the Dus. They had hoped to reap about $15,000 net each month, but they rarely did. Distributors of some foods, beverages, and newspapers refused to stock the store at one point when the Dus failed to pay them. At least one employee, the store's butcher, had a paycheck bounce, twice.[42]

Perhaps most problematically, the Dus did not get along with the local customers. They did not have a high opinion of their clientele, particularly the local blacks. The dislike and disregard was mutual. The Dus eventually tried hiring some neighborhood help, undoubtedly hoping that this would help ease the tension between themselves and their customers. Their first introduction to the Harlins family, in fact, came when Billy Du hired Latasha's uncle, Richard, to bag groceries in their store. This relationship did not portend good things for the future.

Richard Harlins (a.k.a. Richard Brown) became an employee of the Du's in 1990. Some months later, however, Richard quit when Mr. Du ordered him to work overtime without pay. This incident is important because it suggests the manner in which the Du family, or at least their patriarchal head Billy, perceived their African American patrons. Richard explained:

> They fired me because I refused to work overtime. They asked me if I would work overtime for them, and I said no. And he said, "You supposed to work for free, do what Black people are supposed to do." And I looked at him, stamped my foot, and said, "No, I'm not working for free." And he said, "Fine, go home." So I went home.[43]

When asked how the Dus treated him otherwise, Richard Harlins replied: "They treated me nice most times. Although every move I make he would watch me, even in the bathroom. He thinks I take tissue. That really upsets me . . . But otherwise they treated me okay." When asked how the Dus treated the other customers, Richard was unequivocal: "They were really terrible to the customers, never smiling or saying thank you. I would do that when I bagged the groceries."[44] The Dus may not have been overtly or visibly friendly to their customers. Traditional Korean culture would dissuade shopkeepers, particularly female shopkeepers like Soon Ja Du, from looking in the eyes of customers, smiling at them or touching their hands, for example, when returning change or receipts. African Americans, on the other hand, would view this kind of treatment as cold at best, disrespectful and offensive at worst.[45]

Customers also complained about the way the Dus watched them in the store—as if they were all thieves. Joseph Du, they added, would snatch money out of their hands when they tried to pay for an item.[46] Latasha's grandmother had warned her not to go into the Du's store because she believed the owners always thought everyone was trying to steal, and she did not want Latasha to get into trouble. Other girls who knew Latasha at Westchester reported in grief counseling after her murder that they felt harassed when they walked into a Korean-owned store, not just the Dus' establishment. "All of these kids have felt like victims," school psychologist Barbara Snader said. "They walk into a store and feel like people suspect them . . . looking them up and down. It's a very humiliating experience. It's like they're guilty because they're black."[47]

Still, some Korean/Korean-American shopkeepers admired the friendly nature of their black and Latino/s customers. A 1991 survey indicates that these entrepreneurs sometimes preferred black and Latino/a customers to whites because the latter were less friendly.[48] This was, however, perhaps not the case with the Dus and their patrons.

There was one incident, in particular, which branded the Empire Liquor Market in the eyes of the neighborhood as a hostile place and the Dus as uncaring, even mean-spirited. A drive-by shooting occurred one evening in 1990 outside the store, and witnesses ran for cover. Some ran into the Empire Liquor Market. Mr. Du, no doubt hoping to stay out of the fray, forced them out of his store. One of the local black men he forced out subsequently was shot and killed.[49] If there had been any goodwill in the community toward the shop owners before, that incident ended it. And there was something else as well—rumors that Mr. Du was "running around with young black girls."[50] If they were true, it would have meant more problems for the Du marriage and the relationship the Dus had with the black community.

If things were not bad enough, the Dus then came into conflict with a dangerous local gang, the Main Street Crips. Only shortly before the Harlins shooting, the Du family felt compelled to close the store for two weeks in order to defuse an escalating problem with local Crips who had threatened to hurt their eldest son. Joseph Du had promised the District Attorney's Office that he would testify against Michael Hickson and Tyrin Thomas, two alleged Crips members he had accused of stealing from the store and threatening to harm his kin and their property. They all feared Crips's retaliation since the gang, purportedly, had threatened to return to the store and kill the entire family.[51]

Joseph begged Billy to sell the store, but his father could not find a buyer, at least not at the price he wanted. "My mother's biggest prayer was to sell the store," Sandy Du lamented.[52] After months on the market, there still were no takers. Mr. Du went so far as to meet with gang leaders to resolve the situation. He hoped that they could come to some kind of agreement, a truce. But, he confessed, "it was unsuccessful."[53] Afraid, frustrated, and angry, Soon Ja Du went to the store that fateful Saturday morning in an effort to keep peace in her family and to give her son and husband a rest.[54]

The Issue of Race

It probably was not difficult for the Dus to generalize their fear and anger of local Crips members to the larger South Central population. Interviews of Los Angeles Korean shopkeepers in 1989 revealed that most felt blacks were inferior to them and did not deserve to be treated with courtesy and respect.[55]

Many Korean business owners seemed to have been influenced by potent myths within their ethnic community, the larger US urban world, and Korea that characterized African Americans as lazy people who wanted to live off of welfare. Indeed, Korean/Korean-Americans who speak to the issue of black racism in Korea and in their communities in the United States most often locate the origin and nexus of their attitudes toward blacks in the attitudes of white Americans toward blacks. Ji-Yeon Yun, a noted historian of Korean American women, asserts, for example, that Koreans first learned of the racial hierarchy that existed in the United States by observing how blacks were treated differently from whites among the military forces stationed in their country. This hierarchy was reinforced through images found in film and television shows. Once they arrived in the United States, Yun continued, they witnessed how blacks struggled at the bottom of society. "Koreans who dreamed of coming to America were dreaming of upward mobility," she noted, and therefore, they "dreamed of living like whites not like blacks." Unaware of the legacy of racial oppression, "the racial prejudices of Koreans mimicked the racial hierarchy they found in America society."[56] Korean Americans vividly recall the lessons they learned growing up in the United States regarding the status of blacks in their society: "At least you're not black," and "You should be grateful that you are not black," Elaine Kim remembered whites often told her.[57]

While it is difficult to gauge the ways in which Soon Ja Du, her family, or other Korean shopkeepers in Los Angeles may have been influenced by the media or mythical images of blacks that are found in Korea, there is compelling evidence that indeed blacks are stigmatized in that country. Images of blacks that emerge from blackface performers, cartoons, and comedy routines point persuasively to a cultural history that denies black humanity. Whether it is an entertainer painted black imitating black rhythm and blues singers like Louis Armstrong, or a commercial to sell fried chicken that features Africans in "tribal" clothing about to physically assault a Korean man until he whips out a bucket of delicious chicken, the message is the same: blacks are different, and that difference indicates inferiority.[58]

Even in the mid-2000s, visitors to the Republic of Korea were struck by the level of tolerance of black racism in Korean society. The Bubble Sister phenomenon, for example, indicates a significant amount of acceptance of black racism. The Bubble Sisters were a pop group, composed of four young Korean female singers, who dressed and performed in black face. The group, signed by Universal Music Korea, painted their faces and bodies black; wore braided hair, afro wigs, or rollers; sometimes painted their lips white; and performed with exaggerated facial expressions. When asked why they portrayed themselves in this way, the group responded that a producer had told them that they were not attractive enough for their projected audience. They decided, as a marketing strategy, to embrace "ugliness," and thus the blackface costume and makeup.[59]

A Nigerian-Canadian who was teaching English in Seoul at the height of the Bubble Sisters's popularity complained about the phenomenon but had to admit that he was not surprised. Olalekan Waheed Temidire noted that living in South Korea in 2003 was like "living in Western society before the civil rights movement came to be." Temidire added that he became so tired of people calling him "Gum-Doong-Ee" every time he took a subway that he finally asked someone what it meant. It was, he concluded, a word "equated" with the N-word.[60]

Superbowl MVP Hines Ward, whose mother is Korean and whose father is African American, has been quite vocal about the racism he has encountered (years after Soon Ja Du and Latasha Harlins met).

FIGURE 2.3 "Bubble Sisters Album Cover."

Hines went to Korea in 2006 and was stunned by the amount of racism that mixed-race individuals (mixed with African Americans) had to sustain in the country. He noted that biracial adults cannot join the Korean military. He also recounted meeting a young biracial soccer player whose teammates referred to as "nappy-haired boy" and whose coaches told him he would not be allowed to play because of his racial status.[61]

The custom of the social rejection of blacks is particularly apparent in the treatment of Korean women who marry African American men. These relationships became especially prevalent after the US military began to establish a salient presence in Korea during the 1940s. Korean wives of black soldiers and officers paint a clear picture of complete social rejection by other Koreans as a result. Many, for example, believe that these women were not respectable and probably had been prostitutes in Korea. Similar notions, however, did not apply to the women who married white US military personnel. "Because I had married a black person," one Korean woman who migrated to the United States noted, the Korean immigrant women she worked with "would call me a nigger yankee whore and would have nothing to do with me."[62]

Few seem to associate the racialized attitudes toward blacks with personal experiences as the racialized "other" by the Japanese, for example, in their colonization of Korea, or later, the racial oppression they experienced, especially at the hands of whites, once they migrated to the United States. Korean shopkeepers, according to a 1992 survey in New York City, viewed their black customers, when compared with whites, as violent and dishonest. A whopping 70% believed that blacks were more criminally oriented than whites. Equally important, 61% thought blacks to be less intelligent than whites, and a large minority (45%) believed that blacks were lazy, but only a small minority (13%) believed that blacks were poor because of racial discrimination. In other words, many believed that blacks could improve their lot if they were more intelligent, hardworking, and honest.[63]

Soon Ja Du held similar beliefs. When interviewed by Patricia Dwyer of the county probation office in 1992, Du admitted that she was afraid of blacks and that she did not respect them. "They look healthy, young . . . big question why they don't work . . . got welfare money and buying alcoholic beverages and consuming them instead of feeding children." She concluded that it was "their way of living."[64] Faced with what they perceived as black hostility, some Korean/Korean-American shopkeepers did not attribute these bad relations to their own behavior or prejudice, but rather believed that their black customers's resentment derived from their jealousy of Korean industry and success.

African Americans interviewed during the same 1992 survey, however, offered a different analysis. They overwhelmingly attested to the poor, disrespectful, dishonest, and sometimes violent treatment that they suffered at the hands of most Korean shopkeepers in their communities. Others noted that the shop owners charged high prices for low quality goods and demonstrated little or no interest in the community outside of posting a profit. In the survey, for example, the majority of the black customers of Korean-owned markets in New York indicated that these merchants drained resources from their communities. Moreover, significant numbers believed that Korean entrepreneurs exploited their customers and reduced economic opportunities for residents.[65] John Mack, then president of the Los Angeles branch of the Urban League, reiterated this point when he noted in 1987 that "the Urban League continues to receive complaints on a regular basis from blacks who say they resent rude treatment they get from Korean merchants . . . Whether that be because of language difficulties or what, if you're going to do business in a community, it's important to be good neighbors and sensitive, for instance, in showing that by hiring more black employees." He also noted that Korean merchants, when asked to hire from the neighborhood, typically responded that they run family-operated businesses. Mack's response was simple: "when making money off a community that has high unemployment and social problems, it doesn't sit well with people who live there to say you just can't afford to hire some of the people who are keeping you in business."[66] This type of sentiment, black customers implied (and, in this case, that the Dus ran a "liquor" store rather than a "convenience" store) was at the base of the hostile interactions Korean shopkeepers complained they routinely had with their black customers.[67]

African Americans, however, also have racialized Korean Americans and other Asian-descended Americans. Like other Americans, black Americans have resented waves of immigrants whom they believed worsened working conditions for African Americans and competed with them for space in segregated urban landscapes. They too have ridiculed the cultural and physical attributes of Asians from various locales and ethnic groups. To be racist, to be exclusionary of the racial "other," after all, is a fundamentally American point of reference and identity. African Americans, as Americans, hardly have been successful in escaping such prejudices or behaviors.

The Asian "menace" from the African Americans perspective, therefore, was economic, social, and cultural. On the streets of South Central in particular, as in other locales in urban America and increasingly in smaller cities in the late twentieth and early twenty-first centuries, conflict between blacks and Asians has mostly meant conflict between blacks and Koreans. Many shopkeepers, including the Dus, have spoken of the harsh treatment they received from black customers. They only have to recount the harrowing homicide statistics to make their point: 19 Korean shopkeepers were killed in Los Angeles during the 1980s, most of them by African Americans. In 1992, nine Asian American shopkeepers were killed in Washington, DC. The next year, 15 lost their lives in Los Angeles.[68] While these homicides usually occurred during a robbery, anyone can understand Korean shopkeepers's fear that blacks were targeting them as a group. The "BLACK OWNED" signs that saved many businesses during the 1992 riots, while scores of Korean-owned shops burned to the ground, offered them more evidence. Many Korean shopkeepers have felt that this kind of treatment is, indeed, the result of racial hostility that blacks feel for them. Some Asian/Asian-Americans who have not just worked in black communities, but resided in neighborhoods with African Americans, have spoken similarly of experiencing black animosity. Ying Ma, for example, a Chinese immigrant who arrived in Oakland, California, in 1985, at the age of ten, recalled that all Asians, despite their country or culture of origin, were assumed to be the same in her neighborhood and school. The "label 'Chinamen' was dished out indiscriminately to Vietnamese, Koreans, and other Asians," she noted. According to Ying Ma, the taunting that local black children, and later by adolescents and adults, subjected her to was vicious and constant. No one, she explained, attempted to learn her name. She was just "Ching Chong," "dumb Chink," "Chow Mein" or "Chinagirl." Everyone laughed at her culture, language, and race. If she tried to defend herself, she was threatened with violence. As an adult, Ying Ma graduated from Cornell and Stanford Law. Yet, she still witnesses black-on-Asian discrimination. She recalled, for example, watching a black woman screaming at a Korean man on a public bus, "You f—ing Chinese person! Didn't you hear that I asked you to move yo' ass? You too stupid to understand English or something?" Ying Ma, a foreign policy expert, the author of *Chinese Girl in the Ghetto*, and one of the Bay Area organizers of Proposition 209 to end race-based affirmative action in California, also made the observation that, as far as she knew, much of this kind of abuse was class based. "In poor neighborhoods across this country," she explained, "Asians endure daily racial hatred just as I did. Because of their language deficiencies, their small size, [and] their fear of violent confrontations, they endure in silence . . . So each day they grow more bitter against a group that much of America refuses to acknowledge to be capable of racism: African Americans."[69]

Frank Wu, professor of law at Howard University, also has commented on the racism Asian Americans have been subjected to in late twentieth- and early twenty-first-century America. In his book *Yellow*, Wu writes from both personal experience and the results of copious research. Within the response of the "American" to the Asian American, he notes, there is a great contradiction—Asian Americans have a presence, but also are invisible. They inhabit the perceptions of others about them. "I alternate between being conspicuous and vanishing, being stared at or looked through. Although the conditions may seem contradictory, they have in common the loss of control." This "loss of control" of one's own image, Wu maintains, is experienced as a great tragedy. The loss of the right to define oneself individually, prized in American society, he concludes, "is the greatest loss of liberty possible . . . I might as well be a stage prop."[70]

While Wu locates this kind of racism as an American response to the Asian presence, white Americans, rather than blacks, are the focus of his analysis. The murder of Vincent P. Chin, of course, takes center stage in discussions of Asian brutalization by whites. Ronald Ebens and Michael Nitz beat the unarmed Vincent Chin to death with a baseball bat in Detroit on June 19, 1982. Ebens and Nitz supposedly believed that Japanese automakers were the reasons for the Detroit auto industry's problems. Although Chin was Chinese American, not Japanese, one of the men was heard screaming while he beat Chin: "It's because of you little motherfuckers that we're out of work!"[71] Arrested on charges of second-degree murder that later were reduced to manslaughter, Ronald Ebens pled guilty, and his stepson, Nitz pled no contest. The judge in the case, Charles Kaufmann, sentenced both men to three years probation, a $3,000 fine, and $780 in court fees.[72] Many experienced what Helen Zee, a Chinese American journalist and activist, did when she read about the case and the defendants's sentences. Zee confessed that she felt "distraught, betrayed—and furious. The probationary sentences seemed to echo the familiar taunt, 'a Chinaman's chance,' that grim reminder of the days when whites lynched Chinese with impunity."[73] Two years later, Ronald Ebens was found guilty in federal court of violating Vincent Chin's civil rights; Nitz was acquitted. Ebens was sentenced to 25 years in jail, but the case was overturned on appeal due to a technicality. During the retrial—which was held in Cincinnati, Ohio, not Detroit, the jury acquitted Ebens of all charges.[74] Completely disgusted at the inability to win justice for her son, Lily Chin, the victim's mother, gave up her life in the United States and returned to China.[75]

Criminal cases that went against Asian Americans have not been their only complaints of discrimination in the justice system. Some Korean immigrants have noted that cases that involve property also are settled unfairly against them. For example, Kyeyoung Park interviewed a Mr. Kang, who explained: "In 1983 I was sued for lack of heat. In that case, if you are white, you will be fined only $25 or $100, but $2,000 or $3,000 if Chinese, and if Korean, you will be fined $4,000. . . . This reflects community power in the justice system. . . . There are already many Chinese judges. So we badly need second-generation Korean American judges, a district attorney, and lawyers in the future."[76]

As such, it was not just the white working class, Frank Wu acknowledged, who felt and acted on racist notions regarding Asian Americans, but rather a phenomenon shared across class and race boundaries in the United States. It was clear to Wu, as with most others, for example, that most Americans did and do not distinguish between Chinese Americans and other Asian-descended Americans. When analyzing the findings of the 2001 report *American Attitudes Toward Chinese Americans and Asian Americans*, based on a phone survey of "highly educated people," in the nations three most populous cities—New York, Chicago, and Los Angeles—Wu speculated that similar results would have been reached as well had other Asian and Pacific Islander (API) groups, including Koreans, been the subject of the query. The findings were indeed compelling: 25% of those surveyed believed Chinese Americans were harming the ability of other Americans to be employed; one-third believed that Chinese Americans had too much influence in the nation's "high technology" sector and had deeper loyalty to China than to the United States; and almost one-half believed that Chinese Americans passed secret information to China. Moreover, a majority of those surveyed in this study "balked at the idea" that a Chinese American should be a CEO of a major company, preferring instead a Jew, African American, or female to hold such a high-status position.[77]

Rosalind Chou and Joe Feagin, writing on racism that Asian Americans face in the United States, also document that Asian Americans, both those born in the United States and those who become naturalized citizens, face a tremendous amount of racist taunting, physical aggression, and outright discrimination in schools and in the workplace. Noting the impact of white privilege on Asian American aspirations, they assert: "Whites have been educationally, economically, and politically advantaged for all of U.S. history." If a person of color, including Asian Americans, manages to "enter educational or job settings populated heavily by middle-class whites," that person has had to "overachieve" to gain that position and must continue to do so if they hope to continue to excel. Even so, many still encounter the "glass ceiling," while white colleagues do not.[78]

Frank Wu centers most of his analysis on white discrimination, but also included in *Yellow* some direct evidence of black-on-Asian racism. Racism, of course, suggests differential power at play. Many argue that African Americans are less likely to impose racist responses that are meaningful in any significant way because they lack power within American society. Yet, as Wu points out, in certain situations and at some sites, some African Americans do possess the kind of power that allows them to affect others in a racist manner. The obvious scenario is the one that Yin Ma recounts—power in numbers vis-à-vis other racial and cultural groups within a relatively isolated locale, institution, or organization. Ma experienced black racism in the predominantly black public schools in Oakland that she attended through the twelfth grade. Wu offers the example of the abuse of Asian Americans at the hands of blacks in public housing facilities in San Francisco. Asian Americans, he concludes, can feel doubly victimized, "ostracized by whites and terrorized by blacks." In the end, Wu notes, it is a zero-sum game that African Americans and Asian Americans play: "African American children pick on Asian American children, just as whites have done. But Asian Americans who can fight back do so without remorse."[79]

Sylvia Kim might disagree. Kim migrated from Korea to the United States during the late 1940s as an adolescent. Her father founded the first ethnic Korean church in Washington, DC in the early 1950s. After college, Kim eventually married and lived as an adult mostly in Arizona where her husband was a college professor. Kim noted that during most of her life in the United States, she did not think about race or racism. Even when her children reported that they were victims of racial teasing at school, she told them to rise above it. "I always told them just to work harder and prove to everyone else that they were superior. I knew that we were descendants of a proud people with many centuries of culture and civilization . . . I knew we were better."[80] Growing up in Washington, Kim often saw blacks (who were nearly the majority of the city's population) but attended all-white schools. She recalls, however, that she "looked down her nose at them," because she believed that they made too much out of racial victimization and did not "work twice as hard when confronted with racist behavior" as Asians did.[81] Her feelings changed radically about race in the United States and her identity as an Asian American vis-à-vis African Americans, however, when a white man she had never seen before shockingly assaulted her on the streets of San Francisco. Sylvia Kim's anger, pain, and humiliation grew because her white co-workers found it difficult to accept the attack as racially motivated—even though her assailant repeatedly referred to the Korean woman as "Chinese" when he randomly approached her, picked her up, and threw her against a wall, breaking her hip. Her experience with racialized hate caused Kim to rethink her opinion of African Americans. She began to educate herself by reading black history. After doing so, she noted, "I've lived in a vacuum. I realized, 'My gosh, this is what happens to black people all their lives.'"[82] "I now look back on my life and think how blind I was . . . I think what I might have done different if only my eyes had been opened sooner to the racism in our society."[83]

While Sylvia Kim arrived with her family on the East Coast in the 1940s, most Korean immigrants arrived decades later; and most settled on the West Coast. Fewer than 9,000 Koreans and more than 840,000 blacks lived in Los Angeles in 1970. Throughout that decade, however, the Korean population increased almost tenfold while the black population grew slowly. As early as 1974, disputes between the two groups began to be documented. Local high school officials were some of the first to address Korean and African American tension. Confict mounted rather rapidly both locally and nationally.[84] In 1981, blacks boycotted a Korean grocer in Queens, New York, for more than eight weeks after a purported physical altercation between the owner and a black customer. Two years later, the *Los Angeles Sentinel,* like other newspapers in New York and Chicago, found cause to run a series of editorials on the relationship between blacks and Korean/Korean-Americans in South Central, asserting in one article, for example, that the "African American community had literally been taken over by Asians in the past five years." As the number of Korean-owned shops in South Central increased, so too did the numbers of shopkeepers who were physically harmed or killed, usually during a robbery. In September of 1986, for example, four Korean shopkeepers were the victims of murder, a chilling wakeup call for most area storeowners. In that same year, blacks boycotted Asian owned Good Hope Carryout in southeast Washington, DC after a store owner purportedly chased a black female customer who had complained of "discourteous treatment" out of the shop with a .38 caliber revolver.[85] Both communities in Los Angeles feared that relations might continue to erode. Such sentiments helped to inspire the creation of the Black-Korean Alliance in 1986, a coalition of about 30 organizations from both communities that fostered cultural exchange, acceptance, and cooperation through sponsored public forums, scholarships, food drives, and crime-prevention workshops.[86]

Difficulties, nonetheless, mounted. Tensions continued to develop from altercations that subsequently led to public boycotts—sometimes lengthy ones. In the major locales of Korean entrepreneurship and black clientage, boycotts ensued during the 1980s, including ones in Brooklyn, Harlem, Jamaica (Queens), Los Angeles, and Chicago. During the 1990s, the list of cities with such protests grew even longer to include Atlanta, Berkeley (California), Dallas, Fort Worth, Indianapolis, Philadelphia, Washington, Miami, and Orlando.[87]

Patrick Joyce, in his detailed monograph on African-American–Korean relations *No Fire Next Time,* describes the boycotts that occurred in Los Angeles in the years before and after the Dus opened their businesses and documents that these events of black popular protest evolved for a number of related economic and social reasons. Verma Foreman, for example, organized the first of such boycotts in January 1987, centering her efforts on her former place of employment—Young Kim's Finest Market in South Central. She did so, according to Foreman, in order to force the storeowners to stock better produce, to donate to local charities, to lower prices, and to treat their black customers with more courtesy. Although Foreman's boycott lasted only one day, it was successful—resulting in the owner's written agreement to meet all of her demands.[88] That same year, blacks protested at the Crenshaw Swap-meet and the LA Slauson Swapmeet; a similar boycott of the Inglewood Swapmeet took place in 1989. Charles Cook, who led the United Black People of America protest against the Crenshaw Swapmeet in 1987, did so in order to force Korean shop owners to allow blacks to rent stalls there. Swapmeet owners eventually agreed to allow more African American stall representation (five out of fifty-five) after the Justice Department's Community Relations Service (CRS) created a successful arbitration process.[89] The Organization of Mutual Neighborhood In-terest (OMNI), led by local black entrepreneur Ward Wesley, boycotted the Slauson and Inglewood Swapmeets in an effort to get Korean owners and stall renters to reassess the manner in which they treated their black customers. With assistance from the CRS, an agreement eventually was accepted in which Michael Yoon, Slauson Swapmeet owner, promised to hire an "African American customer service representative."[90] The last African American boycott of a Korean-owned shop in Los Angeles during the 1980s took place at the Village Inn Café in the Crenshaw district. It began with a heated disagreement over a food order, lasted more than a month, and was supported by the local NAACP. Eventually, the café's owner was charged with misdemeanor assault of the aggrieved customer, ending the boycott.[91]

Model Minority

Despite early and enduring conflicts of Korean/Korean immigrants with blacks on the urban landscape, the dominant popular image of Asian Americans, including Koreans, in the United States is that of success, of doing well. "For many whites and other Americans, *Asian American* has become associated with 'model minority' success," sociologists Rosalind Chou and Joe Feagin argue.[92] As a group, Frank Wu notes, "we are said to be intelligent, gifted in math and science, polite, hard working, family oriented, law abiding, and successfully entrepreneurial," as well as good to elders and respectful of traditions. The myth of the Asian American as a model minority depicts an immigrant people (Asian Americans typically are regarded similarly by other Americans regardless of their place of birth or descent) who arrive with very little, are denied access to decent jobs because of their foreign educations and lack of English fluency, sacrifice mightily for their children's education, and work tirelessly to succeed financially. As early as 1971, Wu reminds his audience, popular magazines, such as *Newsweek* and *Fortune,* ran stories that characterized Asians as "outwhiting the whites" and labeled them the "superminority" as they overachieved the American dream in record time. While seemingly positive and complimentary, however, the myth is just that—a myth. As Frank Wu notes, it is objectionable for three important reasons: First, it is a one-dimensional, homogenous view of a very diverse and complex population; second, it implicitly mythologizes blacks and other racial minorities who have been less "successful" as lacking merit; and third, it denies the racially charged environment that Asian Americans have had to face.[93]

Indeed, it is little coincidence that the myth first developed a public unveiling in the midst of the civil rights activism of the 1960s. Just as blacks pressed for equal political rights and access to more of the nation's resources, the myth of hard-working, high-achieving, nonactivist Asian Americans emerged. In 1966, for example, the same year that Stokley Carmichael called for "black power," a *U.S. News and World Report* noted: "At a time when it is being proposed that hundreds of billions be spent to uplift the Negroes and other minorities . . . The Nation's 300 thousand Chinese Americans are moving ahead on their own—with no help from anyone else . . . Winning wealth and respect by dint of their own hard work."[94]

The tension engulfing the Empire Liquor Market on the eve of Latasha's murder, therefore, had a history and a future. Much of it was centered on urban racial hierarchies. Some of it derived from class issues. Some of it was intertwined with the history of liquor sales in Los Angeles. After 1975, much of that history, particularly in predominantly black neighborhoods in Southern California, was another chapter in the story of Korean immigration to the United States.

The history of Korean migration to this country is, in some ways, quite different from that of African Americans; and in others, remarkably similar. A few Korean students, traders, and political exiles came as early as the 1880s. The most illustrious, no doubt, was one of the major leaders of the Korean independence movement, Sao Jae Pil (his angli-cized name was Philip Jaisohn), who arrived as a political refugee in 1885. Jaisohn has a number of firsts to his credit: the first naturalized Korean to become a citizen of the United States; the first Korean Ameri-can medical doctor; and the creator of Korea's first modern newspaper.[95] Most Koreans arrived at the beginning of the twentieth century as la-borers, whom prospective employers hoped would work for the barest minimum wages and material support. Plantation owners in Hawaii recruited waves of Asian/Pacific Islander (API) migrant laborers to work in their sugar plantations. Drawing on workers from China, Japan, Korea and the Philippines, the planters hoped to exploit national ri-valries so that the workers would not unite for better treatment.[96]

Between 1903 and 1907, slightly more than 7,200 Koreans came to Hawaii as workers on sugar plantations, replacing, in part, Chinese workers who could no longer be employed because of the Chinese Exclusion Act of 1882.[97] Christian missionaries in Korea were an impor-tant part of the recruitment process—about 50% of those who came were Christian. The first group of 56 men, 21 women, and 25 children arrived on the SS *Gaelic* on January 13, 1903, as indentured workers. Their labor contracts stipulated that they had to work three years to pay off the cost of their travel from Korea. After they fully met the condi-tions of their contracts, Korean immigrants faced extremely discrimina-tory social, economic, legal, and political conditions. As a result, the majority of those who remained in the United States (fully one-half chose to return to their native Korea) became tenant farmers or per-formed menial labor. A few, the lucky ones, were able to open their own small businesses. As such, small-business ownership, such as the Dus's investments several decades later, was a deeply entrenched part of Korean American economic, social, and cultural histories.[98]

Kan Won-Shin, for example, left Korea in 1905 when she was 18 because she believed it was her duty to follow her husband and mother-in-law. Her story is indicative of the many difficulties early immigrants faced. Won-Shin's family was related to an important government official in Korea, but they still were treated as peasants in their new Hawaiian home. They did not even know that they had contracted to be laborers when they agreed to have their passage paid. The work they had to do was brutal. "We . . . were still in our long traditional clothes and wearing woven shoes of dried grass in the fields," she noted of her first day in America. "Suddenly, we were ordered to haul huge sacks across the sugar fields . . . We had never done a day's work in our lives." All of them were forced to work a year in the fields. For an additional ten years, Won Shin labored at menial jobs to support her family and to send her husband to school, as was her duty. Her husband had lofty professional aspirations and set about acquiring one advanced degree after another. Unfortunately, none of those degrees helped him, or his family, to gain the financial stability they sought. Racial and cultural differences proved to be a lingering, and firm, barrier. When Won-Shin's spouse finally gained a doctorate in law, he still could not get a job except in housework and service. Finally, the couple opened a chop suey business.[99]

The vast majority, in excess of 90%, of the early Korean immigrants to the United States were men. They arrived in a country that was overwhelmingly racist in their attitudes toward Asians, who were considered the "Yellow Peril." This racism was reflected in custom and law on local, state, and federal levels. Indeed, there were more than 50 laws passed in the United States between 1850 and 1950 that were meant to exclude and control the Asian immigrant population.[100] The first such legislation that applied to Koreans was the Gentlemen's Agreement of 1907 that barred Japanese immigration. Since Japan had colonial control of Korea from 1906 to 1945, the ban on Japanese immigrants also applied to Koreans. Unlike most early Japanese and Chinese immigrants, however, many Korean immigrant pioneers were from urban, rather than rural, areas of their homeland.[101]

While Africans first came to the land that would be the United States also as laborers in an overwhelmingly agriculturally driven economy and were predominantly male (about two-thirds), they arrived 200 years prior, lived and worked along the eastern seaboard, and were slaves, with not even the most primitive of social or political rights that Korean or other API workers exercised, even on the oppressively harsh plantations of early twentieth-century Hawaii. The experience of black enslavement, then, was followed by at least another hundred years of political, social, educational, and cultural discrimination. Blacks continued to live on the very margins of American society. Even so, by the time Korean immigrants began to arrive in substantial numbers, 250 years of slavery had bought something in the way of political rights for blacks:

citizenship with the ratification of the Fourteenth Amendment in 1868; the right to become naturalized citizens; and the right of black men to vote, made possible by the ratification of the Fifteenth Amendment in 1870, almost everywhere in the nation except in the American South.[102]

Persons of Asian descent born in the United States also were citizens. Still, like African Americans and other persons of color, nineteenth- and twentieth-century Asian Americans, born and reared in the United States, also found customary and legalized discrimination that limited their access to education; employment (beyond menial, agricultural, or criminal work); residential areas; religious expression; and inclusion in social, political, and literary organizations.[103]

Discrimination against Asian/Asian-Americans not only was exclusionary but often was violent. Mobs attacked the "Chinese" in places like San Francisco, Denver, Tacoma, Seattle, and Los Angeles in the 1870s. As early as 1860, Chinese immigrants were petitioning the federal government for protection. Pun Chi, for example, a Chinese merchant, sent an appeal to Congress that year which recounted the history of the immigrants of his generation. Chi noted that the Chinese had been enticed by dishonest labor recruiters during the era of the gold rush to come to this country. Trusting the description of the United States as a place of legal "equality," well-mannered residents, and friendship toward the Chinese, they came only to face great hardship and hostility: "When we Chinese are viewed like thieves and enemies, when in the administration of justice our testimony is not received . . . when in the legal collection of the licenses we are injured and plundered, and villains of other nations are encouraged to rob and do violence to us!"[104]

Moreover whites, and other Americans, did not differentiate between Chinese immigrants and Chinese Americans or, for that matter, other immigrants and natives of API descent. In Los Angeles's Chinatown, 19 men were lynched and $40,000 stolen from them by a mob in 1871.[105] This scene, and others like it, left Asian immigrants, including Koreans and their descendants, at the mercy of angry, lawless mobs, which mirrored similar treatment of blacks in the American South during the same era. Legal protection, to speak nothing of justice, was difficult for them to find.

Koreans also were victims of the abuse, but there was some relief. Despite the Gentleman's Agreement of 1907, for example, 2,000 or so additional Korean immigrants arrived in the United States between 1906 and 1924—some settling in Los Angeles. The agreement banned unskilled male workers, but did allow entry of wives and relatives of those already in the United States. Many of these female immigrants were "picture brides," who came to marry Korean workers. Others were Korean nationalists and students.[106]

Like the Japanese women who arrived with the promise to marry men whom they had not known, or even seen beyond a photograph, Korean picture brides often did not find the men of their dreams waiting for them.[107] Kim Sung-Jin, for example, arrived in Hawaii as a picture bride in 1905. She had left Korea because of a devastating famine: "Young children, old people, everyone was scrounging around for something to eat—anything. Even all the wild plants in the hillside were all gone. . . . We peasants were the worst off."[108] Even ten hours of work a day on the harsh sugar plantations of Hawaii, Sung-Jin concluded, was easier than life in Korea before she left. "It was really hard work . . . in the blazing sun," she recalled. "But it was better than Korea because we were so poor."[109]

Young women left Korea for America at the turn of the twentieth century not just because they were poor and dispossessed. Some sought educational opportunities that their home did not afford them. Others wanted to escape political persecution as a result of their support of Korean nationalism and opposition to Japanese colonization. Some left difficult marriages behind. Most wanted a chance to start over. Kim Suk-eun, for example, arrived in San Francisco in 1913, as a picture bride, but also hoping to gain an education. She came against her parents's wishes who warned her that if "something go wrong, don't tell family. You go drown in the ocean." She was immediately disappointed in her new husband, who, she confided, looked much older than his picture. But she soon found out that there was nothing she could do about her marriage or her desire for an education. Her dreams were not going to come true. Feelings of bitterness and despair accumulated when she realized, "I had been deceived. It was very difficult for me, under the circumstances, to face the realities of my fate."[110] Approximately 1,000 Korean women like Kim Suk-eun arrived as picture brides in the United States. A large majority settled in Hawaii; only about 200 moved to the mainland[111] Fortunately, most did marry, managing to escape the fate of thousands of early Chinese female immigrants who were forced into prostitution.

The stigma of the myth of Chinese female sexual promiscuity also stuck to Korean women. The Chinese first arrived in large numbers as labor for the 1848 gold rush. Later, they helped build transcontinental railroads. Although they also found work in early industries, such as laundries, and as cooks, housekeepers, and so forth, employers almost unanimously sought male workers, not females. The lack of women available for Chinese men to marry and create families soon led to the importation of Chinese women to be used in a developing sex industry.

Indeed, sexual exploitation of Asian immigrant women was rampant on the West Coast during the nineteenth and early twentieth centuries. By 1870, for example, San Francisco's Chinatown had 159 known brothels. While San Francisco, which had the largest urban Chinese population, was infamous for its Asian female sex industry, sexual misuse of Chinese women was found throughout the West as well as in eastern urban locales. The image of the Asian female prostitute was widespread and long-lasting, just as the myth of the black female slave deemed sexually "insatiable" by those most responsible for her abuse. "The Chinese are lustful and sensual in their dispositions; every female is a prostitute of the basest order," an editorial in a New York newspaper read in 1856.[112] These racist images, along with hostility against cheap Chinese labor in a soft economy, helped usher in the Page Act of 1875 which excluded entry into the United States of any "undesirables," including convicted felons, Chinese contract laborers, or Asian prostitutes. Seven years later, the Chinese Exclusion Act of 1882, which excluded all Chinese immigrants for ten years, was passed. It was later extended until 1943.[113]

Japanese immigrant women fared better than the Chinese because the Japanese government made efforts to limit the number of women who left Japan for the sex trade. They feared that these women would leave a bad impression of Japan and cause the United States to ban Japanese immigration as they had Chinese immigration. The similarity between the treatment of blacks and Asians was not lost on these immigrant women.

Korean Kim Suk-eun, for example, lived for a while in San Francisco during the 1930s. She was horrified by the ways in which white residents treated her. She realized that she too was a victim of the prevalent anti-Japanese and anti-Chinese sentiment, even though she was Korean. "We were all so hated as were the Blacks," Suk-uen explained. "Americans called us 'Dirty Japs, dirty Japs.' It didn't matter that we were Koreans. . . . There were many Korean picture brides in San Francisco. It was one of the worst places to be living. To be humiliated and be targets of rock throwers was a common occurrence. I have always been proud to be a Korean. Why should I be ashamed? We have a culture and a language all our own that is more than 5,000 years old. We don't bother anybody."[114]

By the 1920s, about 20% of the Korean population in the United States was female, primarily wives of Korean workers. Like their husbands, they labored on sugar plantations in Hawaii and elsewhere on farms, or worked as gardeners, custodians, and maids.[115] Even though Korean immigrant men outnumbered Korean women by five to one, this gender imbalance was small compared with that of other early API immigrants. Among the first generation of Japanese, for example, men outnumbered women 25 to one; among the Chinese, 19 to one and; and among Filipinas/os, 14 to one.[116] In 1924, the Oriental Exclusion Act disallowed immigration from all of Asia. The annual number of Korean migrants to the United States dwindled immediately, and fewer than ten succeeded in their application to come each year.[117] Those who did arrive in Los Angeles joined a community that had been growing for years.

World War II brought greater public scrutiny to all persons of Asian descent living in the United States. American residents who were Japanese, Korean, Filipino/a, and Chinese all served in the US military in the thousands and sometimes, in the case of the Chinese, in the tens of thousands.[118] The attack of Pearl Harbor on December 7, 1941, however, hastened the public's suspicion, denunciation, and internment of Japanese Americans. In their absence, Los Angeles's Little Tokyo became Bronzeville, the home of African Americans who took over residences and developed a thriving business district.[119] Koreans, Filipinos, South Asian Indians, and the Chinese fared better. A 1942 public opinion poll, for example, indicated that most Americans viewed the Japanese as "sly," "cruel," and "treacherous." In contrast, those polled viewed the Chinese as "honest," "brave," "religious," and "intelligent."[120] Indeed, the exclusion laws that had so severely impacted Chinese immigration were lifted partially in 1943, allowing a small quota to enter the country and those already residing in the United States to become naturalized citizens.[121] Three years later, Filipinos/as and Southern Asians gained similar relief.[122]

It is not certain when African Americans and Koreans first came in contact with one another in the City of Angels. What is probable, however, is that major interaction began during World War II, when the defense industry brought large numbers of African Americans to Los Angeles to work in local factories. These black migrants settled predominantly in South Central, not so far from sites of older Korean communities located between Hoover and Crenshaw and close to Jefferson Boulevard. No doubt there was some contact between these adjacent communities. It was actually another war, however, which deeply enhanced black-Korean encounters.

The Korean War during the early 1950s witnessed the arrival of hundreds of thousands of US soldiers to Korea, some of whom were African American. Since this war also was the first occasion of significant integration of black and white Americans in the US armed forces, there was considerable opportunity for association between Korean and black American military personnel, as well as some contact with civilians. Certainly the interactions would, for the most part, be quite restricted. The limitations were due, primarily, to the reluctance of General Douglas MacArthur, who led the United Nations command in the war until his controversial removal by President Truman in 1951, to actually utilize black soldiers in the war effort. MacArthur thought, according to NAACP lead attorney Thurmond Marshall, that the soldiers were unfit to serve. At the same time, however, blacks were fully integrated in the Navy and Air Force units that served in the war effort. Moreover, MacArthur's successor, General Matthew Ridgway, did deploy blacks in Korea.[123] There were, as well, some social and cultural exchanges, most apparent perhaps through the intermarriage of black soldiers and Korean women. The US military maintained a strong military presence in Korea after the war ended, primarily as a response to the partitioning of the country into South Korea and communist North Korea. Indeed, Cold War policies after the Korean partitioning encouraged greater Korean migration to the United States.

At the same time that African American soldiers were stationed in Korea in the 1950s and communities of black migrants, who had arrived in the mid 1940s, were developing some ties to the communities of Koreans already in Los Angeles, federal legislation was beginning to ease the restrictions against Korean immigration. The McCarran-Walter

Act of 1952, for example, partially repealed the Oriental Exclusion Act of 1924. It not only granted Asian immigrants the right to US citizenship and allowed small numbers of quotas for each individual country, but also sanctioned migration of US soldiers' Korean brides and the adoption of orphans by American couples. By 1980, 50,000 Korean women had married US soldiers.[124] Some of these brides were married to black American soldiers and some of the orphans were the biracial children of black soldiers and Korean women. The vast majority became naturalized citizens. Between 1950 and 1965, approximately 15,000 Koreans, primarily drawn from these two groups—about half women, the other half children—migrated to the United States.[125]

It was not until 1965, however, as part of the broad ramifications of the Civil Rights movement, that Congress passed the Immigration and Naturalization Act that completely overturned the Oriental Exclusion Act of 1924. The Hart Cellar Act of that year allowed immigration based on family unification initiatives, occupations perceived needed in the nation, political refugee status, and a baseline quota of 20,000 persons. This quota, however, did not include family members of persons already residing in the United States. The wives of US military personnel, then, were instrumental in increasing substantially the Korean population as sponsors of their family members who migrated. Some scholars believe, for example, that these women helped to sponsor 40% to 50% of the Korean immigrants who arrived during the first years after the passing of the Hart Cellar Act. For the first time in the twentieth century, Koreans migrated to the United Sates in family groups. Still, the number of women exceeded those of men, primarily because many were wives of military personnel and others were orphaned and abandoned girls. Approximately 100,000 Korean children came to reside in the United States, many as adoptees, from 1960 to the 1990s. Women and children, therefore, characterized much of the Korean immigrant population of the late twentieth century.[126]

Since 1965, Los Angeles has been the site of the largest Korean immigrant community in the United States, and Southern California, the second-largest site of Korean external settlement in the world (Yanbian, China, is the largest). Fifty-six percent of Korean immigrants in California lived in Los Angeles County in 1990.[127]

The year 1965 was indeed momentous. Voting rights and immigration legislation came at the end of decades of entrenched agitation to expand the body politic, especially to include African American southerners and to open the nation's shores to Asia. The hope of the Civil Rights era was in full swing. But for blacks living in South Central Los Angeles, it was too little, too late; or perhaps just not enough. On August 11, a riot erupted in Watts. Six days and $182 million in property damage later, 34 persons were dead and 1,032 injured.[128]

Three years later, as the working-poor black community in South Central Los Angeles struggled to rebuild, Korean immigrant entrepreneurs were opening the first shops in what would become Koreatown. In 1968, for example, the Olympic Market, located at the corner of Olympic and Hobart, was one of the first Korean-owned shops to open in the vicinity. The development of this business and residential area during the 1970s and 1980s was a reflection of the rapidly developing Korean American population in Los Angeles County. These two decades proved to be a heyday for Korean immigration. While the number arriving in 1965 was 2,165; in 1970, 9,300 came; in 1974, 28,000; and in 1976, the year that the Du family arrived, 30,830. By 1985, the annual Korean immigration rate was well in the thirty thousands. Both large numbers of men and women arrived, but the majority of immigrants from 1965 to 1989 were female.[129] Accordingly, the Korean American population in 1990 had a male-female ration of 4:5 (80:100), while the male-female ratio was 95:100 for the general United States and 96:100 for all APIs.[130] As the number of Korean immigrants continued to grow, few lived in communities occupied by African Americans, although their presence, as entrepreneurs, certainly was felt in many traditional African American communities. Moreover, the overall numbers of APIs increased so much that by 1990, they rivaled the number of African Americans in Los Angeles County. That year, blacks comprised 11.17% of all county residents. APIs were 10.77% and growing.[131]

Altogether, the number of Koreans residing in the United States increased by 125.3% between 1980 and 1990, rendering them the fifth-largest group of APIs in the country.[132] By 1990, 33% of the US Korean/Korean-American population lived in California, while only 12% lived in New York. The third-largest concentration of Korean/Korean-Americans lived in Illinois and New Jersey, 5% each. The vast majority lived in urban centers—Los Angeles County, San Francisco, San Diego, Chicago, and the boroughs of New York.[133]

There were many reasons Koreans came to live in the United States after 1965. Some did so because of political unrest and South Korea's uneasy relations with North Korea. Most however, particularly those among an aspiring middle class like the Dus, were attracted to what they believed were economic opportunities and the possibility of a higher standard of living for themselves and their families. Because of the presence of the middle class in the immigrant pool, those Koreans who did arrive represented some of the best educated of all immigrants coming to the United States. Approximately 32% of Korean immigrants, 25 and older, for example, held at least a bachelor's degree by 1980, rising to about 35% in 1990. Both Mr. and Mrs. Du had college degrees. Only immigrants from India and the Philippines exceeded this educational level that year. Only about 20% of the general population in the United States had similar educational backgrounds in 1980. In that year, for example, only 12% of young African American women and 11% of young African American men had completed four years of college; only 22% of young European American women and 25% of young European American men had done so.[134] Many Korean immigrants had been professionals—administrators, executives, physicians, or managers in their homeland.[135]

While men generally were better educated and had a higher occupational status in Korea than women, female Korean migrants were a part of this well educated, professional trend. Prior to arriving in the United States, 20.3% of employed Korean female migrants were professionals; 38.7% were in technical, sales, or administrative occupations; 20.6% were in service; 3.9% were operators and laborers; 5.8% were employed in production, crafts, and repairs; and only 0.4% worked in farming, forestry, or fishing. As such, the paid labor women performed in Korea was quite different from that they had to take on in the United States.[136] In 1990, for example, only 11% of employed Korean women in the United States were in the professional ranks; 9% in managerial; 25% were in sales and technical work; 14% worked in administrative support; 20% in service; 14% as operators; and 6% in production and craft.[137] Males had similar declines in occupational status and the economic, physical, and psychological rewards their status in Korea had allowed.

Years of exposure to US military personnel and their families deployed in South Korea, the impressions given by US missionaries, as well as the middle- and upper-middle class lifestyles depicted in exported American books and films, had convinced many South Koreans that the United States was indeed a land of opportunity, economic opportunity in particular. In 1975, the standard of living in the United States was much higher than that of their home country. Relatedly, per capita annual income in South Korea in 1977 was $843; in 1987, it was $2,100. In striking contrast, the per capita income of the United States in 1987 was $18,841.[138]

The concentration of Korean-owned businesses, residences, and residential property in Los Angeles grew with their population, encompassing the busy thoroughfares of Hoover, Normandie, Melrose, Crenshaw, and Pico, primarily south and west of downtown, expanding to areas quite close to traditional black residential neighborhoods. Korean immigrants first came to live in Koreatown when they arrived in Southern California for several reasons. Although their cohort was characterized by well-educated, middle-class professionals, for businessmen and entrepreneurs like the Dus, language and cultural barriers pushed many to take up residence in this area. Meanwhile, Koreatown's employment opportunities; cultural familiarity; inexpensive services, goods, and housing were key attractions. Elderly family members, in particular, felt comfortable because they could find food that they enjoyed and socialize with others who spoke their language and who had lived for years in Korea.[139] Their stay was usually temporary, a measure of how quickly they could acculturate and gain a solid foothold in the city's economy. While it was a welcoming oasis when migrants first arrived, poor schools, and high crime rates characterized the locale. Most moved as soon as they were able to do so.[140]

The Korean community in Southern California, as in other urban areas such as New York and Chicago, created important resources for its members. While these resources were meant to benefit all Koreans living in a particular locale, they were particularly important to the acclimation of the thousands of new immigrants, like the Dus, who were becoming part of the American urban landscape during the 1970s and 1980s. Sociologists Illsoo Kim and Pyong Gap Min, among others, have argued that Koreans in major US cities reside in "nongeographical communities" derived from "ethnic networks," rather than ones defined by geographical lines.[141] This certainly would appear to be so for Koreans who lived in Southern California as contemporaries of the Dus. Koreatown functioned as a commercial, social, and cultural center. Even though Koreans/Korean-Americans lived in Koreatown, the majority of the locale's population at the time the Dus arrived was Latino/Latina immigrants. Pockets of Korean residential communities developed instead in other parts in Los Angeles and Orange counties. The Dus, for example, initially moved to Inglewood, just southwest of Koreatown, before eventually purchasing a home in Mission Hills, in the San Fernando Valley. The Valley in the early 1990s was home for a substantial number of Korean/Korean-American residents.

Christian denominational churches were, and continue to be, of tremendous importance to the somewhat geographically disparate Korean ethnic community. Almost 75% of Korean immigrants became members of these religious institutions that are predominantly Protestant, particularly Presbyterian.[142] These churches, like other institutions servicing Koreans in Los Angeles, rapidly developed with increased migration after 1970. By 1990, there were approximately 635 Korean Christian churches in Southern California. The largest, the Oriental Mission Church, was created in Koreatown in 1970. Twenty years later, its membership exceeded 6,000. It was not soon, however, before it was rivaled by the Young-Nak Presbyterian Church, created in 1973. By 1990, the Young-Nak membership was 4,500. Thirty other churches in the area also had memberships of more than 2,000 that year.[143]

Korean churches, like black places of worship, provided a haven for its members—spiritually, socially, and culturally. Although only 25% of Koreans in South Korea are Christian,[144] the vast majority of late twentieth-century immigrants became affiliated with these churches because of their vital importance to their survival as new residents. Moreover, since Christian churches headquartered in the United States historically have played an important role in Korea—building, since the late nineteenth century, a number of schools, colleges, hospitals, and other service-oriented institutions[145]—there may have been a psycho-historical attachment that immigrants had to these institutions, if not before, then certainly once arriving in the United States.

Almost all the services have been, and still are, conducted in Korean—making them comfortable language settings for recent immigrants and for Americans of Korean heritage who want to retain their ancestral language. Many of the churches actively promote Korean cultural retention, offering language classes for children on the weekends, providing social hours after church services where traditional Korean food is served, and functioning as safe sites where recent immigrants can meet each other and Koreans of later generations. Churches are the location of celebrations of traditional Korean holidays and important familial rituals—such as marriages and funerals. Often young men and women also meet potential marriage partners and begin courtship rituals in the sanctioned social space that churches make available. Religious institutions also provide important informational bases, formally and informally. It was not unusual, for example, for churches to sponsor seminars on health, finance, and various aspects of their new American life. Informal counseling from ministers and other church leaders to members included topics of interest such as job acquisition, and use of local, state, and federal social services and housing.[146]

As a community resource, Korean Christian churches were perhaps the most important for female immigrants like Soon Ja Du. Since females in Korea of her generation were raised to be modest, with a very prescribed public presence, the church provided the kind of sheltered bridge between their lives in the old country and their new one—a bridge that members of their families who expected homage to traditional patriarchal family structure and paternalistic ethos found acceptable. Older women were expected to, and appreciated for, teaching the younger generation proper Korean female behavior. Younger women, attending these churches, had the advantage of being able to form social and economic bonds with others of their own cohort with similar experiences and expectations.

Soon Ja Du, for example, returned to South Korea for her two sons to be married in the traditional style, but it is clear that her life within the Valley Korean Central Presbyterian Church was the foundation of her social and cultural life in Los Angeles. Du joined Korean Central Presbyterian soon after arriving in 1976, and by 1990, was a deaconess. It was there that she formed friendships with other women of her age and circumstance, and it was from them that she learned about proper decorum for a Korean woman in late twentieth-century Los Angeles. Her dedication to her family and church, and the church's dedication to her, were instrumental during the difficult times that she faced. After she was arrested for shooting Latasha, for example, Soon Ja's church members rallied around her and were a constant means of support. They helped to raise the $30,000 bail money that she needed. More than 100 of them showed up in Judge Lance Ito's court (Ito was the first judge assigned to the case) to help convince him, by virtue of their presence, that she not only had community support, but church support. They demonstrated that Mrs. Du was not a criminal and should not be treated as one. They cheered when Ito granted bail. Each pretrial hearing, each day of the trial, and on the day of the sentencing too, of course, Korean Valley Presbyterian Church members were present—in large numbers.[147]

Other community resources that Korean immigrants came to rely on included ethnic alumni associations, media outlets, and banking institutions.[148] In 1990, there were approximately 145 Korean alumni associations in Southern California. These organizations, which connect graduates from high schools and colleges in Korea living in close proximity in the United States, were particularly important, socially, culturally, and economically.[149]

While Korean Christian church organizations provided a broad class and generational base, operating as a kind of protonationalist, sociocultural institution from which one could carve out his or her social world, alumni associations sharpened the focus. There, persons who had attended the same schools in Korea, who perhaps even knew one another as schoolmates and alumni before migrating, and probably were closer in economic class affiliation, attended ritualized social events together—biannual picnics, annual balls, and graduation parties for children. Members of these organizations also gave more attention to financial issues than churches, typically organizing a rotating-credit apparatus that lent money to members so that they could begin or continue business enterprises. They provided even further financial assistance by offering personal loans, employment opportunities for children of members and their kin, and through various business deals.[150] Females within the Korean community, of course, benefited from this kind of fiscal aid, because families benefited from those of their kin who garnered such support. Many women also were independent business owners and drew directly from this kind of aid. Likewise, young adult women, who were planning on entering the professional or business world, were able to establish potential professional contacts through their parents's alumni organizations. Older women and younger daughters, on the other hand, enjoyed opportunities to expand their social worlds through the alumni associations's sponsored events.

Alumni organizations also helped to emphasize the importance of higher education, an imperative within immigrant and descended Korean communities. Many of their activities celebrated social and financial success derived from diligent academic work. Graduation celebrations of members's children underscored the importance to the younger generation of carrying on the tradition of educational attainment. Koreans in South Korea, and in the United States, viewed an excellent education as foundational for success. Ninety percent of a sample of South Korean parents interviewed in 1987, for example, anticipated that they would support their sons through college; 70% anticipated doing so for their daughters.[151]

The rotating-credit apparatus, the "kye," that existed within Korean alumni organizations was replicated in other institutions as well. Different groups of Koreans who wanted to provide, and receive, financial support from associates created kyes. Usually in a kye, 10 to 20 persons give an equal amount of money each month to create a fund that is lent to each member in rotation. Every member must continue to contribute monthly until each member has received his or her loan. The number of persons involved typically is large enough to generate a substantial loan, but not too large as to be unwieldy or impersonal.[152]

The kye system is based on the honor of each member who has made a verbal promise to contribute his or her monthly payments on time. The size of kye loans vary from small to quite large—one was documented at $10 million to a group of ambitious businessmen in San Francisco in 1988—but they usually were $10,000 to $30,000. The interest rates on the money one received from a kye was higher than a commercial bank (14–20% for example), but members did not have to undergo credit checks, have a credit history, or use collateral to secure the loan.[153]

Surveys conducted in Los Angeles and Chicago suggest that a majority of Korean immigrant small-business owners, like the Dus, relied on a variety and, sometimes, combination of funding sources to initiate their businesses. Personal savings accounted for 41.5%; savings from Korea, 17.5%; loans from family members, 8.1% and money from kyes, 4%. Savings from Korea were a substantial help to those hoping to create a business in the United States. The South Korean government, however, did establish limits on the amount of money emigrants could take with them when they left Korea. The Dus, for example, only would have been able to bring $3,000 per adult and $1,000 per child, or $9,000 maximum, when they migrated to Los Angeles in 1976.[154]

Soon Ja and Billy worked very hard for ten years before they had saved enough to buy their first store. By that time, the Korean government had loosened considerably the limits on the amount of money those emigrating could take with them: $50,000 for the head of the family, and $10,000 for each family member. Still, there were not many who had that much reserve income. According to Korean immigrants in Los Angeles surveyed in 1993 and 1994, for example, they brought, on average, less than $10,000 with them when they arrived.[155] Since it was difficult sometimes for them to acquire loans for businesses in poor urban communities, pooling their resources seemed the appropriate option. Still, approximately 30 to 40% acquired loans from Korean American or American banks. Only about 8% in Los Angeles successfully sought funds from the Small Business Administration.[156]

Acclimation to urban America was difficult for Korean immigrants. Those arriving after 1965 were much better educated and more financially able than earlier generations. Yet, language barriers often precluded their ability to find work in professions in which they had trained in Korea. Cultural differences created a sense of social alienation, especially vis-à-vis the larger society. Many Korean women have noted that their views of the United States prior to their actual arrival were based on Hollywood movies and television programs. Those coming to Los Angeles were not prepared for the racial diversity, poverty, crime, and failing infrastructure too often apparent in the city. Local Korean/Korean-American media services—Korean language newspapers, radio stations, and television networks—helped them understand the world around them and their place in it. Los Angeles had three Korean-language newspapers in 1990, all local editions of papers originating in Seoul; at least 30 "ethnic" publications available either weekly or monthly; five television stations; and four Korean-language radio stations.[157]

Korean immigrants and Korean Americans made great use of their growing community resources. Part of the great success of their community institutions in aiding their constituents was tied to the size and age of the community during the 1970s and 1980s. While it is certain that the first Korean immigrants settled in Los Angeles at the turn of the twentieth century and created their own community-based institutions, the unprecedented migration of tens of thousands of Koreans in two later decades (1970s and 1980s), to a relatively small geographic area (Southern California), meant the development of a dynamic community drawn together by strong commonalities: language; socioeconomic and political status; short and long-term goals; and a desire to retain fundamental cultural attributes in their new home nation. In other words, many Korean immigrants of Du's era quickly developed a nationalist mentality bolstered by internal, separatist institutions such as Korean Christian churches, alumni organizations, banking institutions, and Korean-language media. It was a temporary nationalism, because Korean immigrants mostly hoped to integrate, at least to some extent, into the larger US urban society; and a nationalism that varied in significance depending on one's social and economic circumstances at home and in the United States, as well as other variables. Age, for example, was an important determinant—the younger the immigrant, the more likely he or she was to culturally accommodate quickly or at least to feel comfortable in a culturally integrated American society. Participation in local schools, of course, hurried the process of language and cultural acquisition. Even though many parents required their children to attend Saturday Korean-language schools and ethnically exclusive "cram schools" so they could excel in their studies, children—more than adults and especially more than older adults—learned English and the particularities of American society. Those who did learn English were especially important to their family's eventual success: in 1980, 81% of Koreans living in the Los Angeles-Long Beach area did not speak English well.[158] In the Du family, their eldest—John—seemed to be the child who helped interpret urban America to his parents.

A large percentage of the immigrants of the 1970s and 1980s eventually turned to ownership of small businesses as a means to acquire the better life in America that they sought when they left South Korea. Even though native-born persons of Korean descent chose different employment avenues, working as an entrepreneur was lucrative, particularly in Los Angeles. Indeed, the mean earnings of the self-employed among blacks, APIs, Latinos/as, and whites were greater than the mean earnings gained through either private or government employment in data sampled from 1970, 1980, and 1990. Among APIs, the earnings were almost double in some years.[159]

Koreans/Korean-Americans, as an ethnic niche in Los Angeles, have been the most entrepreneurial since they began to arrive in large numbers during the 1980s. In 1990, for example, 34.5% of Korean immigrant adults of working age (25–64) in LA county were self-employed. Their self-employment rate exceeded all those of minority or immigrant group status, and even the self-employment rates of white Americans. Not only did a larger percentage of Koreans residing in Los Angeles derive their income from small-business ownership than any other ethnic group—it was a national trend. By 1990, 25 years after the U.S. government lifted its ban on Asian immigration, Koreans led the nation in self-employment. Of the hundred ancestry groups that In-Jin Yoo canvassed from the federal census that year, Koreans were ranked first with a 24.3% self-employment rate. The closest in rank of another Asian ethnic group were the Taiwanese, ranked 13th with a self-employment rate of 16.5%.[160] African Americans, on the other hand were ranked 95th with only 3.7% self-employed. The national average for all U.S. ancestry groups was 10.2%.[161]

The dominance of Koreans in the self-employment market is clear, but their overall family income ranking, nationally, was less impressive—32nd in 1990. Still, Koreans had average family incomes that were higher than the national average. Korean family income one decade before the end of the twentieth century, therefore, was substantially above the average for African Americans and above the incomes of other families of African descent who resided in the nation, with the exception of Guyanese immigrants.[162] While the average family income of Korean/Korean-Americans in 1990 was $46,307, that of African Americans was $26, 849. Moreover, the African American national unemployment rate that year was 11.4%; but these rates were several times as high in some working-poor, urban areas. In some residential areas of South Central Los Angeles, where the Harlins family resided, for example, African American male unemployment in 1990 was almost 50%.[163] Despite their financial success, vis-à-vis African Americans, however, Koreans hardly were the most financially successful immigrant group overall, or among other Asian-descended residents. Nationally, Asian Indians, Japanese, Filipinos, Taiwanese, Chinese, and Pakistanis all had higher average family incomes, personal incomes, and rates of employment than did Koreans in 1990.[164] Relatedly, the number of Koreans living below the poverty line was not inconsequential. In 1989, for example, 15% of Korean families living in the United States did so in poverty—while only 10% of all American families did so, and only 12% of all API families.[165] From the perspective of Koreans, therefore, financial security was hardly a given in 1980 or even by 1990. They had found a niche—self-employment in Los Angeles and other urban economies in the United States—but initiating and maintaining a small business were difficult prospects and always fraught with uncertainties.

One of the principal reasons that Korean immigrant families found their income levels lower than those of other APIs was the role of women within their communities. Unlike most other API groups, Korean females substantially outnumbered Korean males. Since males tend to earn more than women in Korea, as well as in the United States, these women typically brought fewer financial resources with them when they immigrated and earned less once they arrived than the "average" API immigrant, who was male. Moreover, fewer than half of the Korean women who immigrated during the 1970s and 1980s were married—only 46.5%. A substantial minority had never married (43.1%).[166] Many of these women, consequently, lived in households that did not benefit from the income of higher earning males, or they resided alone rather than in family households. This was an important distinction: Korean households were earning over $46,000 annually in 1980, but individual Korean women were earning less than $19,000 ten years later.[167] The gender distinction is an important one for African Americans as well. In 1990, for example, 42% of African American female-headed households in the United States, where most African American children resided, were below the poverty line. Only 11% of African American two-headed households, however, were impoverished.[168]

One also must note that while the Korean immigrant population was well educated, by 1990, they were still less educated, overall, than the general API cohort, particularly when compared to South Asians and Filipinos. Likewise, Korean Americans, men and women, were substantially less likely to speak English, a skill quite important in the quest for economic success in the United States. In 1990, for example, 52% of Koreans in the United States who were at least five years old did not speak English "very well," and 35% could not speak it well at all, as compared to 38% and 24% respectively for other API groups.[169] One reason for this disparity is that some API ethnicities, particularly immigrants from the Philippines and India, and to a lesser extent Pakistan, came from societies where most persons of middle-class status spoke English. As such, it was more difficult for Korean immigrants to gain better paying jobs than some other API immigrants, but easier to do so than others who came from less middle-class environments, such as the Hmong, Laotians, and Cambodians.[170] The median annual income for Korean women in the United States in 1990 was $18,760; for other API women it was $21,335, and for U.S. women (of all races/ethnicities combined) it was $19,570.[171]

Soon Ja Du, of course, was married and part of a nuclear, patriarchal family. Her chances for social and financial stability, therefore, were substantial. At first glance—and even second glance—Soon Ja did not present a profile of a person who would be charged with a violent crime that ended in the death of a young girl. Why not? First, men, not women, historically, have committed most violent crimes in the United States. This is true for recent history as well. While the arrests for murder and nonnegligent manslaughters for black and white women, for example, increased by 40% from 1963 to 1979, it increased by 95% for men in those communities.[172] Second, there is little evidence to support any notion, realistically or conjecturally, that Korean (as well as other API) women are likely to commit violent crimes. Both their immigration history and their model minority status have kept statisticians even from attempting to calculate criminality rates. Moreover, they have maintained a popular image as law-abiding citizens. To the contrary, longstanding stereotypes of Asian and Pacific Islander females emphasize passivity and femininity, rather than violent or aggressive behavior. Indeed, these stereotypes are much more apt to indicate the likelihood of their victimization, rather than criminal behavior. This is certainly so when stereotypes of API females are compared with those of black and Latina women, and *even* when compared to stereotypes of white women.[173] Another dissuasive factor is that crime data indicates that when women kill, women of any race or ethnic group, they usually kill someone who is of the same racial or ethnic group. Moreover, women usually kill men, particularly men who previously assaulted them. This is not surprising given that 90% of women who are killed are killed by men. Indeed, the rarest victim-offender scenario, homicide experts note, are those of a female offender of one race/ethnicity and a female victim of another race/ethnicity.[174] How, then, did this 49-year-old Korean immigrant woman—wife, mother, deaconess, shop owner—come to shoot and kill Latasha Harlins on March 16, 1991?

FIGURE 3.1 "The Empire Liquor Market." Photograph by Al Seib, Courtesy of the *Los Angeles Times*.

3

March 16, 1991

Not Just Another Saturday in South Central

The Harlins Family Is Shocked

Word of the murder of a black girl in the Harlins's neighborhood spread quickly that March morning. Murder was not an unusual occurrence, but murder of a black girl, as opposed to a boy or an adult, was unusual. Murder in a local, Korean-owned liquor store contributed a kind of political sensationalism that pumped the rumor mill at full speed. There had been a lot of trouble and a tremendous amount of bad blood between the Dus and the working-class community where they owned a shop. People wanted to know, "What now?"

Between the two eyewitnesses, the growing pool of onlookers outside the crime scene, and the police's canvassing of the neighborhood for a positive identification of the body, there were few in the immediate vicinity who had not heard something about Latasha's death by the end of the day. Still, the Harlins family had not been immediately contacted.

Latasha did not have any identification on her when she went out that morning. Once the police wrapped up their preliminary investigation at the Empire Market, they carried a picture of the dead girl's body door to door, trying to find someone to identify her. When Denise Harlins opened the door and saw the police standing there she knew there was trouble. Instead of telling her that Latasha had been shot, the policeman first asked a question: How old was the girl who lived with her? Shinese, Denise's daughter was at home, so that meant that something had happened to Latasha. When the questions and answers finally ended with the reality that Latasha was dead, the family's responses were a jumble of shock, dismay, hurt, and anger. Ruth, who had seen so many of her family killed over the years, all by gunshot—her two brothers and her daughter—did not scream out, but cried deeply. Shinese took to the streets, displaying her anger to the curious onlookers. "It can't be 'Tasha, it can't be 'Tasha, I know that bitch didn't kill my cousin," she was heard screaming.[1] It was days before the family actually got to see Latasha. She already had been taken to the coroner's when they found out she had died. Latasha's family could not start to say their good-byes until the wake, four days later. One can only imagine what Latasha's younger sister and brother must have felt and thought when they were told that their big sister—the one who had been so protective of them ever since their mom died—now also was dead.

Neighbors gathered in front of the Harlins's apartment building. Frantic, grief-strewn calls came in and went out to family members and friends, and desperate pleas from the family peppered the police department for details of what had happened. The media picked up the story by Monday, the 19th; Latasha's classmates at Westchester High School found out about it when they returned from the weekend. Her middle school friends who had gone to Washington Prep did too. "I was at my locker and this girl came up to me and said 'Latasha was killed.' I said who? 'Latasha, you know your best friend. The black girl with the Chinese eyes, Latasha!' Then our group, me and the two other girls Tunisia and Sandra who had hung with 'Tasha every day at Bret Harte, stood in the hallway together, quiet," JonSandy Campbell, recalled with tears in her eyes. "And that's how I found out. A lot of kids got killed that year, a lot."[2]

Black politicians and Korean business owners began their public responses a few days later.

Danny Bakewell Sr.'s Crusade

The first and most visible organizational response within the South Central black community to Latasha's death came from the Brotherhood Crusade (BC) and their affiliated female organization, Mothers in Action

FIGURE 3.2 "Danny Bakewell, 1991." Courtesy of *Los Angeles Times.*

(MIA). Danny Bakewell, president of the Brotherhood Crusade, was probably the first political activist to offer assistance, financial and political, to the Harlins family. He was an extremely important ally.

Like Ruth Harlins, Bakewell was from the South. But unlike Ruth, he did not grow up in a small rural hamlet in the Black Belt. Danny was born in 1946 in New Orleans. He was Catholic and Creole—light enough to pass for white, but he didn't. The man who had become one of Los Angeles's most prominent activists and entrepreneurs grew up playing football, attending parochial schools, and trying to stay out of trouble. He was a good athlete—good enough in fact to win a scholarship to a college in Arizona. But Danny's heart was in New Orleans. A year after being out west, he returned home to marry his high school sweetheart, Aline. With a new wife, Danny started working at local hotels patronized by tourists. He learned quickly that this was not a life on which he could financially secure his family. He began thinking about moving west again. His father, after all, had come out to Los Angeles some years earlier and had opened a successful check-cashing business in South Central. He wanted Danny to join him and learn the business. Danny obliged. He soon knew much about life as an entrepreneur in a poor neighborhood. It was a blessing—working for yourself and helping your people. But it could also be a burden, even a blight. Desperate people sometimes acted desperately. Danny's father was killed in an armed robbery at his business in South Los Angeles.[3]

Danny's lessons as an entrepreneur coincided with his growing activism, as he joined the Nation of Islam in the mid-1960s. Bakewell was working at UCLA at the time, trying to assist administrators in their efforts to integrate the university's staff. It was a momentous time for black power advocates in Los Angeles, and Danny was at one of the centers of it—a college campus where Angela Davis was on the faculty, Elaine Brown (future leader of the Black Panthers) was a student, and Ron Karenga (founder of The Organization of Us, aka US and Kwanzaa) was a graduate student. His daily associates, therefore, were not only brothers from the Nation, but also important members of two of the most important activist organizations of the day: US and the Black Panthers. Bakewell became a lifelong friend to Karenga. He was at UCLA through the antiwar protests and the sit-ins instituted to create a Black Studies program. Danny was there when two members of the US organization shot and killed two members of the Black Panthers on campus. It was quite an education in racial and racialized politics for him.

The influences of US's cultural nationalism agenda, the Panthers's commitment to providing essential services to poor black communities and children, and the Nation of Islam's self-help, self-determinationist, Pan-African philosophy were not lost on Bakewell. When he joined the Brotherhood Crusade in 1968, an organization that focused on providing funding both for black-activist initiatives and community development, Danny was ready to bring all these ideals to it. But long before he became involved personally, as president of the Brotherhood Crusade, in the Latasha Harlins justice campaign, Bakewell had left his position at UCLA and, over time, became a powerful businessman. By the late 1980s, he was a real estate developer—one of the most successful in Los Angeles—had owned several businesses, many of them in South Central, and had been vice president of a downtown bank. Danny Bakewell's late twentieth-century political stature, therefore, derived not only from his leadership in grassroots activism built on decades-long ties to the black community, but also as a result of his status as a major player in Los Angeles's financial sector.[4]

Smart, ambitious, tenacious, self-assured, handsome, and charismatic— Danny Bakewell was a force to be reckoned with. What Danny wanted, he got. Everyone knew him, and everyone knew that he was not to be trifled with, ignored, or taken for granted. Danny Bakewell had the attention of anyone who hoped to benefit politically from the black community, from the mayor's office, the state legislature, the Congressional Black Caucus, grassroots organizers, the old guard, and the Black Muslims, to the traditional NAACP and Urban League.

But Danny Bakewell was more than an activist and entrepreneur; he was also a father with two daughters and a son. One of his daughters, the youngest, Sabriya, like Latasha, was in high school in 1991. Her vitality and promise too had been cut short. Sabriya was struggling with a life-threatening illness, a battle she would lose over the course of the next year. So well respected was Danny, that the Honorable Mervyn Dymally, past lieutenant governor of California, former state assemblyman, and, at that time, a member of the House of Representatives, read a two-and-a-half-page memorial to Sabriya Bakewell into the official *Congressional Record* on the House floor soon after her death.[5] The tragic shooting of Latasha resonated deeply with him. He reached out to the family immediately, offering financial assistance for Latasha's funeral, and promised that he would do all that he could to make certain that she received justice.

Latasha's murder proved to be an opportune moment for Danny Bakewell and the Brotherhood, which he then led, to showcase their agenda of black self-determination and community ownership and development. Four days after Soon Ja Du shot Latasha, the BC and their sister organization, MIA, borrowing a page from the grassroots organization OMNI (Organization of Mutual Neighborhood Interest), which had successfully boycotted Michael Yoon's Slauson Swapmeet in 1987, held a protest rally and boycott in front of the Empire Liquor Market.[6] It was their intention that, as a monument to Latasha, the store should never reopen, at least not under the ownership of the Dus. "Stop Killing Our Children," protestors chanted while an array of speakers promised that the store would remain closed. "We are declaring here today," Bakewell asserted before the press, "that this store will never reopen. We are putting a sign up here that will declare that we, the African American community, are closing this store because of murder and disrespect on the part of these people towards us and our community."[7]

The protests surrounding Latasha's death had quickly turned into something larger—a campaign to oust rude, disrespectful businessmen from the community. Bakewell intended to use these protests as a way to begin a community-wide effort to levy an ultimatum to anyone who gained financially from the community—comply with the Brotherhood Crusade's guidelines regarding the treatment of black customers or face boycotts and closure. These meetings soon shaped into something of a movement. It was more than a little reminiscent of the "Don't shop where you can't work" protest campaigns, led by prominent blacks like Charlotta Bass in Los Angeles and Adam Clayton Powell in New York, and in other urban locales—Chicago, Toledo, Newark, Pittsburg, Philadelphia, and Detroit. Beginning in the late 1920s and particularly in the 1930s and 1940s, these older protest campaigns sought to gain employment for blacks in their residential communities.[8] While Bakewell was clear to point out that the BC was willing to act against any local shop owner who did not treat his or her customers with respect and courtesy, the message he was sending seemed to be directed at local Korean shopkeepers. The Empire Liquor Market soon became the symbol of "foreign," specifically Korean, offenses. "Wherever we are disrespected," he promised, "we will take action."[9]

Bakewell's Brotherhood Crusade sponsored another boycott a week later. The word of Latasha's death at the hands of a Korean shopkeeper had spread quickly throughout most of South Central and, along with it, false rumors that the alleged perpetrator, Soon Ja Du, had been secreted away to South Korea. The expansive black working-class community was bursting with questions, anger, frustration, and sadness. They vented their feelings to one another, to other shopkeepers, and in meetings and rallies.[10]

As the number of protests and rallies grew, gaining publicity and widening support, the BC's agenda became more ambitious. Now it was not just about Latasha or even abusive "foreign" shopkeepers. The campaign was turning into an all out self-deterministic effort to increase local black entrepreneurship—an ambition that was near and dear to Danny Bakewell's heart and nationalist political strivings.

On April 1, the BC and the MIA held a town-hall meeting as the inaugural event of the African American Unity Center located on South Vermont. Not only was Danny Bakewell present, but also a who's who of local black activists and politicians. Latasha's death was becoming a cause célèbre, and it was bringing tremendous political cachet to anyone who took a leadership role in demanding justice for her. Mark Ridley Thomas, then a candidate for City Council and executive director of SCLC was present. So too was Danny's old, black cultural nationalist comrade Maulana (formerly Ron) Karenga. Meda Chamberlin, executive director of the Southern California National Council of Negro Women; Johnnie Gillman, founder of the National Welfare Rights Organization; and Daniel Morgan of the Church of Religious Science were among the many activists and religious leaders present.[11] Indeed, more than 400 others attended a meeting that was meant to "inspire the African American community to hold disrespectful merchants accountable for their actions." Speaker after speaker took to the podium espousing traditional black-nationalist goals of self-determination and economic development for predominantly black communities. "It is time that we looked at what needs to be done in our community," Danny Bakewell told the audience.[12]

He then went on to link the two articulated initiatives of holding merchants accountable for their relations with customers and improving the economic welfare of the community through black entrepreneurship via his proposal of a Community Economic Development Fund. This fund, Danny explained, would be used to "buyout businesses that refuse to respect African American patrons." Local black would-be entrepreneurs could buy these shops, with the help of the fund, and hire other local blacks to work there. It would be a win-win-win situation for South Central neighborhoods, producing black shopkeepers, black employees, and a well-served black clientele. There was the additional bonus of keeping black dollars in the black community. Bakewell then proposed an oversight organization comprised of three standing committees: a Standards Committee, which would identify appropriate standards of behavior for merchants that would guarantee that shop owners treated their customers with respect; a Complaints Committee, which would register and investigate customer complaints of unfair or rude treatment in local shops; and an Action Committee, which would work to "close down" those merchants who, like the Dus, failed to live up to acceptable standards of customer service. The plan seemed sound to most, but who was going to pay into it? Convenience stores were not cheap and most could hardly hope to afford one on their own, even at a discounted price. If the Bakewell plan was to work, the fund had to be well endowed. It was time for people to put their money where their mouths were, and Danny suggested as much. He even donated $5,000 of his own money to inspire others to help get this initiative off the ground. Two others speakers that day—Mark Ridley-Thomas and Lonnie Bunkley, an old friend and business partner of Danny's—matched his donations.[13]

The Brotherhood Crusade and its supporters continued to closely monitor developments in the Du-Harlins incident and to attend to some of the Harlins family's needs, but they also continued to use the incident to implement their agenda of black self-determination and economic development. Their efforts to use Latasha's death as a launching pad for a black community-ownership campaign was just what the mayor's office and the Korean community, particularly that large faction invested in entrepreneurship, feared would happen.

Mayor Bradley Stays Neutral

Tension had been growing for the past several years between Korean shopkeepers and their black clientele, not only in Los Angeles, but also in New York, Chicago, and other cities with large numbers of Korean shopkeepers whose clientele were largely African American. The political fallout could have dire circumstances for elected officials. Along with other protests discussed elsewhere in *Contested Murder*, there was, for example, the nationally publicized boycott and picketing of the Red Apple Grocery in Brooklyn staged by activists in support of a Haitian immigrant woman, Giselaine Felissainte, purportedly beaten by store manager Bong Ok Jang. The incident, which only concluded in the spring of 1991 when the store owner, Bong Jae Jang, sold his store after 16 months of boycotts, had been a disaster for New York's African American mayor, Donald Dinkins.[14]

Mayor Tom Bradley, therefore, knew all too well that this latest outbreak of interracial tension in Los Angeles could be costly for the city and for him, particularly if he seemed to support one side over the other. Bradley was nearing the end of his fifth term as Los Angeles's mayor. His accomplishments had been remarkable—the development of the downtown skyline and the corporations housed in these buildings; the enormous growth of Los Angeles's business ties with Pacific Rim nations; the development of the Westside; and, of course, the 1984 Summer Olympics. By any measure, Tom Bradley, the son of a sharecropper and the grandson of Texas slaves, had made a tremendous mark on the development of Los Angeles as the second-largest city in the country and as a financial and cultural giant. Moreover, the fact that Bradley, a black man, was the city's mayor and had come so close to a successful gubernatorial race in 1986 underscored the city's diversity, reigniting old myths of Los Angeles as a mecca for the "racial other" that were good for LA's international profile and for the business that derived from it. Korean Americans believed they had a stake in Bradley's loyalty. They had generously supported his gubernatorial campaign and their businesses were an important source of the city's tax revenue. But, African Americans noted, they had voted overwhelmingly for Bradley in all his elections. Bradley walked a tightrope, and he knew it. On March 23, the mayor released a brief statement, worded to suggest a neutral position.

"I share the sorrow and distress expressed by leaders in both the African American and Korean American communities in response to the tragic murder of Latasha Harlins," the press release read. But as "I am deeply concerned about the potential for this incident to divide our city along ethnic lines . . . aggressive efforts must be undertaken in order to establish and maintain relationships based upon mutual respect and understanding."[15] Neither community was satisfied.

Korean Business Leaders Marginalize the Dus

The Los Angeles Korean/Korean-American merchant community was acutely aware of the kinds of problems they might face as a result of Latasha's murder. They had read, and heard from kin, friends, and associates, stories about the financially crippling boycotts in other cities and had lived through the swapmeet debacle. They also realized that the hostility that they routinely faced in their laundries, swapmeets, liquor stores, dry cleaners, groceries, fish restaurants, hair boutiques, and nail salons was going to get worse—they just did not know how much worse. Many worried about black retaliation in the forms of burglary, vandalism, physical threats, or rioting.[16] Edward Chang, a professor of history and founding member of the Black-Korean Alliance, tried to assuage the feelings of black Los Angeles. On the same day that Bradley released his statement, Chang released one of his own from his community: "We, the Korean-American community leaders," Chang declared, "would like to express our deepest regret and sympathy to [Latasha Harlins's] family and friends." He added, "We are shocked and outraged by this tragic loss of life."[17] He offered no public support for the Dus. Others, taking a leadership position to try to calm the waters, also spoke out.

On April 1, Yang Il Kim, president of the national Korean American Grocers Association, stepped into the discourse. Again, the Dus found no solace. Piggybacking on Chang's message, Kim assured Los Angeles that Soon Ja Du's shooting of Latasha Harlins was "an isolated incident" and without "racial overtone." No one should conclude, he observed, that this was the typical behavior of Korean businesspeople located in black communities. Kim came right to the point—this event should not be allowed to undermine the attempts, made over the years, to bridge the gap between Koreans and blacks in Los Angeles. "It is," he noted "our sincere hope that this event is treated as a dispute between a retail store owner and a customer . . . and that this event is not looked on as a racial one or exploited for cynical political reasons."[18] That same week, the *Korea Times* indicated in its editorial that Korean merchants and interested members of the community were donating "Gifts of Love" to aid the Harlins family.[19] It was clear that the Korean business community, the same business community that the Dus had struggled to become part of, and had been part of for several years, were closing ranks—and not around them. The Dus could not look to their fellow Korean entrepreneurs to help them with their legal problems.

Other Asian/Asian-American ethnic groups also responded, trying to develop a broader initiative of cross-ethnic understanding and cooperation, rather than focusing specifically on the Du-Harlins tragedy. The Asian Pacific American League Center (APALC), initiated a few weeks after the shooting, hosted a Leadership Development in Interethnic Relations (LDIR) program, meant to assist communities in their adjustment to swift demographic change so as to ameliorate interethnic tensions. The program, directed by Kathleen Hiyake, was comprised of two parts, both to be implemented within a nine-month time period. The first phase was a three-month educational program, teaching 20 to 30 participants about various ethnicities and cultures represented in their neighborhoods. It also would provide them with conflict-resolution skills. The second part of the program would facilitate participants analyzing current problems, and brainstorming possible solutions for them, in three separate neighborhoods determined to be at risk for conflict. Two of the areas targeted were Koreatown and South Central Los Angeles.[20]

Still, the Korean merchant community was not completely unified against the Dus. Too many Koreans had died at the hands of blacks, some noted in frustration, for the public to just ignore the dangerous context in which they all worked.

The Press and Local Interethnic Organizations

Even the Los Angeles press corps weighed in, trying to devise a program that would help ease interethnic tensions. Most realized that strain between the city's different racial communities seemed to be growing exponentially every day. It was not just, of course, Latasha's death, but Rodney King's beating as well. One reporter for the *Los Angeles Times* noted that in discussions during local political meetings concerned with upcoming City Council elections, "In questions from the audience, or in casual conversation, the Harlins killing and the King beating inevitably are tied together in a single expression of outrage."[21] On April 2, representatives of the *Los Angeles Sentinel*, *La Opinion*, *Jewish Journal*, *Korea Times*, and *Frontiers*, along with Mayor Bradley, and County Commissioner Raul Garza (also chairman of the New Arrival Committee of the Human Relations Commission) met to discuss the increase in interethnic tensions "due to the formation of new immigrant communities" (clearly the new code phrase for deteriorating black-Korean relations). Forming the Council of Multicultural Publications, they initiated a plan that purportedly would, among other things, attempt to improve relations between various ethnic communities by publishing informative articles emphasizing significant aspects of the cultural lives of Los Angeles residents and monitor the "mainstream media" to insure the quality of articles published about "people of color."[22]

Some members of the black press, in particular, used their access to a broad African American readership to call for calm. They implored their readers to trust in the courts to render justice. "Standing in front of Soon Ja Du's shuttered store while hurling epithets and insults at Koreans serves no useful purpose," the editor of the *Los Angeles Sentinel* wrote in his editorial on March 28. "Quite the contrary, it makes matters that much more volatile and adds fuel to a fire that is already raging out of control." The answer, he went on to assert, was to "place our trust in the judicial process just this once. After all, given the irrefutable evidence of the video recording, this is a clear case of a 'smoking gun' if there ever was one." Even in his calls for calm and trust in the judicial system, however, the editor also reiterated the Brotherhood Crusade's mandate for economic self-determination, and how important it was to patronize black-owned businesses: "Keep the money in our own communities."[23] Other public activists, such as Larry Aubry, also a writer for the *Los Angeles Sentinel* and a consultant to the Los Angeles County Human Relations Committee, tried to contextualize the problem in a column he wrote for the *Korea Times*'s special edition on the Harlins case. There, Aubrey focused on the broader, systemic problems in

South Central that had to be addressed, rather than the explosive case seemingly on everyone's mind—the community's high crime rate, economic blight, housing shortage, high unemployment rates, and poor-performing schools,[24]

There were some joint efforts committed to brokering the problem as well. Blacks and Koreans, working through the Black-Korean Alliance, which had formed in 1986, sponsored a meeting between members of both communities on April 8 at the Greater New Unity Baptist Church in Watts to identify ways to "diffuse tensions that have erupted anew in wake of the Latasha Harlins shooting" and to design measures to utilize Du's shooting of Latasha to build bridges between the two groups.[25] The two-hour meeting was one of the first ever held in Los Angeles between merchants and their client base. Richard Fruto, who covered the event for the *Korea Times*, described the opening remarks as "the same old accusations against Korean merchants." He went on to note, however, that other attendants quickly pushed acrimony aside and moved on to what he believed was a more constructive dialogue. Although the gathering ended with little more accomplished than an agreement that the two groups should "work together" and try to "understand each other," the Black-Korean Alliance believed that it had made a step in the right direction.[26]

Activist institutions, such as the Black-Korean Christian Coalition, established in 1984, built on the joint membership of black and Korean Christians from area churches, also participated as individual denominations in both the Korean American and black neighborhoods engaged in dialogue and donated money to the Harlins family. Since the mid-1980s, churches had been the most consistent arenas of constructive dialogue between the two groups. Korean-based churches, usually under the auspices of the Council of Korean Churches in Southern California, for example, had provided rather consistent scholarship money for students at their "sister" black churches. They also sponsored numerous goodwill and cultural trips for local blacks to travel to South Korea. "We did it first to have good relations with the black community and secondly because we are brothers and sisters," noted Rev. John Song, who was an assistant minister at Oriental Mission Church.[27]

Many residents of South Central remained unimpressed. To them, it seemed as if the Korean merchants and leaders were more concerned with their profits and protection than they were for Latasha or her family. It is certain that the Dus shared the concerns of fellow merchants. They remained unable to visit the Empire Liquor Market, much less open it for business. Still, the 24-hour police patrol guarding their liquor market since the shooting only reaffirmed the black community's belief that the police and city hall were on the side of the Dus. When asked about the constant surveillance, Sgt. Landry of the Southeast Bureau of the LAPD responded that "because other crimes against Koreans have been committed as a result of Harlins' death," they feared acts of "vigilantism" and "vandalism."[28] The Brotherhood Crusade and other protestors were not dissuaded. They did not call for violent repercussions but rather moved forward with their plan to impose financial damage. The BC continued to boycott and eventually closed the Empire Liquor Market. The sign painted on the store left nothing to the imagination. It read: "Closed for Murder and the General Disrespect of Black People."

The Du's establishment was not the only Korean-owned market affected. Boycotters also focused their attention on another neighborhood store, the Watts Market, located at Wilmington and Alameda and owned by Chung Lee. According to Mr. Lee, a local black storeowner who wanted Lee's customers, began a false rumor that Chung's wife was the sister of Soon Ja Du. Any merchant related to Soon Ja Du, of course, was a target. As a result, six days after Latasha's murder, about 35 people began to picket Lee's store, telling potential customers that Lee and Du were "blood relations." Lee acted quickly to deny the connection. He circulated flyers that denied any relationship to Du and temporarily closed his store so that he could talk to the protesters himself. Until that incident, Mr. Lee actually had had quite friendly relations with most of his clientele. Sophia Kyung Kim, covering this story for the *Korea Times*, noted that Chung Lee was "known for his marathon love affair with the black community." Mr. Lee admitted, "My heart is broke now." The boycott lasted less than a week, but the dye had been cast.[29]

Harlins Family Fights for Justice

As the Harlins family slowly came to grips with their tragedy, Denise Harlins emerged as its public face. "It was my intention," she noted as she reflected back on her efforts, "to make certain that Latasha didn't die for

FIGURE 3.3 "Harlins's relatives (Aunt Anheva, Cousin Shinese, Aunt Denise), at Press Conference, March 21, 1991," Photograph by Al Seib. Courtesy of the *Los Angeles Times*.

nothing . . . I had to make a lot of sacrifices—I quit my job, everything— to keep this issue alive, to fight for justice—for Latasha."[30] Looking back on the death of Latasha's mother, Crystal, and how little jail time her assailant had received, the Harlins family was keenly aware that seeking justice for their latest victim would be a battle. But it was a fight they felt they had to win. They had been shocked and immobilized when Crystal was killed. But this was Crystal's daughter, and they had made a pledge to take care of Latasha, Vester Jr. and Christina. They had to do it for Latasha; they had to do it for Crystal; and they had to do it for the other kids in their family. Denise worried that her work for Latasha's justice would keep her from addressing the needs of her own daughter, 15-year-old Shinese. In the end, however, she knew what she had to do: she held on tightly to Shinese as she armed herself for the fight.

Denise soon realized that the family did not have to fight alone. By the first of May 1991, the Harlins family's friends and supporters had created the Latasha Harlins Justice Committee (LHJC). Their grassroots organization lacked the star quality of Bakewell's Brotherhood Crusade, local politicians, popular ministers, or activist Hollywood movers and shakers. It did, however, have a heartfelt membership of 10 to 15 persons, and they attracted even more people to their rallies, vigils, and news conferences.[31] More important, the LHJC only had one goal—justice for Latasha. For them, that meant making certain that Du would be found guilty of murder and serve the maximum sentence for her crime. In this quest, they solicited the attention of the print and TV media, using them to communicate to the public the family's feelings about what had happened to their loved one and how the courts should handle the case.[32]

The committee worked hard, very hard, and they did so on a shoestring budget. External support came and went, and then came and went again. In the first few months after Latasha's death, the LHJC, especially aunt Denise, received a lot of media attention and community support. As the face of the LHJC, Denise soon found out that she was important to the politicians, activists, church leaders, and members of the media who needed a member of Latasha's family present in order to legitimate their agendas. Denise had the ear of Danny Bakewell, Mark Ridley-Thomas, Maxine Waters, Walter Tucker, Patricia Moore, and even Jesse Jackson. The Fruit of Islam, the security arm of the Black Muslims, provided her with protection whenever she appeared in public. Her thoughts were chronicled in the *Los Angeles Times*, the *Los Angeles Sentinel*, and the *Korea Times*. And that was not all.

Representatives of KAGRO (Korean American Grocers Organization) contacted Denise and extended the promise of financial support. Anna Devere Smith negotiated with her for the rights to include Latasha's story in her famed one-woman show *Twilight*. All this made for good press, and good press benefited the agenda of seemingly everyone involved. But was it good for the Harlins family's quest for justice? There appeared a disconnect between the media hype and action on the ground specifically focused on Latasha. The LHJC, for example, rarely had more than 30 or 40 people attend their events. Denise was vocal about her frustration over what she took as a lack of consistent community commitment to justice for Latasha. In mid-May, on the eve of Soon Ja Du's pretrial, the committee held a candlelight vigil in memory of Latasha. It actually was at that event that the committee outlined its "justice" mandates: revocation of Du's bail; prosecution of Du to the "fullest extent of the law"; and that the Dus make financial reparations to the Harlins family. While the press covered the story, much of the articles detailed Denise's disappointment at the small number who attended the event. "I thought there would have been many more people out there to support our family," she told Marsha Mitchell of the *Los Angeles Sentinel*. "This tragedy has affected our family, but it could have been anyone's child. I just thought more people would have come out to let people know that the Black community is not going to stand for this injustice." Still, they persevered. By May 16, they had collected in excess of 1,000 signatures on a petition requesting that Soon Ja Du's bail be revoked.[33]

While Denise and other Harlins family members worked hard to push the legal system to hold Du accountable for Latasha's death, another family member quickly sought monetary redress. By the end of April, Vester Acoff had filed a $10 million wrongful death lawsuit against Soon Ja and her husband Heung Ki Du. The suit, "for unspecified compensatory damages and $10 million in punitive damages," was filed on behalf of Latasha's siblings, Vester Acoff Jr. and Christina.[34]

Grandmother and care provider Ruth Harlins too had initiated a wrongful death suit, but had been told by her attorney that she would not be able to pursue it given that she was not Latasha's "legal guardian." Denise was furious, both at Vester and at their attorney. Vester, after all, had hardly been a father. He was known more in the Harlins family for his abuse of Crystal, his part in her death, and his criminal behavior, than as a father to Latasha and her siblings, whom he had not seen in years. Denise claimed that Vester had even asked her mother, and his own relatives, to raise money for him to attend Latasha's funeral. They gave him the money, but he never showed. And his attorney, Geraldine Green, had been the Harlins's family attorney. After she realized that Ruth was not the legal guardian, Denise surmised, Green found Vester Sr. and pursued the civil suit in his name. In the end, Vester's case failed because he could not prove paternity—his name is not listed on Latasha's birth certificate.[35]

Denise also worried intuitively about how to keep the press interested in the cause of her niece, and not to let them, or herself, become distracted. For better or worse, deteriorating relations between Korean/Korean-American shopkeepers and black customers kept references to Latasha's murder in the media. Interest was especially kindled after an African American man, Lee Arthur Mitchell, was shot and killed in a local Korean-owned liquor store several weeks later.

Lee Arthur Mitchell

On the night of June 4, Lee Arthur Mitchell, age 42, died in John's Liquor store, located in the 7900 block of South Western Avenue. Tae Sam Park, the store's owner, killed Mitchell in a purported attempted robbery. Park reported to the police investigating the murder that Mitchell, a local resident and boxing trainer, attempted to buy alcohol but did not present the cashier with enough money for the item he had chosen. He was 25 cents short, although some believed Mitchell actually had enough money on hand to pay for it. According to Park, however, Mitchell tried to pay the additional quarter with a piece of jewelry instead of the coin. He supposedly offered Park's wife, Kumoch Park, who was working behind the counter, a gold chain, to make up the shortage. She refused it. Mr. Park then reported that Mitchell, whose autopsy proved that he had some traces of cocaine in his blood, acted as if he was carrying a gun and ordered them to open the cash register. Then Lee supposedly went behind the counter. Mrs. Park began to scream. Her husband came into the room and a "scuffle" ensued between the two men. Park reached under the counter, pulled out a gun and shot at Mr. Mitchell several times, hitting him five times in all—three times in his chest. The police pronounced Lee Arthur Mitchell dead when they arrived on the scene.[36]

Unlike the Latasha Harlins shooting, there was no videotape of what happened to Lee and no eyewitnesses except those who worked in the store. In their police report, investigators said that Tae Sam Park was "under attack and shot Lee in self-defense." Mr. Park did sustain injuries in the fight with Mitchell—three broken ribs. The storeowner maintained that he had acted appropriately. "I have done nothing other than defend my wife and my business," he told news reporters. "The crime they [the local black community] are accusing me of is based more on racial differences than fact." The police decided not to press charges against Tae Sam Park in the shooting death of Lee Arthur Mitchell.[37]

Coming close on the heels of Latasha's murder, black residents of South Central were bitterly angry when they heard of Mitchell's death. He was a respected and liked member of the community, known for his own boxing career and his work with young, professional boxers at the Hoover Street Gym. People who knew Lee well commented widely that the story that the Parks told did not seem possible. "I have known Lee for more than 10 years," one of his associates noted. "In that time he has always been a very level headed gentlemen. I have never seen him behave in a violent manner. Unless Lee had another side to him," he added, "I just can't believe that he would do the things that he is accused of doing."[38] There was no question as far as Lee's family, friends, and community associates were concerned: justice had not been served—a black man was dead over 25 cents at the hands of a Korean, and no one was going to be charged with the killing.

The community was not about to take Arthur's murder and the complete exoneration of Tae Sam Park sitting down. On June 11, community leaders and representatives of the LAPD met near John's Liquor at the Bethel AME Church to discuss the incident, particularly the police's decision not to charge Park. While some wanted to know precisely what had happened to Lee Arthur Mitchell, others met to try to allay predictable interethnic violence. Community activists, spearheaded by the Reverend Edgar E. Boyd, the minister of the Bethel AME Church, and Danny Bakewell had decided prior to the public meeting to boycott John's Liquor in an effort to close it down. Indeed, a collection of black religious organizations and activist groups had asked potential customers to boycott the store for 90 days. Community residents, as well as Lee Arthur Mitchell's wife, advocated doing so largely because

District Attorney Ira Reiner had decided not to press charges against Park. The boycott's mandate, however, also was part of the more comprehensive directive indicated in Bakewell's Community Economic Development Fund plan to "oust uncooperative and abusive merchants from predominantly black neighborhoods."[39] Bakewell, along with other protestors on the scene, held a news conference in which they also asked the district attorney to reopen the case. "The man had no weapon on him. Someone should have recognized it," Bakewell asserted.[40]

The protest was a little more personal for Rev. Edgar Boyd. John's Liquor store had been a thorn in his side for some time. Located directly across the street from his church, Boyd had complained long and hard about the negative impact that neighborhood liquor stores had on the vicinity, the social problems created by storekeepers who do not even live in the neighborhood, and the kind of "bad element" such business establishments attracted. Most of the protestors picketing the store, however, centered their complaints on the issue of respect, that is, the lack of respect that store owners demonstrated toward their customers. Approximately 25 boycotters consistently marched with placards that read: "Don't shop where you can't work," "We will not shop with killers," "Take a Stand Now!," "Respect Us, or Leave Us . . . Our $ Is Green Too," and "Stop the Killing!" while chanting "Boycott Korea," and "No justice, no peace."[41] A week after the protests started, someone tossed a Molotov cocktail onto the roof of the store—it was an ominous foreshadowing.[42]

Denise Harlins and other members of the LHJC were present both at the news conference and the protest. Denise was not only deeply affected by the death of another black customer in a Korean-owned store, she also was frightened by the district attorney's decision not to charge Park. If the criminal justice system, in the form of District Attorney Ira Reiner, had decided that Park acted "in self-defense," then what would that same system—in the form of the jury and judge—decide about Soon Ja Du's murder of Latasha? Gender politics should also have caused Denise concern. Tae Sam Park had raised the issue of the threat to women, Korean women specifically, that black customers posed. He had acted, he stated over and over again, to protect his business and his wife—an Asian woman who was being threatened by a black male. The scenario was only too familiar—nonblack women had to be protected from aggressive, dangerous blacks at all costs. Denise appeared at the meetings and boycotts to make certain that no one forgot about Latasha, to connect Mitchell's and her niece's deaths within the minds of the community, and to ask that the community continue to stand behind her and her family in their quest for justice.[43] The Dus continued to stay out of the limelight as much as possible. Their days were taken up with lawyer meetings, a few preliminary court appearances, medical examinations, finding the right interpreters, and prayer within the family and with supportive church members. The district attorney's decision in the Mitchell case must have given them the first glimmer of hope that Soon Ja might be exonerated.

That Long Hot Summer

Many affected organizations in the black and Korean communities, politicians, and activists had hoped that with Latasha's death two-months old and Du on her way to a jury trial on charges of first-degree murder, that black-Korean relations would get back on track. The Lee Arthur Mitchell killing dashed those hopes. But that shooting was only one of several which occurred that spring and summer of 1991. Ten days before the John's Liquor store shooting that left Mitchell dead, an African American man, in the commission of a robbery in South Central, shot and killed two recent Korean immigrants who worked in a liquor store near 35th Street and Central Avenue. According to witnesses, the two employees complied with the robber's demands, but he still shot them. Moreover, about ten days after the Mitchell shooting, on June 13, another African American man was accidentally shot and killed by his accomplice during a struggle with the Korean owner of an auto parts store that the two were trying to purportedly rob.[44] That made five deaths in four months in Korean shops in South Central. The tension between blacks and Koreans was greater than ever.

The pressure was mounting and organizations like the Black-Korean Alliance worked hard to try to calm the situation. Some in the black and Korean communities complained openly that Mayor Bradley, the City Council, and the County Board of Commissioners had not tried very hard to end the conflict. "The situation is very volatile," Larry Aubry of the Black-Korean Alliance noted in frustration. "And there has not been the political will to do something about it." Bradley responded by asking the Los Angeles Human Relations Commission to prepare a report on the state of "intercultural relations" in the metropolis.[45]

Things changed for Tom Bradley, however, in the next two months, forcing him to become more publicly proactive. The killings and protests had not ceased. The boycott of John's Liquor store had gone on for 109 days. Bradley asked Bakewell to meet with him to negotiate an end to the "selective buying campaign," but Bakewell refused. In August, Bradley met with the other activist leader, Reverend Boyd, but to little avail. Then on September 12, about two weeks before Soon Ja Du's trial began, the *Los Angeles Sentinel* carried a story about the "gathering of forces." Bakewell and others were planning a mass boycott. "A group of 30 or more organizations will meet Saturday morning at Bethel AME Church," Dennis Schatzman reported in his article, "to launch a selective buying campaign" that was planned to last for three months.[46] This boycott seemed more related to the "injustices" associated with the Lee Arthur Mitchell death than Latasha's. Still the LHJC was on board. This close to the trial, they hardly could afford to pull away from a vital support network in order to reassert their singular agenda of justice for Latasha.

Danny Bakewell served as spokesman for the coalition. "This selective buying campaign," Bakewell explained, "is designed to serve notice on merchants who had shown a history of disrespect to consumers in African American neighborhoods that is was time to change their ways or move on." He went on, "And we are here to serve notice that we are fortified and unified in our resilience and commitment to African American people."[47] Bakewell called on an expansive cadre of black organizations—clubs, churches, sororities, fraternities, and individuals—for support. In so doing, he and the other leaders were not only able to tap into a large pool of potential black activists that cut across class lines, but also employ some of the tactics of grassroots organizing that had been so popular during an earlier black-nationalist era in Los Angeles. This umbrella organization, the African American Honor Committee, was more than a little reminiscent of the powerful Black Congress through which black protest groups like the Black Panthers, US, the Nation of Islam, and the Organization of African American Unity had worked cooperatively during the mid to late 1960s. At the same moment that Bakewell was calling for the three-month boycott to "establish a lethal force to invoke economic paralysis on any business that chooses to operate with disrespect and disregard for African-Americans and the community in which we live," he also was keeping the door open for negotiation. Bakewell and Boyd announced that the Honor Committee was still willing to meet with those interested in ending the dispute.[48] The Du and Harlins families, however, were more than a little distracted from Bakewell's efforts by the end of summer—the trial was about to begin.

Despite the threatened economic and political pressures that Danny Bakewell and his Honor Committee were ready to levy, the two sides involved in the boycott remained at an impasse through much of Soon Ja Du's trial. Tae Sam Park was determined that he would not close his store. Bakewell, Boyd, and their coalition, who were focused on the plight of black constituents forced to shop in what they believed was a hostile and racist environment, were determined, on the other hand, to force Park to close his business. Mayor Bradley, and newly elected City Councilman Mark Ridley-Thomas, reportedly worked furiously behind the scenes to broker a compromise of sorts: John's Liquor store would close and a resolution center, meant to mediate "disagreements" between blacks and Koreans, would be created.[49] The timing could not have been more auspicious—the announcement came on the last day of Soon Ja Du's trial for the murder of Latasha.[50]

A Truce of Sorts

Deputy Mayor Mark Fabiani told the press that an agreement had been reached after a series of meetings held at the Hilton Hotel in Universal City. The negotiators included Danny Bakewell; Yang Il Kim, president of the national KAGRO; other Korean community leaders; and Councilman Michael Woo. The "treaty" purportedly gave African Americans, through the African American Honor Committee (Bakewell and other activists were part of this committee), an opportunity to purchase the store from Park. It also created a "Merchants Code of Ethics" that was to guide how shop owners treated their customers. It was a beginning, Councilman Woo noted, and that was something. "This is only a starting point for a lot of work that has to be done to try to get the Korean community and African American community to understand each other," Woo told the *Los Angeles Times.* "It will take more than a piece of paper."[51]

The terms of the agreement included a temporary store closure and suspension of the boycott. Still, it was clear that Park was going to have to settle for the eventual sale of his store, probably to the African American Honor Committee. This committee and KAGRO also promised to cooperate in creating a "dispute resolution center" that would handle future disputes of a similar nature. They also hoped to create a jobs program that would encourage Korean merchants to hire local residents to work in their shops and provide, as well, customer-cultural sensitivity training for Koreans who wanted to open shops locally.[52]

The agreement, on paper, clearly was a victory for Bakewell, Boyd, and the African American Honor Committee—KAGRO and Park had agreed to all their demands. The one demand that was not met—the decision to reopen the case of Lee Arthur Miller's shooting—was in the hands of the district attorney, and he refused. Bakewell reported that Mitchell's family, with whom he had worked closely, had "released that condition," thereby allowing him to sign the agreement. "We are very satisfied with what we appear to have and we think it is going to make [the Mitchell family] feel very, very vindicated in this whole process," Bakewell told the press. "We're talking about jobs, we're talking about an infusion of African-American capital into the community . . . More importantly it represents the restoring of dignity to the community. That's what we set out to achieve."[53]

As one might imagine, Tae Sam Park and other Korean merchants who had shops in South Central felt quite differently. Indeed, the peace that had been crafted was so fragile that the two sides held separate news conferences. For the Korean shopkeepers, the agreement was a stinging defeat. Park maintained that he had not acted in error or illegally but still was being punished. "Because I didn't do anything wrong, it is regrettable for me to lose the business," he noted sadly. David Kim, president of the local KAGRO, echoed Park's feelings. "We're not too happy about it but we are willing to do it for the peace of the community," he told reporters.[54] Kim must have felt subdued for other reasons as well, not the least of which was the role that KAGRO's national president, Yang Il Kim, played in the negotiations. For Yang Il Kim, the sacrifice of Park's store was a necessary one that would ease the tensions of a three-month-old boycott, which could have had national implications. But for David Kim and Tae Sam Park, the settlement ignored the violence Korean shopkeepers had suffered at the hands of black customers and put into place a scenario whereby merchants were at the mercy of customers who, in their estimation, could be unreasonable and unruly. They felt no "justice" had been rendered.

Still, the agreement was in place and after a very long, hot summer a slight calm hovered. Now, if they could just get through the impending results of the Soon Ja Du trial. Hope of that was shallow—Danny Bakewell already was calling for a massive boycott if the verdict did not go the way he believed it should.[55]

FIGURE 4.1 "Soon Ja Du." Courtesy of *Los Angeles Times*.

4

People v. Du

The Trial

After the preliminary investigation held at the site of the shooting, the police arrested Soon Ja Du on suspicion of first-degree murder with the special circumstance of using a hand-gun in the commission of a felony. She then was taken to the Martin Luther King Jr. Medical Center and treated for her injuries. The doctors who saw her later reported to the police that Mrs. Du had feigned severe injuries—acting as if she were unconscious when she was being examined, but suddenly waking up and looking around when she believed that she was alone.[1] Afterward, Du was held without bail at the Sybil Brand Institute for Women for ten days, where she reported that she was physically and verbally abused.[2] On March 19, she appeared at the Compton Municipal Court with her lawyer, Tyson Park. Park asked for a delay so that he could get Mrs. Du a Korean translator and so that she could have her injuries further examined. Judge Morris Jones granted the delay. Three days later, Du reappeared at court, this time with a different, but very powerful, defense lawyer: Charles Lloyd.

Lawyers, Prosecutors, and Judges

The Du family hit the proverbial jackpot when they chose their second attorney to represent Soon Ja. Charles Earl Lloyd was one of the most respected and successful lawyers in Los Angeles. It also did not hurt, they must have believed, to have a black attorney defend a Korean woman accused of killing a black teen. If blacks on the jury could relate to their black attorney, maybe Soon Ja had a chance of beating the first-degree murder charge she faced.

Charles Lloyd's story was the golden American dream of acquired wealth, success, and status that so many newcomers, like the Harlins family or the Dus, hoped and prayed would be theirs. Born in 1934 in Indianola, Mississippi, the second child of seven to Katie and William Lloyd, Charles Lloyd showed early signs of leadership ability and a commitment to success. At Indianola Colored High School, he was quarterback and captain of the football team as well as president of his graduating class of 1952. He left Mississippi after graduation and headed for California. Lore has it that he arrived with a hole in one pocket and 12 cents in the other. Lloyd became a student at Cal State LA and three years later joined the LAPD. He continued college while working as a policeman and graduated in 1957. Lloyd went to USC law school, graduating in 1961. With his law degree in hand, he resigned from the LAPD and promptly became a prosecuting attorney in the Criminal Division of the LA City Attorney's Office. There Lloyd became a legendary figure. It seemed as if no defense attorney could beat the brilliant, charismatic prosecutor once the case went to jury. Charles Lloyd won a record 144 jury trials out of 145. It is no wonder that he was promoted to chief trial deputy, supervising 25 prosecutors—the first African American to hold that distinction in the city.

Lloyd took his success in the public sector and parlayed it to equal success in the private legal sector. He began his own firm (Berman, Lloyd, and Goldstein) in 1964, but he quickly moved on to become a senior partner in Lloyd, Bradley, Burrell, and Nelson in 1965. The Bradley in the firm's name was Tom Bradley, who would go on to become Los Angeles's first black mayor, a position he held for an unprecedented five terms. Lloyd and Bradley were great friends. They had been in the police force together and attended law school together. They were business partners as well, jointly purchasing land and buildings in Koreatown and other parts of the city. Lloyd even had a building on Western Avenue that he sold to Koreans who developed it into the Korean Community Center.[3]

Rumor had it that Mayor Thomas Bradley had personally asked Charles Lloyd to take Soon Ja Du as a client, fearing that the case and the incendiary relations between LA blacks and Koreans might be as politically damaging for him as the Family Red Apple case (where black-Korean relations were severely damaged)[4] had been for his friend and peer Mayor David Dinkins in New York.[5] And it was Charles Lloyd who suggested to the Du family that they hire Richard Leonard to work along with him.[6] Leonard joined the defense after Lloyd's unsuccessful first appearance in Judge Lois Anderson-Smaltz's courtroom on July 29 to ask for a continuance of Du's case.

Lloyd was used to getting his way when he appeared before most judges in the county. He did not, though, with Anderson-Smaltz. She was a novice to the Superior Court bench—just appointed in 1991, but she knew her way around a courtroom, having served as a judge in the Los Angeles Municipal Court the four previous years.[7] Anderson-Smaltz denied Lloyd's motion. He persisted, telling Judge Smaltz that he would need another six months to prepare for trial. The judge called him "irresponsible" and let Mrs. Du know that under no circumstances could she avoid going to trial by choosing a lawyer who could not prepare her case in a timely manner. Lloyd, playing the injured victim, appeared insulted by the Judge's words. He insisted that he would give back Mrs. Du's retainer if his client wanted him to do so. A slight delay was had after all because they had to wait for a courtroom to hear the case.[8] In the interim, Charles Lloyd called on Richard Leonard for help.

Leonard too had come from the South, but his journey to prominence had been quite different from that of Charles Lloyd. Born and raised in Texas, Leonard attended, but did not graduate from, the University of Dallas. After dropping out, he bought and worked in his own liquor store for a couple of years, but then he was drafted and went off to fight in Vietnam. When he returned, Richard moved to Los Angeles, finished his college degree at Pepperdine and went on to law school, the then unaccredited Glendale College of Law. He graduated and, a few years later, passed the bar. His first job was with Wesley Russell, a local black attorney. It was through him that Leonard met Johnny Cochran, Earl Brody, and other black elites of the legal profession. His first jury trial was one in which he assisted Russell. It was a serial murderer, death penalty case. It stamped him. Leonard established his own law office in South Central in 1985, and he quickly went on to become nationally renowned for his work on high-profile murder cases and particularly as defense counsel for potential death penalty felons. On two of the 18 death penalty cases he handled before 1991, he brought in Charles Lloyd to assist him, and the two had become friendly.[9]

Lloyd and Leonard were quite a pair. Charles Lloyd was the affable, somewhat folksy, but always well-mannered, black southerner who dressed immaculately, drove a black Corniche Rolls Royce with personalized license plates, occupied a suite of offices in one of the most posh buildings in downtown LA, and was not likely to get through a trial without multiple references to his belief in God. Richard Leonard was the friendly, white, "good-old-boy" Texan—smart and articulate, equally comfortable with death-row criminals as with upper-class judges; his modest office, located close to South Central, was decorated with a full-grown, stuffed bull elk, mounted big-game fish, and beautiful family photos. Both were charmers in and out of the courtroom, and their charm was known to work in their collective favor with juries and with judges.[10]

Charged with first-degree murder, Soon Ja Du pled not guilty. Judge Jones released her on $250,000 bail and the court's retention of her passport. Roxane Carvajal, deputy district attorney, represented the people.[11] Ms. Carvajal was a stark contrast to the team of Lloyd and Leonard. Like her male adversaries, she was experienced, accomplished, ambitious, and successful. Like the judge who would eventually sit for the trial, she was much younger than the defense counsel. She was, at one time, considered seriously for a judgeship. But unlike Du's attorneys, Carvajal could seem cold, formal, and arrogant when interacting with the defense counsel and judges. As the case unfolded in court, it was clear that she had no time to engage in friendly banter with Lloyd and Leonard, and she was not afraid to challenge Judge Joyce Karlin on her rulings. Carvajal knew that she was not part of the old boy network. She probably did not want to be. What she wanted instead, and achieved, was to be the consummate legal professional who executed her job extremely well. And she obviously felt passionately about this case. From the very beginning of the pretrial hearings, Carvajal perceived Du as the aggressor in the fight between her and Latasha; she thought of the shopkeeper as a murderer. When Charles Lloyd applied for bail for Du, for example, he carefully described his client as a mother and wife who was no threat to society. "In this case," Carvajal snapped back, "she apparently killed a fifteen year old for no reason."[12] This deputy district attorney expected to impress her juries with tight, evidentiary-driven cases meticulously constructed and passionately argued. Charles Lloyd and Richard Leonard were impressive enough handling evidence and witnesses, but they had another asset. They willfully courted the kindness of their juries and, especially, their judges. There were four judges who heard parts of Soon Ja Du's case, and they all eventually ruled in favor of key motions and requests made by Leonard and Lloyd.[13]

The Honorable Morris Jones was the first judge assigned to the case. On March 19, 1991, he sat through Du's arraignment on first-degree murder charges, but ordered that she be held, without bail, until an interpreter could be present when she entered a plea. A week later, Jones released Du on $250,000 bail and her surrendered passport. Lance Ito, of O. J. Simpson double-murder trial fame, was next, presiding over the case during a hearing in which Roxane Carvajal asked that Du's bail be revoked—there were fears that Soon Ja would escape to her native South Korea. Ito decided that Du was not a flight risk, noting in his ruling Soon Ja Du's substantial family and community support as indicators that she would stay put. A trial date of July 29, 1991, was set, but later postponed.

Judge Lois Anderson-Smaltz came aboard in time to hear arguments about a change of venue and to determine a new trial date. When, in July 1991, she heard defense counsel Charles Lloyd and Richard Leonard argue that Soon Ja Du could not receive a fair trial in Compton, Anderson-Smaltz disagreed and refused to move the trial's location. By August, however, she had changed her mind, citing the pressure that some witnesses and key trial personnel might feel, or fear, if the trial was held in Compton. Accordingly, Judge Anderson-Smaltz ordered that the case be moved to downtown Los Angeles and begin as soon as a courtroom was secured. "This is a political trial," the judge noted in her deliberations on August 26. "The potential for bias lies in the process of coming to court and being influenced by the various contingents. There is a high level of tension due to the serious nature of the facts in this case. My concern is that there will be a great deal of pressure from the local community in the Compton area on the witnesses, the jurors, and the court staff. . . . It's not that an impartial jury could not be impaneled. It's more the pressure that surrounds this particular courthouse in

Compton."[14] Anderson-Smaltz had eliminated Compton as a place where justice could be rendered simply because of the race of the majority of the community's residents. The Harlins family and supporters were incensed, and not a little worried about how this change in venue might affect the justice they sought.

Day One, September 30: Opening Remarks

Soon Ja Du's trial began on Monday, September 30, 1991, amid deep and sustained controversy and racial tension. The Harlins family publicly criticized the trial's relocation. But they had other problems as well. Much of their strategy for justice relied on keeping the case in the public eye, and, until that time, the media largely had obliged. But the week of the trial, another case took top billing. Instead of focusing on the Du trial, the nation was obsessed with the Anita Hill-Clarence Thomas "event" that was being televised from Washington, DC that same week. Who wanted to hear about a poor black girl being killed by some Korean shopkeeper when they could hear about black sexual fantasies instead? And this was no run-of-the-mill black sex story, the kind that has made Jerry Springer a household name. This scandal concerned the elite of the national legal community—one of who was nominated for the Supreme Court! Salacious televised trials about black Yalies caught up in a lurid sex scandal was stiff competition for *People v. Du*. The Charles Keating financial scandal case also began that week and was being held in the same courthouse as Du's trial. Judge Ito was now presiding jurist over that case. There was just incredible room for public distraction.

The Harlins family were not the only ones who wanted justice and who feared they would not get it. Du family members and supporters complained bitterly that the police were scapegoating Mrs. Du to appease the black community after the Rodney King beating.[15] They also complained that out of the 135 perspective jurors interviewed, none were Korean. The 12 jurors selected were five African Americans, four Latinos, and three whites. Race reared its head again even before the actual proceedings could start. Everyone was aware of the mounting tension in the elevators leading up to and in the hallway outside the courtroom. Harlins family supporters chanted, shoved, yelled insults, and whispered threats in English. Du family supporters pushed back and spoke excitedly and angrily in Korean. The press hurried to capture it all and to catch snippets of interviews with persons on both sides. Charles Lloyd, "the black man defending the Korean child killer," was the center of much of the anger from Harlins family supporters. Mrs. Du was denounced as a "murderer." The anguish and anger threatened to spill into the courtroom in the rush for seats.[16]

The trial of *The People of the State of California vs. Soon Ja Du*, case no. BA 037738, the Honorable Joyce A. Karlin presiding, began at approximately 9:50 a.m. that late September morning.[17] Along with a packed audience of Du supporters and Harlins sympathizers were members of the press; policemen; court personnel; Mrs. Du with her two attorneys, Lloyd and Leonard, and two interpreters, Wongsup Kim and Paul H. Yi. Roxane Carvajal was seated with Detective J. C. Johnson of the LAPD, the investigating officer. Judge Karlin began the trial with the usual greetings followed by a stern warning to her audience: "There will be no talking in the courtroom during the testimony of witnesses and during the opening statements by counsel. If anyone is disruptive in any fashion, the bailiffs have been asked by me to ask you to leave permanently. You will not be allowed back in."[18] The jury then entered and received from Karlin typical instructions and the suggestion that the trial probably would not last longer than a week.[19] Roxane Carvajal began the opening statements.

Carvajal turned to the jury and explained her perception of the altercation that had cost Latasha her life. She drew her conclusions, she explained, from the videotape of the shooting captured on the store's security camera and the preliminary testimony of two eyewitnesses, Ismail Ali and Lakeshia Combs. Her re-creation of the argument between Du and Harlins that preceded the shooting was taken directly from her interview of Ali and Combs, their testimony during the preliminary hearing, and other interviews. The videotape did not have audio, so the re-creation of the verbal argument had to be based on Du's accounts and those of the eyewitnesses.

March 16, Carvajal began, was a Saturday morning. According to the district attorney, Latasha went to the Empire Liquor Market to buy some orange juice for breakfast. She took the juice from the refrigerated case and stuck it partially inside her backpack. She then proceeded to the counter. When she reached the counter, Soon Ja Du, who had been watching her in the security mirror, asked Latasha if she was trying to steal the juice. Latasha then turned around to show Du the juice in her backpack and told her that she wanted to pay for it. Du then began tugging on the arm of Latasha's sweater, trying to retrieve the juice by pulling the backpack off. Mrs. Du continued holding Latasha's arm and tried to pull her across the counter. In an attempt to protect herself from Du's aggression, Latasha punched the shopkeeper in the face four times. As a result, Du fell down twice. When she stood up the first time, Du threw the stool that was behind the counter at Latasha and missed. When the shopkeeper stood up the second time, Soon Ja had a holstered gun in her hand. Seeing Du with the gun, Latasha picked up the orange juice, which had fallen out of the backpack onto the floor, and placed it on the counter in front of Du. Instead of taking the orange juice and ending the confrontation, Du swatted it away and proceeded to take her gun out of the holster. Latasha then turned and started to walk out of the store. Holding the gun with both hands, "one under the other," Du took a shot. "Latasha is hit in the back of the head. Latasha immediately falls to the ground."[20]

Throughout her opening statement Roxane Carvajal was careful to characterize Du as the aggressor in the altercation with Latasha. She was the one, the assistant district attorney told the jury, who accused Latasha of stealing just as she approached the counter. Du was the one who grabbed the girl's arm. She was the one who threw a stool at Latasha. She was the one who swatted away the juice when Latasha tried to give it to her. She was the one who pulled out a gun, held it with both hands, and shot it as Latasha walked away. Latasha, according to Carvajal, clearly was the victim; she hit Du in self-defense after Du grabbed her arm, held on to it, and tried to take her backpack away. Latasha, Carvajal informed her audience, just stood there when Du finally wrestled the backpack off and threw it behind the counter. Latasha just stood and watched when Du emerged from behind the counter and threw a stool at her. Latasha remained still when Du knocked away the juice after Latasha picked it up from the floor and placed it on the counter. It was Latasha who turned to walk away when Du confronted her with a gun. It was Latasha who was shot in the back of her head.[21]

Defense attorney Charles Lloyd wasted no time telling the jury, in his opening statement, that he believed that the events of March 16 unfolded radically differently than Carvajal suggested. It was not Soon Ja Du, he asserted, who acted aggressively, but Latasha Harlins. Soon Ja Du was a shopkeeper, he began, suspicious that a customer was shoplifting, so she did the logical thing—she grabbed Latasha's sweater to investigate what was in her backpack. Du had, in Lloyd's opinion, every right to investigate her suspicions. It was then Latasha who acted aggressively, "very viciously" in Lloyd's words. She struck Mrs. Du in the face "four times," so forcefully that the shopkeeper fell down twice. "Mrs. Du never struck her," Lloyd argued. It was because Mrs. Du was "half knocked out of her wits from those blows," because of her fear that Latasha would kill her that she first picked up the "defective gun." According to Lloyd, whose re-creation was based on his interviews with Mrs. Du, Latasha threatened to kill Soon Ja. "She didn't go after this gun until she had been knocked down twice, and then the young girl picks up the orange juice and said, 'Bitch, I told you I was going to kill you.'" Once Mrs. Du got the gun out of the holster, it "accidentally goes off." Lloyd concluded by pressing his contention of an accidental shooting. "Mrs. Du, even though she pulled up that gun, never intended—never, never intended to kill Miss Harlins. You'll notice [from the videotape] how hysterical she is after and how surprised she looks when this gun goes off, how remorseful she is. It's sad."[22]

After opening statements, Carvajal began calling witnesses. The first to testify were the eyewitnesses to the fight and the shooting: nine-year-old Ismail Ali, who was a fifth grader at the 97th Street School; and his sister, 13-year-old Lakeshia Combs. The two lived on the same block as the Empire Liquor Market. They had come to the store that morning to purchase some hair gel for their mother, but had lingered to play video games. Ismail and Lakeshia had finished at the cash register and were headed toward the video games located near the store's entrance when Latasha reached the counter.[23]

According to the youngsters, Latasha approached the counter with cash in her hand and was about to pay for her purchase when Mrs. Du grabbed her. "This girl walked into the store, and she went straight to the juice section," Ismail began his description of the events.

> And then she didn't go nowhere else and came straight up to the counter and was going to pay for it, the juice, and she had it in her backpack where you could see it. And the oriental lady

started pulling on her shirt, her sweater, and telling her, "That's my orange juice," and kept pulling it. And the girl says she was going to pay for it. And the girl was telling her to let her go, but she wouldn't.[24]

Ismail went on to testify about the angry words Du and Harlins exchanged. Latasha repeatedly demanded that Du "Let [her] go," but, according to Ismail, the shopkeeper would not. When asked if he saw any money that Latasha might have had while at the counter, Ismail recalled that she had money in her hand and that she showed the money to Du when she told her "she was going to pay for it and 'let me go.'"[25] Court records indicate that Latasha Harlins had two $1 bills. The juice was $1.79.[26] District Attorney Carvajal then had Ismail watch the video-tape of the altercation and provide the missing dialogue.

Ismail's sister recalled a similar chain of events. She also remembered that Du had grabbed Latasha's arm while asking her if she was stealing and that the two then exchanged angry words. Reiterating the point that Harlins approached the counter "with her money in her hand," Lakeshia Combs confirmed that Du seemed to believe that Harlins was trying to steal the juice. Ignoring the money in front of her, she asked Latasha: "Are you trying to steal my orange juice?" According to the witness, Latasha answered, "No." Du supposedly repeated the question, and Harlins re-peated her response, while attempting to place the money on the counter and telling Du, "I'm trying to pay for it."[27] Lakeshia also recalled that Lata-sha demanded that Du "let [her] go." A fight ensued as Du tried to take Harlins's backpack, and Harlins tried to get Du to release her sweater. Harlins punched Du forcefully in the face four times. Stunned, Du fell behind the counter but was able to hold onto the backpack. As they pulled the backpack back and forth across the counter, the two exchanged more words: "The black girl called the clerk a bitch first and then the oriental lady asked her . . .bitch, are you trying to steal my orange juice." Accord-ing to Lakeshia, Harlins and Du "just kept cursing back and forth."[28]

Both children testified that during the scuffle between Du and Lata-sha, the disputed bottle of orange juice fell in front of the counter and that Latasha bent down to pick it up. They also both saw Du stand up from behind the counter with a holstered gun in her hand. Latasha, they then testified, placed the juice on the counter and turned to walk away.[29]

CARVAJAL: When the clerk had the gun out in the holster, what was the black girl doing?

LAKESHIA COMBS: She was trying to walk out the store.

CARVAJAL: Was she saying anything to the lady at that point?

LAKESHIA COMBS: No.[30]

Charles Lloyd's cross-examination of both Ismail Ali and Lakeshia Combs was an attempt to erode their integrity as witnesses—first, on the grounds that they were children; second, because, as members of the South Central community, he argued, they might have been influenced by the community to give exaggerated or distorted accounts of the events. Attorney Lloyd was able to establish that there were some inconsistencies in their testimonies: neither child could remember exactly how many times Harlins hit Du; they may have forgotten just where they were standing when the shooting occurred; they could not recall precisely when Du started calling for her husband; they did not know which hand Latasha used to punch Du; and Ismail could not remember that Latasha had called Du "bitch."

Yet, the attorney for the defense could not shake the children's powerful testimony that implicated Du as the aggressor in the fight and that established Latasha intended to pay for the juice and actually tried to give Du the money.

CARVAJAL: What happened after you saw her put the orange juice in the backpack?

LAKESHIA COMBS: She walked up to the counter and was ready to pay for the juice.

CARVAJAL: Okay. When you say she "was ready to pay for the juice," why do you say that?

LAKESHIA COMBS: Because she walked up to the counter with her money in her hand. It was—she was holding it towards the counter.

Nor could he get Lakeshia to testify that Harlins ever verbalized a threat to kill Du:

CARVAJAL: Did you ever hear the black girl say anything else to the clerk other than "I'm trying to pay for it" and calling her a bitch?

LAKESHIA COMBS: No.

CARVAJAL: Those are the only two things that you heard the—the
girl say to the clerk?

LAKESHIA COMBS: Yes.[31]

Defense Attorney Lloyd also asked Lakeshia what she recalled of the
conversation between Du and Harlins.

LLOYD: Now, did you hear the girl say to Mrs. Du four or five times,
"I'm going to kill you?"

LAKESHIA COMBS: No.[32]

and again:

LLOYD: You moved back away [from the store's checkout counter] . . .
because you heard the girl say "I'm going to kill you," didn't you?

LAKESHIA COMBS: No, I didn't.[33]

He also could not get Lakeshia to say that Du's hand shook when she
held the gun.

LLOYD: All right. Did you see Mrs. Du when she—when she came
up with the gun?

LAKESHIA COMBS: Yes.

LLOYD: Was the gun shaking in her hand?

LAKESHIA COMBS: No.

LLOYD: It wasn't shaking in her hand at all?

LAKESHIA COMBS: No.[34]

Officers Jeffrey Alley, Lewis Parker, and Ralph Spinello, members of
the LAPD Southeast division, were the next to testify. The three had
been among several law enforcement officers who had responded to
Billy Du's call that he was being robbed and that his wife "had shot the
robber lady." Parker was the first officer to arrive at the scene.

Officer Parker testified that when he entered the store, Latasha was
lying on her stomach in front of the counter with "what appeared to be
a bullet hole through the forehead."[35] He noted that his first act was to
call for an ambulance. His second act, after speaking to dispatch, was to
recover a "revolver weapon" and other weapons from Billy Du. Parker
handed the revolver to Officer Spinello when he arrived a little later.
Shortly thereafter, Parker searched Latasha for weapons. It was then he
observed money by her hand.[36] Officer Jeffrey Alley testified that when
he arrived, at approximately 9:40 a.m., Latasha was suffering from a

gunshot wound to the head and was lying on the floor; Mrs. Du had "passed out" behind the counter; and Mr. Du was on the phone.[37] He then stated that paramedics arrived some 15 to 20 minutes later. They tried to revive Latasha with CPR and defibrillation but both failed. He also noticed money close to Latasha's left hand.[38] Officer Spinello, Alley's partner, confirmed the testimony of his colleagues. He received Du's revolver, noticed that it still had bullets in it, and placed it, for safekeeping, in the trunk of his patrol car. After Spinello secured the gun, he returned to the store. It was then, he testified, that he checked Latasha for a pulse. There was none.[39] Spinello also testified that he secured the backpack that Latasha had had with her. He found it behind the counter, still resting where Du had thrown it during their fight.[40] While behind the counter, Spinello also found a "carbon rifle" and ammunition for it. And, he observed something unusual—Mr. Du was behind the counter with his wife, slapping her, supposedly attempting to revive her.

> CARVAJAL: What did you see?
> SPINELLO: I saw Mr. Du slap Mrs. Du in an attempt to revive her.
>   She was—. . .—she seemed to be passed out at the time, and
>   Mr. Du began slapping her across the face . . . from right to left.
> CARVAJAL: Approximately how many times did you see . . . Mr. Du
>   slapping Mrs. Du in the face[?]
> SPINELLO: Several times at which they started not so hard and kind
>   of graduated into very hard slaps at which time I had to stop it.
> CARVAJAL: Why did you stop him?
> SPINELLO: Because of the force that he was using.
> CARVAJAL: Were you concerned at that point about Mrs. Du?
> SPINELLO: Yes, I was.[41]

Under cross-examination from co-defense counsel Lloyd, however, Spinello conceded that Mr. Du's slaps to his wife's face were not as powerful as the four punches that Latasha had given her.[42]

Day Two: October 1, 1991

The videotape was the center of attention during the second day of the trial. Roxane Carvajal had an additional tape made in which a portion was slowed and slightly enlarged so that it would be clearer to the viewing audience. The graininess of the tape remained, however. David Micheal Muehsam, a videotape expert then employed at Westcoast Post, testified that the graininess was due to the extensive use of the tape; that is, many recordings and erasures had been made on that same tape prior to the recording on March 16, the day Latasha was shot. Each time taped material was erased, he explained, it lowered the quality of the tape's visibility. Muehsam noted that he had "no ability to sharpen something that is fuzzy," but he added that computer enhancing, "something that costs hundreds of thousands of dollars," could possibly improve its quality.[43]

Roxane Carvajal had directed Michael Muehsam to place arrows and circles on a version of the taped encounter so that the jurors could understand the movement of Du and Harlins during and after their altercation. Co-defense attorneys Lloyd and Leonard objected to the use of highlights, stating that it "emphasize[d] certain portions of the tape, what is going on for the jurors to see it." Judge Karlin, however, did not believe that doing so made the tape "prejudicial" in any way and overruled their objections.[44]

Clearly the most dramatic development in the case that day, however, came after the lunch break. Co-defense counsel Richard Leonard, made a 1118 motion, that is, a motion to dismiss, which was entered away from the jury. He offered two principal reasons that the case against Mrs. Du should not be heard. First, Leonard argued, Du only was acting out of self-defense and within the legal limits of store owners when she shot Latasha. It was Harlins, not Du, Leonard asserted, who began the fight and Mrs. Du acted only to protect herself. Although she had grabbed Latasha's sweater, Leonard conceded, it was within her purview as a store owner to try to "detain a person" long enough to determine whether he or she was stealing. Latasha, he continued, overreacted to Du's tugging on her, striking the woman in her face several times. Second, the gun discharged accidentally because of a faulty (altered) trigger function. "The fact that this gun was inherently dangerous and the trigger pull was—hair trigger that could go off very easily with just being touched it would appear that this was an accidental shooting."[45] Leonard then added that if Judge Karlin disagreed that the case should be dismissed based on these two reasons, then she should consider the "imperfect self-defense; that is, Mrs. Du felt that . . . her life was in danger." This "imperfect self-defense" reasoning should prompt Karlin to at least reduce Du's charges from murder to manslaughter, specifically involuntary manslaughter.[46]

Roxane Carvajal forcefully countered Leonard's arguments on the dismissal and reduction of charge motions, noting that the evidence entered in the court record thus far did not substantiate the proposed "imperfect self-defense;" that lethal force cannot be used in response to "fists alone unless there's some evidence that there is fear of great bodily injury or death," and there was no evidence that Du felt that way. To the contrary, the district attorney argued, it was Du who assaulted Latasha when she grabbed the girl's backpack. Likewise, Carvajal insisted, there was no evidence to substantiate an "accidental shooting." Moreover, the evidence that had been entered into the trial thus far was "sufficient" to warrant a first-degree murder charge. Mrs. Du, Carvajal explained, is seen in the videotape getting her gun, taking it out of its holster, aiming it "in the direction of the victim," and shooting it: "Clearly enough evidence for premeditation . . . Premeditation is not measured by the amount of time. It's just a decision to kill, and there was certainly enough evidence so far to let that question go to the jury."[47] Judge Karlin agreed with Carvajal. It was, the jurist noted, "premature for the defense to make such a motion," although she would take it "under submission" until the end of the defense's case.[48]

A subsequent discussion, also away from the jury that day, centered on the relevance of testimony regarding the terror the Dus had withstood at the Empire Liquor market from local gang members. Attorneys Lloyd and Leonard wanted the Dus—Soon Ja, her husband Billy, and their son Joseph—given wide breadth in their testimony regarding the negative, hostile experiences they had experienced at the store since purchasing it: robberies, burglaries, threats of arson and murder, and extortion. Judge Karlin agreed to some testimony, but not an extensive amount. It was made clear in the discussion, however, that the Dus' testimony would speak to the shopkeeper and her family's personal and familial terror by local gang members, but that there was no evidence that Latasha Harlins belonged to a gang.[49]

The testimony of Billy and Joseph did detail the difficulties and violence that the family had sustained from customers at their Figueroa Street store. Billy Du testified with the help of a Korean translator. Soon Ja Du's husband explained that the store had been "burglarized" three times since he had purchased it in 1989 and that he had been "person-ally" robbed once, on March 9 or 10 of 1991.[50] Billy also was aware that his son had been threatened by gang members during a violent incident in December 1990. Joseph Du reported the incident to the police and later testified against the purported assailants, leading to the incarcera-tion of six men.[51] "Every day," Mr. Du noted, "the gangsters were coming in and threatening to kill my son." He finally discovered the identities of these men and tried to "resolve" the conflict by meeting with them, but his attempts were "unsuccessful." Gang members tried to force him to hire them, but he refused.

> LEONARD: Were you ever forced to hire any gang members to work inside your store?
> BILLY DU: I was—continued the pressure by these gang members to the—due to hire somebody to work in the store, but I declined, and I closed the store.[52]

Du went on to note that in 1981, he purchased, for "self-defense," the gun that killed Latasha Harlins. He was the gun's third owner. In 1988, it was stolen from the Du's Bouquet Canyon store. The Santa Clarita Police Department eventually recovered the gun and returned the weapon to Billy Du in late 1990. The storeowner testified that he brought the pistol to his Figueroa store only a month before Latasha's shooting.[53]

When it was her turn to cross-examine Billy Du, the district at-torney wasted no time going back over the details of the difficult rela-tions his family had with neighborhood customers. She then wanted Mr. Du to recount what he had seen and heard on the morning that Latasha was killed. Carvajal was particularly interested in the 911 call that Billy Du made after the shooting. When queried by the DA, Mr. Du stated emphatically that he had not seen a wound on Latasha when he called the police. He also testified that he had not, in his 911 call, charac-terized the events that had taken place between Soon Ja and Latasha as part of a robbery.

> CARVAJAL: Did you tell the people at 911 . . . that this was a holdup, that you had a holdup?
> BILLY DU: No, I did not. No, the police said everything.

CARVAJAL: Okay. You did not—when you called 911, you did not tell the people "I just had a holdup in my store"; is that correct?

BILLY DU: I did not.

CARVAJAL: Did you tell . . . the lady who answered the 911 call that the girl, Latasha, was trying to take the money out of the . . . cash register?

BILLY DU: No, I did not.[54]

Carvajal then produced the 911 audiotape and had it played for Mr. Du and the jury. Afterward, Soon Ja Du's husband had to concede that he had, indeed, reported to the 911 dispatcher that "we got a holdup," and that she [Latasha] had taken money out of the cash register. He also had to admit that he had seen a "lot of blood" coming from the victim when he first walked into his store.[55] Carvajal continued to press Mr. Du about discrepancies between his court testimony and his 911 statement. She finally got Mr. Du to confess that when he entered his store, he did not think that there was anyone there except for Latasha and Soon Ja. He also had to acknowledge that he actually did report that "my wife shoot the robber lady," not only to the 911 dispatcher, but also to the first police personnel who came into the store after the shooting. Carvajal pushed Mr. Du as well to state that when he first walked into the store, Soon Ja Du asked him, "Where is that customer that is standing here? I'm not sure whether she's dead or not." Earlier, Mr. Du denied that Soon Ja Du had asked if Latasha was alive.[56]

Throughout his cross-examination, Mr. Du tried to portray Soon Ja as equally victimized as Latasha, repeatedly stating that when he came into his store, he saw two people dying—both his wife and the girl. Indeed, after being questioned for a few minutes, it seemed clear that Mr. Du wanted to equate what he called Soon Ja Du's "collapse" on the floor with the 15-year-old lying in a pool of blood. "At the time two people were dying," he said on one occasion; on another, "there were two people both dying."[57] Billy Du's insistence not only cast the defendant as equal victim to the dead girl, but also served as a ready excuse for the inconsistencies in his testimony. When asked why his testimony differed so much from his 911 call he noted, for example, "I was trying to recall the incidents, but I still cannot recall exactly because at that time two people were dying, and I really was in a panic."[58] In the end, however,

FIGURE 4.2 "Soon Ja Du leaves court with her husband Billy Hong Ki Du," Photograph by Chris Martinez. Courtesy of *Associated Press*.

Mr. Du proved a rather weak witness for the defense because his story had changed so much from when he made the 911 call, certainly leaving his credibility in great question.

Day Three: October 2, 1991

Before Mr. Du continued his testimony on the third day of the trial, District Attorney Roxane Carvajal complained to Judge Karlin that counsels for the defense had withheld vital evidence, thereby not complying with her earlier motions for discovery, filed in June 1991. She was referring to Billy Du's indication in his testimony the previous day that the .38 revolver that Soon Ja Du shot Latasha Harlins with had been stolen two years prior and only returned to him in late 1990. Although Charles Lloyd (not Richard Leonard) had received a copy of the Santa Clarita police report from Mr. Du detailing the gun's theft and subsequent return to the Dus, he never disclosed this information to the district attorney. When faced with Carvajal's accusation in conference with the judge, Lloyd simply replied that the report had slipped his mind. "I lost sight of the fact that the gun was stolen . . . It was just an oversight." Carvajal pursued her point, noting that she anticipated that defense counsel would use this information to argue that whoever had stolen the gun, had altered it. If the Dus did not know the gun had been altered to facilitate the firing mechanism, then Lloyd and Leonard had a stronger case for an accidental shooting. Lloyd denied his intent to use this line of reasoning, stating emphatically, "No, that's not true." Carvajal then countered that her ability to question police officers who had returned the gun about the details of its altering, along with other appropriate preparation to address this vital issue, had been "taken away" because Lloyd had not given her the report when she requested information months before.[59]

Judge Karlin was not convinced that Carvajal's concern had great merit. "Let's do this," she declared, "I accept your [Lloyd] representation that it was an oversight, but I do think that Miss Carvajal can do some legitimate investigation with it. Let's give her the report immediately, and if she needs some time to pursue, I'm going to give it to her." Carvajal fired back that she wanted Karlin to issue a 1054 Disclosure to the jury that would inform them that she had a right to the information regarding the gun, that she had requested it, and that Lloyd had not given it to her. "Mr. Lloyd has been the attorney of record for months," she argued, "and I have been absolutely asking and begging and yelling every single time [to] give me whatever information you have. Give me whatever information you have." Karlin resolutely refused Carvajal's request for the second time. "I really don't think it's appropriate," the judge answered, "because I accept the representation that Mr. Leonard didn't even know about it [and regarding Mr. Lloyd] I think it was a good faith oversight rather than intentional withholding."[60] Assistant district attorney Carvajal was not pleased with the judge's ruling.

Joseph Du was the second member of Soon Ja Du's family to testify. Early on, he told a reporter for the Los Angeles Times how he felt about the case: "My mother is made a scapegoat of Korean-Black tensions," he declared. "She was merely trying to protect herself. Why is it they never publicize all the Koreans who were killed?"[61] Joseph testified in Korean and was assisted by translator Wongsup Kim. It seemed clear to attorneys Lloyd and Leonard that they could not convince a jury that Soon Ja Du had not shot and killed Latasha Harlins—the videotape that both sides played repeatedly during the trial clearly proved otherwise. One defense strategy was to establish—just as Carvajal had feared when she complained of the lack of disclosure regarding the gun, and Lloyd had forcefully denied it—that the weapon had been tampered with to such an extent that it went off without Du pulling the trigger. The other principal defense strategy was to emphasize the provocation behind the shooting. Joseph's testimony was meant to support the defense team's contention that Soon Ja Du had been conditioned to fear black patrons frequenting the Empire Liquor Market because of the trouble that her son and her husband had at the store during the two years that Billy Du owned it. Allowing Mrs. Du, her son Joseph, and her husband Billy to describe in detail the terror that they had suffered at the South Central store at the hands of Crips gang members, the attorneys pieced together a situational context of black juvenile violence and criminality that was so frightening to Du that she felt she had no alternative but to defend her life against Latasha. They argued that Du's killing of Harlins was tragic and it should never have occurred, but they blamed her death on the "situation," not Du. Fear of the racial other, specifically young blacks, was the centerpiece of Soon Ja Du's defense for her shooting Latasha.

Under direct testimony, Joseph Du outlined the two years of trouble that his family had from South Central customers—constant shoplifting, burglaries, robberies, verbal abuse, and physical threats. Perhaps trying to repair some of the damage his father had done when forced to admit a number of embarrassing discrepancies in his testimony, Joseph exaggerated the problems at the store:

LEONARD: Tell me how many times that you have been burglarized
   that you reported it to the police?

JOSEPH DU: . . . Around 14 times . . .

LEONARD: How many times would you say that the store
   was burglarized where you did not report it to the police,
   approximately? . . .

JOSEPH DU: For a week . . . over 40 times.

LEONARD: Would you see these people come inside the store and
   take something and leave without paying?

JOSEPH DU: I see it every day.

LEONARD: . . . Why didn't you stop these people?

JOSEPH DU: If I tried to stop them, they show me their guns.

LEONARD: Sir, when you're working at that store, did anybody ever
   threaten to kill you?
JOSEPH DU: Yes.
LEONARD: How many times have you been threatened?
JOSEPH DU: Too many times. So many people came in and threaten
   me. So I cannot recall even how many times.
LEONARD: Well, if you had to put a figure on it and estimate?
JOSEPH DU: Over 30 times.
LEONARD: And has anybody ever come into the store and threaten
   to burn down your store, sir?
JOSEPH DU: Yes.
LEONARD: And approximately how many times . . . before March 16th.
JOSEPH DU: Over 20 times.
LEONARD: Have gang members ever come into your store and
   threaten—threaten you?
JOSEPH DU: Of course.
LEONARD: And did you testify . . . against these gang
   members[?]. . .
JOSEPH DU: Yes.[62]

Prompted by Judge Karlin, and perhaps fearing Du's son was per-
juring himself, Mr. Leonard explained to Joseph the difference between
shoplifting and burglary. Soon Ja's 30-year-old son still insisted that
there were over 40 burglaries per week.[63] Joseph Du's testimony was
outlandish, because it was not only inflated to the point of perjury, but
because it also conflicted with his father's earlier testimony. When
Billy Du was asked the day before about the number of robberies and
burglaries that had occurred at the store since their ownership, he had
responded that they had been robbed once and burglarized three
times. He had filed police reports each time.[64] Frustrated at what the
jury would clearly see as incorrect testimony by Joseph, one of the
defendant's key witnesses, attorney Richard Leonard moved on to
what he hoped would be safer ground. He wanted to establish that
Joseph Du had shared with his mother the terror associated with
working in the store.

LEONARD: Now, all these threats that have been made to you
   regarding killing you, burning down your store, and these gang

members that come in and terrorized you, did you discuss this with your mother?

JOSEPH DU: I told her of it every day.[65]

Roxane Carvajal quickly underscored for the benefit of the jury the problems in Joseph Du's testimony. Under cross-examination, she revisited his sworn testimony that he had been robbed twice—on December 16 and 19, 1990. Joseph Du noted that on the 16th, an armed black man whom he had never seen before robbed him at gunpoint and took an unknown amount of cash. He also testified that, while there were two guns under the counter, the .38 that killed Latasha and a shotgun, he had not used them to thwart the robbery. Carvajal then revealed, however, that when Joseph reported the incident on December 16 to the police, he had spoken of two men, not one, and he stated that he actually did know them, identifying them as Tyrone Thomas and Eric Ross. (Both were arrested after the report was filed and Joseph Du testified against them.) According to the statement Joseph Du gave to the police, Ross and Thomas had threatened him, not in the commission of a robbery, as he had just testified in court, but because he refused to give them jobs. Joseph Du apparently also had reported to the police that he had drawn the .38 caliber on the two men, and that he pulled the gun out of his pocket. But under oath in his mother's trial, Joseph changed his statement. There he testified that he had not used a gun when confronted by Ross and Thomas and that the gun remained under the cash register.[66] Judge Karlin called for a 15-minute recess, probably to allow Joseph to compose himself. When he returned to court, however, Joseph Du still refused to change his story, even though his statement to the police was substantially different.[67]

The district attorney later focused her questioning on the coincidental similarity between the story that Joseph told the court about his "robbery" and the story that Soon Ja Du reported about her "robbery." While Carvajal obviously had no admissible evidence that Joseph had fed his mother a story which she later used to defend her actions against Latasha, the DA did try to push this possibility at the end of her cross-examination.

CARVAJAL: And why was it that you took out your gun?

JOSEPH DU: Because I felt that my life was threatened.

CARVAJAL: What did the person do to make you feel that way?

JOSEPH DU: The person hit me first and then try to grab the money.

CARVAJAL: Did the person do anything else besides hit you and try to grab the money?

JOSEPH DU: The other—the person look like he trying to grab something from the back, and I thought that—that it could be a gun. So I grabbed for the gun, and just as I was about to pull the trigger, the person ran out . . .

CARVAJAL: When you went home that evening, did you tell your mother what had happened?

JOSEPH DU: Yes, I did.

CARVAJAL: Did you tell your mother that some black man came in the store, hit you, tried to grab the money, and then you took out your gun?

JOSEPH DU: Yes.

CARVAJAL: Did your mother know where the gun was kept, if you know?

JOSEPH DU: Well, she had eyes. So she—I'm sure she's able to see where the gun—gun was . . .

CARVAJAL: And did your mother tell you that Latasha was going for the cash register?

JOSEPH DU: Yes.[68]

Despite the difficulties that both Billy, and particularly Joseph, Du had relaying accurately the particulars about their difficulties at the Empire Liquor Market since Billy had purchased it two years prior to Latasha's death, the jury no doubt understood that the Dus worked in an environment that could be intermittently, and spontaneously, very hostile and dangerous. Soon Ja Du's testimony centered on the impression of such an environment that her husband, and especially her son, had given her. Indeed, Soon Ja Du testified that much of her fear of Latasha Harlins stemmed from her son's description of what gang members wore and, most important, how dangerous they were. Soon Ja Du repeatedly stated that she believed that Latasha was dressed like a gang member when she came into her store that Saturday morning—that she believed that Harlins was a member of a gang.

CARVAJAL: Did Latasha look like a gang member to you?

SOON JA DU: Yes.

CARVAJAL: . . . Did you think she was a gang member?

SOON JA DU: Yes, because I asked my son "how do gang members in America look like?" because he told me he was getting continually threatened. So I asked him to describe how they looked like because I have to be careful when they come in. And when I asked, he said either they wear some pants and some jackets, and they wear light sneakers, and they either wear a cap or hairband, headband. And they have some kind of satchel, and there were some thick jackets. And he told me to be careful with those jackets sticking out. And when she hit me with that iron like fist, what I heard from my son and her description how she was dressed was similar, and that's what I thought.[69]

Before Carvajal cross-examined Mrs. Du, her lawyers gave her an opportunity to tell her story of the events that happened before Latasha's death. Her interpreter was Paul H. Yi. Du began with the reason why she was at the Empire Liquor Market that day. It was only to help her son, Soon Ja told the jury, because otherwise she never went to work there on the weekends. During the weekdays, she typically worked at their Valley store, the Bouquet Canyon Liquor store in Valencia. "As a mother," she declared to the court, "I felt so terrible that I really felt that I should go and try to help my son; so I would go there and work there with my husband, and that was about three to four times."[70]

According to Soon Ja Du, she and her husband arrived at the Empire Liquor Market at approximately 8:00 a.m. It had been their intention that both she and her husband work behind the counter, but her husband was so tired that "even though my husband resisted . . . I insisted and pushed him out so that he could go . . . and get some rest."[71] About an hour and a half later, Du recalled, the shooting took place. About ten customers had come and gone before Latasha. She was ringing up the purchase of Lakeshia Combs and Ismail Ali when Harlins came into the store. Du found it easy to watch customers' whereabouts through the mounted security mirrors. She saw, she recalled, Latasha enter the store, go directly to the freezer, pick up a bottle of juice, and place it in her backpack. Then, she came "directly toward the check stand."[72] At that point, Du's statements matched those of the two eyewitnesses, Lakeshia and Ismail.

Once Latasha reached the counter, the stories recounted by the eye-witnesses and the defendant began to differ in significant ways. Du maintained, for example, that she did not see any money in Latasha's hand: "I'm a business operator," she explained. "If she had the money, I would try to grab the money rather than the orange juice since she already had the orange juice in her backpack." Du also maintained that Latasha never told her that she was trying to pay for the juice. In fact, she never said anything else to her except to threaten to kill her, and she and Latasha never had a verbal argument; she just started punching after Du grabbed her sweater. "She did not say anything," she noted. "And all of a sudden . . . she punched me in the eyes with her fist. The fist felt like an iron."[73]

Soon Ja Du freely admitted that she had grabbed Latasha's arm first, trying to reach the juice that she could see protruding out of her back-pack. She was suspicious of Latasha because she had placed the juice in her backpack. Her hands were free, Du reasoned, so why didn't she just carry the juice instead of partially concealing it? Latasha's behavior re-garding the placement of the juice in the backpack fit, in Soon Ja Du's estimation, a pattern of shoplifting that she had noticed at the Empire Liquor Market during the three or four times that she had worked there:

When I was working there, I noticed that the people who were shoplifting—they would take the merchandise, would place it inside the bra or anyplace where the owner would not notice, and they would come up to the check stand, to the counter, and buy some small items and pay for it and leave.

There were a lot of times when I noticed that that's what the people who were shoplifting were doing. And when I saw her place it in—the orange juice in the back-pack, I noticed that she was walking toward the counter, and I saw this specifically.[74]

Mrs. Du then went on to describe the beating she suffered at the hands of Latasha. The 15-year-old, whom she had first mistaken as a boy because of her clothing and the hat that was pulled closely over her hair, first hit her twice, she recalled. After that, she was "dazed and shocked" and, therefore, could not remember what exactly happened next. She did, however, manage to recall some details of the brawl. "The girl," she noted, "was holding on to the backpack with all [her] might." Because

Latasha would not let go of the backpack, Du believed that she had a weapon in it. Du then too held onto it. "That's why maybe perhaps I was struck more than—more than what really was needed," she added. Latasha's blows were powerful and Du remembered that when she fell down behind the counter she thought, "Oh, my God. I'm going to die." She threw the stool at Latasha to defend herself. Then she remembered the gun under the counter: "Every now and then," she recalled, "when I go to work there, I noticed the gun was underneath the paper bags."[75]

Du confessed that she was "in a state of panic" when she took the gun. "I grabbed something underneath," she explained of her action after the second time she fell behind the counter. "And it was the gun holster." Du repeatedly declared, however, that she did not mean to shoot Latasha, and that she did not even recall shooting her.

> LEONARD: When you grabbed this gun, did you intend to kill that young lady?
> SOON JA DU: No. No. Not at all. I had no such thought at all. And it was because I was punched in my eyes all of a sudden, and I was very dazed. It's not—it—it never happened[.] I never thought that way . . .
> LEONARD: At any point in time, do you remember pointing this gun at the back of the head of that young lady and pulling the trigger?
> SOON JA DU: I don't even know where the focus of the trigger is, and I don't know that I even touched it. . . .
> LEONARD: When was the first time you knew that the girl had been shot with the gun that you had in your hand?
> SOON JA DU: After I went to the hospital.[76]

According to Mrs. Du, her son never told her that he had used the gun to scare away gang members, in contrast to what Joseph Du testified; and she never told her husband or son that Latasha was trying to steal money from her, as both Joseph and Billy Du testified she had.[77] The court could easily have concluded that, according to Soon Ja's testimony, both Joseph and Billy had lied under oath.

Under cross-examination, District Attorney Carvajal grilled Mrs. Du on any knowledge she had about guns and their usage before March 16. She even had Mrs. Du hold the gun and shoot it (there were no bullets in the gun) the way she had seen on television, because she testified that she only had seen guns shot on TV programs. Du then held the gun by its handle and shook it. She refused to acknowledge that she knew that one had to pull a trigger before a gun fired.[78] Du stated that she also could not recall pulling the trigger, or hearing more than "a little small sound" when the gun went off, or dropping the gun after it fired.[79] When Carvajal asked her why she was so concerned about Latasha after the gun discharged, she replied:

SOON JA DU: About her killing me because she said, "Bitch, I'll kill you."

CARVAJAL: All right. I'm sorry Mrs. Du, I don't understand. The gun goes off. The girl falls out of sight, and you are concerned about her because she said she was going to kill you. Were you afraid she was going to come—come up and get you?

SOON JA DU: Yes.[80]

The district attorney continued to fire questions at Mrs. Du. As with Billy and Joseph Du, her strategy was to get Soon Ja to commit to a certain scenario, ask her if she was confused, and then play the videotape which would clearly contradict what she said. The point Carvajal really centered on was the action of Latasha Harlins just prior to Du shooting her. The district attorney suggested that Du was perhaps more angry than afraid for her life when she shot the girl. "So this—this black girl who you think is a gang member hits you in the eye where it causes you a great deal of pain, and you don't get angry at that?"[81] Carvajal asked. Du insisted that her only emotion was derived from her fear of being killed. Then Carvajal wanted to know precisely what was taking place at the time Du shot the girl:

CARVAJAL: Now, you also told us that after you threw the chair at Latasha, she came up to you, and she hit you some—some more, and you fell to the ground, and that's when you picked up the gun. Do you remember saying that?

SOON JA DU: Yes.

CARVAJAL: Is that what happened?

SOON JA DU: Yes . . .

[Carvajal then plays some of the tape of the incident.]

CARVAJAL: Do you see Latasha coming over to the counter and hitting you again?

SOON JA DU: Yes. After that moment she came back and hit me again.

Roxane Carvajal, referencing the video again, asked Mrs. Du again what she saw.

SOON JA DU: Well, I was somewhat dazed so perhaps I didn't know what was going on. I think at that moment I had felt—fallen down for the second time.

CARVAJAL: All right. Miss Du, I'm going to play it again, and you show me where you fall down the second time . . .

SOON JA DU: That moment I asked to get—give the money, and then she said something like "bitch." Right there.

CARVAJAL: Mrs. Du, you're saying that you fell down there.

SOON JA DU: Yes.

CARVAJAL: How did you fall down?

SOON JA DU: Because I was struck from the impact.

CARVAJAL: Mrs. Du, isn't it true that all you're doing right there is bending over and picking up the gun that's under the counter?

SOON JA DU: No. No . . .

CARVAJAL: And isn't it true that Latasha is nowhere near you when you go under the counter?

SOON JA DU: She was not near the counter, but I . . . was already in the state of being down, and didn't know exactly where she was . . .

CARVAJAL: Mrs. Du, when you fired the gun, where was Latasha?

SOON JA DU: I guess she was inside.

CARVAJAL: Was she walking toward you?

SOON JA DU: At that time I recall that she was just standing there . . . But at that time she was putting something up on the counter, and she said, "Bitch," and she said, "I kill you." She said it twice.

CARVAJAL: And that's when you fired the gun?

SOON JA DU: I do not recall even discharging the gun. I don't even remember the bullet going out of the gun.[82]

Carvajal ended her cross-examination of Mrs. Du, but then asked that the 911 tapes—one from the burglary company and one from Mr. Du—be entered as evidence. She also asked that the second part of Mr. Du's 911 tape be played and entered in the court record. During his 911 call, Mr. Du's other store-phone rang. He is heard in the background of his 911 call speaking in Korean to a family member on the other phone. Carvajal had the interpreter translate his statement: "Let me talk to Jinchul right away. Let me talk to Jinchul right away . . . Please come over here right away. Your mother shot somebody," Billy Du told whomever was on the phone.[83]

The drama of the courtroom spilled out into the hallways. The following day, for example, two bailiffs, Mr. Upland and Mr. D. Johnson, who were escorting Mrs. Du from the court at the end of proceedings on the previous day, had witnessed someone from the Harlins camp threaten Mrs. Du. "You're going to get yours," the person (identified as a Harlins family member) yelled at her. Judge Karlin took the threat very seriously. After all, security had been a key issue regarding the Du family and their supporters—the trial had to be moved from Compton to downtown Los Angeles; the defendant sat behind bullet-proof glass; and while in the court, Du was escorted by armed bailiffs. "I'll tell counsel and whoever is in the audience—and I will repeat this to others when they are next in court"—Karlin began her admonishment, "but I intend to take any such threats very seriously. I think they will be referred for prosecution. If there is any indication of another threat directly or indirectly to the defendant, there will be severe consequences to whoever is responsible for those threats."[84]

Testimony ended on Wednesday afternoon. Karlin had decided by the next morning that she was removing the charge of first-degree murder before she instructed jurors. "It's my intention to give the instructions on second degree, voluntary, involuntarily excusable," she informed Carvajal, Lloyd, and Leonard.[85] The four also agreed that she would instruct the jurors of this change before they heard closing statements from both sides. The Harlins family could feel the justice they sought slipping away. The Dus, however, were regaining hope—at least Soon Ja would not face life in prison or the death penalty if she was found guilty.

Day Four, October 3, 1991: Closing Arguments

Roxane Carvajal presented the first closing statement, making clear to the jury that they should find Soon Ja Du guilty of murder in the second degree, not voluntary or involuntary manslaughter. She began by attacking Du's self-defense argument.

"Let's assume for the sake of argument," Carvajal noted to the jury, "that at this point, when Latasha hits Mrs. Du in the face, in the eyes, that Mrs. Du has the right to defend herself. Absolutely, that's a given."[86] But, Carvajal contended, Mrs. Du still did not have the right to kill Latasha because she was not in "imminent" danger of dying. Latasha, Carvajal continued, had picked up the orange juice from the floor, placed it on the checkout counter, and was standing five feet away from Mrs. Du—actions that suggested to a "reasonable person" that she was no longer a threat to the shopkeeper. Moreover, Du's right to self-defense ended when Latasha turned her back on her. "You can't shoot somebody in the back. The minute Latasha turns around it's over. You cannot use self-defense. The danger is no longer imminent. The danger is non-apparent," Carvajal hammered.[87] Indeed, the district attorney went on to argue, Du never had a right to self-defense because she was the original aggressor—the fray began when the storekeeper grabbed Latasha's sweater. It was Latasha, striking Du back, who was acting in self-defense. It was Du, not Harlins, who had committed battery.[88]

The issue of self-defense, of course, was key to both the prosecution's and the defense's cases. Who had acted aggressively? and, Who had defended herself? were key to Du's conviction or exoneration. Both sides had argued forcefully, and repeatedly, regarding this issue. The questions are historically important in cases involving women. Many female defendants have been found not guilty for reasons of self-defense. Other female victims of violence have been found culpable and, therefore, unable to pursue a case of wrongdoing against them, because of what legal scholars label "victim precipitation."

Cora Mae Mann, a leading scholar on females in the criminal justice system, explains that if a female victim of a crime (usually a violent one) is found to have instigated the event which led to her victimization, then it would be difficult to prosecute the supposed perpetrator or to prosecute on the most severe charge available, because the victim is deemed culpable in some way. If defense attorneys Lloyd and Leonard, therefore, could succeed in convincing the jury, or the judge, that their defendant was actually acting only in response to Latasha's physical aggression (punching Du in the face), then they would have proven that Latasha's actions directly resulted in her being shot by Du. According to Mann, when one considers the phenomenon of women murdering women, many of the cases are determined to be the result of "victim precipitation." Consequently, less than half those arrested and tried in these cases receive jail time. "Because of the victim's contributory role in her homicide," Mann notes, "prison sentences were assigned in only 41.4 percent of the cases, and time to be served in prison averaged only 6.4 years."[89] Given the videotaped event that clearly displayed Latasha punching Ms. Du, Carvajal had her work cut out for her. The DA had to try to erase images that could be interpreted as Latasha demonstrating physical prowess and aggression toward Du.

After meticulously detailing the reasons that Soon Ja should be found guilty of second-degree murder rather than a lesser charge, Carvajal peppered the jury with declarations of Mrs. Du's dishonesty and selective memory, reminding them of the many inconsistencies, reversals, and memory lapses in her testimony. The DA argued three damning contentions. First, that while under oath, Mrs. Du deliberately hid the motives and thoughts she had when she pulled out the gun, aimed, and shot Latasha. How is it, Carvajal asked the jury, that Soon Ja Du could remember every other detail of that day and the days that followed, but she could not remember those details? "When we get to the crucial, crucial point, the reason why we're here, the gun, she can't tell you anymore. That's it. I don't remember anymore." Second, Carvajal maintained that Du lied about knowing how to shoot the gun. "She told you the very first time that I asked . . . her," Carvajal reminded the jury, "How do you fire a gun?" Du responded, "I see it in the movies. You pull the trigger." But a few minutes later during cross-examination, Du stated: "Oh, no, I didn't know that. I didn't know that at all. Not until now. Not until you show me that that's how it's done."[90] And third, Carvajal declared, Du lied about Latasha trying to steal money from her. It was Carvajal's contention that Billy Du told the 911 dispatcher that his wife had reported a robbery and then lied about it under oath because Mrs. Du really did tell him that she had shot a robber when he first rushed into the store. She also told her son that she had been robbed. When Billy Du later discovered that Latasha had not robbed the store, he changed his story under oath. He was undone, however, when Carvajal produced the 911 tape with him saying clearly that Latasha was trying to rob his wife, and Mrs. Du shot her. Crime photos taken immediately after the shooting displayed that no money from the store cash register was "scattered," which indeed would have suggested that a robbery, or attempted robbery, had taken place. "The only money at the scene that day," Carvajal added, "was the $2 that was in Latasha's hand when she was shot."[91] The story about the robber, Carvajal deduced, was one that Soon Ja took from her son's experiences that he had reported to her. "So ladies and gentlemen, what Mrs. Du did that day when her husband came in was she used her son's story—she [Latasha] hit me. She was going for the cash register, so I shot her."[92]

Carvajal concluded her summation by indicting Mrs. Du, her husband Billy, and her son Joseph as liars—pointing out again the discrepancies between their testimonies in court, evidence from police reports, the 911 audiotape, and the security videotape. They all lied, she concluded, because they wanted the jury to believe that Soon Ja Du's shooting of Latasha was an accident. Their lying was, the district attorney noted several times, an intentional act. Soon Ja Du had shot Latasha with both "express" and "intentional malice." She "never even gave Latasha a chance."[93]

Richard Leonard provided the closing remarks for the defense team. Soon Ja Du, Leonard reiterated time and time again, was not guilty. He laid out several reasons to support his conclusion. First, Du did not initiate the argument by grabbing Latasha's arm because she had a right, as a merchant, to detain a customer whom she thought was stealing. Second, Soon Ja also was entitled to pull out the gun to defend herself against what she perceived as a murder threat. Third, the gun went off accidentally while Soon Ja Du was holding it. His argument about Du's orientation to the .38 caliber Smith and Wesson was especially important: "Mrs. Du knew that the gun was there. She had seen the gun. She never handled the gun before, never knew how to use a gun, was never taught how to use a gun, didn't know the gun was loaded. There is no evidence that she pulled the trigger." As such, the defense attorney concluded, Mrs. Du certainly was not guilty of second-degree murder or voluntary manslaughter—there was no intent to kill, he argued. If the jury found her guilty of anything, Leonard proclaimed, and he was not in the least suggesting that they should or legally could, then it would have to be involuntary manslaughter.[94]

Going back over the case and, in particular, the concluding remarks of Carvajal, Richard Leonard tried to convince the jury that the district attorney had a weak case. It is because she has a weak case, he reasoned, that she spent so much time impeaching the honesty of the Du family.

One could find inconsistencies in witnesses for "the people" as well, he noted, particularly in the testimony of the nine-year-old Ismail Ali. Brushing aside Roxane Carvajal's contention that Billy, Joseph, and Soon Ja Du lied under oath to protect Soon Ja from being convicted of murder or voluntary manslaughter, Leonard tried to get the audience to believe Du's story and to empathize with her. It was her fear created by constant threats to her family, her impaired judgment due to Latasha's beating, her unfamiliarity with English, her "defective" gun and gun holster, her age and physical frailty in relation to Latasha's size and youth, and Latasha's anger, he argued, that caused Du to be part of a tragic, accidental shooting and to be confused at the time of her testimony. "You think if you're punched like that, if you're— . . . —49 . . . you're an old woman by this young lady, that you might have a hard time remembering exactly what had happened during that short period of time?"[95]

If Latasha was not the aggressor, defense co-counsel went on to argue, then at least she provoked Du to believe that she was shoplifting. "Why did she put the juice in her backpack to begin with?" he asked rhetorically. "Why didn't she just carry it in her hand and place it on the counter? What merchant in a store known to have rampant shoplifting would not suspect someone who picked up an item and placed it in his or her backpack?" Leonard quoted part of the jury instruction package to substantiate his point: "A merchant may detain a person for a reasonable time for the purpose of conducting an investigation in a reasonable manner whenever the merchant has probable cause to believe the person to be detained is attempting to unlawfully take . . . merchandise from the merchant's premises."[96] "That I submit," he added, "gave Mrs. Du the right to go over and to grab that young lady's sweater."[97]

Roxane Carvajal attempted to respond to all of Richard Leonard's major points in her rebuttal. She largely succeeded. At the end of her remarks, however, the jury probably still had a few questions. First, did Mrs. Du have the right to grab Latasha's arm as a merchant trying to protect her interest from a shoplifter? as Leonard argued. Or were her actions tantamount to assault of Latasha as the district attorney asserted? Did the gun go off accidentally? as Leonard concluded, or did Du grip the gun with both hands, brace herself, and pull the trigger? as Carvajal reiterated. Surely, it was not an easy case to deliberate—the trial lasted three-and-a-half days, and it took the jury over three days to reach a verdict. And in the midst of their deliberations, a controversy erupted—jury members were overheard in the hallway of the Criminal Courts building arguing about the case.

Itabari Njeri, a reporter for the *Los Angeles Times* on leave in order to chronicle the case for a book that she was preparing, reported to Judge Karlin that she overheard the jury members. Andrea Ford, the *Times* reporter actually covering the case for the newspaper, confirmed that she too had heard the two jurors arguing. Karlin had instructed the jurors not to discuss the case outside the jury room, and standard jury rules prohibit them from any discussion without the entire jury present. She halted the case for hours while investigating their allegations. Andrea Ford confessed that she had heard two male members of the jury "arguing loudly" outside the courtroom about whether Du should be convicted of voluntary or involuntary manslaughter. She also overheard one of the jurors insist: "It's hard to convince a jury that she thought that gun would fire if she shook it. That's insulting to my intelligence." The judge, after talking to Njeri and Ford, eventually ruled that she believed that "the integrity of the jury deliberation process has not been compromised" and chose not to replace the jurors in question with alternates.[98]

The Verdict Is In

Slightly after 1 p.m. on Friday, October 11, the foreman read the following verdict:

> We, the jury in the above-entitled action, find the defendant, Soon Ja Du, guilty of voluntary manslaughter, in violation of Penal Code Section 192 (A), a felony, a lesser included offense to that charge in count 1 of the indictment. We further find the allegation that in the commission and attempted commission of the above offense the defendant personally used a firearm within the meaning of penal code section 120306(A) (1) and 12022.5 to be true.[99]

Immediately following the reading of the verdict, Roxane Carvajal asked that Du's bail be revoked, citing that she was a possible flight risk. Charles Lloyd objected, noting that Mrs. Du had surrendered her passport as a condition of her posting bail; that she had ties in Southern California, not in South Korea; and that she really was no "threat to the community." The two argued back and forth, but in the end, Judge Karlin allowed Mrs. Du to remain free on bail until the sentencing hearing, with the stipulation that she phone her counsel once per day. Karlin then indicated that the sentencing hearing probably would be held on November 15. Lloyd requested more time; Carvajal opposed, and Karlin maintained her original date—November 15, 1991, at 3:00 p.m.[100]

FIGURE 5.1 "Joyce Karlin." Courtesy of the *Los Angeles Times*.

5

Judge Joyce Karlin

"I Would Dream of Closing Arguments"

In the hot, late summer of 1991, Joyce Karlin no doubt was proud of her latest professional achievement, and she had every right to be. California Governor Pete Wilson swore her in as Superior Court judge on September 3, 1991. Gaining a judgeship in the Superior Court of Los Angeles County is not an easy feat; it was one of those career milestones that many lawyers dreamed of, but most would never reach. In order for Governor Wilson to choose Karlin, his advisors had to believe that she had superior intellectual acumen as well as an impressive degree of professional experience with the law and the culture of criminality. Anyone who wanted to be a judge had to have all that, as well as be beyond public reproach and have enough political savvy to either be selected by a sitting governor to fill a midterm vacancy, or to mount and win a competitive campaign for the position. It was clear that Joyce Karlin felt honored by Governor Wilson's appointment, and she was certainly thrilled by the work that she would be doing. Twenty-seven days after she took the oath of office, Judge Joyce Karlin's first trial by jury began. It was the *People of California v. Soon Ja Du.*

Perhaps the other more experienced judges, like Lance Ito, Morris Jones, and Lois Anderson-Smaltz who had handled earlier motions for the case, had realized that the *People v. Du* was a political and social hot potato and had managed to avoid its burn. There was hardly any glory to be had by a jurist who presided over the case. If Du was found guilty, a significant faction of the Los Angeles community would question Karlin's notion of justice, no matter what sentence she handed down. If the case went well for the prosecution, the business community and her more conservative constituents also might disapprove. If, on the other hand, the case went well for the defense, much of the black community and political liberals clearly would be incensed. In her first real trial, a very public trial, Karlin was up against the proverbial rock and a hard place.

Of course, from the perspective of Latasha Harlins's family and their supporters, the pretrial rulings of Judge Ito regarding bail and Judge Anderson-Smaltz regarding change of venue that had taken place prior to the case landing on Joyce Karlin's calendar were cause for great scrutiny of, protest against, and continued pressure on the judicial system. They immediately began to question what kind of justice Latasha would receive outside of her community. Soon Ja Du's family and supporters also believed they had cause for concern. Would the vocal criticism and direct-action protest demonstrations of the black community influence court proceedings against her? When a downtown courtroom was finally secured, Anderson-Smaltz was no longer the sitting judge, her novice colleague—Joyce Karlin—was. In the incestuous social and professional world of big city lawyers and judges, the two women certainly were not strangers to each other—Joyce Karlin's husband was a partner in the law firm headed by Lois Anderson-Smaltz's spouse.

Joyce Karlin had to view *People v. Soon Ja Du* as an extremely important trial in her career. It was her first criminal case that would not end in a plea bargain; the first case that she would see all the way through the sentencing phase. It was a ripe opportunity to prove that Governor Wilson had made the appropriate choice in her appointment to the bench—that neither her gender, her ethnicity, her social status, nor her political affiliation had influenced Wilson's decision more than her professional readiness. Certainly this case held the promise of enhanced public awareness of her ability as a judge and, if all went well, greater respect from her peers and the voting public she would have to face if her judgeship was to be extended. This case, obviously, would be a difficult one, fraught with all kinds of political rhetoric and racial tension that had played itself out in the media and in the streets of South Central for months. There was a lot riding on this case, personally and professionally, for Judge Karlin. This is her story.

Early Life

Joyce Ann Karlin was born in Caracas, Venezuela, on January 5, 1951, into a wealthy, Jewish American family. By the time of her birth, Joyce's father, Myron, was an extremely successful film-studio executive who rose through the ranks to eventually become president of Warner Bros., International. Myron Karlin's career took the family— his wife Charlotte and his two young daughters, Joyce and Cheri— around the world. It was a privileged life indeed for young Joyce. Records of airline flights the family took, for example, document Joyce flying from Venezuela, Paris, and Germany to New York all before she was in the second grade.[1] From Venezuela in the early 1950s, where her father was an executive with MGM, the family moved to Ecuador, then to Italy, Germany, and Argentina. Joyce recalled having movie stars come to her home for parties and going to the set of *Ben Hur* in Rome (the only film that has ever won 11 Oscars).

Judge Joyce Karlin, therefore, grew up in a home charged with intellect, sophistication, and power. Her father was smart, ambitious, and exceptionally successful. His career took him and his family into the inner circles of some of the most popular film stars, brilliant writers, and visionary directors of more than one generation. Myron Karlin was an A-lister—a leader in a business (the "only" business as far as much of LA is concerned) that produced great wealth and power and that propelled equally great careers. Karlin's work in the film industry not only made him a star maker, but also made him an international cultural architect. It was at the helm of one of the most influential film studios in the world, and later as president of one of the industry's most important organizations, that Myron Karlin showered the world with cultural images and icons created in Hollywood. He helped shape American popular culture in the 1950s, 1960s, 1970s, and 1980s and exported it around the globe. The world saw, and accepted, the America that Karlin created on the screen. Karlin's work in Hollywood was a different path from the one on which he started, and it was extremely different from the one his immigrant ancestors could have ever imagined.

Immigrants from Russia

Judge Joyce Karlin's paternal great grandparents, Morris and Rose Karlinsky (Karlinski/y was their Russian surname), along with their six children, migrated from Kiev, Russia, to Boston, Massachusetts, during the first decade of the twentieth century. The family seems to have lived in or near Kiev at the time of their immigration but also had resided in the Ukraine of Chernigov. There were, indeed, a great number of persons living in that part of Russia with names so similar—Karlinski, Karlinsky, and the Karlens from nearby Smolensk as well as Kiev, for example—that clearly Morris and Rose were part of a large clan.

Like so many other Russian Jews at the time, the Karlinskys no doubt fled to escape state-sanctioned violence and discrimination that touched all aspects of their lives. The records indicate, for example, that several families tied to them left Russia between 1890 and 1925. Kiev was the largest city in and the capital of Ukraine. Located on the Dneiper River, Kiev, like Boston, was a center of business and trade. Chernigov, their earlier home, also was located on the Dneiper and was the site of one of the oldest Jewish settlements in the Ukraine, dating back to the thirteenth century. There, Jews formed a significant minority—about 40% (11,000) of the population at the turn of the century. Most were merchants or craftsmen.[2] Both cities had anti-Semitic laws and the Ukraine in general was plagued by pogroms for much of the nineteenth century. Jews were more numerous in Kiev, where they numbered about 20,000 in 1902. Most, however, did not live directly in the city, but in a segregated Jewish quarter. Life had been particularly difficult since the government officially expelled Jews in 1825, but had improved somewhat under the reign of Czar Alexander II. These positive developments, however, ended abruptly with the anti-Jewish riots of 1881. After that, general police repression, economic and educational sanctions, and social as well as cultural exclusion and vilification followed. Jews were subject to even more harsh and discriminatory treatment after the failed revolutionary attempt of 1905, which ended with many Jews being labeled anti-czarist. Their enemies destroyed Jewish businesses and homes, beat and killed men, women, and children indiscriminately, and raped women and girls. Pogroms in their home city of Kiev in 1881 and 1905, and in other places in Russia in 1828, 1848, 1856, 1865, 1871, as well as 1903, convinced many, including the Karlinskys, to seek asylum in the United States.

Like African Americans who fled the vicious repression of the racist, segregated South, Jews left Russia in search of safety and protection for their families, greater freedom, economic promise, and hope for a brighter future for their children.[3] Indeed, if Joyce Karlin's great grandparents from Russia had ever met those of Latasha Harlins from Mississippi and Alabama, the two sets of ancestors would have recognized a common horror in their stories about what it was like to be a despised people living outside the protection of the law. And why shouldn't the Karlinskys have looked forward to a better life in the United States? They were arriving at a time when economic and educational opportunities were at least sufficient; when friends and relatives from Russia were forming large communities; when Jewish local institutions could provide support and encouragement; and when large, national institutions, like the Jewish Theological Seminary, the American Jewish Historical Society, the National Council of Jewish Women, *The Jewish Quarterly Review*, and Jewish teacher colleges were beginning to solidify a sense of Jewish permanence and prosperity. Still, their new home was not without anti-Jewish prejudice. Indeed, this large wave of Russian and central European Jewish immigrants witnessed increasing hostility throughout the United States.[4]

Immigration records indicate that Morris Karlinski (y) traveled on the Cunard shipping line's RMS *Saxonia* to Boston, which left Liverpool, England, on August 11, 1903, and arrived on August 20. Morris, who was approximately 38 at the time, had been living in London and was a tailor by occupation. He intended to stay initially with his brother-in-law, Max Nofonsky, who lived at 23 Ware Street. Upon reaching Boston, Morris was examined by immigration officers and certified that he was neither a polygamist nor an anarchist and was in good health. He reported that he carried with him five dollars. The *Saxonia* was part of the Cunard line that shipped persons from all over Europe to Boston. After leaving Liverpool, the ship typically stopped at Queenstown to pick up Irish passengers. The passenger manifest for Morris's trip indeed indicates that there were passengers from England and Ireland, as well as Sweden, Finland, Denmark, Russia and Germany. Although no information remains regarding what class of passenger Morris was, most Jewish immigrants traveled in third class or steerage—far from a luxury cruise. Two years later, Louis Karlinsky, Morris's eldest son, arrived. The father's plan, no doubt, was for him and his son to find lucrative work and prepare a home. Louis was 14 in 1905, old enough to work doing odd jobs while he attended school. He could not only work some, but Louis was probably also able to learn English faster than his father. English acquisition would be important for the family's acculturation and eventual success in their new home. Other members of Morris's extended family began to arrive and continued to do so for the next decade. Elia Kurlansky, a tailor, for example, traveled to Boston on the *Saxonia* from Liverpool in March 1906 at age 18.[5] Eight years later, Mones Karlinsky arrived, reuniting with his wife Rivka.[6] Others moved on to locales in New York, Ohio, and even Los Angeles.

In September 26, 1906, Rose, Morris's wife, arrived from Liverpool on the SS *Arabic* of the White Star Shipping Line. She declared $11 in cash and, like her husband, had to swear to immigration officials in Boston that she had paid for her own fare. She told them that she was going to stay with her husband. The couple's other five children—Minnie, Millie, Joseph, Sarah and little Myer, who was only four at the time—traveled with her. Joseph, who was born in 1897, was the future father of Myron and the grandfather of Joyce Karlin.[7]

The Karlinsky family settled in Boston's Ward Eight in the West End, a neighborhood filled with Russian Jewish immigrants who worked as butchers, tailors, bookkeepers, peddlers, and upholsterers. Like most of their peers, the Karlinskys read Hebrew and Yiddish, with Yiddish as their lingua franca. In a few years, they all spoke at least some English. They were not wealthy. Morris continued his work as a tailor. The children began to work as soon as they could—the males as newsboys selling papers in the streets, and the girls as seamstresses. Working as a newsboy was a popular occupation for West End Jewish boys because it allowed them time to attend school. The eldest children also began to marry and start their own families. Those who did not find spouses in Boston resorted to finding husbands and wives in other communities along the northeastern seaboard. Four years after she arrived, for example, Minnie was listed in the 1910 federal census as still living in her father's Boston home, but married to 23-year-old Charles Shafran.[8] Charles was the son of Davis and Dora Shafrans, Russian Jewish émigrés who lived in New York. Charles also came from a family of tailors and seamstresses, although he had found a more lucrative job as a butcher. Kosher butchers were in high demand in orthodox Jewish communities like the West End. Charles's

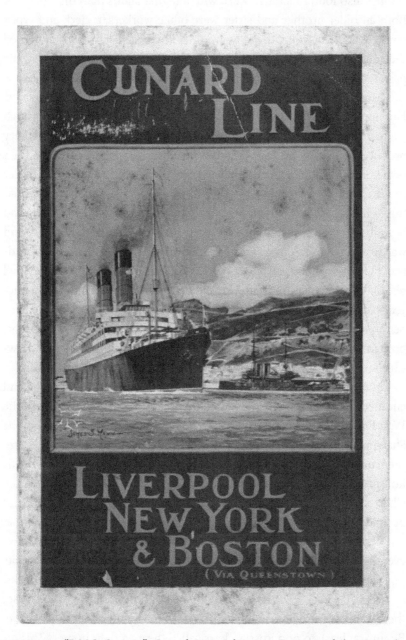

FIGURE 5.2 "R.M.S. Saxonia," Cunard Line, July 1909. Courtesy of the Gjenvick-Gjonvik Archives.

siblings also found lucrative work with a higher status than their parents. Both an older brother and sister were office workers, a clerk and typist respectively. Not coincidentally, by 1910, the Karlinsky's had shortened their surname to Karlin; although Morris, in a persistent nod to his ethnic past, sometimes still appeared in the Boston city directory as Karlinsky.[9]

Morris, Rose, and their children became naturalized citizens in 1915. Hoping to improve his own family's financial status, the family patriarch augmented his work as a tailor with a managerial position at the local dairy produce factory. As his sons matured and married, they moved into their own homes. Louis, for example, lived in Roxbury, worked as a news dealer in 1920, and was married to a Jewish woman named Dora. The couple had three children. Dora's parents were from Poland and Hungary, but she had been born in Massachusetts.[10] Joseph also had married by 1920 and was working as a salesman in a grocery. He and his wife Sadie, a second-generation Jewish woman whose parents had emigrated from Germany, had two children by then—a three-year-old daughter named Judith, and a one-year-old son, Myron. Joyce Karlin's father was born to the couple on September 21, 1918.[11] Joseph and Sadie went on to have two more children—Selma, born in 1922, and Robert, born in 1926. Sadie was from another largely Jewish community of first- and second-generation immigrants from Russia.[12]

The neighborhood that Morris and his family came to call home had endured waves of settlements before their arrival. Early in the 1800s, the West End, located along the Charles River on the northwest portion of the Shawmut Peninsula, was known as a community of wealthy, white entrepreneurs with large mansions, most famously the Harrison Gray Otis house, and such landmarks as Massachusetts General Hospital and the Charles Street Jail. As those wealthy families moved out to Bunker Hill and beyond, large numbers of free African Americans came and stayed. Irish immigrants followed at midcentury. Many of the Irish and blacks, however, had started to relocate by the end of the century. New immigrants replaced them, including Armenians, Lebanese, Italians, Syrians, Greeks, as well as families from Lithuania, Poland, Ukraine, and Russia. In 1880, there were only 100 Jews living in the West End; by 1895, there were 6,300. By 1910, at least 40,000 Russian Jews called the area their home.[13] This diversity was manifest in the various languages heard on the street, the different food shops which catered to the culinary needs of residents, and a variety of churches and synagogues, representing the different religious faiths of the residents. The back and forth of migrants was especially reflected in spaces of worship. Indeed, by 1909, the trustees of five historically black churches in the West End had sold their buildings to Jewish congregations. On the other hand, two of the black congregations who left the West End—The AME Zion and Twelfth Baptist—purchased, and then occupied, two synagogues, Adath Israel and Mishkan Tefila.[14]

By the time that Morris Karlinsky arrived in 1903, the West End was fast becoming a place dominated by central European and Russian Jews. The neighborhood, as well as the city, also was witnessing a change in the cultural background of its Jewish residents. Before the 1880s, the vast majority of Jewish immigrants to Boston had come from Germany, with smaller numbers coming from Poland, Prussia, and Lithuania.[15] All this changed by the 1890s.[16] The typical immigrant family to Boston during this era was like the Karlinskys—a Russian couple with small children. Most of the men were literate and held skilled occupations. There were few professionals. It was not unusual for Russian immigrants to encounter the disdain of Jews who had arrived earlier and from other areas in Europe—a disdain centered on their cultural and class differences. Most Russian Jews, for example, were more orthodox worshippers, less educated and poorer than many who arrived from Germany.[17]

Although this community represented several occupational spheres, many Jewish immigrants focused on owning small businesses, such as tailor establishments and kosher butcher shops and groceries, which serviced the needs of their communities. The widespread needle trade provided plenty of work in local shops and factories in the garment district, even though wages were low and working conditions poor. Many Jews of the Karlinsky generation in Boston found it difficult to improve their economic status. Like contemporary African American migrants leaving the South, as well as Korean immigrants arriving more than half a century later, Jewish immigrants like the Karlinskys faced discrimination. As a result, they created banks and lending institutions that aided not only their own community, but also the larger society. Jewish women, ever cognizant of the limits to their financial independence given the patriarchal world they inhabited, also created lending organizations to help other women.

Jewish women of this generation worked outside the home because their families needed their income, but their defining work, as Jewish women, was within their domestic circle. The Boston *Jewish Advocate* carried an editorial in 1908, for example, that argued that the home should be women's most important priority. Mothers and wives were to encourage "loyalty to Judaism in those who love them," and put aside their own "personal pleasures and enjoyments" to instill in their children and other kin "a spirit of race and constancy to principle."[18] Many in Boston heeded this message and, as a result, most wage-earning women were young and single.

Mary Antin, in her autobiographical account of her life as a Jewish child in Russia and later as an immigrant in Boston, was clear about her family's priorities regarding girl children. When her sister Frieda, after being in Boston for only two years, received an offer of marriage, her father did not hesitate to let her go, even though his family desperately needed Frieda's earnings from sewing. To begin her own family, her father insisted, was much more important.[19] Their lives were not easy. Their homes were small and cramped. The streets narrow, busy, dirty, and sometimes dangerous. Streetcars crisscrossed lanes and alleys. There were saloons and houses of ill-repute mixed in with Chinese laundries, small workshops, and basement groceries. Antin described her family's home in a neighborhood not far from the Karlinsky's as "five small rooms up two flights of stairs with the right of way through the dark corridors. In the 'parlor' the dingy paper hung in rags and the plaster fell in chunks. One of the bedrooms was absolutely dark and air-tight. The kitchen windows looked out on a dirty court, at the back of which was the rear tenement."[20]

Those who worked in the factories of Boston had a difficult time of it—laboring in what could only be called sweatshops that were dirty, dangerous, and paid little. It was not long before some of these women began to seek redress through collective bargaining and union formation. In 1902, for example, Philip Davis, a Russian Jewish graduate of Harvard, who had taken a particular interest in the plight of female workers in Boston, along with Samuel Gompers of the AFL, helped them to organize the Waist-makers, the Wrap-Makers, and the White-goods Workers Unions which, a year later, became part of the International Union.[21]

The diverse occupational, legal, and cultural histories that these Jewish settlers experienced in their various European homelands translated into different ways of life, languages, and religious expression that they pursued once in Boston. The Jewish community that the Karlinskys entered, therefore, was not necessarily a united one, with regard to class or culture, but it was one that typically worked together to provide services and support institutions that benefited most. Family, work, education, religion, and acculturation were at the center of their lives and their community efforts. Building on an older tradition of community institutions, businesses, and service-oriented organizations, Jews in Boston's West End managed to construct synagogues, libraries, orphanages, lending societies, social clubs, settlement houses, and health centers, as well as organize labor unions—all organizations that would have benefited Joyce Karlin's ancestors.

Most important among the community institutions that serviced Jewish women were educational and self-help organizations. Linda Hectt, for example, founded the Hebrew Industrial School in 1890 in order to teach Jewish girls in Boston how to sew and cook. She began to admit boys soon after the school's founding. By 1896, it is estimated that at least 1,000 Jewish immigrant children had attended the Hebrew Industrial School and had gained the skills to become active "wage earners, breadwinners and self-respecting intelligent citizens." Jewish women also organized locally based kindergartens that provided generations with spiritual guidance and religious education.[22]

Development of their own community institutions and communities, however, did not mean that West End Jewish immigrants, like the Karlinskys, were not interested in being a part of mainstream American society. Indeed, most passionately embraced not just citizenship but also "being American." Many centered their attention on assimilating the customs of their new nation, acculturating as quickly as possible. This process meant not only the rapid acquisition of English but also "reforming" religious rituals and expression that gave new residents an opportunity to more fully embrace the American lifestyle and political and social philosophies, while still remaining adherents of their faith. Mary Antin, for example, explained of her family's experience that in the attempt to "fit in" as Americans, her father insisted that their entire family move away from orthodoxy. In America, not nearly as much time in the Antin home would be spent in prayer, the men would shave their faces, and Mrs. Antin was not to bring her wig from Russia. Mary's mother kept kosher, but her father insisted that the children could eat at the homes of Gentiles. They also had to attend school on holy days, except

Yom Kippur. It was, Antin insisted, a difficult transition for her mother, but given her father's strict patriarchy, which the mother respected dearly, it was a new lifestyle her mother had to learn to accept.[23]

Anti-Immigrant Fervor

Jewish immigrants struggled mightily to make and take advantage of opportunities to achieve family and community stability as well as individual success in their new country. Like most immigrants, their welcome was a mixed bag. Not atypically, as the numbers of immigrants from Russia and eastern and central Europe climbed, the American response hardened. Indeed, the arrival of Jewish immigrants at the turn of the twentieth century coincided with one of the most vehement anti-immigration campaigns in the nation's history. The laws on immigration and naturalization that affected Jews (as well as those from Asia, Africa, and southern Europe) mounted from the 1880s on. New immigration laws, for example, charged taxes for all nonresident persons arriving in the United Sates; excluded those with serious illnesses and with documented moral flaws; and refused to admit "known" anarchists and political leftists, as well as the illiterate. These laws also created immigrant quotas. The Immigration Act of 1924 limited the number of European immigrants to 2% of the number of people who lived in the United States from their native countries in 1890, reducing substantially the flow of Jews from central Europe.[24] Laws were not the only efforts put in place to quell immigration. In Boston, where the Karlinskys first arrived, for example, the Immigrant Restriction League, an organization founded by men of elite New England families and Harvard graduates, had as its principal goal to "keep America for the Americans." For example, the League sponsored the immigrant literacy-requirement bills before Congress. It eventually grew to a national organization with offices in New York, San Francisco, and other urban centers. According to a League officer, the purpose of trying to restrict immigrants from southern and eastern Europe was to limit those:

- destitute of resources, either in money or still more in ability
  or knowledge of the means to support itself; which is generally
  ignorant; which has criminal tendencies; is averse to country life
  and congregates in our city slums; which has a low standard of

living and little ambition a better [one]; and which has no permanent interests in this country.[25]

The Immigration Protection League, on the other hand, was an example of organized efforts to fight immigration restrictions. Interestingly, William Lloyd Garrison, the most important white abolitionist of the nineteenth century, served as the Protection League's vice president.[26]

Amidst the nation's xenophobic response to immigrants, Jews suffered a criminalization that was not dissimilar from that which both Asian immigrants encountered in the nineteenth century and African Americans have experienced since the colonial era. The attack on Jews also mirrored the centuries of malicious mistrust and vilification they had been subject to across Europe. Popular stereotypes of Jews as argumentative, untrustworthy, greedy, emotional, insular, and clannish merged with "scientific racism" that posited Jews as inferior to white (i.e., Christian) Europeans.[27] Simply put, many regarded Jews as inferior culturally, physically, and morally. Jewish women were caught in this ugly net as well as men. Both, for example, were accused of participating in the urban sex trade. Indeed, one of the most salacious anti-Semitic documents to emerge at the turn of the century was George Kibbe Turner's 1909 article in *McClure* magazine in which he accused Jewish "pimps" of procuring literally thousands of immigrant Jewish girls and women from Russia, Hungary, and Austria to use as prostitutes, at first in New York, and then in other major cities of the nation, including Boston, Philadelphia, Seattle, Chicago, New Orleans, St. Louis, Los Angeles, and San Francisco.[28] These types of accusations caused middle-class Jewish women to be particularly interested in helping immigrant Jewish females to acquire lucrative skills and to find safe work and housing through the creation of settlement houses and other philanthropic organizations. This anti-Jewish propaganda also helped to fuel the continual scrutiny of, and opposition to, Jewish immigration.[29]

The Family Moves to California

Anti-Semitism grew rapidly during this era, but immigrants and their children continued to seek solace in the US from the more extreme forms of repression and discrimination they faced in Europe. Once they arrived in the United States, they sought the most welcoming environment in which to succeed. Boston certainly had thriving Jewish communities in the early decades of the twentieth century, for example, but in the quest to find the most opportune location to raise families and prosper, many younger immigrants, or their children, moved onward. Some went almost immediately to New York. Others stayed in the Boston area and relocated to nearby neighborhoods. Some moved to cities in the Midwest and West. Joyce Karlin's paternal grandparents—Joseph and Sadie—decided to move to California. They might have been lured to Los Angeles by Harry and Jennie Karlin.

Harry Karlin was born in 1891 and probably was Joseph's paternal uncle or a cousin. Immigration records indicate, for example, that both Harry and Jennie arrived from Russia in 1907, about the same time as Joseph's immediate family and many of the other extended family members came. By 1920, the couple was living in Los Angeles with their two children, Aaron and Hilda, and Harry had found work as a carpenter. Ten years later, Joseph, Sadie and their four children, including Joyce Karlin's father, had made their home in the same building as Harry and Jennie. They were living in what is now the heart of downtown Los Angeles, at West 1st Street between Broadway and Spring.[30] Joseph found work as a salesman in an advertising company. Their new neighborhood, like those in Massachusetts where they had resided, was one of the central Jewish communities in Los Angeles at the time.[31]

Jews, of course, had been living in the City of Angels for several decades prior to the Karlins's arrival. Various records indicate that by the time that California became a state in 1850, there were eight Jews, 15 blacks, and two Chinese living in the city of 1,600 residents.[32] The Jewish community grew slowly, but certainly. Most were immigrants from Germany, but a few also came from Poland (Prussia) or were Sephardic. Horace Bell visited the city in 1852 when he described it as "a nice looking place" with "neat," "clean," "whitewashed" houses and numerous businesses. "Most of the merchants," he added "were Jews, and all seemed to be doing a paying business."[33]

By 1854, there were enough Jewish residents that they had regular religious services led by a lay leader named Joseph Newmark. Eight years later, the city's first rabbi, Abraham Wolf Edelman, came to stay. Early efforts at community self-help and philanthropy resulted in creation of the

Hebrew Benevolent Society. This association, which was one of the first charitable organizations founded in Los Angeles (1854), provided burial services and sites, charity to Jews and Gentiles alike, and religious services and financial support to Jews in Palestine. Others within the community helped to create the city's Chamber of Commerce, Library Association, Board of Trade, and the Los Angeles Athletic Club.[34]

Jewish settlers also quickly found a place in the city's government and legal institutions. Of the eight members of the Jewish community found in the census in 1850, for example, one—Morris Goldman—served on the city's first City Council. Maurice Kremer became city treasurer in 1859 and also served on the City Council, Board of Supervisors, and Board of Education. Indeed, eight Jewish men had been elected to the City Council by 1870. Other nineteenth-century members of this community held positions such as city attorney, city clerk, and were school board members. Blacks too were members of early Los Angeles' and California's governing institutions. Several mixed-race families (African, Spanish, and Native American), for example, arrived during the late eighteenth century when California was still owned and governed by Mexico. Most famously perhaps were the Picos (of Pico Boulevard, Pico Rivera, and the Pico House), who acquired thousands of acres of land in San Diego and the San Fernando Valley; constructed the elegant Pico House Hotel; and held important positions in early Los Angeles and California, including that of governor. By the late nineteenth century, however, most of these early mixed-race families had disappeared into other group designations, including mestizos, *espanoles, californios*, and Mexicans.[35]

In 1870, the Jewish community in Los Angeles was more than 300 in a city of 5,800 residents. Jewish Angelenos created the city's first synagogue in 1872. Their Southern California community was small, but among it were notable business, banking, civic, educational, and philanthropic leaders. Jewish men, for example, were found in the local police department; Emil Harris, who had been born in Prussia, served as police chief in the late 1870s. Bernard Cohn served on the City Council for several terms and also was mayor pro tem. The Jewish community in Los Angeles also created the Order of the B'nai B'rith in 1874.[36] Successful Jewish merchants established lucrative clothing and department stores. Peter Kahn, a political prisoner from Kiev, like the Karlins, arrived in Los Angeles in 1907, and created the successful Kahn Produce Company, while also serving as an activist for workers and local Native Americans.[37] Bankers helped create many of the state's earliest banks. Isaias Hellman was perhaps the most successful within the community's financial sector. He created three banks in the state—Farmers and Merchants in Los Angeles, the Nevada Bank in San Francisco, and Wells Fargo Bank. Eventually his banks would become the basis for Bank of America. Entrepreneur par excellence, Hellman also provided city businessmen and residents with real estate as well as business and personal loans that helped spark a number of statewide and local industries, including oil, wine, and transportation. Hellman also donated part of the land that became California's first institution of higher learning—the University of Southern California. The state recognized these accomplishments and appointed Hellman as a regent for the newly created University of California system in 1881. His wife, Esther, like most wealthy women of her era, fulfilled the demands of gender convention—using her wealth and social cachet to help the needy.[38]

Local Jewish women organized the Ladies Hebrew Benevolent Society in 1870, noted for its assistance to new immigrants and the financially needy, including the ill. Later in that decade, Emma Marwedel, a German immigrant, arrived and along with Caroline Severance, a feminist activist from Boston, opened Marwedel's California Model Kindergarten, the first kindergarten in California. Other organizations they helped to create and support included the German Ladies' Benevolent Society, the Orphans' Home Society, the Boys' Home Society, and the Flower Festival Society. Most of their services aided children, women, and the poor, for whom they raised money and provided shelter. The Flower Festival Society, for example, established a boardinghouse for the elderly as well as for young, single, female laborers. Other important female philanthropic and charity organizations that were in place by the time Sadie Karlin arrived included the Jewish Sisterhood, the Jewish Women's Foreign Relief Association, the Home for Jewish Working Girls, the Council of Jewish Women, the Temple Sewing Circle, the Young Women's Hebrew Association, and the Jewish Ladies Auxiliary Society.[39]

The Karlins made it to Los Angeles during the late 1920s and soon faced, like the rest of the nation, a city on the brink of financial disaster. The stock market crash of 1929 was as devastating to immigrant communities in the West as to those in the East. The community provided relief efforts through their various charitable organizations. Fortunately, by the 1930s, many Jewish families still were experiencing upward mobility. Education, usually in public and Hebrew schools, along with hard work and the ability to find unique places within the economy allowed many to continue to advance.

Jewish progress, in turn, fueled more anti-Semitism. "If the 1920s saw the building up of a substantial edifice of anti-Jewish rhetoric and behavior," one important historian of the American Jewish experience notes, "the 1930s represented anti-Semitism's apex."[40] Jews faced growing public outrage over their presence, voiced in popular media outlets, in the corridors of government, and in the communities in which they worked and owned businesses. For the first time, African Americans in urban communities, for example, began criticizing Jewish shopkeepers for what they believed were discriminatory hiring practices. They held "Don't shop where you can't work" campaigns in neighborhoods in New York and Chicago. Moreover, the Harlem race riot of 1935 witnessed blacks and other residents targeting Jewish-owned shops. This, unfortunately, was the beginning of a trend. Thirty years later, the Los Angeles riots also resulted in the looting of Jewish-owned stores in predominantly black neighborhoods and for some of the same purported reasons. The burning of Koreatown 27 years later also was due to perceptions by African Americans of racist repression and discrimination—both Jewish and Korean.[41]

Still blacks did not plan, lead, or execute the anti-Semitic campaigns in the United States, not during the era of the Depression or later. This tone was set much higher in the nation's sociopolitical hierarchy. Some of the nation's most heralded institutions and citizens led these efforts—locally, regionally, and nationally. Father Charles Coughlin, for example, a Catholic priest who had a popular radio show and newspaper, *Social Justice*, tried to convince his audience of 30 million plus that Jews controlled America and that the vicious 1938 pogrom Kristallnacht was justified.[42] Anti-Semitic organizations like William Dudley Pelley's Silver Shirts or the German American Bund attracted relatively small followings (15,000 or so each), but their presence, and their propaganda, was felt mightily in Jewish communities, particularly in light of what was happening in Germany at the time.[43]

In Southern California, as throughout the Southwest, numerous anti-Semitic organizations existed. The KKK was prominent in Los Angeles, San Diego, Orange County, and other locales, with its members winning local elections as well as serving on grand juries and as policemen. In 1924, for example, four members of the Klan became Anaheim City Council members, and one, council president. A few months into office, they held a huge Klan rally in a local park that drew 10,000 persons. The majority of the Anaheim Police Department also were Klan members.[44] In 1929, local Klan leader John Clinton Porter became mayor of Los Angles. Throughout the region, the organization harassed, threatened, and terrorized Mexican and Mexican Americans, blacks, Catholics, and Jews, burning crosses, mocking worshippers leaving synagogues, and marching through Jewish neighborhoods.[45] During the 1930s, some local braches joined forces with the Silver Shirts and other racist groups, such as the Minute Men and the White Guards. By the 1940s, Los Angeles served as the center of KKK activity in the state and a large swath of the Southwest. It was also in that decade, however, that popular opposition to the Klan's rhetoric of hatred won out. In 1946, their charter was revoked and the organization no longer was allowed to operate in the state.[46]

Joyce Karlin's grandparents moved to Los Angeles during this era of Klan resurgence. While not much is known of their feelings about this kind of anti-Semitic environment, it is clear that the family was able to progress during the years between World Wars I and II. One indicator was their ability to move. Most Jewish immigrants began their residence in a new place by living in neighborhoods occupied principally by other Jews. This had been the case for the Karlins in Boston and in Los Angeles. As they gained greater economic stability, however, many moved to neighborhoods that boasted better homes, schools, and neighborhood services. By the mid-1930s, Joseph and Sadie had moved from the business district of downtown and were living at 26½ Thornton Avenue in the Venice district, about one block from the Pacific Ocean. Joseph was a salesman and Sadie a housewife.[47] Ten years later, the family moved again. This time they took up residence at 136 Hill Street in Santa Monica. At the time, Santa Monica and Venice were important sites of the Jewish elite. The beachside communities were so popular, in fact, that services for B'nai B'rith were held there during the summer months. The family was mostly still intact—Judith and Selma, who had not yet married, were living at home. Myron, Joyce's father, also probably was still there but attending college. A student at UCLA, he received his BA degree in Spanish in 1939 and, two years later, his MA.[48]

War, Movies and Moving

That generation of Karlins was reaching adulthood, beginning their work lives and their own families. On July 26, 1942, a year after finishing his graduate degree, Myron married the woman who was to become Joyce Karlin's mother—20-year-old Charlotte Siletzky from Denver. Her parents—Solomon, a watchmaker, and Fannie—like Myron's grandparents, had emigrated from Russia.[49]

World War II was well underway by the time that Myron and Charlotte married. He was one of 50 million whom the government required to register for selective service and 10 million later inducted. Myron Karlin enlisted in the United States Army on April 24, 1943. Europe was bursting with war and Myron went. He soon was chosen, because of the ease in which he learned foreign languages, to be part of the Office of Strategic Services (OSS), precursor to the CIA.[50] Deployed as an intelligence agent in France, his work took him away from his wife into a life of secrecy that he could not share with her or any of his family. Karlin recalled that he could not tell Charlotte where he was stationed or the nature of the work he was doing. His French was so good that Myron was able to establish himself in Paris as a local during the German occupation, extremely dangerous work because he was not just a spy, but a Jewish spy.[51] Karlin provided important intelligence for the French and other Allies that contributed, like the work of so many others, to the defeat of Hitler's Nazi Germany and an end to the genocides being implemented throughout Europe. The French government was so thankful for his services that they honored him with the prestigious Croix de Guerre. Myron Karlin also received the distinction of Commander, Order of Leopold II of Belgium, and Knight of the Italian Republic. He finished his tour of duty in 1946.[52]

Myron Karlin's life in France and Europe during the war included cultural experiences and language training that must have helped him advance in the film industry. The movie business, of course, was a particularly lucrative sector of the Los Angeles economy with tremendous Jewish influence. Jewish businessmen had founded most of the major studios by the time Myron began his work in Hollywood, including Columbia Pictures, Universal Studios, Metro-Goldwyn-Mayer (MGM), Warner Bros., and Paramount Pictures. Indeed, MGM was founded by Louis B. Mayer, whose biography was not so different from those of an earlier generation of men in Karlin's family. Mayer too was from Russia (Minsk), had migrated to North America (at first Canada), and eventually came to reside in Boston before moving to Los Angeles.[53]

Myron's college and graduate degrees, language training, and experience living abroad were all accoutrements that benefited his new career. He began as an executive in the business. Karlin's Spanish was excellent, and in 1946, Myron began serving as general manager of MGM in Ecuador, before moving on to head other MGM offices in Venezuela, Germany, and Argentina. In the late 1950s, he also served as general manager for United Artists in Italy. Myron Karlin had been in the movie business for almost fifteen years when he decided to take his career in another direction. He remained in the corporate world, but left Europe, and moved back to America in 1960. Perhaps it was that he needed a new career challenge. Maybe he moved back so that his girls, Joyce and Cheri, could complete their education in America. Not that they were not receiving a fine education in Latin America and Europe—Joyce was fluent in both Spanish and Italian. Myron also might have decided to return stateside so that he could be close to his ailing father. Or perhaps he got a job offer that he could not resist. Whatever the reason(s), Myron Karlin and his family moved home, taking up residence in a posh Chicago neighborhood. There, he served as president of Brunswick International Corporation, a Fortune 500 company that was a leader in sports equipment, particularly billiards and bowling.[54]

After eight years in Chicago, Myron Karlin was ready to head back to Europe and back to the film industry. He spent the next two years as vice president of MGM's UK, Europe, Middle East, and Africa offices. It was a tumultuous time for MGM, characterized by frequent changes in studio heads and downsizing of their European operations. Not surprisingly, Myron left. This time, it was only the company he left behind, not the industry. He was at the peak of his game. In 1972, Myron Karlin became president of Warner Bros., International. Like MGM, Warner Bros. had been founded by East European Jews who, like the Karlins, had migrated from Russia to North America.[55] It was a position that Myron would maintain for the next 13 years. Even after leaving this post in 1985, Karlin immediately became the studio's executive vice president of international affairs. His responsibilities included a focus on "government issues and problems" that impacted Warner Bros.' products in 80 or so countries.[56] Ten years later he retired, but he continued to be one of the most important advocates and protectors of Hollywood abroad, assuming the presidency of the Motion Picture Export Association of America, a.k.a. the Motion Picture Association of America (MPAA).[57] It was because of this position that Karlin literally spent eight out of 12 months each year traveling abroad in order to find quality foreign films and to promote US films internationally.[58]

In "the business," Karlin was much liked and well honored for his work and his philanthropy. Jack Valenti, for example, another powerful Hollywood executive who also served as president of the MPAA, described Myron as a man who was a "guide when it came to doing what was necessary . . . to help[ing] others who could not always do that for themselves."[59] In 1984, France's National Cinema Center honored Myron as a Knight of Arts and Letters. Two years later, the Los Angeles Friends of Shaare Zedek Medical Center bestowed on him its Jerusalem Award, for his continued support of Jerusalem's major research hospital.[60]

Joyce Karlin's upbringing no doubt fueled her own ambition. Her father's great success in the military, intelligence-gathering circles, the corporate world, and the movie industry—at home and abroad—certainly would have made her extremely comfortable with her own professional aspirations. Likewise, Myron Karlin's honored work that helped free the French from Nazi control, as well as his philanthropic commitments later in life, no doubt inspired his daughter to think of a career that might aid others. Joyce's intellect and her family's financial resources meant that she could have pursued any professional career she desired. She chose, fairly early in life, the legal profession as the occupational avenue she would pursue. It was during her childhood, actually, that she began to think of becoming an attorney. "I would write murder mysteries when I was little," she remembered. "I would dream of closing arguments."[61]

The women in Joyce Karlin's immediate family did not have to work outside their home since Myron certainly provided a wealthy lifestyle for his wife and two daughters. When the family eventually moved from Europe to the United States in 1960, Joyce was an early adolescent. Their hometown was, and is, a community of the very affluent. Sitting atop a bluff and bordered by miles of lakefront, the Chicago suburb was famous for its majestic, historic homes, designed by notable architects. It also was known for its parks, luxurious golf courses, superior public schools, and lack of diversity. More than 95% of its population was European American. Two percent were African American and less than one percent was Asian/Pacific Islander.[62]

The constant moving proved difficult for Joyce. Each place she went meant finding new friends and adjusting to a new school. Young Karlin, who was then a brunette, was very bright and she excelled intellectually, so much so that school officials allowed Joyce to skip two grades before she was nine. Instead of helping her gain entrance to the social world of her peers, however, her intellectual acumen left her on the margins. Her small stature heightened her sense of social alienation. "I've always been very small, and I looked young" she noted. "I was 9 years old in sixth grade. It was very hard for me."[63]

It was there that Joyce, "Joy" to her family and friends, attended Deerfield High School, a model public school brimming with excellence and opportunity. Deerfield offered not only the regular courses and sporting activities, for example, but also a magnificent library with secondary and primary source materials; a language arts department with a language lab that offered four years of instruction in French, Spanish, German, and Latin; courses in sociology and economics; studio art, sculpture and painting; and advance placement classes in all the major disciplines. Like most Chicago-area high schools during that era, Deerfield was racially segregated. In 1965, Joyce's sophomore year, no black students attended the high school; only two Asian American pupils contributed any kind of racial diversity.[64]

After her graduation, Joyce's parents moved back to Europe. She remained and entered Northern Illinois University in 1967. Northern Illinois, located in DeKalb, is the second-largest university in the state but began as a normal (i.e., educational) school in 1857. Joyce was at the school during a very interesting moment. Like many colleges and universities at the end of the 1960s, Northern Illinois was the site of influential social experiments and changes, particularly the antiwar movement and a protracted effort to create African American Studies on campus and to increase the numbers of black students and faculty. Demonstrations, marches, sit-ins, heated speeches, and editorials were part of the order of the day. The Kent State student killings by the National Guard on May 4, 1970, and the murder of two students at Jackson State ten days later, proved to be especially provocative, leading to marches, unrest, arrests, class closures, and destruction of university property.[65] One wonders what Joyce Karlin, who was only 18 at the time and a junior, felt about all that was happening around her. A year later, she graduated and was on her way to Loyola University Law School in Chicago.[66]

Joyce's actual work in the legal profession began, like most lawyers, while she was a student, and she worked for the Chicago Public Defender's office and the US Attorney's office. When she graduated Loyola in 1974, Joyce Karlin started her career working in law firms in Chicago and then Los Angeles. She quickly passed the Illinois state exam and was admitted to the state bar in 1975. The next year, she passed the California state exam, perhaps the most rigorous in the nation, and was admitted to the California bar.[67]

Jewish Women, Education, and Professionalization

Joyce Karlin's childhood dream to become a legal professional was not one that was new to Jewish women in this country, especially not to those of her generation. Large numbers of Jewish American women became part of the professionalization of the nation's female workforce in the decades after the 1950s, forming substantial cohorts among physicians and lawyers, as well as in higher education, art, and entertainment.[68] These women's success in the job market was related directly to educational attainment as an ethnic/cultural mandate within their families and communities that allowed them to take advantage of dramatic increases in access to higher education for females.

The educational history of Jewish women in the United States is one that underscores both their access to and acquisition of higher education in numbers well beyond other women of various races and ethnicities. While Jewish women did not have the same or as many educational opportunities as Jewish men, they benefited from a number of variables that supported lofty educational aspirations. These variables included, but were not limited to, a high cultural value placed on educational attainment that did not exclude secular educational realization for females; the settlement of large waves of Jewish immigrants, from 1881 to 1924 for example, in places where public secondary schools provided particularly rich educational opportunities; and their general belief, as immigrants or the children of immigrants, that education was key to socioeconomic advancement in the United States.

Significant numbers of Jewish immigrants, for example, came to settle in New York City at the turn of the twentieth century. There, many females, as well as males, were able to take advantage of the expanding educational opportunities that included the creation of the city college system. In 1910, for instance, 40% of female night school students were Jewish. Fifteen years later, one-fourth of Hunter College graduates were Eastern European derived Jewish women. By 1934, more than half the women in college in New York City were Jewish.[69]

This trend of Jewish women's exceptional educational attainment established them as the leading cohort of American women seeking higher education; a trend that continued through the century. One study from the mid-twentieth century, for example, indicates that, at one high school, more than 50% of Jewish women attended college, when only 34% of other white women did at the same time. By 1990, the cohort had grown to 85% of Jewish American women with college degrees, and 30% had gone on to graduate or professional schools.[70] Six percent of Jewish women, like Joyce Karlin, had law degrees, representing 27% of the law degrees held by Jewish Americans. European American women who were not Jewish held only 13% of the law degrees in their racial group.[71]

Most women of color, as noted in earlier chapters, had different educational histories. African American women were much less able to take advantage of educational opportunities available to the white and urbanized population that Jewish females availed. This is not to say that acquiring undergraduate or graduate and professional degrees for Jewish women was easy. Many worked full time and took care of family responsibilities while seeking their degrees as part time students. For some, it was a stop-and-go experience. Not everyone could count on his or her family's support, even moral support. In the end, however, they found a way. Black women also had the will, but the way was filled with even greater obstacles. While the numbers who held college or advanced degrees steadily grew, the pace was anything but fast. Only 8.3% of African American females over 25 years old, for example, had attained college or higher degrees by 1970; only 4.6% had done so the previous decade. The numbers of black women able to reach this educational milestone grew at a slightly quicker rate after the Civil Rights era. By 1980, fairly equal numbers of black women and men had at least acquired a BA degree. While black women eventually moved ahead of the men in their cohort, a significant difference between them and other women (Jewish and European American) existed. Black women's educational strides were more similar to those of Hispanic women. By 1990, less than 12% of black women held a BA degree, compared with nearly 19% of their white counterparts.[72]

Educational opportunities for Asian immigrant and Asian American women also were limited. Like African Americans, many had to attend poorly funded, segregated lower schools. Racism, sexism (internal and external), and economic hardship hampered educational accomplishment. So too did migration patterns. Just as the vast numbers of Jewish immigrants settling in the northeast, particularly New York City, benefited mightily from the availability of public secondary schools and colleges, Asian migrants settling largely in California could not benefit from a similar movement. Local and state officials, like the mayor of San Francisco, branded Asian immigrants as "unassimilable." Attempts to enroll children in school met with popular outcries, voiced in the local newspapers as part of the "yellow peril." In 1906, for example, the city of San Francisco passed a resolution to establish segregated schools for Japanese children. After a long anti-segregation campaign mounted by Japanese Americans, city and school officials agreed to allow Japanese and Japanese American children to attend the same schools as white children. Exclusionary laws, however, kept the numbers of Asian and Asian American children living in the nation extremely low.[73]

While waves of Jewish immigrants from the colonial period forward had proven that, indeed, they were assimilable, the large numbers of Eastern European and Russian Jews who arrived at the end of the nineteenth century and first few decades of the twentieth elicited a similar response to that which Asian immigrants had received. Jewish women and men, despite their substantial academic achievements, still faced educational discrimination, particularly in post-secondary elite institutions of learning that complained that they did not want to become "too Jewish."[74] This particular dislike of Jewish students who hailed from Russian and East European immigrant homes was based on a popular racialized stereotype of the Jewish political radical—supporters of anarchy, communism, and socialism. Moreover, the obvious cultural difference of these new immigrants and their lack of wealth also pushed this discriminatory response.[75] These prejudices were reflected in immigration polices and supported the "scientific racism" of the day.[76] Immigrants and their children, especially, felt the brunt, but the impact was much more widespread. A developing scientific racism painted all Jews, as a distinct, inferior "race."[77]

During the 1920s, 1930s, and 1940s, many, if not most, colleges and universities restricted the number of Jewish students they admitted. In 1918, for example, the Association of New England Deans met to consider their common "Jewish problem."[78] Ivy League institutions established Jewish quotas, despite the academic credentials of those excluded. Harvard only allowed an incoming class to be 10% to 12% Jewish; Yale, 10%; Columbia, 20%; and Princeton, 3%. Other distinguished universities along the eastern seaboard, as well as state institutions in the South, Midwest, and West, acted accordingly.[79] Both Jewish men and women faced this discrimination. Rutgers University insisted on a cap on Jewish students so that it would not become "denominational." The New Jersey College for women followed suit. In 1930, it accepted 61% of all its applicants, except Jews. It only accepted 31% of Jewish women who applied.[80] At Barnard, the first college that admitted females in New York City, Virginia Gildersleeves, an alumnus who went on to become its longtime dean, was clear in her denunciation of Jewish girls of Eastern European immigrant origin. "Many of our Jewish students have been charming and cultivated beings," she began. "On the other hand . . . the intense ambition of the Jews for education has brought to college girls from a lower social level than most of the non-Jewish students." The Seven Sister colleges typically limited Jewish enrollment to between 6 and 12%.[81]

Professional school administrations were just as prejudiced. Admissions boards at medical, business, and law schools used surnames or face-to-face interviews to indentify Jewish applicants. Yale Medical School marked applications with an "H" for Hebrew. At Cornell in 1940, the dean of their medical school admitted that the Jewish student quota had to mirror the percentage of Jewish state residents. At Columbia's College of Physicians and Surgeons, a quota on Jewish students resulted in a 41% decline in Jewish enrollment in the years between 1920 and 1940.[82] Law schools were slightly less discriminatory, at least at first. During the early 1930s, for example, Jews were 25% of the nation's law students (more than 50% of New York's law students). Later that same decade, however, the percentages of Jewish law students began to decline precipitously.[83]

The Civil Rights movement changed this phenomenon for Jewish Americans, just as it did for Asian Americans and African Americans. The movement eventually eliminated not only segregated public schools, but also discriminatory practices in universities and professional school admissions.

Jewish American women not only created or found opportunities to acquire higher education, but their history as paid laborers, particularly in urban settings, paved the way for them to use their new educational credentials. Many early twentieth-century female immigrants worked because of financial necessity. Working-poor Jewish women, like those in the first generation of Joyce Karlin's immigrant ancestors, performed all kinds of industrial labor, particularly in the garment trades. Their labor in US cities had pre-immigration precedence—European Jewish women had worked sometimes to allow their husbands the financial freedom to pursue Talmudic studies. Still, Jewish wives, in distinction from single Jewish women, rarely worked outside of the home. Susan Glenn, in her groundbreaking study *Daughters of the Shtetl: Life and Labor in the Immigrant Generation*, underscored the comparatively small number of married immigrant Jewish wives who worked outside their homes. Utilizing data collected by the United States Immigration Commission in 1907–1908, Glenn concluded: "Jewish immigrant wives had a lower rate of labor force participation than all other groups, immigrant or nonimmigrant."[84] Indeed, the commission indicated that while only 8% of married Russian Jewish wives worked, 68% of black married women in their sample worked.[85]

Early- and mid-twentieth-century middle-class Jewish women, however, did work in their homes and in family-centered businesses, not unlike the work that Soon Ja Du would do in her stores decades later. Soon Ja Du also worked as a seamstress when she arrived in Los Angeles, as did earlier generations of urbanized Jewish immigrant women who worked in the needle trades. These were feminized sites of labor that routinely excluded black women. Historian Pamela Nadell notes that middle-class Jewish American female labor, however, often was "masked" as just "helping out," rather than identified as having full-fledged labor market participation. A growing national trend found many middle- and upper-class Jewish women entering the work world during the third-quarter of the twentieth century. The numbers continued to grow so that by 1990, 75% of Jewish women aged 25–44 and 66% aged 45–64 were working. The majority were teachers, clerical workers and secretaries, sales clerks, managers, and administrators. Smaller numbers were employed as bookkeepers, social workers, registered nurses, real estate agents, accountants, and other professionals.[86]

Higher educational attainment also meant higher status within the job market.[87] Jewish women still clearly were relegated to a small arena of job titles compared with men, but more than 30% of these women worked as professionals in 1990, substantially more than the 17% of other white female groups who worked as professionals. That same year, only 7% of Jewish women in the United States held blue-collar jobs, while 28% of other European American working women did.[88]

Joyce Karlin graduated law school at a time when females were just beginning to make an impact on the legal profession. During that decade alone, the number of female attorneys in the United States increased by more than five times, and for the first time in American history, they numbered more than 15,000. By the end of the decade, women were more than 14% of all lawyers. A mere 20 years before, they were only 3.4% of the group.[89] It was a time marked by, as one expert noted, "perhaps the single most radical formation in the modern legal profession—the massive influx of women."[90] Indeed, while the number of female attorneys admitted to the bar continued to increase during the 1970s and into the 1980s by a whopping 300%, the number of males increased by a moderate 44%.[91]

Females leaving law school during the same generation as Joyce Karlin entered all sectors of the profession. Their choices largely were similar to those of men, but there are some discernible differences. Government agencies were the first choice for female attorneys, even though they were less lucrative positions. Men preferred firms. Women often chose to work in federal agencies like the Department of Justice, or in their own independent offices, because these positions tended to have shorter work weeks (40 hours instead of 60) and afforded greater schedule flexibility than firm culture.[92] As a single woman with great professional ambition, Joyce began her career in a large, private firm in Chicago. When she later moved to Los Angeles, Karlin was taking up practice in a region not nearly as well-endowed by the legal profession—only 12.6% of the nation's lawyers worked along the Pacific Coast, as opposed to 22% in the Midwest.[93]

Female attorneys in Joyce's era realized a number of wonderful opportunities on the one hand, and a number of painful obstacles on the other. Their entrance in such spectacular numbers during the 1970s signaled the beginning of the end of male dominance in the legal profession, but the domination did not end quietly or happily. The sexism that historically had limited the admission of women into this bastion of male professional work did not disappear or dissipate quickly. Many found themselves in the untenable position of being the only woman, even in large firms; the "token" female, with all that implied with regard to their worth and their acceptance. Substantial numbers complained about sexual harassment, being given unattractive or less lucrative work assignments deemed in the "women's sphere," and being assigned work more appropriate for a legal secretary rather than an attorney. Male-dominated, exclusionary social networks, nasty office politics, and a lack of on-site, female role models added to the uncomfortable professional environment. Many felt isolated and ignored and believed that they had little chance of becoming partners. While certainly some advances had been made since women like Anne Schlezinger, one of the nation's first female Jewish judges who, began working as a lawyer in the 1940s and served as a judge for the National Labor Relations Board in the 1960s and 1970s, no one could argue that this first, large generation of female lawyers faced a level playing field. In 1980, for example, 98.4% of the partners in firms with both associates and partners were male. Even a decade later, male attorneys had almost 50% more advantage in becoming a partner than females.[94] If office politics were unsatisfactory, they were just a preview of work in the courtroom. There, it was not unusual for opposing counsel to try to minimize the professional demeanor of female attorneys by referring to them as "girls," commenting on their clothes and makeup, and asking them about their personal lives, in the presence of judges, other attorneys, juries, and clients.[95]

Karlin's first job was as a junior associate at the Chicago firm of Schippers, Betar, Lamandelle, O'Brien that specialized in labor and trust law, but also had a criminal defense division of which Karlin was a part. She stayed with the firm for two years (1973–1975), before moving to Los Angeles. David Schippers was keen on hiring Loyola graduates like Joyce—he had been both an undergraduate and law student there. His career as a successful attorney and as a politician must have inspired admiration among his younger colleagues. Schippers had worked in the Justice Department: first serving as a member and later chief of the Organized Crime and Racketeering Section of the US Department of Justice in Chicago. He also had served as an assistant US attorney. Long after Karlin had moved to Los Angeles, Schippers went on to gain national prominence in his role as chief counsel to the US House of Representatives's managers for the impeachment trial of President Clinton. Karlin left Schippers's law firm soon after she passed the Illinois bar, but followed in his footsteps. She worked in a criminal defense law firm in Los Angeles (Bruton, Marks) only one year (1976), before she became an assistant U. S. attorney in that city—a position that she held for 14 years. Like her former boss, Joyce became politically active.[96]

Joyce Karlin moved to Los Angeles in the mid-1970s and began to put down roots. Her father was already there—living in Beverly Hills, working as a high-ranking executive at Warner Bros. Studios. Karlin joined the US Attorney's office in 1977, where her specialty was in the Corruption/Violent Crimes Division. It was an opportunity, Karlin recalled, "to guarantee defendants a fair trial and a fair sentence." She also "enjoyed representing victims of crimes." She was a workaholic for years, and her dedication and long hours clearly reaped great benefits for her career. The work, however, might have harmed her personal life.

Joyce married Joel M. Babst at the Stephen S. Wise Temple on May 1, 1977. Like Joyce, Joel was Jewish, well educated, and a professional. After graduating from Rutgers, he earned a master's degree in Public Administration from Syracuse University. At the time of their marriage, Babst was the administrative director of Hemodialysis Services of Beverly Hills.[97]

The marriage did not last. Seven years later, Joyce and Joel divorced.[98] Five months after the divorce was finalized, Joel remarried.[99] A year later, so did Joyce.

Special attention to the needs of children has been a continual theme in her career. Joyce Karlin first made a name for herself, for example, as deputy chief of the Major Narcotics Violators Unit, prosecuting defendants charged with child pornography, crimes against children, and police corruption.[100] Karlin helped establish and coordinate the multiagency Southern California Child Exploitation Task Force. She also was a member of the Interagency Council on Child Abuse and Neglect for several years, chairing its Legal Issues Committee, which assesses legislation that might impact children. Karlin served as well on the Board of Directors for the Crippled Children's Society.[101]

While much of her work in the US Attorney's office centered on the protection of children, Joyce Karlin certainly made other significant contributions to her unit. When Karlin became chief of the Major Crimes Unit and Senior Litigation Counsel, for example, she supervised all the work on arson, sex crimes, narcotics conspiracies, and frauds that came through the office. To have held this position at the same time that crack cocaine and methamphetamine were being centrally manufactured in and distributed from Los Angeles in record amounts must have been extremely challenging. Of course, it was the crack cocaine epidemic of the 1980s, during Karlin's tenure as chief of the Majors Crime Unit, that ravaged South Central, reaching into the home of Latasha Harlins, for one, with devastating consequences. It also was the money from the sale of crack and meth, both businesses monopolized by black gangs in Los Angeles, that provided the high-powered weapons on the street that thugs and crack addicts alike used to terrorize both the black populace and local business owners, like the Du family.[102]

Joyce Karlin received special media and professional attention for her contribution to the conviction of federal DEA agent Darnell Garcia and for the convictions of defendants charged with the kidnapping, torture, and killing of DEA agent Enrique Camarena.[103] The execution-style murder of Camarena had sent shivers through the Justice Department because it reeked of insider corruption. The convictions and the lengthy sentences that Karlin's team produced were very important to the

Justice Department's war on drugs, serving notice to "dirty" agents that they would be exposed, tried, and sentenced. Karlin also helped prosecute members of the Aryan Brotherhood, securing convictions for murders they committed in Lompoc prison.[104] These were quite significant accomplishments for the petite, curly top, rich girl with Hollywood connections.

During her lengthy stint as a federal prosecutor, therefore, Joyce Karlin built a reputation as a consummate professional, but also one who was tough and did not necessarily play it safe. "She's independent," Robert Corbin—a criminal attorney and civil litigator who had, earlier in his career, served as deputy federal public defender and staff counsel for the Christopher Commission—noted. "She's taken tough cases." Former employer David Schippers added that Karlin was not just some "spoiled rich kid," relying on her wealth or social prestige to make it in a competitive world of top-ranked legal professionals. "She waited tables to pay her way through law school."[105]

Joyce Karlin left the US Attorney's office in 1991, after Governor Wilson appointed her as a judge to replace retiring jurist Richard A. Lavine. Superior Court judges in Los Angeles serve a term of six years and can either be selected by the governor to replace a retiring, sitting judge or be elected by popular vote. The only stated qualification for the appointee is that he or she must have had a minimum of ten years of work as a lawyer in the state or service as a judge.[106] A governor's appointee for judgeship is vetted by the Commission on Judicial Nominees Evaluation, made up of lawyers and private citizens of various backgrounds. Judge Lavine, whom she was to replace, had served as supervising judge of the Family Law Department in downtown Los Angeles and, like Karlin, had worked in private practice and the US Attorney's office before being appointed judge by then Governor Jerry Brown in 1980.[107]

Karlin too had asked to be placed in the family court, a good fit she thought, given her proven interests in legal rights advocacy for children. Her initial assignment, however, was in the county criminal courts division, probably because most of her legal work had been centered on criminal cases, rather than family law issues, and because of the large backlog of such cases in Los Angeles. Karlin's appointment was for two years, the time that remained of retiring Judge Lavine's tenure. Any additional time she would have as a Superior Court judge would have to be through popular election.

A Woman's Court

Appointment to the court was, of course, another feather in Joyce's professional cap—a big one. Women made up merely 18% of Superior Court judges in Los Angeles at the time; a position only possible for them to hold since the 1930s.[108] Even 20 years later, female judges were a "rare exception."[109] Georgia Phillips Bullock was the first female Superior Court judge in Los Angeles—as well as in California—appointed 60 years earlier than Judge Karlin by then Governor James Rudolph Jr. Bullock served until 1955, retiring at the age of 76.[110] Despite the decades between their appointments, both by Republican governors, similar themes echoed in the professional careers of Bullock and Karlin, particularly with regard to Karlin's role in *People v. Du.*

The overwhelming presence of women—the defendant, the prosecutor, the victim, the court secretary, and, of course, the judge—that was characteristic of the courtroom scene in the murder trial of Soon Ja Du made it oddly reminiscent of Judge Georgia Bullock's courtroom. Indeed, one can imagine that they were removed decades backward in time to when women's courts handled much of the legal problems of Los Angeles's females. Before being appointed to the Superior Court, Georgia Bullock was the first female "judge" in California's sex-segregated "women's courts."

In 1914, three years after women received the right to vote in California, Judge Thomas P. White (a Los Angeles police judge, a.k.a. metropolitan court judge) feared that his elected position might be threatened if recently enfranchised female voters found reason to disapprove of the manner in which he handled misdemeanor cases involving women. In an attempt to win their support, White advocated for female judges to hear the cases of women and juveniles. His idea was not a novel one, nor was it one that evolved among male jurists. Chicago had adopted a similar process in 1912. Male jurists in that city had felt forced into doing so by female political activists, organized through women's clubs and professional organizations. They wanted a woman—a "city mother," if you will—to hear and decide the cases of "wayward" women and juveniles, not a male jurist whom they believed had little sympathy for, or understanding of, the special needs of errant women, girls, and male adolescents. Drawing on popular notions of women's distinct gender attributes—particularly their compassion, high moral aptitude, and distinct maternal instincts—Judge White successfully introduced a bill into the California legislature that created the state's first women's court. White would be present in the court, as presiding judge, but assisted by a female judge—Georgia Bullock—along with a female probation officer, a female policewoman, and a female clerk when such cases were heard.[111]

As this special court for females and juveniles evolved, other women became involved. Judges White and Bullock were assisted in their decisions by two committees of women created out of the membership of 20 local women's clubs. One committee would help the jurists decide what punishment should be levied on guilty parties; the other served as a support network for convicted women once their sentences had been completed. Interestingly, a "colored" representative from an African American female club addressed the "interests of African American offenders," and a "nationality representative" did so for those who were immigrants.[112] All the women involved, including Judge Bullock, were considered volunteers. None were paid for their services, not even Bullock, who was a graduate of USC law school and worked otherwise as a paid attorney in Los Angeles.[113]

Georgia Bullock took quite seriously her role as "mother" to the women and juveniles who came into her court. Although educated with men at law school, she too believed that she had a unique role, as a female jurist, to put on the right track the lives of the children and women who appeared in her courtroom. She hoped to do so by being an example of appropriate moral female decorum and behavior and by protecting these women and youth from the potential of further male abuse and exploitation. Bullock intended to "protect" and "discipline" the women in her court "in conformity to cultural gender role norms" of her day. The State of California had given her, as it had to Joyce Karlin so many decades later, the public authority to "judge," "punish," and "rehabilitate" women. Both were to do so within the conservative, gendered, cultural norms created by their society and so deeply embedded in the legal culture that they inherited.[114]

Much had changed, obviously, since the era of Bullock's first work as a judge in a women's court to the time that Karlin received her appointment to the Superior Court. Georgia Bullock's legal career even progressed tremendously over the decades of the twentieth century. She went from her women's court appointment to a paid position in the metropolitan court, to eventually becoming an elected Superior Court judge with a 24-year tenure—18 years as the county's only female Superior Court judge. In order to gain the support of male voters, Georgia altered her campaign strategies from one in which she depicted herself as a woman with special moral abilities to guide and rehabilitate females to the image of a capable, experienced jurist who could efficiently and effectively try cases of all types. In other words, she convinced her electorate that "she could do a male judge's job."[115] Still, Judge Georgia Bullock never was able to move outside of the "female sphere" that had become the tradition of female jurists within the Los Angeles and national court system—the cases that came before her court were about children, adoption, or other "domestic relations."[116]

Karlin's role in the *People v. Du* is reminiscent of Bullock's position because she, like Bullock, had been part of a hierarchy of women within the justice system—the top rung of the hierarchy. It was a role, however, that a powerful male—Governor Pete Wilson—had determined. And it was Joyce Karlin, like Georgia Bullock, who seemed to bring to bear on her judgment in this case her sense of women's particular role in society.

Even given her years of very hard work as a top federal prosecutor, her professionalism, her obvious intellectual ability, and her proven capacity as an administrator in some of the most challenging units of the US Attorney's office, Joyce Karlin was young—only 40 when appointed as Superior Court judge. She also was largely unknown by the defense attorneys, prosecutors, judges, police officers, and other personnel who worked in and around the local courthouses. Karlin's work in the US Attorney's office had kept her at a distance from this realm of legal work; a typical scenario for new judges who came from other arenas of the profession. Her role as a judge clearly was quite unlike the experiences she had as a federal prosecutor or a criminal defense attorney. The general sexual bias that affected females in the legal profession, however, was little different for those with the elevated rank of jurist. Indeed, given their heightened status, the bias might have even been greater.

Female judges faced scrutiny and doubt that male judges did not. Evidence of gender bias during the era that Joyce Karlin began her tenure on the bench emerges from a number of sources. The Colorado Supreme Court, for example, requested a Task Force Report in 1990 that investigated such allegations. The results were telling. Female judges faced "hostility and lack of respect" from the attorneys in their courtrooms and from male judges. Counsel would "argue with women judges more often, scrutinize them more closely and criticize them more frequently." Another analysis, emerging from 1992, confirmed these results. When assessing the performance ratings of judges, the experts found that female judges were ranked "significantly lower than male judges . . . on every attribute measured." Male attorneys were particularly harsh, although female attorneys also ranked them lower than male judges. Attorneys routinely rated female judges lowest on their sentences and rulings on motions. Female attorneys also seemed to be exceptionally critical of the demeanor of women judges—complaining that female jurists seemed to lack "compassion" and "courtesy" in their courts.[117] These characterizations, no doubt, affected Karlin as they did her peers. Perhaps they even affected her "demeanor" in the *People v. Du* trial.

No matter what difficulties Joyce Karlin might have anticipated when offered the judgeship, it clearly was a position that she wanted. After all, she had to submit to the rigorous review all potential judges withstand before gaining the position. The judgeship was a clear signal that she had political clout because the road to gaining a Superior Court appointment meant, in part, that she had the blessing of the state and local bar associations as well as the movers and shakers of the governor's political party—in Joyce's case, the Republican Party. She received her official appointment on July 25, 1991.

Marriage (Again)

At the same time that she was building a successful legal career in Los Angeles, Joyce Karlin also was starting her own family. In 1985, she married another young assistant US attorney, William Fahey. Her spouse was born in Chicago (November 8, 1951) and educated in Los Angeles, earning his undergraduate degree at USC, where he graduated magna cum laude, and then gaining a law degree from UCLA. Bill Fahey was an up-and-coming legal professional on a similar fast track as his future wife. Fahey credits John and Robert Kennedy as the role models who motivated him to become an attorney. "They were my inspiration: young, idealistic and committed to public service. I think a lot of people in my generation were caught up in the Kennedy mystique."[118]

After graduating with honors from law school, Bill clerked for the Honorable US District Court Judge Laughlin Waters. "That's a great way for a young lawyer to start out," he recalled. "I got an opportunity to see some of the best judges and lawyers our system has to offer. Watching Judge Laughlin Waters in action probably inspired me to want to be a judge someday."[119] He then entered the law firm of Sullivan, Jones, and Archer in San Diego. In 1980, Fahey became a US Attorney in the Central District of California, in the same Los Angeles office where Joyce already had worked for four years.

There, Fahey first worked as a trial deputy, but eventually became head of the Government Fraud and Public Corruption Section, then first assistant chief of the Criminal Division. He was quite successful, winning particular acclaim for garnering a conviction against the aerospace giant Northrop.[120] The Department of Justice twice publicly recognized Bill Fahey's excellence and leadership, awarding him the Directors Award in 1987 and the John Marshall Award in 1991.[121]

Bill Fahey and Joyce Karlin clearly had a lot in common. Besides their quite remarkably similar career paths, they were both born in 1951 and both had spent much of their youth in Chicago, although Bill was raised Catholic and Joyce, Jewish. They worked together in the Justice Department where Bill remained for one year after his wife's departure to become a judge.[122] Both he and Joyce were active in the local and state Republican Party. Joyce was distinct in her political affiliation, given that large swathes of local Jewish communities were Democrats. In 1992, Fahey left the Justice Department to run for Congress from the 36th District, but lost in the primary. That same year, he chaired the failed Bush-Qualye presidential campaign in Los Angeles County.[123] "That ended my career in politics," he admitted. "I got into it for the best of reasons—to discuss issues and find solutions to problems. But the fundraising, the never-ending quest for money, really wore me down. Frankly,

I hated it."[124] William Fahey then joined, as a partner, the law firm of Smaltz, Anderson, and Fahey in 1993. The two other senior partners of this law firm, Donald Smaltz and Lois Anderson-Smaltz, were married and professional, as well as social, associates of Fahey and Karlin.[125]

While working at Anderson, Smaltz, and Fahey, Bill assisted the firm's senior partner, Donald Smaltz, when he was independent counsel in the prosecution of Agriculture Secretary Mike Espy. It was a position that won Fahey few friends. "Bill was on the firing line, like we all were," remembered Smaltz. Fahey eventually did convict Espy's chief of staff, Ronald H. Blackley, for covering up a $22,000 contribution from agribusiness firms. In 1998, Fahey, who had been spending large amounts of time in Washington on this case, returned to Los Angeles to join, as a partner, the Los Angeles firm of Hanna and Morton. "I wanted to try the [Espy]case," he noted, "but I knew a slot on the bench would open up while the trial was in progress. I couldn't afford to take that risk."[126] On September 1 of that year, Governor Pete Wilson appointed him as a Los Angeles County Superior Court judge. In the end, the independent counsel was not successful in convicting Espy, who was found not guilty on all counts. Fahey insisted that they had a "good case," but that the jury "was not in a mood to accept the prosecution evidence," because of the public's response to the independent counsel's performance in other Clinton administration investigations.[127]

Judge Karlin was, understandably, proud of her husband's placement on the bench. She was, he recalled, "extremely supportive. She said to go for it: I would derive a great deal of personal and professional satisfaction from serving on the bench," and she was right.[128]

William Fahey's tenure as a judge has not been marked by a single notorious case, as has his wife's career, although he has had his share of celebrity (this is Los Angeles!) cases before his court. Generally, many regard him as an intelligent, tough judge, formal in his demeanor, rather pro-prosecution and somewhat antagonistic to defense attorneys. Reviews by lawyers have run the gamut from positive to negative. Some have applauded his work. "Judge Fahey is very thorough, very deliberate," deputy district attorney Richard J. Healey noted. "He agonizes a great deal over cases because he wants to achieve the right result."[129] Deputy public defender Geoffrey D. Crowther had similar comments: "He's extremely patient, especially with defendants. He has the ability to calm down hostile defendants and convince them they'll get a fair deal in his courtroom." Frank Rorie, a well known defense attorney, labeled Fahey as a "top-notch" judge who is "attentive, even-handed and a stickler for detail."[130] Some lawyers were particularly struck by his preparation for trials, his breadth of legal knowledge, and his overall rigorous standards. Others have been less complimentary. While one local prosecutor concluded that Fahey had a "very formal demeanor," he generally believed him "as efficient as any judge I've seen." That same prosecutor, however, thought that Judge Fahey "has a tendency to consider himself 'God, Jr.,'" believed to be a common problem exhibited by judges who had been US attorneys.[131] A defense attorney added: "He belittles people. I think he belittles mostly defense attorneys, but I've seen him belittle prosecutors as well, although mostly when they argue with him."[132] Prosecutors tended to be less critical, concluding that he was "antagonistic" but "efficient."[133]

The discussion in Fahey's profile that concerned the "attitude" or "culture" of county judges coming from the ranks of federal prosecutors perhaps could shed some light on Joyce Karlin's demeanor in her first jury trial. "It's not unusual that former assistant U.S. attorneys who come over have very high standards about what the prosecution should do and how they should do it," one attorney who had argued in Fahey's court noted. "They're sometimes tougher on the deputy D.A.'s than a former D.A."[134] Karlin may have brought such standards to bear on the case that Roxanne Carvajal presented.

Joyce Karlin and William Fahey were a formidable pair, a power couple by any definition. They both were poised to do great things in Los Angeles as part of the younger generation of a legal elite. The couple had settled in affluent Manhattan Beach in a large corner-lot home, part of a picturesque community along the Pacific, miles away, literally and figuratively, from the San Fernando Valley home of the Dus and the South Central home of the Harlins.

Like her community outside Chicago, like all the communities she had lived in, in Latin America, Europe, and the United States, Joyce Karlin's Manhattan Beach community was wealthy and white: almost 113,000 whites lived there in 1990, as compared with 1,500 blacks, and 7,000 persons of Asian/Pacific Islander descent (618 of whom identified themselves as Korean). The median price for a home in Manhattan

Beach in 1990 was $501,000—three times the average price of a home in the Dus' community of Mission Hills, and five times those in Latasha's neighborhood.[135] Of course, Latasha's family had never been able to purchase a home in their poor, working-class neighborhood. They lived in an inexpensive rental property on a street known for its high drug-related crime rate, haunting murder rates, and "take no prisoners" arrogant police patrols. Clearly, Joyce Karlin had little opportunity to come into contact with persons of Miss Harlins's class or culture except at her place of work. They simply were not part of her social, cultural, or political worlds. Nor was Soon Ja Du.

Jews, Blacks, and Asian Americans

The Jewish experience with persons of African descent within the United States extends back to the colonial period, where it mimicked that typically attributed to whites and blacks. As Hasia Diner notes, Jews throughout the colonies owned slaves and participated in the slave trade. Moreover, "nothing in their letters, wills and other writings indicat[ed] any ambivalence about the practice; indeed, following this fashion helped them to be more like their neighbors."[136] Unlike Europe, where class, religion, and race were dividing elements, the single most important badge worn in the colonies, and later in the nation, was that of color. The lighter one's color, the more privileges afforded one. As such, blacks found themselves at the bottom of social (and judicial) structures. Jews during the colonial era, on the other hand, benefited from their white skin. Diner adds, for example, that "in America, to be 'white' meant to be free, and not being white meant enduring enslavement." As such, "Jews in the colonies had an asset that served them well: they were white. They no longer bore the burden of being the stigmatized group whom others reviled and oppressed."[137] Historian Cheryl Greenberg agrees, concluding that "(European) Jews in the United States have benefitted from having white skin, even when they rejected a white identity, and that whiteness has informed their politics more than they recognize."[138] Still, Jews were not universally thought of as white. This was particularly so when culture, especially religion and language, carried great social significance. Moreover, diversity within their own ranks later in US history (Hasidic Orthodox, non-Hasidic

Orthodox, Reformed, Conservative, and Reconstructionist) created internal hierarchies that sometimes were externally exploited and even racialized.[139]

Historically, blacks, as well as whites and Asian/Asian-Americans, have related to Jews both as whites and nonwhites, friend and foe. Jews, themselves, struggled with this dual identity in the United States—of being Jewish and white, segregated or assimilated, accepted or rejected, living either in the mainstream or on the margins, or both, concurrently. Of course, their changing relationships with blacks, Asians, and other racialized minorities depended in large measure on their own perceived racial/ethnic identity, both as part of a group and as individuals at a specific time and place.[140] As whites, blacks perceived Jews as oppressive and exploitative, greeting them with animosity and, sometimes, anti-Semitism.[141] This was particularly so when Jews exercised inordinate power vis à vis blacks as landlords and employers. As nonwhites, on the other hand, blacks have recognized the hardships Jews faced in Europe, America, and elsewhere, thus fostering a kind of kinship. They also have much appreciated the willingness of some in Jewish communities to promote human and civil rights across color, class, and regional lines. The history between the two groups, therefore, is a complex one.

During the colonial and antebellum eras, equality *before* the law, or *in* the law, between the two groups was not possible. Jews could be citizens; blacks could not. Jews were free; the vast majority of blacks were enslaved. After the Civil War, Jews again were distinguishable from blacks in law and treatment. Yet, both were targets of discrimination. The release of four million blacks out of slavery in 1865 led, within a few years, to a repressive Jim Crow regime in the South, where most blacks lived. Life was somewhat better, but not substantially, in other parts of the nation. Blacks were not welcome anywhere. Immigrant Jews from Eastern Europe and Russia also faced a harsh backlash because of their religious and cultural differences. As the nineteenth century ended, white Americans embraced a racial and cultural chauvinism that placed anyone who was not European American and Protestant on the margins of respectable society.

This marginality, of course, also included those from Asia. Historian Najia Aarim-Heriot is right, therefore, when she links Asian immigrants (and by extension Jewish immigrants) with blacks, asserting that, in the

United States, there was a "dual doctrine of nationalism for foreign immigration and states' rights for Negro mobility"—the presence of black and "foreign" bodies had to be, and was, carefully controlled.[142] In contemporary society, most scholars link the experiences of Jewish Americans and Asian Americans through their eventual designation as model minorities. As legal scholar and social commentator Frank Wu notes, "To the extent that Asian Americans are compared with anyone else at all, it is with American Jews of an earlier era. Asian immigrants are sometimes called the New Jews."[143]

Yet, during the late nineteenth and early twentieth centuries, Jews and Asians living in the United States were considered anything but model. Historian Gary Okihiro is correct when he asserts: "The Asian work ethic, family values, self-help, culture and religiosity, and intermarriage—all elements of the model minority—can also be read as components of the yellow peril."[144] Both groups, like blacks, were considered racially and culturally inferior. All three were exoticized, criminalized, sexualized, and racialized. All were considered to be the purveyors of filth and disease. Women from each group were depicted as promiscuous sex workers; men—their pimps. They were all, as far as mainstream white America was concerned, an affront to decent, hardworking, Christian, white Americans. None deserved to be treated as citizens or to reap the benefits of that citizenship. Russian Jewish immigrants, in particular, also were demonized as political anarchists. Asian (Chinese, and later the Japanese, for example) continued to be tainted with a perception of "foreignness" that signified "peril" of all types and disloyalty as well.[145] Asian and Jewish threats to American democracy, therefore, were deemed as considerable as the threat of "intellectually inferior" blacks allowed to participate in electoral politics. Political cartoons from the era vividly display the vehement hostility members of each group faced and how the white imagination linked all three as enemies of American progress, decency, and democracy. (See, for example, figure 5.3.)

The San Francisco *Wasp*, a magazine founded by three brothers from Bohemia in the mid-1870s, for example, was known for cartoons that depicted the yellow peril, often in full color. The magazine also printed cartoons, such as "Uncle Sam's Troublesome Bedfellows," that spoke broadly to fears of the racial "other." The "troublesome bedfellows" include the Chinese, Native Americans, Russian immigrants (who primarily were Jewish), and blacks—all threats to the "American" way of life.[146]

The *Wasp* was hardly the only popular periodical that captured fears of the racial other. Frank Beard, one of the most popular political cartoonists of the late nineteenth century, published a cartoon in the *Judge*, for example, that was aptly titled "Columbia's Unwanted Guests." Included among Beard's "unwelcome" were blacks, Jews, Asians, and others. Another cartoon of Beard's published in 1896 and titled "The Stranger at Our Gate," specifically depicts a Jewish immigrant, but deliberately colors the stranger, so that he does not appear racially white, but some darker race. It connects this Jewish immigrant, shown as loaded with baggage and clothing marked "anarchy," "Sabbath desecration," "poverty," "superstition," "intoxication" and "disease" with blacks and Asians through darkened skin color.[147]

Jewish immigrants were not only darkened in some political cartoons, but many during that era also considered them not to be white. In Europe, and in certain "scientific" circles, the color of Jews had been regarded as other than white for some time. Sander Gilman notes in *The Jew's Body*, for example: "The general consensus of the ethnological literature of the late nineteenth century was that the Jews were 'black,' or at least 'swarthy.'"[148] Gilman added that "for the eighteenth and nineteenth century scientist the 'blackness' of the Jew was not only a mark of racial inferiority, but also an indicator of the diseased nature of the Jew."[149] Gilman went on to explain that Jews were considered "black" by nineteenth century "racial scientists" since they were not deemed a "pure" race, "because they are a race which has come from Africa."[150] Others went so far to state that blacks and Jews looked alike—with "lips very full," prominent noses, eyes close together, and so forth.[151] Scientific racism of the era designated Jews, particularly those from Eastern Europe, as not only inferior to "whites" but also connected, perhaps biologically, to blacks through previous incidences of intermarriage.[152] "The Jews were quite literally seen as black."[153]

If some viewed Jews as black; others perceived them as Asian, or at least "Oriental." The image of the "Oriental Jew" from the "East" of the Middle East also was used to marginalize and exclude Jewish immigrants.

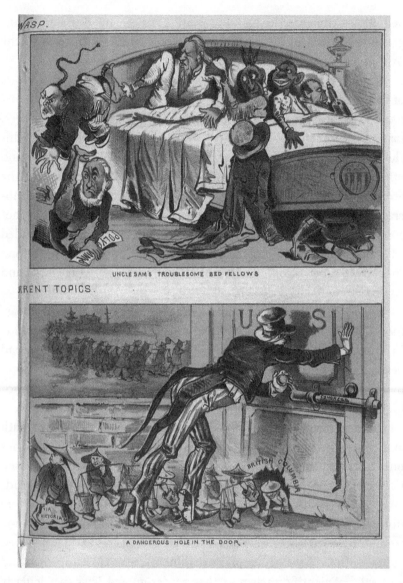

FIGURE 5.3 "Uncle Sam's Troublesome Bedfellows," and "A Dangerous Hole in the Door," *The Wasp*, February 8, 1879. Courtesy of Bancroft Library, University of California, Berkeley.

Jews were called, Peter Langman notes, "Asiatic and Mongoloid," and "'primitive, tribal, Oriental'" in the United States. "Thus," he asserts, "the idea that Jews are White is relatively new."[154]

What did these popular, and discriminatory, ideas that connected blacks, Jews, and Asians in America so profoundly as the racial "other"

FIGURE 5.4 Frank Beard, "Columbia's Unwelcome Guests," February 7, 1885. Courtesy of the Granger Collection.

mean for those who were female? Women, of course, shared in these negative stereotypes of biological, intellectual, and moral inferiority along with the notion that the "other" could not assimilate. Women were regarded equally dangerous as their men, because just as the men could seduce white women, women of color could lure white men into sexual relationships with them. The most significant image imposed on these women, after all, was the one of promiscuity. If allowed to have social access, therefore, these women would entice white men into sexual intercourse that would not only threaten the health of these men with venereal disease, but also produce inferior, "impure" children. Laws regarding miscegenation at the turn of the century codified this fear of whiteness lost. European and European American dread of sexual contact with the racial female "other" undergird the fear of racial impurity that would "infect" the white race.[155]

Editorials in newspapers around the country, but especially where Jewish and Asian immigrants were more likely to migrate, such as New York and San Francisco, bemoaned the arrival of these women—the vehicle by which the white race would be lost. Likewise, white society regarded black women, historically and continuously, as sexually aggressive, even insatiable. One of the most potent fears regarding black

THE STRANGER AT OUR GATE.

EMIGRANT.—Can I come in?   UNCLE SAM.—I 'spose you can; there's no law to keep you out.

FIGURE 5.5 Frank Beard, "The Immigrant: Stranger at Our Gate," April 25, 1896. Courtesy of the Billy Ireland Cartoon Library and Museum, Ohio State University.

emancipation, after all, was that the white race would become a "mulatto" one. And nothing was considered more indicative of shared racial flaws of people of color than the spectacle of marriage across racial lines when both races were nonwhite. Consider for example the 1897 cover for the Billy Johnson and Bob Cole song, "The Marriage of the Chinee and the Coon," a song that originally was to be part of the musical, "A Trip to Coontown."[156] In this portrait of this "exotic" coupling, the "strangeness" (read ridiculousness) of black manhood, portrayed in physical stereotype, is equaled with the "strangeness" of Asian (stereo-typed Chinese in this particular depiction) womanhood. Part of the lyrics for the first stanza read, for example: "This strange amalgamation of these two funny nations gwine to cause an awful jumble soon."[157] Indeed, this storyline must have appeared to have been a perfect solution to the worry of miscegenation and the darkening of the white race—let the two inferior races marry one another. The portrayal is even more suggestive when one realizes that it was produced for a song written by two African American musicians, Cole and Johnson. Such minstrel-like depictions of the racial other in popular entertainment and art genres from the nineteenth through the twentieth and into the twenty-first centuries, meant for the pleasure of all audiences despite their racial affiliation, indicate how much a part of American culture these stereotypes were and still are.

Yet, while it is true that Jewish, Asian, and black women were all maligned as inferior, and socially marginal (or invisible), the impact of European American racism did not affect them "equally." Skin color and the ability and desire to culturally assimilate influenced one's access to acceptance. The racial hierarchy of women, therefore, was balanced by one's closeness to whiteness in appearance, language, behavior, education, religion, and wealth. None of these attributes could completely erase color, but it certainly could diminish the impact of it. Jews, who had the whitest skin among these women, could, and did, benefit from their racial invisibility. As the outer accouterments of their distinct cultures also disappeared, access to white privilege increased. Blacks, of course, could not lose their color, no matter how much they culturally assimilated. Nor could Asian/Asian-Americans disappear into the white, middle-class norm of American society. Educational gains and financial success certainly helped members of all these groups. Growing political strength, particularly exercised by Jewish Americans and black Americans, also was influential. Still, one's color, hair texture, and phenotype continue to have great significance. Those who are perceived to be most like whites find it easier to reach the top of the nation's racial hierarchy. Those who are less like whites have traditionally found themselves on the bottom. This hierarchy certainly was operative with regard to blacks and Jews because, as historian Cheryl Greenberg notes, regarding the relationships between the two groups during the early days

FIGURE 5.6 Bob Cole, "The Wedding of the Chinee and the Coon," 1907. Courtesy of the Brown Hay Library, Brown University Library.

of the twentieth century, most were "deeply unequal. Black and Jewish experiences might appear parallel, but in fact most interactions between them were hierarchical."[158]

Still, blacks and Jews found themselves bound by a long history of racial and cultural oppression that prompted cooperation for much of the twentieth century. Each had some investment in the success of the other. It is of great significance, for example, that the seminal civil rights organizations of the twentieth century mostly associated with the acquisition of black rights and protections under the law, the NAACP and the Urban League, began with a strong Jewish presence within their membership and their leadership. Civil rights marches, boycotts, sit-ins, and freedom rides all witnessed black-Jewish collaboration. Blacks in the earlier twentieth century, on the other hand, participated in antiracist socialist organizations, national and international, that had a significant Jewish contingent. Relatedly, black workers benefited from Jewish support of their inclusion in early- to mid-twentieth-century trade unions. They worked together to end social exclusion, residential segregation, denial of higher education, and negative stereotyping that demeaned and dehumanized both. Jewish professionals, such as doctors, dentists, and lawyers, offered blacks medical and legal aid when professional school training for blacks was practically nonexistent, and other white professionals, particularly in the Jim Crow South, refused to do so. During the World War II era, Black newspapers, such as the Chicago *Defender*, hired Jewish journalists and printed numerous stories that helped to expose the Jewish holocaust, linking it to the plight of black Americans at home.[159] Jewish newspapers, like the *Forward*, the *Tageblatt*, and the *Jewish Daily Courier*, countered by publicizing and criticizing antiblack racism and violence.[160]

Black and Jewish women did not sit on the sidelines in this relationship. Indeed, they often were the pioneers who first participated in the cooperative efforts to expand rights for both groups. The National Association of Colored Women and the National Council of Jewish Women (NCJW), for example, were working together as early as the 1920s.[161] Black women in the YWCA reached out to the families of Jewish soldiers during World War I. Jewish women in the NCJW protested early twentieth-century race riots and lynchings. Jewish women in the New York International Ladies' Garment Workers' Union (ILGWU) also encouraged black women in the needle trades to join their union as early as 1929.[162] These activities occurred, as historian Cheryl Greenberg notes, a full decade before male groups caught up with the organized efforts of women's groups.[163]

Cooperation between Jewish women and black women continued, on and off, throughout the twentieth century. The NCJW, for example, lobbied congressional committees to end lynching as early as 1935, as well as opposed restrictive housing covenants and poll tax stipulations for voting during the 1940s.[164] There was perhaps no greater period of joint efforts for the expansion of human rights than during the Civil Rights era. Jewish women, more than any other nonblack racial or ethnic women, traveled to the South to participate in marches, sit-ins, freedom rides, hunger strikes, and voter registration efforts. Life in the South for these women mirrored those of their African American female peers. They were, after all, Jewish, not Christians and, as such, faced extreme cultural hostility from white southerners. Even under the best circumstances, they still faced segregation and exclusion from elite southern social and cultural institutions. Moreover, their gender cast them in a secondary leadership role, by blacks and whites. Once they, as civil rights workers in interracial associations, crossed the racial divide that was so pervasive in the South, they too became the offensive "racial other": "white n—s."[165] They were beaten; sexually harassed; thrown in prison; verbally assaulted; threatened; and vilified in the southern press, where they were depicted as promiscuous, left-ists, troublemaking outsiders who, if harmed, deserved what they got.[166] It was a struggle, as one might imagine, for these antiracist Jew-ish female activists to accomplish what they set out to do. Who were these women who interrupted their educations and risked their lives to help in the cause? Debra Schultz, who has written extensively on the topic, explains:

> They were relatively privileged, well-educated northern students who chose to go south to work in a social justice movement; still they often felt outside the mainstream. They were Jewish women from families and a culture that both encouraged and limited their life choices. They were children of Jews struggling to assimilate into American culture without losing their Jewish connection entirely . . . They were competent and experienced, willing to take action before the Feminist movement made it legitimate to do so. They were secular Jews in a Black Christian movement working in the anti-Semitic and virulently racist South.[167]

Relations between the black and Jewish women in the Civil Rights movement were generally positive and filled with respect and con-cern for each other's well-being. Still tensions arose over leadership, competition for certain work assignments, political consciousness, activist strategies, and what were perceived to be different levels of commitment.[168] Politically, it was difficult for some of the Jewish female volunteers to openly criticize the federal administration that typically had the electoral support of Jews. Most were from liberal Democratic families and were a little reticent to criticize either the Kennedy or Johnson administrations. Most also came from a tradition where violent abuse was met with nonviolence; although, in the face of so much violence in the South, they began to feel differently. "Love thy neighbor," Carol Ruth Silver noted in her diary that she kept while involved in the movement, "does not come easily to me."[169] Were they ready to die for the cause? Although black women extended whatever protective measures they could, some questioned whether these women, who could go back North and pick up their relatively free status without difficulty, were as committed as those whose homes and families were in the South. Joan Trumpanuer explained that, as a black woman, she had "come to Jackson prepared to suffer anything—mobs, beatings, death itself—before turning back."[170]

There always were tensions around competing social and political agendas and questions over who was best able to lead. There also always was a racialized tension. Neither group was exempt from the racist, classist ideology that permeates US society. This tension became especially palpable as blacks found themselves lingering at the bottom of the nation's socioeconomic strata while Jews moved further and further up and away. The reality was, as one historian notes, that "increasing numbers of black migrants moved into Jewish neighborhoods and met Jews as employers, teachers, landlords, and shopkeepers, not as fellow oppressed people. Jewish impresarios and producers hired black musicians, actors, and entertainers; Jewish union leaders represented black workers."[171]

These discrepancies in status and wealth were particularly apparent in the urban communities where both Jewish immigrants (along with their descendants) and black migrants landed in the first half of the twentieth century. While blacks and Jews found the opportunity to cooperate greatly during the Civil Rights era, these ties waned as strategies for acquiring expanded black rights evolved from interracial, nonviolent direct action and legal challenges to the more separatist and confrontational attitudes associated with a growing black political and cultural nationalism. Some blacks no longer regarded Jews as part of the solution, but rather as part of the problem. They believed that Jews had indeed become "white."[172] It was at this moment that an impasse of sorts was reached. Were they incorrect? Legal scholar Beverly Horsburg believes that, in some important ways, they were not. Writing of the relationship between Jewish and black women, she notes: "Assimilation into the dominant culture cannot eradicate racial hatred or discrimination. The minority person who is in the economic position to assimilate and who learns the grammar of the dominant language also internalizes that culture's hierarchy and prejudice."[173] It also meant that those who remained on the outside or on the margins of the "dominant culture" lost a sense of connection to those within it.

There is no better indication of the growing disconnect between blacks and Jews in urban America than in the opposing roles they played in the race riots of the 1960s. Racial unrest in Philadelphia in 1963 and 1964, Los Angeles in 1965, and Newark and Detroit in 1967 all witnessed blacks targeting "white" Jewish businesses and real estate in a similar fashion to the ways in which Korean shops were targeted during the Los Angeles riots of 1992. Indeed, in August 1991, at the same time that blacks and Koreans were having a "mini" race war in South Central related to the *People v. Du*, rioting that resulted in looting and violence erupted between blacks (African American and Afro-Caribbean) and Hasidic Jews in Crown Heights after a car accident ended in the death of the small son of Guyanese immigrants who lived in the neighborhood.[174] Blacks accused Jews of being racist and oppressive; Jews accused blacks of being anti-Semitic and destructive.[175]

After the riots of the 1960s, however, moderates on both sides still were able to craft important interracial cooperative councils in many major cities, including Newark, Philadelphia, New York, and Los Angeles.[176] Jews and blacks also continued to work together to press for black rights and an end to urban blight—including advocacy for better jobs, housing, education, and economic opportunities. As some struggled to keep relations positive and move forward, many Jews who owned real estate and businesses in predominantly black urban communities were ready to throw in the towel. The American Jewish

Congress and the National Community Relations Advisory Committee both reported at the end of the 1960s that 50% of shopkeepers were "very anxious to sell their places of business," and most realized that younger members of their families would not carry on their operations.[177] Many did sell—to blacks, but also to new waves of immigrants, such as Koreans, Latinos, South Asians, and Middle Easterners. Differing views on Israel and Palestine, beginning in the 1960s, also deepened the divide in some quarters between blacks and Jews. Likewise, opposing views on the role of Jewish teachers in predominantly African American classrooms as well as the lingering benefits of affirmative action as a means of access to higher education provided new sources of conflict during the 1970s and beyond.[178]

Still, there were ties that bound even beyond the Civil Rights era. One of the most significant examples of black-Jewish coalition building, of course, was the support that Mayor Tom Bradley secured from large numbers of Jewish Angelenos who lived on the Westside. With their support, and that of most African Americans, Bradley garnered a record five terms as mayor of the city. Still, issues that had undermined other such coalitions eventually struck this one as well. Minister Louis Farrakhan's visit to Los Angeles in 1985, for example, was particularly galling to Bradley's Jewish support network.[179]

The political ties and the civil and human rights work shared by blacks and Jews over the decades of the twentieth century represent, perhaps, the most significant heritage of cross-racial and cross-ethnic cooperation in US history. Such lengthy and complex bonds have not been created between African Americans and Jewish Americans with Asians Americans. The most noteworthy cooperation, perhaps, came in the late 1960s when students and community activists, from many racial or ethnic backgrounds, worked collectively to expand rights for not only blacks, but for other ethnic groups as well. Asian Americans were a part of this movement and were influenced by black nationalist activists, particularly Malcolm X.[180] As Glenn Omatsu notes, "the birth of the Asian American movement coincided . . . with the . . . demand for black liberation." The principal goal of this activism, Omatsu adds, was, like that of black militants, "not one of seeking legitimacy and representation within American society but the larger goal of liberation."[181] The San Francisco State University strike, the longest student campus strike in the nation's history, beginning on November 6, 1968, and ending on March 20, 1969, was especially crucial in developing political-activist ties between blacks and Asian Americans. The two groups worked cooperatively, African Americans via the Black Student Union and Asian Americans via the umbrella organization Third World Liberation Front. The strike culminated with the creation of the first College of Ethnic Studies in the nation, providing scholarly programs not in just African American, but also in Asian American, Native American and Chicano/a studies. It was a model for a revolution of ethnic studies programs that would soon be created at colleges and universities across the nation.[182] The experiment in interracial political and social cooperation and radicalization, however, was less successful in the long term.[183]

Other attempts at cooperation between blacks and Koreans usually came in response to hostilities between the two. In most of the major cities of the United States where Korean immigrants settled and established businesses in predominantly black communities, some attempt was made to form organizations whose goals were to aid relations between the two groups. In Los Angeles, as noted elsewhere in this book, the Black-Korean Christian Coalition was founded in 1984 and the umbrella organization Black-Korean Alliance in 1986.[184]

Jews and Korean Americans did not necessarily "bond" instantly upon contact with each other in urban environments, but they did have business ties that elicited both positive and negative contact. Many Korean Americans bought their first businesses from Jewish American entrepreneurs or rented business space from them. Pyong Gap Min, in his groundbreaking work on Korean entrepreneurs in Los Angles and New York, for example, documents that some Korean immigrants viewed Jewish business people through stereotypes of Jewish greed. In an interview with Korean garment subcontractors in New York, for example, one asserted angrily that "Jewish landlords have no tears, no blood; they will do anything to exploit renters." The respondent also was quick to generalize his beliefs beyond landlords, noting: "Being tough about money is not limited to Jewish landlords. Jewish wholesalers, Jewish manufacturers, and all other Jewish merchants are tough about money. That's why Jews are so successful in business."[185]

Despite some hostilities, the belief held by many Korean shop-keepers and wholesalers that Jews had much to offer through examples of success, along with the opportunities many received through the purchase of Jewish businesses, were bases for economic cooperation and cultural appreciation. Moreover, their similar histories as immigrants and immigrant entrepreneurs also helped to forge ties. Korean shopkeepers in New York, for example, were heartened by those Jews who spoke out on their behalf when blacks boycotted their shops and provided legal assistance in times of need.[186]

These similarities between Jews and Koreans, as immigrants and as immigrant entrepreneurs, undoubtedly were not lost on Judge Karlin when she came to encounter Soon Ja Du in her courtroom. Joyce Karlin, after all, descended from Jewish immigrant shopkeepers and independent entrepreneurs in the needle, grocery, and jewelry trades. She, no doubt, grew up appreciating the hard work and sacrifices that her grandparents and great-grandparents made when they moved from Russia to the United States to create a better life for their families. It was the same sacrifice Soon Ja Du and her husband had been willing to make for their family when they moved from Korea to Los Angeles. Just as her family had suffered hardship and hostility, some of it from other racial groups, to achieve success, Joyce Karlin must have assumed, so too had the Dus.

While blacks and Jews in the last decades of the twentieth century struggled to find common ground on issues that exposed a deepening gulf in political, social, and economic perspectives, Koreans and Jews were finding mutual accord. Koreans did not fill all the spaces that Jewish businessmen and women vacated, such as landlords, teachers, physicians, and other professional and business related occupations, but the late twentieth century Korean presence in urban centers of black residential life, such as Brooklyn and South Central, certainly seemed reminiscent of Jewish property owners.[187] Both groups recognized that the commonality of experience extended beyond the economic sector.

Rabbi Douglas Kahn, for one, saw many similarities between Jews and Asians, including Koreans. Speaking to the Council of Jewish Federations General Assembly in 1990, Kahn encouraged his audience to build a deeper connection between the two because "we have too many common interests and too few explosive flashpoints to let these relations suffer from benign neglect."[188] Among the connective tissue was, of course, Kahn noted, the immigrant experience; but there were other factors at work, too. Both are victimized through stereotypes and targets of race-based violence, he explained; both were disliked because of their relationship to their homelands; both had experienced the trauma of internment; and both are opposed to reverse discrimination.[189]

Koreans were, as the press repeatedly touted in the 1980s and 1990s, the "new Jews." Some of the similarities were striking—a shared immigrant ethos of familial deprivation and hard work deemed necessary to succeed at any cost; strong patriarchal families and community structures; pursuit of economic success through entrepreneurship; location of businesses in working-poor communities of racially/ethnically different people; a willingness to culturally assimilate and a profoundly deep investment in educational attainment for their children because it provided future generations with a clear path to success. They, along with other Asian immigrant and immigrant-derived groups from Japan, China, India, the Philippines, and so forth, were, indeed, the new model minority, capable of not only seeking but also acquiring the American dream. Despite the narrow and inaccurate depiction that the "model minority" label has come to denote (see chapter 2), the term also signifies a kind of success that both Asian Americans and Jewish Americans accept as theirs on some level. This acceptance, and the reality of their accomplishments, placed them both at odds with blacks by the end of the twentieth century, and for similar reasons.

While it is certain that the history of cooperative interactions for a common good that blacks and Jews shared for much of the twentieth century does not characterize the relations between Asian Americans and Jewish Americans, they do recognize a kind of commonality of condition lending itself to mutual admiration. Today in South Korea, for example, Koreans are not shy about the esteem they hold for Jews. They readily admit that they respect Jewish accomplishments and perceive them as role models for success. This admiration has lent itself to a requirement for all elementary school children in South Korea to read the Talmud. Why? Because South Koreans believe that Jews are very intelligent, an intelligence that has, along with a perceived strong work ethos, led to their success. They suppose that the Talmud, which Jewish children also read, has contributed to their intelligence and success. As one mother noted, "The stereotype of Jews here is that they are ultra-intelligent people. Jews have come out of nowhere to become business chiefs, media bosses, Nobel Prize winners—we want our children to do the same. If that means studying Talmud, Torah, whatever, so be it."[190] The Korean ambassador to Israel, Young Sam Mah, was equally clear: "We tried to understand why the Jews are geniuses, and we came to the conclusion that it is because they study Talmud . . . Jews study the Talmud at a young age, and it helps them, in our opinion, to develop mental capabilities. This understanding led us to teach our children as well. We believe that if we teach our children Talmud, they will also become geniuses."[191] And in the United States, Asian women, Koreans included, purportedly have become the "new shiksas." Song Ho, who wrote an article on this popular myth for the online version of the *Jewish Journal* in 2003 concluded that while there was plenty of anecdotal evidence to support the claim, she could not find hard facts. She did find out from Asian and Jewish couples who were married, however, that they felt the two groups had strong similarities which eased their romance. "All the couples," she noted, "list similarities between Jewish culture and Asian culture—both Jews and Asians place great importance on education, family, [and] respect for elders, they said."[192] Oddly enough, if one had queried Soon Ja Du, Joyce Karlin, or Ruth Harlins (Latasha's surrogate mother), they all would have described their cultural beliefs in this way. Perhaps that is why intermarriage between African Americans and Jewish Americans has been especially prevalent.[193]

What most people do not recognize, of course, is that African Americans also share in the model minority stereotype and all that it connotes about hard work, ambition, family stability, and potential contributions to American society. They are, however, immigrant African Americans, not those born in the United States. Since emancipation, and even before in the elite literary salons, clubs, and churches of free born blacks, African Americans tried to fashion a public face of "model" Americans—in gender convention, military service, educational status, and economic stability. Blacks never abandoned this tradition. By the end of the twentieth century, the title finally had arrived, but those who held it, like Jews and Asians, were linked to a significant history of voluntary immigration. According to some in the United States and in Britain, black Caribbean and African immigrants are the true holders of the model minority mantle. The *London Daily Times* reported in 1993, for example, that "Black Africans have emerged as the most highly educated members of British society, surpassing even the Chinese as the most academically successful ethnic minority."[194] According to sociologist John Logan of Brown University, African immigrants also have acquired the highest educational status within the United States. Logan notes that as of the year 2000, "43.8 percent of African immigrants have achieved a college degree, compared to 42.5 percent of Asian Americans, 23.9 percent for immigrants from Europe, Russia and Canada, and 23.1 percent of the US population as a whole."[195]

Immigrant blacks, of course, are quite distinct from native born African Americans like those who comprised the Harlins family. John Logan goes on to explain of his statistics, which are drawn from 1990 and 2000 census data, that "the larger picture is that differences between whites and Asians are small to begin with, and the main message . . . is the larger gap between these two groups and [native] blacks or Hispanics."[196] Lumped as they were in the popular perception that native born blacks are the least desirable of Americans, the Harlins family never would have been characterized as model.

Regardless of each group's status as a model, they all remained a minority and, as such, have experienced—and still do today—a certain degree of marginalization. Jews, who often appear physically white, have been the least marginalized when compared with Koreans or blacks. No amount of cultural assimilation or similarity, education, nuclear kinship structure, or middle-class ownership has lessened the stigma of being physically distinct for African Americans and Asian Americans. In US society, physical difference equals racial difference and racial difference means inferiority.

Today, as throughout the nation's past, blacks are most vilified as the racial other. Hate crimes statistics are a telling measure: African Americans are most likely to be the victims of hate crimes. Jews, however, are the second most likely.[197] In 2009, for example, the FBI documented that most hate crimes stemmed from racial animosity, and that blacks typically were the intended victims of these crimes. That year, 71.5% of racially motivated hate crimes derived from "prejudice against blacks." While hate crimes associated with religion were much less in overall number, Jews usually were those victims—71.9%, for example, that same year.[198] The year that Latasha Harlins died, the FBI documented 4,558 hate crimes nationally; with blacks and Jews leading as victims.[199] What is not usually documented, though, is how many hate crimes one group of color instigates against another group of color.

Perhaps even more difficult to document quantitatively are racial/ ethnic group feelings of cultural distance and affinity. A survey taken in Los Angeles in 1992 of business owners, however, indicated that, of all major ethnic/racial groups, black entrepreneurs felt "closest" to Jews, and then whites and then Latinos/as. Korean American entrepreneurs in the study, on the other hand, felt "closest" to other Asian Americans, followed by whites, Jews, and Latinos in that order. Both blacks and Korean Americans entrepreneurs in LA reported that they felt least close to each other.[200] These feelings were not new. An earlier poll taken in 1988 of African Americans and Korean Americans in Los Angeles across occupational and class lines revealed similar results. In that survey, Asians emerged as the least liked of ethnic/racial groups among African Americans and vice versa. The only major difference was in the status that Jews held with African Americans—those surveyed four years earlier felt significantly less close to Jews than they did other whites or Spanish-speaking residents.[201] A national study released in 1990 that measured some aspects of Jewish feelings toward blacks, however, indicated that among whites, they were the most supportive of racial integration.[202] Slight shifts in racial/ethnic/cultural alliances, no doubt, occur often.

When surveying the outcome of *People v. Du*, however, most people would have cause to believe that the US racial hierarchy, and its relationship to the workings of the criminal justice system, were more predictable over time than not. The outcry from blacks was loud and clear: a Korean woman killed a black girl, and a Jewish female judge let her get away with it.

FIGURE 6.1 "Judge Joyce Karlin on first day back after her controversial sentencing," Photograph by Larry Davis. Courtesy of the *Los Angeles Times*.

6

People v. Du

Sentencing

It was the most flagrant demonstration of injustice against the African American community.

—Danny Bakewell

The Sentencing Hearing

The courtroom was quiet as everyone prepared to hear Judge Karlin pronounce sentencing in *People v. Du*. All during the trial, there had been an obvious enmity among the two principal groups camped out in her courtroom—the family and supporters of Soon Ja Du, who turned out in the hundreds on some days and often monopolized much of the seating; and the much smaller, but more visibly angry, family and supporters of Latasha Harlins. It was not unusual for there to be physical jostling and an exchange of angry words between the two sides in front of the court building, in the elevators, and in the corridors, that spilled over into the courtroom. Karlin struggled to contain order, threatening more than once to expel some members of the audience. Neither side took a liking to the judge right away. Harlins's kin remembered seeing Joyce Karlin in the courthouse elevators on several occasions. They had expected that she would give them some sign of sympathy or at least speak. In African American culture, speaking—saying hello, how are you? or even a slight nod of the head and eye contact are important indicators of respect, a respect the Harlins family knew they deserved given their devastating loss. Karlin repeatedly gave no indication of recognition outside her courtroom. Likewise, Du's family and friends worried that the judge, as part of the larger Los Angeles criminal justice system, was going to "scapegoat" Soon Ja, in order to divert attention from the police beating of Rodney King. Still, Judge Karlin's key rulings at the time of the trial, particularly her decision to take first-degree murder off of the table, underscored the Harlins family's suspicions and encouraged hope among the Dus.

Between Trial and Error

During those five weeks between the rendering of the verdict in the case and the sentencing, several key activities directly related to the case took place. Both the district attorney and Du's lawyers prepared written arguments detailing their recommendations for Du's sentence before the hearing began. Still, most of the presentencing maneuvers were those on Soon Ja's team. Shockingly, Richard Leonard had a major heart attack leading to multiple bypass surgery in late October, taking him away from the case. Charles Lloyd no doubt understood that he would have to rely on his charm and wit more than ever to persuade Judge Karlin since he would not have his co-counsel at his side. This change in the defense counsel table undoubtedly unsettled the Dus. Still, Lloyd pressed on and made certain that his client continued to pursue every avenue to help her case.

Soon Ja Du had undergone a psychiatric evaluation and was interviewed by Patricia Dwyer of the Los Angeles County Probation Office so that both might make a recommendation about sentencing to Judge Karlin. Lloyd and Leonard had acted strategically in acquiring the "psych eval." Instead of having Mrs. Du examined by the resident psychiatric team at the Correctional Facility at Chino Hills—the usual route—they had hired a private firm, "their own firm," as Leonard called it, to evaluate her.[1] It paid off—the team recommended probation rather than incarceration. The Du family and friends also orchestrated a letter-writing campaign at Soon Ja Du's church that poured scores of letters into Judge Karlin's chambers asking the judge to have mercy on their friend and fellow church member, as well Du's family. Mrs. Du sent a letter as well, expressing her remorse and repentance.[2] Charles Lloyd and Richard Leonard also petitioned the court for a new trial, "alleging insufficiency of the evidence." But the Dus's friends and associates were not the only ones who tried to sway the judge's opinion during the weeks before sentencing. Danny Bakewell, for one, held rallies and spoke often on the issue publicly. So too did members of the Latasha Harlins Justice Committee.[3] Supporters of the Harlins family also exerted some effort at influence. Judge Karlin no doubt reviewed all these documents carefully before rendering her sentence. While she must have been impressed by the defense's numerous tactics to assist Du, Karlin was not about to dismiss the case. She denied the motion as soon as the sentencing hearing began.[4]

The psychologist's report on Soon Ja Du was sealed, but some of it did enter the court's record because of the multiple references to it that District Attorney Carvajal made during her verbal argument at the sentencing hearing. Most important, the report concluded that Mrs. Du was not a threat to society and did not need to serve a jail sentence. In her rebuttal, Carvajal argued that these findings may have been heavily influenced by a clear predisposition indicated in the report, where Latasha's death was described as resulting from a "shooting accident."[5] This report, Carvajal asserted, went on to describe at length Soon Ja Du's upper-class upbringing. The psychiatrist who examined her noted that it lent the shopkeeper an air of superiority, a feeling that she should be "treated differently."[6]

The report also detailed the "mentality" with which Mrs. Du approached her occasional work at the Empire Liquor Market: any member of her family working there "would be attacked or possibly killed by any of the people that come in the store, and that would affect the whole family . . . any one of them can come in and kill me."[7] According to the psychiatrist, Soon Ja Du noted in their conversation that while she was in the brawl with Latasha she was thinking to herself that she was "happy it was her and not one of her children."[8] Du also purportedly told the doctor that she was certain that Latasha had a gun in her backpack, but that Du had picked up her handgun only to scare the teen. Soon Ja Du also spoke about her sense of cultural alienation, particularly when she first arrived in the United States and of her great remorse for Latasha's *mother* for having lost her child. Of course, Latasha's mother had been dead for years—a point that Carvajal seized on in her sentencing recommendation to indicate how disinterested Du actually was in the plight of the Harlins family and in the loss of her victim's life.[9]

Patricia Dwyer was the veteran probation officer charged with interviewing the convicted felon and rendering a sentencing recommendation to the court. Dwyer's suggestion was startlingly different from that of Du's psychiatric team. She sent her 39-page report to Judge Karlin with a recommendation that Du serve the maximum sentence allowed for her conviction—16 years. Dwyer explained her reasoning carefully. In it, she noted that after shooting Latasha, Du "took no action to assist the victim, exaggerated her injuries and feigned unconsciousness. This can only be viewed as a deliberate attempt to manipulate public opinion and underscores her unrepentant attitude."[10] Her recommendation, the court officer went on to state, was drawn mostly from her impression that Du was not remorseful about her actions, refused to take responsibility for the shooting, and when asked what she would do if confronted with the same situation, answered: "I would do the same thing again."[11] The remorse that Du did express, as assessed by both the probation officer and the psychiatrist, was for the damage that her legal troubles had on her life: the possibility of her going to prison; her loss of face in Korea, in her church, and in her community; and the pain that all this had caused her family including, no doubt, their financial losses. She did not express remorse for her victim or her victim's family.[12]

As one might imagine, the written arguments to Judge Karlin from Carvajal and Lloyd regarding Du's sentence varied greatly. When Charles Lloyd wrote to Karlin and spoke openly at the sentencing hearing, he pleaded with the judge not to incarcerate Soon Ja. After all, no matter which way Carvajal chose to use the contents of Du's psychological evaluation, the report still carried a recommendation for probation. "This case," Lloyd asserted, "does not fall within the parameters of anything other than straight probation."[13] In her defense, Lloyd emphasized that Soon Ja had never committed a crime before, and that she would not commit a crime in the future—she was not a threat to society. The psychiatric report, he added, confirmed his contention. The killing of Latasha, Lloyd reiterated, was accidental because her gun was defective. Du's role in the girl's death was tragic and strictly "situational" because Mrs. Du had only pulled out the gun to protect herself. She was the defenseless one in that crime-ridden store, he argued, not Latasha: "Mrs. Du in this case was vulnerable, not Miss Harlins. You look at the tape. There is no contest. No contest. Smashed her in the face."[14]

Lloyd had to address the probation report's recommendation of maximum jail time. He openly challenged Patricia Dwyer's conclusion regarding Du's lack of remorse. She was, he countered, extremely remorseful and genuinely apologetic to the Harlins family. "There isn't anything Mrs. Du wouldn't do to undo what has happened," he pled. Sometimes sounding like a country preacher, Lloyd's presentation before the court was filled with emotion, references to injustices he had suffered in his life and the injustices that Mrs. Du, as an immigrant, had suffered. "I am not asking for anything for Mrs. Du that she's not entitled to," he assured Judge Karlin. "The good Lord above knows I don't know how to ask for anything less than she's entitled to."[15]

Part of Lloyd's strategy was to attack Carvajal's sentencing recommendation. Conflating the district attorney's views with those of the African American community—he accused both of playing the race card. "Now the people are making so much to do about race," he noted on one occasion. On another, he spoke specifically of the pressure that the black community was trying to place on the sentencing outcome: "People have tried to make this a racial case . . . There was nothing alluded to during the trial of this case about race."[16]

The probation officer's report, however, did suggest that Mrs. Du had racist notions concerning the black people who frequented the Empire Liquor Market. Du admitted to Ms. Dwyer that she was afraid of blacks and did not respect them. "They look healthy, young . . . big question why they don't work . . . got welfare money and buying alcoholic beverages and consuming them instead of feeding children." She concluded that it was "their way of living."[17] Du's statements to Ms. Dwyer about Latasha and her family also suggested her racism: "I . . . pray for her [Latasha] thinking that if she was born in a better family,"[18] she would not have done what she did.

Roxane Carvajal countered Lloyd's contention that she had played the race card by reminding the judge that defense counsel had first brought race into the discussion. "It was Mr. Lloyd and Mr. Leonard," she noted, "who presented the evidence to the jury of all the problems that they have had with the black customers in the community . . . As a matter of fact, Mr. Lloyd indicates that she was vulnerable, and she was scared, and she had a right to be because of everything that had happened in that community."[19] Lloyd was eager, she added, to let those in the courtroom believe that Mrs. Du's fear was logical, given "all the black people who were coming in and threatening her son or stealing from her." Once Lloyd opened the door, Carvajal asserted, she had a right to pursue the question of whether Du reacted to Latasha in the manner that she did because of "racial bias."[20] Turning to Dwyer's report, Carvajal pointed out that it was the probation officer's opinion that race had played an important role in Soon Ja Du's actions vis-à-vis Latasha that fateful Saturday morning. "She views black people with suspicion, fear and contempt," Carvajal concluded. "It was this attitude that caused her to [put] in motion a chain of events which led to the death of a 15 year old."[21] The district attorney moved quickly forward.

Recalling Lloyd's rhetorical question posed in his petition: "What is to be gained by sending Mrs. Du to prison?" "My response to that is . . . one word and it's very simple," Carvajal answered emotionally: "Justice."[22] Deputy District Attorney Carvajal defined justice in the Du case as the maximum allowable sentence for voluntary manslaughter with the use of a firearm—16 years in a state prison. Carvajal gave an impassioned speech during the sentencing hearing, not only reiterating Du's guilt, but also the defendant's apparent lack of remorse and the threat to society if released. Carvajal repeatedly returned to the probation officer's report, which emphasized the apparent lack of remorse Mrs. Du had for killing Latasha. "She has killed a 15 year old girl, a beautiful, 15 year old girl," Carvajal cried to Judge Karlin, and she is not sorry. Carvajal retold the story of Du's meetings with the probation officer. Patricia Dwyer was so struck by Soon Ja's apparent lack of remorse that she was certain it was because something was being lost in translation. Dwyer concluded the meeting and asked that Du return with a different interpreter. During their subsequent meeting, Dwyer repeatedly asked Du if she felt remorse. A friend who had accompanied Mrs. Du reminded her that she should express remorse for killing Latasha, but her response then was, "Do you mean me, right away?"[23] And the district attorney also wanted the judge to realize that Du's actions had devastated Latasha's family. She harshly contrasted the "emotional turmoil" that the Harlins had suffered to that of the Du family, emphasizing that Du's loss was monetary, not physical—"because they're not getting their $15,000 a month that they were getting before,"[24] she asserted.

The deputy district attorney then asked Latasha's grandmother, Ruth, to speak for her family. "As a [result] of my granddaughter's death," the matriarch said, "my family and I have grieved severely. . . . I think about my granddaughter all the time. . . . It hurts me so much on the inside that I have missed days from work, and I have had many sleepless nights thinking about Latasha and reliving memories of the times we shared together which will be no more." Harlins weighed in on the issue of Du's remorse. "Each time that my family and I appeared in court and Soon Ja Du testified," she added, "she never showed or expressed any sympathy, no remorse, or regret. Not even 'I'm sorry.' . . . I don't know how Soon Ja Du, the mother of three grown children, could take the life of another mother's 15-year old child without any mercy."[25] Ruth Harlins asked for justice for her granddaughter, pleading with Judge Karlin to prescribe the maximum sentence. "Soon Ja Du has taken the life of a 15-year old child[,] my granddaughter," Mrs. Harlins began. "And I believe that she should get the maximum sentence for the crime that she has committed, and I would be very disappointed if Soon Ja Du get[s] away with probation."[26]

Roxane Carvajal did not just build her case for the maximum sentence on the issue of racial justice. It was just plain justice. She began by summarizing, again, the case that had ended with the jury rendering a guilty verdict, concluding that Du had intended to kill Latasha. Carvajal went on to make a case for assigning Soon Ja the maximum sentence: Du had willfully killed an unarmed child; she had shown no remorse; she had indicated that she would act similarly again under the same circumstances. She meticulously surveyed every standard noted in the California state sentencing guidelines that had to be addressed when determining the proper sentence for a conviction. In order for a judge to sentence Du to probation rather than to prison time, Carvajal asserted, the court had to define this case as an "unusual one" with specific factors—there was no use of a gun in the commission of the crime, or that Du committed manslaughter under "circumstances of great provocation, coercion, or duress."[27]

Carvajal then explained why Soon Ja Du's case failed to meet these conditions. There was no great provocation, coercion, or duress, she argued, because being punched in the eye, even more than once, did not justify pulling out a gun and shooting someone in the back of the head. Moreover, the jury had examined the "extenuating" circumstances of Du's actions and, accordingly, rendered her guilty of the lesser charge of voluntary manslaughter, rather than second-degree murder. In other words, Soon Ja already had benefited once from the court's consideration of the hostile environment in which she worked. The district attorney also reviewed the argument that Latasha's youth and strength, in the face of Mrs. Du's "aged" and "frail" person, caused the defendant to fear for her life, and thus provoked her to shoot the girl. "I submit to the court," Carvajal asserted, "that being 49 . . . is not aged." Nor should one consider, she argued, Du's fears of Latasha being a gang member as reasonable. "Latasha," she asserted, "was not a gang member and there was no evidence to suggest otherwise. Latasha was unarmed. Latasha had stopped moving toward Du. The backpack Du claimed she feared had a gun in it was in Du's possession. And Latasha had turned and was walking toward the door with the two dollars in her hand that she had intended to pay for the juice with, when Du pulled the trigger and killed her."[28] "This killing was merciless, unnecessary," the district attorney concluded, and Du should receive the maximum sentence.[29]

The Sentencing

"Does society need Mrs. Du to be incarcerated in order to be protected? I think not. Is the defendant a danger to society? I think not. Is state prison needed in order to encourage the defendant to lead a law-abiding life or isolate her so that she cannot commit other crimes. I think not. Is state prison needed to punish Mrs. Du? Perhaps." So began Judge Karlin's sentencing statement. It was enough to indicate to the Harlins family that she was not going to honor their wishes and order Du to serve the maximum prison term. In fact, she was not going to order any prison time for Du.[30] Instead, Joyce Karlin ordered that Soon Ja Du receive a suspended ten-year term in the state penitentiary; five years probation; 400 hours of community service; a $500 fine; and the cost of Latasha Harlins's funeral and medical expenses.[31]

The Harlins family stood up and walked out of the courtroom as Judge Karlin read her statement.[32] They were hurt and angry beyond belief in what they took to be a massive miscarriage of justice. It was clear to them that Judge Karlin disagreed with almost everything that district attorney Carvajal argued and agreed wholeheartedly with the case that Lloyd presented. They left before Karlin began to explain her sentence. If they had stayed, they would have heard the judge note that she was "required by law, to consider Mrs. Du as an individual in the context of the crime with which she's been convicted."[33] Karlin added that each case of voluntary manslaughter was unique and, as such, the sentences varied greatly. According to her, those convicted of this crime in the Superior Courts of California during 1990 had received sentences that ranged from "probation with no jail time to incarceration in state prison for many years."[34] Joyce Karlin then explained her rationale with specific reference to Mrs. Du. She would have been eligible for a jail sentence, Karlin explained, if her case had not been an unusual one— but it was an unusual one. And Soon Ja Du's crime, Karlin reiterated, was a result of "great duress and provocation," and as such, this convicted felon deserved special consideration, despite Carvajal's opposite conclusion.

According to Judge Karlin, Soon Ja Du used the gun as a shopkeeper "who lawfully possesses firearms for their own protection," not as a criminal about to commit a crime. She had no prior criminal record, and there was no indication, Karlin argued, that she would commit another crime. Lastly, Du did shoot Latasha "under circumstances of great provocation, coercion and duress."[35] It was Latasha, and not Du, who was the aggressor, Karlin noted. It was Du, and not Latasha, who was vulnerable in the Empire Liquor Market. And it was not Du, but Latasha—if she had lived—who probably would be before the court on an assault charge. "The District Attorney argues that Latasha Harlins was justified in her assault on Mrs. Du," Karlin explained, but "our courts are filled with cases which suggest otherwise. Our courts are filled with the defendants who are charged with assault as a result of attacks on shopkeepers, including shopkeepers who rightfully or wrongfully accuse of . . . shoplifting."[36]

Karlin went on to note that she believed the "altered" gun had been a key element in Latasha's death. Its altered state, she concluded, made it "an automatic weapon with a hairpin trigger . . . I have serious questions in my mind whether this crime should have been committed at all but for the altered gun."[37] The last rhetorical questions Karlin posed in her sentencing statement were: "Did Mrs. Du react inappropriately to Latasha Harlins?" Her answer: "Absolutely . . . But was that overreaction understandable? I think it was."[38]

Joyce Karlin ironically added that she hoped that the case of *People v. Du* would serve as a basis for a healing dialogue between the black and Korean communities in Los Angeles. "Latasha Harlins's death," she lectured, "should be remembered as a catalyst that must force members of the African-American and Korean communities to confront an intolerable situation by the creating of solutions, and by creating solutions, hopefully a better understanding and acceptance can result so that similar tragedies will never be repeated."[39] Karlin noted as welll that she believed that any and all comments made during the trial regarding race harmed this potential healing process, rather than helping it. "To suggest that any sentence that this court might give," she spoke pointedly to Carvajal, "results in the conclusion that young black children don't receive full protection of the law—I'm sorry, Miss Carvajal, but that is dangerous rhetoric, and that is unjustified."[40]

The Burning Question of Injustice

Backtracking to the week in late September/early October when the trial was taking place, Mayor Bradley clearly was pleased with the end of the Danny Bakewell led boycott of Korean grocers. It could not have come at a more opportune moment. But it was soon clear that little had been gained in terms of easing tension between local Korean shopkeepers and the blacks they served. Judge Karlin's decision that same day to reduce the possible charges from first-degree murder to either second-degree murder or manslaughter brought on, the following day, another slate of angry protests from the African American community and provocative editorials in local newspapers. Outspoken black pundits hoped for a first-degree murder conviction. Supporters of Du wanted her found not guilty. Neither side got their way. The jury's decision days later to convict Soon Ja Du of voluntary manslaughter gave Harlins's family members and supporters additional media coverage to express their frustration and anger with the criminal justice "system" in Los Angeles.

It must have seemed like déjà vu—the murder of Crystal Harlins six years earlier had been ruled manslaughter as well, even though some argued that Cora Mae Anderson had sought out Latasha's mother in the bar that Thanksgiving night in 1985; she had sought her out with a loaded gun in her purse. "She got away with murder," Denise Harlins spoke out with tears flowing after she heard the Du verdict. Ruth Harlins, angry enough to confront the press, echoed her daughter's pained revelation, insisting on Soon Ja Du's guilt. So too did Gina Rae, one of the leaders of the Harlins Justice Committee, who threatened continued protest until justice was served. "The system stinks . . . There is no justice."[41]

The Harlins family and their friends were even more upset the next day when they heard Charles Lloyd's response to the jury's verdict. Lloyd admitted that the voluntary manslaughter conviction was a disappointment; he had hoped that Soon Ja would have been exonerated. He also briefly outlined for the press his next step in defense of Du—he and his co-counsel were going to have Mrs. Du undergo psychological testing so that they could argue in the sentencing hearing that the shooting was only "situational" and that "Mrs. Du is no danger." Charles Lloyd told the public that day he was going to ask Judge Karlin to sentence Soon Ja Du to probation.[42]

The advocates for both sides sprang into action. Soon Ja Du submitted to psychological testing. Women who were close to her prepped her for her interviews with the assigned probation officer, Patricia Dwyer. Beneath so much coaching, it was difficult for Du's own notion of justice to emerge. But if the public could barely detect a weak, muffled response from Soon Ja Du on this question, what they heard from the Harlins camp stood out in bold, and loud, contrast.

"Soon Ja Du is getting away with murder!" was the cry blasted through microphones across South Central as Harlins family representative, Denise Harlins, members of the Latasha Harlins Justice Committee, Danny Bakewell and his Brotherhood Crusade, Mothers in Action, and others organized and appeared at rally after rally.

In the wake of controversy over the conviction of Soon Ja Du for voluntary manslaughter rather than first-degree murder, tension between the two communities grew, particularly in South Central Los Angeles shops and convenience stores. At about 6:45 a.m. on October 26, for example, two black men, while robbing a gas-convenience store owned by Hang and Soon Kang, shot the Kangs's nine-year-old daughter, Yuri, in the chest. Yuri was critically wounded but survived. Some witnesses to the robbery repeatedly noted that the shooting occurred after the Kangs had fully cooperated and the robbers were leaving the store. Others suggested that the thief, who got away with more than $500, shot Yuri because she had looked at him after he demanded that she not do so. "Apparently the girl failed to follow the gunman's instructions to avoid looking at him during the robbery, and he shot the child in the chest for not obeying him,"[43] one *Los Angeles Times* reporter explained. Yuri's parents, however, were not physically harmed.

The parallel between Yuri's shooting and Latasha's was apparent to many. Indeed, the two events seemed so tied to one another that activists who had been busy protesting Du's voluntary manslaughter conviction as too lenient, took a break long enough to go on record against Yuri's attempted murder. Danny Bakewell spoke out quickly and forcefully, noting that he was incensed by the shooting. No one in the community, he noted, would accept this kind of harm toward a child, any child.[44] Bakewell then went on to publicly link Yuri's and Latasha's victimization, asserting that whoever harmed Yuri should receive a substantial punishment just as Du should for killing Latasha.[45] Mark Ridley-Thomas added to the outcry against Kang's shooting and proposed that the city offer a $5,000 reward for information that might lead to the prosecution of her assailant. The city agreed. Mayor Thomas Bradley, who had refused contact with the Harlins family after Latasha's death, called the Kangs and offered his sympathy and reassurance that the crime against their daughter would not go unpunished.[46]

The Korean community also took the opportunity to use Yuri's shooting as a clear indication of the violent threat many entrepreneurs and their families faced. Gary Kim, president of the Korean American Coalition, for example, noted that the attempted murder of the nine-year-old Kang was typical of the attacks Korean Americans often face, bemoaning the fact that few outside the Korean American community seemed to care about the large number of their merchants who are killed and robbed in Los Angeles County.[47] Others promised that from that point on, Koreatown community leaders would be more vocal about their victimization, asserting that the media largely gave favorable coverage to the concerns of blacks as opposed to those of Korean Americans.[48]

The Harlins family too was shaken by the Kang shooting, but could not help but contrast the public's response to the shooting of a Korean girl with the public's response to Latasha's murder. Still angry and frustrated due to Du's conviction on a lesser charge, Denise Harlins wanted to know: "Where was the support of any of our so called Black leaders at the beginning of this crisis?" She believed that black politicians carefully timed their public show of concern to have the most positive impact on their public image. "It smacks of political hypocrisy," she asserted.[49] The family was particularly incensed because they believed that Mayor Bradley had given them the cold shoulder. They complained that the mayor had not contacted their family nor offered them condolences and support after Latasha was killed as he had done for the Kang family. "I felt that it was an insult that we could not get Bradley to come out and even condemn the murder of Latasha, but as soon as nine-year-old Yuri Kang was shot, he immediately came out and expressed outrage," Denise told a reporter.[50] Latasha's family had tried to meet with Mayor Bradley before the trial took place. The Latasha Harlins Justice Committee had asked him to make a show of "public support for her family," but he would not. To do so, members of the committee asserted, would have "calm[ed] down the neighborhood." Instead, Bradley left many of them believing that he supported the Korean community instead because they had "a lot more money than the black community to give." When they finally did get the meeting, Denise concluded, it was "a complete waste of our time. [Bradley was] antagonistic [and] defensive."[51]

Two weeks after Yuri was shot, burglars murdered another Korean shopkeeper in South Los Angeles and vandals burned a Korean-owned store. On Wednesday October 30, the *Los Angeles Times* reported that a Korean shopkeeper, 33-year-old Kwang Yui Chun, was shot and killed the previous Monday evening at Century Fashion, his beauty supply store on Jefferson Boulevard, while being robbed. The same article reported that early the next morning, the Korean-owned Imperial Highway Liquor store near Whittier was burned in an act of arson. Damages were estimated to be $135,000.[52] Richard Foster, a black pharmacist who worked in close proximity to Chun's shop, like others who did not want to worsen interethnic relations, attributed the Korean businessman's murder to the drug epidemic rather than to racial hostility. "We have a lot of people on drugs that would just as easily kill me as they would anyone else," he noted. Korean leaders, however, again both mourned the loss of one of their own and used Chun's death to emphasize the difficult position that their shopkeepers found themselves struggling to overcome. It was this kind of violence, they argued, which fed the suspicions of other entrepreneurs. Most South Central blacks recoiled from the growing violence. Others, ignoring the human tragedies these crimes wrought, whispered: "No justice, no peace."

If this violence was in any way related to the jury's decision to convict Du on the lesser charge of voluntary manslaughter, imagine the black community's response after Judge Karlin's no jail time sentence. To say that this decision was controversial, would be a gross understatement. Responses from the black community, the Harlins family, and the District Attorney's Office were immediate.

This Is a Slap in the Face of Every African American Citizen

Black community activists rendered the most vocal opposition to Karlin's sentencing decisions, but were joined by an array of other political and social leaders. Even some in the Korean community spoke against it. "Some justice," K. W. Lee, the editor of the English version *Korea Times* wrote, insisting that he spoke for many other Korean and Korean American residents. "Not one day in jail for taking a human life. In stark contrast to her fellow Korean immigrant Brendan Sheen, who has been given 30 days in county jail for abusing his dog."[53] Lee's referral to the case of 26-year-old Brendan Sheen who had been convicted of physically abusing his eight-month-old cocker spaniel, named Baby, was one that was repeatedly referenced. The idea that a Korean immigrant was sentenced to a month in jail for hurting a dog, but that another Korean immigrant, Soon Ja Du, did not receive any prison time for the death of a 15-year-old African American girl was proof, many said, that Los Angeles's criminal justice system was completely biased against African Americans, including African American women and children. And it was not just that Baby was protected through the justice system: well-wishers poured their hearts out in newspapers, with cards, and with donations that totaled well over $10,000 for Baby.[54] The black community was incensed.

Herschel Hunt of Placentia, like many others, could not get past the image that a dog's life seemed more valued and protected in the justice system than a black girl's life. "I have been trying to understand the judge's decision to give Soon Ja Du probation in [the] murder trial of a Black teenager, Latasha Harlins," Hunt wrote in a letter to the editor of the *Los Angeles Sentinel*:

I have followed the trial very carefully over the last several weeks. I have also followed a trial, in Orange County, where a White teenager accidentally shot and killed another White teenager at a senior prom party. In that case, the judge handed down the maximum sentence of 17 years in prison. With these two cases as a background . . . another case, a Korean was sentenced to 30 days in prison for kicking his dog. Suddenly, everything was very clear to me. In my mind at this moment, a Black person's life is not worth as much as a dog.[55]

A black woman who lived in Los Angeles was equally poignant in her letter to the *Los Angeles Times*. There, she wrote of "weeping" when she heard the sentence and fearing for the lives of her children. "Until now I did not think it was possible to be killed twice," she added. "However that is just what happened to 15-year-old Latasha Harlins at the hands of our justice system. A woman who was convicted of voluntary manslaughter was given probation, community service and a $500 fine! This is a slap in the face of every African-American citizen. . . . Judge Joyce A. Karlin has just told us that it is open season on our children."[56]

Sickened from the sense of complete judicial unfairness, community leaders, along with average citizens, acted swiftly. On the evening after Judge Karlin pronounced her sentence, more than 500 met at the Bethel AME church to protest. This meeting had not been planned—it had been scheduled as a community-wide discussion of the rising number of local violent crimes. Little time was spent on this important issue because most felt the need to vent their incredulity and frustration at Karlin's decision.[57] Rev. George C. Stallings, bishop of the Imani Temple in Washington, DC, began with a call to action. "Wake up Los Angeles. Wake up! We will not allow Latasha Harlins's death to be in vain," he shouted.[58] Maxine Waters, the Democratic US Representative from that area, challenged constituents to use their voting power to end Karlin's judgeship:

"We can vote her out of office," she assured the crowd, who gave her a standing ovation.[59] An angry black resident wore a T-shirt on which someone had written, "Fuck the judge. Justice B Damned!!!"[60] Wilbur Thomas, a local merchant, carried an "Enough is Enough" sign and suggested that protest might take a violent turn. "I don't know what it's going to lead to but a lot of people are fired up and they just can't seem to take it anymore," he reported.[61]

That meeting was just the beginning. Local black churches, as they historically had, protested what they believed was a damning miscarriage of justice. One of the city's most prestigious megachurches, First African Methodist Episcopal (FAME) had its members fill out postcards addressed to District Attorney Ira Reiner demanding that he appeal Du's sentence.[62] Kerman Maddox led the Committee of Justice to deliver 20,000 such cards to the DA.[63] That same first weekend after the sentencing, another local black church distributed petitions in which signers called on the US Attorney's Office and the Committee on Judicial Performance to review Judge Karlin's actions.[64]

The Brotherhood Crusade, the Compton City Council, and several local churches held another protest rally four days later. This time they took their message to the heart of the criminal justice system in South Los Angeles—the Compton Courthouse. The initial plan was to form a human chain around the building, but given the logistical difficulties of doing that, they took their protest inside, hoping to reach Judge Karlin's courtroom. More than 350 protestors pushed there way into the courthouse chanting "Karlin must go!" While they never made it to Karlin's tenth-floor courtroom, press coverage made certain all of Los Angeles was talking about Karlin that evening. "I think a lot of people expect people to stay outside and that's not where I come from. We went in peacefully. We went in big numbers, but I don't think anyone was out of hand," Danny Bakewell explained.[65] The mayor of Compton, Walter R. Tucker III, also wanted the public to know that everyone had acted peacefully while exercising their First Amendment right. "It began as a peaceful demonstration and it ended as a peaceful demonstration. We were certainly not there to hurt anyone. But it easily could have become a dangerous situation," he warned. He also said they wanted to "send a message that we as a people are strong and we're going to stand up and be counted . . . People know her decision was blatantly and egregiously wrong." Comparing Karlin to the national leader of the KKK, Tucker asserted: "We don't need David Duke and we don't need Judge Karlin."[66] The mayor then promised that similar protests would continue to take place until justice had been won for Latasha and her family.[67] The Reverend Richard Sanders reiterated Tucker's sentiments, noting: "We decided to go in peacefully, to take the demonstration inside to make the powers that be aware that we are not going to take this blatant injustice sitting down."[68] Danny Bakewell, who labeled Karlin a racist, vowed to take the protest to her home in Manhattan Beach.

While most protestors's remarks centered on Karlin, Soon Ja Du's role was not forgotten. The Reverend Edgar Boyd, who had sustained the protest against John's Liquor store after the murder of Lee Arthur Mitchell, was quick to add that day: "We cannot stand idly by and see those who . . . came on the scene just some 20 years ago succeed, excel and progress while we are left behind. If you commit a crime in our community, you are going to be accountable to the authorities." That failing, he concluded, "you're also going to be accountable to us, because we're not going to allow you to misuse us and abuse us any more."[69]

Early African American protesters included an impressive array of community members and activists, including those mentioned above and Joseph Duff, president of the Los Angeles branch of the NAACP; and Yvonne Braithwaite Burke, county supervisor and former state congresswoman. A day after protestors went to the Compton Courthouse, 30 civil rights, religious, political, and grass-roots leaders met on Tuesday, November 20, 1991, to continue their public display of outrage against what they believed was a blatant act of injustice. "We believe her decision is racist, insensitive, inaccurate, unjust and reaffirms the nightmare in the minds of African Americans that our children can be killed right before our eyes . . . and the only justice we can count on getting from the criminal justice system is injustice," Danny Bakewell of the Brotherhood Crusade concluded angrily.[70] "They say the punishment should always fit the crime, a theory that only applies when the life is not that of an African American. Kill an African American—go free," Bakewell told his angry audience.[71] Those assembled asked for Judge Karlin's immediate resignation and, that failing, that the black community unite and defeat her in her election scheduled for June 1992.[72]

Deputy district attorney Roxane Carvajal also was quick to denounce the sentencing and to draw criticism away from her role in the trial. "My function is not to sentence the defendant," she told reporters outside the courtroom. She, after all, had managed to get Du convicted of a crime that potentially carried a hefty incarceration period—16 years. "That's the court's job and I disagree with the court."[73] Ira Reiner, district attorney for Los Angeles County, told the press that Karlin's sentence "has shown she has no credibility" and threatened a boycott of the young jurist through affidavit. That is, Reiner asked his assistant DAs to petition for reassignment to another judge should they have a case initially assigned to Karlin. "This was such a stunning miscarriage of justice that Judge Karlin cannot continue to hear criminal cases with any public credibility," Reiner told the press. "It is so beyond the pale . . . that I cannot, in good conscience, send my deputies into that courtroom."[74] After hearing Karlin defend her sentence, Reiner also believed he had the legal grounds to appeal it. He told the media that Karlin's sentencing statement clearly indicated that she believed that Du's shooting of Latasha was accidental. That reasoning, Reiner asserted, meant that Karlin had not accepted the jury's verdict of voluntary manslaughter, even though she instructed them to deliberate on that offense. If she had accepted this verdict, the DA went on to explain, she would not later have characterized the shooting as "accidental"—a term that would have indicated involuntary manslaughter.[75]

Other members of the legal community also publicly disagreed with Judge Karlin's sentence. Laurie Levenson, who then was associate professor at Loyola Law School, for example, sympathized with the black community's fury. "The community is understandably outraged at Judge Joyce A. Karlin's fundamentally wrong sentence of Korean-born grocer Soon Ja Du," she wrote in an article published in the *Los Angeles Times*. "Anyone who voluntarily kills another human being under circumstances such as those that led to the death of 15-year old Latasha Harlins should be sentenced to a term of imprisonment." Levenson suggested that Karlin's decision might have been as a result of inexperience. Underscoring the fact that Du's trial was the judge's first by jury, and that three other seasoned judges had managed to wiggle themselves out of what everyone guessed would be a media and judicial powder keg, Levenson believed Karlin also might have been a victim. She certainly thought that district attorney Reiner's attempt to sanction the judge after the sentencing was unfair. Indeed, most members of the legal community seemed to have believed that Reiner's publicly announced decision not to allow his deputy district attorneys to try cases before Judge Karlin was a gross attempt at judiciary manipulation and intimidation. "Does Reiner really believe that Karlin's four-month tenure on the bench demonstrates an inability to be fair and impartial to the prosecution in every criminal case that may come before her?" Levenson asked. "There is only one reason for Reiner's blanket threat: to intimidate and control the judiciary."[76]

Ricardo Torres, presiding judge of the Los Angeles Superior Court at the time, was livid at Reiner's public remarks. Like Laurie Levenson, Torres perceived Reiner's denouncement of Karlin as politically motivated and manipulative. "This is his campaign," Torres told the *Daily News.* "He can try to intimidate us, but he can't overcome the separation of powers." As for Judge Karlin, Torres concluded, she was not soft on criminals, as some had asserted when she sentenced Du no jail time, but rather a "law and order, pro-prosecutorial judge."[77] Torres wrote a public letter to Reiner asking him to reconsider his decision to boycott Karlin's court, asserting: "While recognizing your strong feelings concerning the sentence and your right as the district attorney to express such disagreement, nonetheless, it is important that the administration of the Superior Court be accorded the necessary flexibility to make what it considers to be appropriate judicial assignments." Torres cautioned Reiner to rethink the boycott of Karlin or risk ending the "excellent rapport between the Superior Court and the District Attorney's Office."[78] Even some members of the black community became a little squeamish at Reiner's pronouncement. Joseph Duff of the local NAACP wanted Reiner to do what he could to make certain that Soon Ja Du received jail time, but he did not want the district attorney to use this case to grab more power vis-à-vis the general discretion judges exercised.[79]

Many believed that Reiner gave into the pressure and recanted. Others thought he and Torres came to a quiet understanding that if Reiner backed down, Torres would eventually remove Karlin from the criminal court. Although Reiner announced that he would not keep his assistant DAs from trying cases in Karlin's courtroom, he still seemed determined to have her sentence of Soon Ja overturned. He promised to appeal it. Some in the black community resented the DA's flip-flop, regarding it as just another example of injustice toward blacks. Joseph Duff and some members of the black community, however, were cautiously optimistic at Reiner's apparent determination to undue Karlin's sentencing. "People want to know that they are heard, that their anger is heard," Duff said. "The judge appeared to ignore the people, as if they didn't count. Any attempt to return this case to the legal process will only aid the healing process."[80] Curtis R. Tucker, chairman of the California Legislative Black Caucus, wrote to Reiner in an open letter in an effort to persuade him to actually appeal the sentence: "Justice may still be served to a family, and a race, that have long hungered for it. You as our elected district attorney have the power to appeal this decision. It is incumbent upon you to act swiftly."[81] Patricia Moore, Compton councilwoman, was clear in her reasons for supporting the promised appeal process—if Du's sentence is not overturned, it will signal to shopkeepers that they can "use guns whenever they choose," with little fear of substantial consequences.[82]

It Took A Lot of Guts

The defense team, Du, her family, and church members's immediate response to Judge Karlin's sentencing, of course, was elation. Attorney Charles Lloyd was happy to pronounce that justice had been done. But even his co-counsel, Richard Leonard, had to admit he was a little surprised at Karlin's sentence. "It took a lot of guts," he noted. "Given the verdict, most judges who felt the way she did probably would have sentenced her to minimum time."[83] The elation soon quieted. The Dus were devastated by Reiner's public pronouncement to appeal the sentence. They had hoped that their legal troubles had ended when Soon Ja walked out of the courtroom that November day. Lloyd labeled Reiner's outcry as one of a desperate elected official pandering to his voter base and "throwing kerosene" on an incendiary situation.[84]

In the weeks following Du's release, her husband Billy was able to rally friends, fellow church members, and some extended family to provide continued financial and moral support. The larger Korean business community, however, was split in their feelings about the case. Many openly blamed the Dus for not trying harder to get along with their black customers and Soon Ja Du in particular for shooting Latasha. Others publicly supported Soon Ja Du and Karlin's sentencing, criticizing those Koreans who did not. Jerry Yu of the Korean American Coalition, for example, announced he was glad that Du received a lenient sentence.[85] Marcia Choo, director of the Asian Pacific American Dispute Resolution Center, received death threats when she publicly announced that she believed Du's sentence was too mild and that Du should not have shot Latasha.[86] When Kim Bong Hwan, working with the Black-Korean Alliance, took a stand against the discretionary sentencing power of judges like Karlin, some members of the Korean community lashed out in menacing phone calls and ugly newspaper stories: "Who is this Kim Bong Hwan anyway, a Korean or a nigger?" one read.[87] Others in the Korean community, especially those invested in small shops located in black communities, extended their sympathy to the Harlins family, their friends, and supporters, but they denied that it was a racially charged incident. Yang Il Kim, president of the national Korean-American Grocers Association, for example, was quick to reiterate the "cultural differences" between African Americans and Korean/Korean-Americans, but then proposed that Latasha's shooting was an "isolated incident, without racial overtones."[88] But there was no convincing black people otherwise. Joseph Duff of the NAACP quite pointedly asserted the issue of race. "I think one cannot ignore," he said, "the racial aspects of the incident."[89]

The larger Asian American community probably understood how African Americans felt. After all, they had felt similarly when members of their communities had been killed by persons of other races and received extremely light sentences from the court. Few could forget the 1982 murder of 27-year-old Vincent Chin in Detroit by two white assailants who attacked Chin because they believed he was Japanese and resented the growing Japanese dominance in the auto industry. Neither served time in jail or paid the judgment in the civil suit.[90] So devastating was that case that many believed it inspired a national consciousness among Asian Americans. "Before Vincent Chin," Henry Der, who was executive director of the Chinese for Affirmative Action organization in San Francisco, noted, "people dealt with hate violence at the local level. But Vincent Chin galvanized the political consciousness among Asian

Americans . . . The lack of a meaningful penalty for the murder was egregious. It was something that could not be ignored."[91] Many in the Korean American community might not have thought that Latasha's death was as a result of a hate crime, but those who spoke out publicly against Karlin's sentencing did believe that Soon Ja Du should have served jail time.

Members of the Harlins family were so upset in the days following the sentencing hearing that only Denise appeared in public to convey their feelings. In a December 5 interview with the *Los Angeles Sentinel*, Latasha's aunt's raw emotion was on full display. The judge, she asserted, was "stupid" and an "idiot."[92] Certain now that they could rely on no one but themselves to acquire justice, Denise vowed to fight on until Du was behind bars. The Latasha Harlins Justice Committee was right by her side and was determined to keep the issue before the public in numerous ways. They began with picketing Karlin's court at least once a week, every week, and outside her Manhattan Beach home, as well as at places where she appeared publicly. Joyce tried to avoid them, but that proved difficult. Initially, she was able to get a restraining order to keep the LHJC 500 feet away from her home, but in January 1992, Los Angeles Superior Court Judge Stephen O'Neil overturned it, labeling the original restraining order "an unlawful prior restraint on First Amendment activity."[93] Karlin's husband, Bill Fahey, who was still an assistant US attorney, then asked the Manhattan Beach City Council to enact an ordinance that would ban picketing in front of their home, noting that "politicians, judges or any individuals carrying out the duties of their offices should be afforded such protection." The Council, however, decided to table the matter for the time being, noting that if the protestors disturbed the peace while picketing the Fahey-Karlin home, there were rules and laws already on the books that could handle that situation. Mayor Bob Holmes explained: "We felt we could protect the neighborhood and assure the safety of Judge Karlin and her family without this ordinance. We have not seen at this time a significant problem develop."[94] Karlin certainly was not finding uniform support among her judicial peers or even among the powerbrokers in her residential community. Frustration and anger must have set in as the pressure continued. Husband Bill Fahey was accused of running over the foot of one of the protestors. Members of the LHJC reported in February 1992 that

Fahey ran over a protestor's foot at a home in Bel-Air where a fund-raiser for Judge Karlin's reelection campaign was occurring. Members of the committee asked the LAPD to open an investigation into the incident after police at the scene purportedly refused to act. Fahey denied that he had done anything wrong, asserting instead that one of the protestors had kicked his car when he pulled in the driveway to pick up his wife.[95]

The protests were moderately successful in keeping the question of justice for Latasha in the public eye. Less public campaigns were mounted to keep Soon Ja Du from leaving the country to visit South Korea. They also traveled to Washington D.C.to petition the Justice Department to file civil rights violation charges against Du. The LHJC, however, was clear that Soon Ja was not the only person who had harmed Latasha. They held Karlin equally accountable for the justice that had been denied them and their loved one. They shifted their attention back and forth from the woman who shot Latasha to the woman who had let the convicted felon off without a jail sentence. The LHJC and other activists involved in the case mounted a tremendous effort to remove Karlin from the bench. They organized two recall measures and sponsored opponents in the election in which Karlin had to run to maintain her office.[96]

In the meantime, the violence between blacks and Koreans in South Central continued. On November 21, less than a week after Du's sentencing, a Korean shopkeeper in South Central shot an unarmed black man who ran into his store to seek shelter from a drive-by shooting. The store owner claimed that he thought the man wanted to rob him. Police investigating the case believed the proprietor, calling the incident a reasonable "mistake." According to Police Lieutenant Bruce Hagerty, the shopkeeper believed he was about to be robbed.[97] Danny Bakewell, among other activists involved in the protest of the Du sentencing, was quick to link the two cases together. "There are merchants operating in our community who see a gang member, or a life that is not worth valuing, behind the face of every black man, woman and child who goes into his store," Bakewell argued. "They don't see hard-working men and women. They see criminals, and they are reinforced by the attitude of Judge Karlin."[98] City Councilwoman Rita Roberts, who is African American, wondered "if the shopkeeper's reaction would have been the same if whites had run into his store instead."[99]

Still, the Korean community wanted to place the shooting in a different kind of context. They wanted the public to understand the tremendous fear most shopkeepers felt toward their customer base, a fear they asserted that was well warranted. Charles Park, chairman of the Korean Crime Task Force, noted, for example, that 15 Korean-born merchants had been killed in the Los Angeles area in the previous 18 months. "This is such unfortunate timing," Park added. "I hope that this doesn't fuel the tension. But from the standpoint of the Korean merchant, I think it is very understandable."[100]

What Park did not know, however, was that that number of victims was about to increase, along with incidences of violence initiated on both sides. Less than two weeks later, on December 4, two black men attacked an Asian woman who was seated in her car at a Compton intersection. Wielding a baseball bat, they broke out her windows and pulled her from the car. Her face and neck were cut from the glass fragments, but she survived the attack. When Joe Duff of the NAACP shunned the attack, some Compton residents, numbering about 15, along with their City Councilwoman Patricia Moore, heckled him. One Compton businessman also told Duff: "You do not live here and you cannot speak for us."[101] Ten days later, two black men shot and killed 46-year-old Paul Park, who had owned the Superior Liquor store, just south of Koreatown, for ten years. It was not certain whether the men had meant to rob Park or just to murder him. Witnesses said the men came into the store at about 6 p.m. and shot Mr. Park five times, leaving the dying man with bullets in his stomach, arm, and leg.[102] At the same time that the Korean grocer community seemed under attack, a Korean grocer in nearby Hawthorne was charged on December 19 with six counts of assault and child endangerment for purportedly attacking a 12-year-old black girl he accused of stealing. Fifty-nine-year-old Wha Young Choi, proprietor of Don's Market, supposedly attacked Keisha Williams for stealing candy, leading to protests at his store. Keisha asserted that Choi hit her in the lower lip and kicked her in the stomach. Memories of Latasha were not about to fade away.[103]

The California Appeals Court Weighs In

District Attorney Ira Reiner made good on his promise to appeal Du's sentence before the California Court of Appeals (Second District, Division Five) in March 1992. At the time that he explained his decision in the press, Reiner admitted that he believed his efforts were a "long shot," but that Karlin's "illegal sentence" had to be addressed. "It is virtually unheard of for a person who engages in an intentional killing and is convicted of voluntary manslaughter to walk scot-free with probation," Reiner said. "The sentence is wholly inappropriate for the conduct that was involved," he reiterated.[104] Reiner was correct in assuming that his was an uphill battle. Most jurists and legal scholars agree that judges have broad discretion in sentencing, and appeals courts usually act to protect that discretion. Moreover, even if he were successful before the appeals court, they would still send the case back to Judge Karlin to reassess her original sentence. The Court of Appeals could not actually remove her power to sentence Du.

Reiner pushed forward with the appeal even though his efforts became a point of attack his opponents used in his upcoming electoral race. In a January 1992 article in the *Los Angeles Times,* for example, Gil Garcetti, Reiner's major opponent in the race, was relentless. He described the district attorney's actions vis-à-vis Judge Karlin as a political trick and abuse of power. Garcetti admitted that he too disagreed strongly with Karlin's sentence, but it was the responsibility of Reiner, as district attorney, to maintain positive relations with the courts and this was not the way to do it, he insisted.[105] Reiner, Garcetti added, should not have criticized Karlin openly because it only incensed African Americans, and his derision of Karlin would be interpreted as an attack on judicial discretion, thereby possibly alienating other judges who would hear future cases. Reiner's other opponents for the office were just as critical. Beverly Hills city councilman, former Beverly Hills mayor, and acclaimed author Robert K. Tanenbaum hoped to unseat Reiner on a campaign that centered on the city's growing crime rate, but he also used his campaign platform to describe the district attorney's actions concerning the Du case as outright pandering to the African American community.[106] Another candidate, Sterling Norris, added that Reiner had "crucified" Judge Karlin.[107]

Reiner retaliated by telling a largely black audience at the Inglewood Public Library, at a preelection event cosponsored by the John M. Langston Bar Association and the Black Women's Lawyer's Association, that his opponents in the district attorney race were participating in the "politics of silence" because they refused to address the Du sentence. Reiner noted that his criticism of Karlin's sentence was like John

Kennedy's criticism of the jailing of Martin Luther King. "Gil [Garcetti] has accused me of being political in taking action against Judge Karlin," he explained. "Well that was not political; that was simple justice."[108] William Fahey, Karlin's husband who was then a Republican candidate for Congress, registered similar denunciations of Reiner's assessment of his wife's role in the Du case. Like Garcetti, he accused the DA of "inflaming" the black community. Fahey added that Reiner had no interest in the "healing process," but instead was counting on "racial tension" to assist him with his reelection.[109]

If Reiner was using the Du sentencing controversy to win his election, his tactics did not work. That June, he only garnered 26% of the popular vote, roundly losing the primary election to Gil Garcetti. Reiner bowed out of the run-off election against Garcetti that following September, just one week shy of the first anniversary of the beginning of the trial *People v. Du*.[110]

At the time the case went up for appeal, all parties were represented. Soon Ja Du retained her trial lawyers—Charles Lloyd and Richard Leonard—and obtained the additional services of Richard Rome. Judge Karlin's attorney was Donald Etra. Attorney and judge had similar legal pasts—Etra, like Karlin, had worked in a large firm in Chicago and also in the central California branch of the Justice Department. Etra has since become known as the attorney of such celebrities as Fran Drescher, Snoop Dogg, and Rhianna and has acquired a slew of large corporate clients. He also has maintained, over the years, a significant presence in the local Jewish community, serving on the Board of Directors for the Jewish Community Relations Council and also as vice chair of the United Jewish Fund.[111] Public defenders Wilbur Littlefield, Laurence Sarnoff, and Albert Menaster represented Latasha Harlins's interest. Assistant district attorney Glenn Britton presented the case for the district attorney's Office. Justices Margaret Grignon (who had graduated from Loyola Law School as had Judge Karlin), Herbert Ashby, and Roger Boren presided.[112]

Etra and Britton made most of the presentations before the Court of Appeals. Britton recounted the district attorney's objections to Judge Karlin's light sentencing of Du after she had been convicted of voluntary manslaughter, arguing that the judge had "overstepped her bounds" when she did not assign Soon Ja Du jail time for killing Latasha Harlins.

Britton further explained that Karlin had misinterpreted a California state law that required a prison term for a felon convicted of using a gun for a crime. (At the time of sentencing, Karlin asserted that particular law did not apply to Du because this legislation was not aimed at shopkeepers who kept guns to protect themselves at their places of business.)[113] Britton went on to contend that Karlin had treated the fight between Harlins and Du before the shooting as if *that* were the crime, not Du's shooting of Harlins. He also reminded the jurists that Latasha was walking away from Du when the latter shot her.

Donald Etra countered Britton's accusations by stating forcefully that Judge Karlin had followed "every letter and sub-letter of the law." Etra asserted that it was Latasha who had "provoked" Du who, before her encounter with the teen, had no prior problems with the law. As such, Etra concluded, Du was "not a threat," as Karlin had indicated in her sentencing statement. He conceded that Karlin may have made some errors, but they were not serious enough for the sentence to be altered. Outside the courtroom, Etra reiterated for the press his belief that Judge Karlin's sentence was appropriate, noting that while it was "unpopular" with some factions, "race" had not been an issue. Du's camp indicated that they believed that they would prevail. The LHJC offered a grim assessment through their spokesperson Gina Rae: "I do not feel confident of those three white judges turning against this other white judge."[114] The California Court of Appeals issued its decision on April 21, 1992.[115]

Despite statistics culled from the sentencing records in Los Angeles County for 1990 that indicated that every person convicted of a similar charge as Du had received some jail time, the Second District Court of Appeals unanimously upheld Karlin's sentencing of Soon Ja, citing the judge's right to exercise broad discretion in sentencing.[116] The opinion, authored by Justice Ashby, centered on whether California law mandated Judge Karlin to assign a jail sentence to Du once she had been convicted of a felony with the use of a firearm. Ashby noted that the judge did have room to avoid a mandatory jail sentence "in unusual cases where the interests of justice would best be served if the person is granted probation."[117] It was then up to the appeals court to decide whether *People v. Du* was an "unusual" case and, as a result, if Judge Karlin had abused the power of "discretion." It was the role of this court to decide if Karlin had exceeded "the bounds of reason, all of the circumstances being considered."[118] Ashby noted in particular, perhaps addressing head on Etra's contention that negative public opinion and political manipulation partly motivated Reiner's request for the appeal, that, "It is the duty of the trial court to exercise its discretion unswayed by partisan interest, public clamor, or fear of criticism."[119] After reviewing court transcripts, listening to the arguments of assistant district attorney Britton and attorney Etra, the justices decided that the *People v. Du* case had been "unusual," and Judge Karlin's court "did not abuse its discretion in determining that the statutory conditions for probation were satisfied in this case."[120] And with regard to those statistics that indicated that those convicted of committing a crime with the use of a gun had to serve jail time, Justice Ashby was clear—it was not just the statistics that mattered, but rather the details of the specific case.[121] Judge Karlin's sentence of Soon Ja Du would stand.

Judge Karlin Must Go!

Ira Reiner had predicted correctly the Court of Appeals's decision. Members of the LHJC wanted the district attorney to pursue the issue of Judge Karlin's light sentence of Du to the California Supreme Court. Reiner made no such commitment. Caught up with his upcoming re-election bid, the loss of the equally important case of the Rodney King beating, followed by the momentous events of the Los Angeles riots and rebellion of 1992, which began only eight days after the appeals court affirmed Karlin's sentence of Du, Reiner was under extreme pressure. The LHJC was disappointed, but had not placed all its eggs in one basket. While Reiner was trying to get the sentence overturned before the Court of Appeals, the group had pursued other avenues to "justice." The LHJC had announced a recall effort of Judge Karlin a few weeks after she had pronounced sentence.

The recall effort, like the appeals effort, was a long shot—but they took it. The committee would have to gather 385,162 registered-voter signatures by mid-February if they were to get the measure on the ballot.[122] Official recall papers were sent to Karlin's home in Manhattan Beach where her husband accepted them from a process server.[123] Karlin was up for reelection in June 1992, but many members of the Compton community, South Central, and other parts of Los Angeles as well, wanted to send a strong statement of condemnation of the judge by seeking to have her recalled during a special election that would be held before the general June contest. They were trying to recall not only Karlin, but also Los Angeles Superior Court Presiding Judge Ricardo Torres, whom the committee perceived was Karlin's great supporter. Torres, of course, was the most powerful judge on the Superior Court at the time. His recall would be a tall order for the activists to fill.[124]

Two leaders of the recall movement in early 1992 were the Reverend Richard Sanders of the Mount Pilgrim Baptist Church in Compton and Compton City Councilwoman Patricia Moore. Sanders was adamant that the efforts to receive justice for Latasha, that is, jail time for Soon Ja, would not die quickly or easily. "Karlin was hoping this would all blow over," he told a *Los Angeles Times* reporter in early January, "But it won't." Sanders's congregation was 1,200 members strong, and he used his pulpit to remind his church members weekly of the injustice.[125] Patricia Moore was certain that recall was what her constituents wanted, and what many throughout the city at large wanted. And it was clear that Moore wanted to please her constituents. The FBI secretly recorded her confessing that she hoped Karlin would be recalled, but she personally needed to "keep the issue alive until election" in order to "have more notoriety and more publicity" than her rivals.[126] Moore reported that she received between 50 to 100 calls each day concerning Karlin's sentencing of Du. These calls, she made clear, did not come only from traditionally black and Latino communities, but from across the city, including the Westside, Hollywood, and the San Fernando Valley.[127] Kerman Maddox reiterated Sanders's assertion that the controversy surrounding Karlin's actions would not be soon forgotten. It was part of a trend he insisted that included Rodney King's beating and KKK President David Duke's run for political office. "This is a people's protest," Maddox asserted, a fire that is "going to keep on burning."[128] "No black person will get justice with her on the bench," a local black woman shopping on Compton Boulevard added.[129]

According to Al Martinez, a *Los Angeles Times* reporter, blacks in Compton regarded Joyce Karlin as a "Barbie doll judge" whose light sentence for Du was an act of racism.[130] The image of Barbie, of course, pointed to gendered biases of female professional incompetence. Karlin's economic status and physical attributes—long, curly blonde hair; petite stature; and immaculate dress—all played into this sexist image. Lost, at least for the moment, was her Jewish ethnicity that might have conjured up other stereotypes that those hostile to her position on Du might have tried to utilize to their advantage in the public discourse. Karlin's change of hair color (from dark brown to blonde) erased her ethnicity; blacks saw her as "just white." She was, in their imagination, a racist, blonde bimbo.[131]

Despite the LHJC's best efforts and garnering more than 200,000 signatures, the recall petitions still lacked the 300,000 plus names needed. With this recall measure unsuccessful, community members switched gears to focus on Judge Karlin's upcoming election and, that failing, to mount a second recall initiative.

By the time the June 1992 county-wide elections that would seal the professional fate of district attorney Reiner and Superior Court Judge Joyce Karlin took place, the Los Angeles riots already had occurred. The Latasha Harlins case remained central to all these events. The three opponents Judge Karlin faced all argued that her sentence of Du proved that she was unfit to serve as a Superior Court judge. The outcome of this case, they confessed, was the principal reason why they were trying to take her seat.

Of the 82 Superior Court elections with incumbents that were held in Los Angeles County that June, Judge Karlin's seat was the only one contested. Many compared the attempt to unseat her with that of another famous jurist six years prior—California's first female Supreme Court Chief Justice, Rose Bird, who had been ousted in the 1986 election because of her anti-death-penalty stance.[132] While there was not a great deal of public discussion in the Jewish community regarding Karlin's decision in the Du case, Marlene Adler Marks, then managing editor of the *Jewish Journal of Greater Los Angeles*, suggested that the Jewish community support Karlin in her reelection campaign because she was Jewish, even though Marks personally felt that Karlin had been too lenient when she sentenced Soon Ja Du. Certainly members of the Jewish community, and that of the Korean, contributed financially to her bid for reelection and in her fight against the recall mounted by the LHJC. But these were not the only communities that did so, and even these groups were not united behind Karlin.[133] The judge faced three opponents whose race and gender helped frame the election: Donald Barnett, European American, was a personal injury attorney in tony Century City; Thomasina Reed, African American, was an Inglewood School Board member and family law attorney; and Deputy Attorney General Robert Henry, who also was African American.[134]

As the race intensified, so too did the efforts to unseat Judge Karlin. She became, as some observing these events noted, a symbol of power and oppression that blacks should challenge. They could "find power at the ballot box by removing her from office."[135] While the vast majority of the black community seemed opposed to Judge Karlin, her defeat was not guaranteed. Some constituents in Los Angeles may have agreed with the way in which Karlin handled the Du-Harlins case, particularly those in the merchant class. Others undoubtedly were affected by the Los Angeles riots that occurred barely a month before, finding new appreciation for a judge who had stood up to public and political criticism from large factions of the black community—a community now viewed as the perpetrators of the deadliest and costliest riot in US history. They also may have been influenced by the California Court of Appeals' decision not to have Du resentenced—a decision that had been announced only weeks before. Still, the legal community could not seem to make up its mind regarding Karlin. The Los Angeles County Bar Association's Judicial Evaluation Committee, for example, certainly sent a mixed message about Judge Karlin's qualifications, giving her a "qualified" rating, not the usual "very qualified" stamp of approval that most incumbents received. But another branch of the Bar, the Los Angeles County Bar Association's Criminal Justice Section had awarded, on May 21, Joyce Karlin the "Trial Judge of the Year" title and Charles Lloyd, Soon Ja Du's attorney, "Trial Attorney of the Year" title, in a clear statement of support for their part in the Du trial.[136] Denise Harlins and other members of the LHJC placed themselves strategically at the Biltmore that evening to protest the outcome of the awards ceremony. "All you people sitting, applauding over a child killer," Harlins yelled, at one point while the ceremony was in full swing. "Latasha was defenseless. She didn't do nothing!"[137]

Despite what seemed a conflicted attitude about Judge Karlin's performance as a jurist, the Bar was clear concerning her opponents. They deemed only one qualified—Deputy State Attorney General Robert

Henry. Henry, who held a BA from Berkeley and a law degree from Harvard, had been in the Attorney General's Office for 18 years and distinguished himself from his opponents by emphasizing that he was the only qualified candidate. Henry also was very open about his reasons for running—he wanted Judge Karlin off the bench. She had, in his estimation, rendered an "abysmally stupid," sentence of Du. Henry had the endorsement of Rep. Maxine Waters (D-Los Angeles) and Mervyn M. Dymally (D-Compton).[138] The Bar labeled both Thomasina Reed and Donald Barnett unqualified. The former because they believed she had demonstrated difficulty in working cooperatively with others, which the Bar noted was central to being an effective judge. Reed countered that she had been deemed difficult because of the racist and sexist contexts in which she often worked. She even referenced embattled Oklahoma Law School professor and sexual harassment accuser, Anita Hill, when speaking of the difficulties she (Reed) had as a legal professional working in a world largely occupied by European American men. Despite the Bar's rating, attorney Reed garnered the endorsement of Compton City Councilwoman Patricia Moore, because of Reed's proven connection to Los Angeles's black community. She lived on the Southside and had worked with Moore on the Judge Karlin recall initiative.[139] Denise Harlins also personally wanted to support Thomasina Reed, but the Latasha Harlins Justice Committee chose Donald Barnett instead, even though the Bar found Barnett unqualified because of his lack of experience and legal knowledge. The reason for the LHJC's decision ironically echoed the LHJC's own racial and sexual bias—Barnett, they argued, had a better chance of beating Judge Karlin because he was white and male.[140]

Judge Karlin campaigned strenuously, spending about $150,000—most of it on a statement she had published and television appearances that focused on the importance of an independent judiciary. Joseph Cerrell of Cerrell Associates devised Karlin's campaign strategy. The public relations firm took full advantage of the controversy surrounding the Du case to gain access to free media coverage for Karlin. According to Cerrell, the firm devised a carefully scripted media blitz that focused on Karlin's insistence on judicial freedom—freedom from public opinion, voter intimidation, and prosecutorial backlash. Cerrell bet that if the larger voting public saw the entire videotaped incident between Latasha and Soon Ja, followed immediately with a long interview with

Karlin about her decision in the case, they would see it her way. She was featured in six long newspaper interviews, and she was seen on one major network (NBC) and 15 local and ethnic television news programs in one night. According to Cerrell, this kind of media coverage for a candidate of a county judgeship was unprecedented and garnered Karlin tremendous advantage.[141] In her statement that appeared in the *Los Angeles Times* just before the election, Karlin defended her sentencing of Du, which she characterized as "well within legal and judicial guidelines," and one which the California Court of Appeals had supported. Judges, she insisted, should not have to render "politically correct" decisions.[142] Donald Barnett spent slightly less money on his campaign than Karlin, but Reed and Henry only spent about $10,000 each.[143]

Despite their best, albeit split, efforts, Judge Karlin won 50.7% of the popular vote, retaining her seat on the bench. Her closest competitor, Deputy Attorney General Bob Henry won 24.7% of the vote. Thomasina Reed managed to get 14.9%, and Donald Barnett, the candidate that the LHJC chose to support, received the fewest votes—only 9.9%.[144] Election observers noted that Karlin's win was due both to substantial support in the white Angeleno community and to a lack of voter turnout in the black community.[145] The county seemed to vote along racial lines. In the areas with the largest percentage of white voters, for example, Karlin won substantial voter support in the four-way race, and, correspondingly, a very low percentage of the vote in those areas with a large number of black voters. Comparing the three areas with the largest white voter registration versus the three areas of the county with the largest black voter registration, Judge Karlin secured 57%, 59%, and 61% of the white vote compared with only 7%, 11%, and 21% of the black vote.[146] Judge Karlin trumpeted her success as a win for judicial independence and keeping a "small, vocal minority" from imposing its "will on the majority," a message she had repeatedly invoked during her campaign. Karlin also labeled her win as a result of "rational judgment." She concluded, "Justice was not for sale, and never would be."[147]

Judge Karlin's supporters took to the offensive, publicly calling for the furor over her sentencing of Du, personal criticism of the judge, and efforts to recall her to end. Angeleno Walter Kennedy, for example, wrote a letter to the *Los Angeles Times* a week after the election, extolling the virtues of Judge Karlin and congratulating her determination not to waiver in the face of public criticism from "some" in the African American community who "didn't get exactly what they wanted." He believed Karlin was a "very literate, sensitive and caring" person who should be a judge.[148] Roxanna Fransconi wrote that she believed Judge Karlin had made "a wise decision" in her sentencing of Du and voted accordingly.[149]

Of course, many disagreed. Mark Oliver, for example, wrote to the *Times* to describe Karlin as having "no remorse, no understanding, no compassion," for the Harlins family and not valuing the life of a black person.[150] Brenda Bankhead wrote to the *Times* as well, perhaps in a not too veiled allusion to Karlin's Jewish ethnicity, comparing the plight of African Americans with those of Jews in Nazi Germany. Emphasizing Karlin's use of coded racial language to refer to blacks ("vocal minority") in her campaign and criticizing what the judge had labeled as a majority versus a minority, Bankhead asked the burning question—what majority was being silenced or undermined by what minority? She reminded Karlin that *the jury* had found Du guilty of voluntary manslaughter—a jury that represented the majority of people in Los Angeles—not a "vocal" black minority. Bankhead went on to note that she was glad that blacks had spoken out against what they believed was an act of racist judicial authority in the case of Karlin's sentencing of Du. "The Jewish people of Nazi Germany were a minority, a silenced one," she added, "and look what happened to them."[151]

Black leaders, including Compton City Councilwoman Patricia Moore and Brotherhood Crusade leader Danny Bakewell, bemoaned Judge Karlin's win, but were ready to continue the fight. They, along with the Latasha Harlins Justice Committee, began a new recall movement almost immediately. Gina Rae, the spokesperson for the LHJC, was clear—she would never consider Judge Karlin the "winner." The LHJC would continue their tireless efforts to remove Karlin from the bench and to have Soon Ja Du serve jail time for murdering Latasha.[152]

While the committee planned its next move on Judge Karlin, they also put other strategies in play that they hoped would reap some form of justice. They contacted the Justice Department to try to convince them to charge Soon Ja Du with a violation of Latasha's civil rights—the same strategy that eventually led to the conviction and prison sentences of the defendants in the Rodney King beating case. They also requested that the Justice Department not allow Soon Ja Du to travel to Korea while they were deciding potential charges. In January 1992, Linda K. Davis, who was chief of the criminal section of the Justice Department's Civil Rights Division, requested that the LA Superior Court, which was considering Du's application to return to her homeland while on probation, not allow her to do so during Davis's investigation of possible civil rights violations in the murder of Latasha. Billy Du explained that they wanted to go back to Korea for a while to escape the continuous telephone harassment they received. The constant threats, he noted, had kept his wife from being able to rest or eat.[153]

The LHJC also tried to raise enough money to purchase the Empire Liquor Market, the site where Latasha was killed. They planned to purchase the building, assessed at around $680,000, from the California Korea Bank and to turn it into a youth center named for Latasha.[154] The committee also continued their protests against Judge Karlin in front of the courthouse where she worked. Karlin no longer worked in Compton, but instead at the Edmund D. Edelman Juvenile Courthouse in Monterey.

It was true that Joyce Karlin had won her election and a new six-year term in June 1992, but in January 1992, only two months after she had sentenced Du, Presiding Judge Ricardo Torres assigned her to the Juvenile Dependency Court, thus removing her from hearing criminal cases of adults. His action, of course, raised suspicion that Torres either had bowed to pressure to remove the controversial Karlin from the spotlight, or that he, too, had been dissatisfied with how Judge Karlin handled the Du case and symbolically demoted her. When queried about the transfer, Judge Karlin responded that she always had wanted to work in the juvenile justice system.[155] Whatever the reasons for her leaving the criminal court system, the LHJC still wanted her off the bench, any court bench, and by the fourth of July of 1992, they already had gained 10,000 of the 385,162 signatures needed on the petition to place a recall measure for Judge Karlin on the November 1992 ballot. Karlin responded to the effort by asserting that it was divisive, incendiary, and a waste of the taxpayer's money.[156]

The second recall effort, like the first, did not use any taxpayer's money, because it also failed. So too did the effort to get the Justice Department to file civil rights charges against Du. The LHJC also was not able to purchase the Empire Liquor Market. While the siblings of Latasha were awarded a reported $300,000 (they had sued for several million) in the civil suit against the Dus (paid by their insurance company), there certainly was not enough money privately among the Harlins family for the purchase, and the committee had not been able to raise the substantial amount necessary.[157] There would be no youth center bearing Latasha's name. The LHJC continued their efforts to publicize the "injustice" of Du's sentence, marking Latasha's birthday and the day of her murder with marches in front of Soon Ja Du's house, outside of Judge Karlin's court-room, and sometimes at her Manhattan Beach home as well. Four years after Latasha's passing, aunt Denise was still protesting. When asked when she would stop appearing at Soon Ja Du's home, Denise Harlins's reply emphasized her resolve to never stop. "I come here to make sure that the injustice is never forgotten and Latasha is never forgotten," she answered.[158]

Not that black youth in South Central or throughout the county and beyond would forget. Latasha's story lived on in the lyrics of such famed rappers as Ice Cube and Tupac Shakur. Ice Cube's "Black Korea," released in 1991, a few months after Latasha's death, was an angry rap ballad that accused Korean merchants in black neighborhoods of being greedy and racist—attitudes that could lead to violence, boycotts, or the destruction of their shops: "So pay respect to the black fist / or we'll burn your store right down to a crisp."[159] Using lyrics that directly related the story of Latasha Harlins and the community's response to her death (Soon Ja Du's accusa-tion that Latasha was stealing, the pounding of Latasha's fist on Soon Ja, the subsequent boycott, and threat to burn the store down), Ice Cube summa-rized Latasha's community's understanding of what had occurred, despite Judge Karlin's lenient sentencing of Du. Tupac Shakur dedicated his video of "Keep Ya Head Up" to Latasha.[160] His rap song was meant to honor and support girls and women struggling in poor neighborhoods. It was released to great critical and fan acclaim in 1993, peaking at number seven on Bill-board's Hip-Hop chart and number twelve overall.[161] In Shakur's famed "Hellrazor," released a year after his murder in 1996, and five years after Latasha lost her life, Tupac reignited the community's memory of Latasha and her tragic loss. There he actually speaks her name, memorializing her in an entire stanza in which she dies at the hands of "busta girl," Soon Ja Du. Shakur's "Hellrazor," fundamentally, is a prayer to God to help him, Latasha, and others to escape the violence of "life in the ghetto, do or die."[162]

For the famed rapper and so many members of his audience, the memory of Latasha was still deeply felt—a "little girl" whose death was a murder that should not have happened: "Dear Lord if ya hear me, tell me why / Little girl like LaTasha, had to die."[163] Tupac also mentioned Latasha in three other songs: "Something 2 Die 4 (Interlude)," in which he reminds his audience, "Latasha Harlins, remember that name . . . 'Cause a bottle of juice is not something to die for"; "Thugz Mansion," and "That's Just the Way It Is." In the latter, Shakur linked Latasha's death with the Rodney King beating and other cases in which he asserts blacks were denied justice because of the low value placed on black life: "Tell me what's a black life worth / A bottle of juice is no excuse, the truth hurts / . . . Ask Rodney, Latasha, and many more."[164] Tupac Shakur's tribute songs to Harlins have become part of his creative and political legacies, have been on his albums that went multiplatinum, and were rereleased multiple times after his death.[165]

Other artistic tributes have included theater pieces performed locally and the one-woman theatrical show, *Twilight*, written, performed, and later published by Anna Deavere Smith.[166] There also remain memorials to Latasha Harlins that have taken advantage of internet developments since her death: a Latasha Harlins Memorial Page on Myspace; a Facebook page bearing her name; and a blog on Tumblr featuring videos of persons discussing her death and their sense of injustice, as well as connecting hers to more recent deaths of black children—such as that of Trayvon Martin, shot and killed by George Zimmerman in Sanford, Florida, on February 26, 2012—and the reluctance of the criminal justice system to render "justice."[167] A different memorial page was posted on "Lipstick Alley" to commemorate the 20th anniversary of Harlins's death. There, a series of public comments indicate that the case, the sense of injustice associated with it, and the case's link to the 1992 Los Angeles riots have not been forgotten.[168]

Images and Intersections

Clearly the lives and experiences of Judge Joyce Karlin, Soon Ja Du, and Latasha Harlins depict a complex of hierarchies that traditionally, or historically, have privileged some at the expense of others. Indeed, in an urban arena such as Los Angeles, purportedly the most "culturally

diverse" city in the United States at the time of Latasha's death, and perhaps even more so now, racial/ethnic, class, cultural, generational, and
gender diversity have meant an unequal distribution of resources and
power, deeply affecting the quality of one's life experiences and expectations. It also can immensely affect the quality of one's justice.

The case of the *People of California v. Soon Ja Du* holds important
symbolic and real implications for one's understanding of female social
status and relationships in contemporary urban society, particularly
their relationships to power and their use of power in relation to one
another. As a wealthy, relatively young, European American (Jewish)
judge, Joyce Karlin certainly sat at the pinnacle of the hierarchies located
within this case. She had the racial and cultural affiliation, the class
status, the education, and the occupation to place her in the position,
literally, to judge two women whose lives and communities were very
different from hers. Once a jury of Soon Ja Du's peers returned a guilty
verdict for voluntary manslaughter, Judge Karlin had the state's relegated authority to render justice in the form of sentencing the defendant. In terms of their power relationships, Judge Karlin clearly had the
upper hand. Several relevant questions emerge from this scenario; two
of them addressed here: What were the underlying influences weighing
on Joyce Karlin's sentencing of Du? And how, if at all, did they relate to
significant social variables?

Although Judge Karlin's critics immediately branded her sentencing
"racist," some even resorting to the sexist epithet of Barbie judge as a
reference to her physical attributes and what they believed was her professional incompetence, it is important to investigate fully how gender,
class, culture, and generation "intersected" with race and figured into
her decisions about the case.[169] Judge Karlin probably would eschew any
such analysis. She openly chastised deputy district attorney Roxane
Carvajal for bringing the race issue into the case during her sentencing
speech. "It is not a time for rhetoric," she snapped in response to Carvajal's contention that Karlin's sentencing of Soon Ja Du would have implications on local race relations. "To suggest that any sentence that this
court might give results in the conclusion that young black children
don't receive full protection of the law—I'm sorry, Miss Carvajal but
that is dangerous rhetoric, and that is unjustified." Karlin then added,
"Justice is never served when public opinion, prejudice, revenge or

unwarranted sympathy are considered by the sentencing court in attempting to resolve the case."[170] As far as Judge Karlin was concerned, she had clear, legally established reasons to place Soon Ja on probation, and none of them had to do with race, or for that matter class, gender, or any other variable found outside the law.[171]

The judge's statement at the time of sentencing that exposed the bare bones of her judicial decision-making, however, suggest otherwise. Recall from previous discussion of the sentence that Judge Karlin brushed aside with one broad sweep that sector of public pressure that insisted she sentence Du jail time. Instead, she assured the public that Soon Ja Du "will be punished for the rest of her life" because she will have to live with the memory of the crime, "every day of her life." Moreover, "no matter what sentence is imposed . . . Mrs. Du will not be able to make up for the loss of Latasha Harlins." The judge then asserted that society did not "need" Mrs. Du to be "incarcerated in order to be protected," because Soon Ja Du was not a "danger to society," she was not a "criminal." Rather, Karlin explained, Du was a shopkeeper who "lawfully" possessed a gun for her "own protection," and only took out the gun to protect herself from Latasha who had beaten her. Finally, Karlin surmised, Du's "participation" in the crime that led to her conviction only occurred because of "circumstances of great provocation, coercion and duress" and because of the "hairpin" triggered gun.[172]

Judge Karlin never spoke directly of Soon Ja Du's race or ethnicity, culture, class, age, or gender as considerations in her sentencing. Yet a close reading of her comments at the time of sentencing, along with an interview the judge gave after the case was terminated, suggests that she was influenced by these factors in determining Du's basic character and potential criminality. These variables also distinguished the ways in which Joyce Karlin perceived Soon Ja Du's actions vis-à-vis Latasha Harlins's and the manner in which she regarded Latasha's character and actions regarding Du. Karlin explained, for example, that Soon Ja Du's "vulnerability" and "victimization" helped shape her decision not to send her to jail. When one investigates why the judge viewed Du, rather than Harlins—the decedent—as the vulnerable victim, then gendered, racist, class, and culturally derived notions of difference between Du and Harlins surface. In her interview with the most prominent local black newspaper, the *Los Angeles Sentinel* in March 1991, Judge Karlin entertained questions about victims's rights.

REPORTER: What is your feeling about victims' rights? You seem to be a little bit more concerned about the defendant than Latasha Harlins.

KARLIN: I have to be. It's not a little bit more. I have to deal with things before me. Victims' rights takes on all sorts of things. . . . I feel very, very strong about victims' rights. But those are victims who are here. Victims for whom something can be done. Victims who have their rights, their needs, and they need the system to protect them and to work with them. Victims who have competing interests . . . If you've got a victim who is dead, you've got to look at who's before the court.[173]

In this interview with the *Sentinel*, Karlin argued that she dismissed Harlins's victimization and her family's concerns for justice because Latasha was "dead" and nothing could be done to bring her back. Soon Ja Du and her family, on the other hand, still needed her "protection" because they were the ones "before" her court. Yet, the judge's actual statement at the time of sentencing points to other reasoning. In that text, Karlin made clear that she did not consider Latasha Harlins to be a victim. As such, any justice she fashioned would necessarily exclude Harlins's victimization. In Karlin's estimation, Latasha was largely responsible for maneuvering her own tragic end. She was the violent perpetrator who set out to victimize Soon Ja Du and, while doing so, was accidentally shot. Karlin told the court, for example, that in "deciding whether or not probation is appropriate" for Du she had to "determine the vulnerability" of the "victim." "Although Latasha Harlins was not armed with a weapon at the time of her death," the judge concluded, "she had used her fists as weapons just seconds before the shooting." Elaborating on her denial of Harlins's status as a victim, Karlin added:

The District Attorney argues that Latasha Harlins was justified in her assault on Mrs. Du. Our courts are filled with cases which suggest otherwise. Our courts are filled with the defendants who are charged with assault as a result of attacks on shopkeepers, including shopkeepers who rightfully or wrongfully accuse of . . . shoplifting.

Had Latasha Harlins not been shot and had the incident which preceded the shooting been reported, it is my opinion that the district attorney would have relied on the videotape and Mrs.

Du's testimony in making a determination whether to prosecute Latasha Harlins for assault. (Author's emphasis added).[174]

Karlin's perception of Latasha resonates soundly with historical views of the black female other. The image of black women as victims has never been largely accepted in this society, particularly in relation to other women.[175] Even the more positive depictions of the African or African American female in America (among blacks as well as among others) have emphasized "masculine" qualities—strong, aggressive, productive— qualities which vigorously deny claims of female vulnerability or victim- ization. The black female is more likely thought of as the black beast or brute herself, as in Karlin's depiction of Latasha, rather than as a victim of brutalization.

Despite the jury's conviction of Du on voluntary manslaughter charges, therefore, Judge Karlin repeatedly underscored her belief that Soon Ja Du was not a criminal and, therefore, should not be treated like one. In Karlin's estimation, she was the victim, not Latasha. In her own words, Karlin described what she had "observed" of Du: she was a "50- year old woman with no criminal history and no history of violence." Karlin then compared her perception of Soon Ja Du with what she had drawn of Latasha from the videotape, Mrs. Du's testimony, and defense lawyers' arguments. In so doing, she concluded that Latasha, unlike Soon Ja Du, was a violent person who had used her violence against Du ("she had used her fists as weapons").[176]

By positing Du as a vulnerable, nonviolent, middle-aged woman, as well as a mother and wife later in her sentencing statement, Judge Karlin exposed some of the basis for her less formalized discretionary "reasoning"— Du's age, gender, and family status had been influential.[177] These traits helped convince Karlin that Du was more victim than criminal. Latasha Harlins's youthful age and physicality, on the other hand, helped Du and her defense attorneys convince Judge Karlin that the 15-year-old was more criminal than victim. During the trial, for example, defense attorney Charles Lloyd insisted on entering Latasha's height and weight into the offi- cial court record. Soon Ja Du was considerably shorter and weighed less than Harlins.

LLOYD: Respectfully inviting your attention to page 3 of the autopsy report, was a determination made as to the weight of the victim?

DR. SOLOMON RILEY: Our investigation determined the . . . weight to
be 152 pounds and height to be 66 inches.[178]

Lloyd succeeded, in Karlin's estimation, in proving that Latasha's
general physical advantage, due to her age and size, contributed to
Du's victimization. So too did the defense team's intimation that Latasha was accustomed to fighting, while Du was not. Under reexamina-
tion of the coroner, Dr. Riley, for example, attorney Lloyd repeatedly
asked Riley about the scars on Latasha's knuckles, inferring that she
was a seasoned fighter.[179] The defense team succeeded in portraying
Latasha Harlins as the young, violent batterer and Soon Ja Du as the
battered, older, female victim. Du's defense attorneys, in fact, used
Harlins's youth and her muscular build to reverse Latasha's gender,
from that of a "girl" to that of a "guy," from a female (the traditional,
vulnerable victim) to a male (the traditional, violent assailant). In his
summation, for example, Richard Leonard pushed Soon Ja Du's
self-defense motive:

> Why did she [Du] take this gun when she went down? Because
> she's in fear of her life, thought the girl was going to kill her if
> the girl punched her two more times. Well, you might say . . . I
> can take a couple of punches . . . Well, maybe the average person
> can. But you have to look at how hard this young lady punched
> Mrs. Du, and you have to look at the age of Mrs. Du, 49, how
> small—how small Mrs. Du is and what was going through her
> mind at that time. I mean, this young lady then punched like a
> 15-year old girl. Take a look at her knuckles. *She punched awfully
> hard, possibly as tough as any guy at the same age.* (Author's
> emphasis added).[180]

Add Latasha's race, class, and culture to Leonard's characterization
of her as a "guy at the same age," and Latasha Harlins is no longer the
vulnerable "child" that District Attorney Roxane Carvajal and the Harlins family and their supporters tried to depict. She became in the mind
of the court, that is, Judge Karlin, the fearsome image of a black, male
teen from South Central Los Angeles so grotesquely criminalized in
contemporary urban society—a violent, black beast so prominent in the
historic depiction of blacks in American society.[181]

FIGURE 6.2 "The Negro A Beast or In the Image of God," cover of the same named book by Charles Carroll, 1900.

This image of poor, black, adolescent, urban born-and-raised Latasha whose mother had died violently and whose abusive father had abandoned the family stood in stark, if not horrifying, contrast to that image which Karlin obviously was convinced was Soon Ja Du—a hardworking, middle-aged immigrant, devoted wife and mother who had pulled herself up to become a respectable businesswoman. Stereotypes embedded in race, class, culture, age, and gender became problematically intertwined and intersected in this case. Popular perceptions of city-dwelling Koreans as the latest Asian model minority and all that entails regarding character, social location, worth, and worthiness of legal protection compared with perhaps even more widespread, and certainly more long-lasting, notions of urban blacks as anything but model, with little social worth and, therefore, hardly worthy of protection from criminal victimization, certainly placed Du in a more favorable position in Karlin's court than Harlins. Discussion of their different class affiliations and cultures—family structure, and lifestyles—served only to reinforce prejudicial ideas about how the two females related to each other on that momentous Saturday morning and how the case about them should be settled.[182]

The labeling of Asian Americans as model minorities, especially in relation to urban African Americans, along with misinformed ideas of the passive Asian in the United States has had the effect of feminizing their image. African Americans in the urban arena, however, historically have conjured up an opposite image—one of brute force, violence, and aggressiveness—that has been crudely characterized as masculine. Black men and women, boys and girls, share in this characterization. Indeed, black women in American society traditionally have been stereotyped by nonblacks as being more like "men" than "women." While both stereotypes manipulate and exploit these racial minorities, each group, and others as well, have used them, mostly against each other, for their benefit. In this particular case, while Latasha became masculinized in the defense attorney's rhetoric, Du's image took on some of the exaggerated feminine characteristics that are part of the racialized gender stereotyping of Asian/Asian-Americans across ethnic lines.

Again, the class differences Du and Harlins represented reiterated the former's femininity and the latter's masculinity. These racist- and class-driven ideas were foundational to the defense's, and subsequently Karlin's, assertions of Soon Ja Du's victimization at the hands of Latasha Harlins. In Judge Karlin's estimation, Du was only defending herself against a real threat, the threat of the vicious, uncontrollable "black beast."[183]

Judge Karlin's statements at the time of sentencing validated Soon Ja Du's perceptions of Latasha as a deadly threat. Like Du, Karlin was not able to distinguish Latasha Harlins from the black male gang members who were terrorizing the Du family. The judge explained in her sentencing statement: "The District Attorney would have this court ignore the very real terror that was experienced by the Du family before the shooting and the fear, whether it was reasonable or unreasonable, but the fear experienced by Mrs. Du on the day of the shooting. But these are things that I cannot ignore."[184]

Culturally, therefore, Latasha was brushed with the same paint as the gangbangers who sometimes frequented the Empire Liquor Market.[185] The defense team had gone to great length to profile most of the store's surrounding black community as potential gang members, thieves, and thugs. Du thought, they argued, that Latasha was a gang member. She dressed like a gang member, they stressed. She fought like a gang member. Culturally, they implied, Latasha was a gang member—violent, unpredictable, criminal, and uncivilized. Du had to protect herself from such a "very real terror." Such conclusions regarding blacks in the courts, law scholar Cynthia Lee notes, is not unusual because blacks are viewed, stereotypically, as criminals. This "Black as Criminal" image allows the court to view a black victim as actually the criminal, "to more readily believe the defendant's claim that he honestly and reasonably believed he needed to act in self-defense."[186] This stereotype, Lee adds, is not just relegated to black men because "Black women are also subject to the Black-as-Criminal stereotype."[187]

Judge Karlin and Soon Ja Du also shared similar ideals about appropriate gender behavior for females, and those ideals excluded Latasha. Explaining her presence at the Empire Liquor Market on March 16, for example, the defendant argued that "as a mother, I felt so terrible that I really felt that I should go and try to help my son." Once there, she was determined to tend the register alone because her husband "was so tired" she "insisted . . . that he could go . . . and get some rest."[188] Karlin was impressed by Soon Ja Du's traditional, middle-class female values, noting in her sentencing statement: "And I cannot ignore the reason that Mrs. Du was in the store that day . . . The Du's son . . . had been the victim over and over of robberies and terrorism in that same store. And on the day of the shooting, Mrs. Du went to work with her husband so that her son would not have to face another day of fear."[189]

Thus, Judge Karlin could add to her already positive female characterization of Soon Ja Du this image of responsible motherhood. There was a connection with Du as a woman that the judge never felt with Latasha. Judge Karlin could not envision Latasha Harlins as more than someone who acted like a violent "gang member." Karlin concluded of her assessment of the two females that "Mrs. Du had led a crime-free life until the day that Latasha Harlins walked into her store."[190] Joyce Karlin's sentencing decision regarding Du seemed to derive from conservative, middle-class notions of female behavior, morality, and victimization. Indeed, some legal experts argue that gender stereotypes often play heavily in every aspect of legal cases that involve females. Elizabeth Stanko, for example, asserts that "stereotypical assumptions about women in general and about their behavior as victims and complainants play a considerable role in the screening of felony arrests."[191] In Judge Karlin's estimation, Latasha Harlins had physically victimized Mrs. Du, causing the shopkeeper to fall from her lofty status as a model minority member and a woman of middle-class respectability. Karlin used her sentencing to right this wrong.

Judge Karlin's images of Latasha Harlins and Soon Ja Du were those argued by the defense. Although the jury, the district attorney, and the probation officer, Patricia Dwyer, clearly were influenced by other criteria and images, their perspectives did not carry the day in the sentencing of Du. One must wonder, therefore, if Judge Karlin would have viewed Latasha as a victim if Roxane Carvajal had devoted more time to crafting a courtroom image of Latasha as the vulnerable, innocent child who was Du's unwitting victim. Unlike defense attorneys Charles Lloyd and Richard Leonard, for example, Carvajal called no character witnesses to support Latasha's image as a victimized child. Lloyd and Leonard called as witnesses on Soon Ja Du's behalf both her son and husband, neither of whom witnessed the shooting. The witnesses asserted to the judge that Soon Ja Du worked in an atmosphere of terror, and that context influenced her actions on March 16, 1991. Their testimonies no doubt went a long way to convince Judge Karlin that Soon Ja had reason to be frightened when she and Latasha began fighting.

Roxane Carvajal tried, with obviously mixed results, to convince the court of Du's guilt and Harlins's psychological and physical victimization. The videotape shows clearly, for example, that Du was the aggressor, she argued. As Latasha approached the counter, Du immediately accused her of stealing—a psychological assault based on racial profiling. Du also was the first to initiate a physical assault—forcefully grabbing the arm of Latasha's jacket as she stood in front of the counter, the district attorney noted. In order to counter the defense's argument that Soon Ja Du acted out of a context of urban black terror, the prosecution would have had to explain that Latasha acted out of a context of Korean shopkeeper persecution. It might have been useful for Carvajal to call witnesses who could attest to the Du family's history of abuse of its customers via racial, class, and generational profiling that resulted in customary hostility, suspicion, and persecution. Latasha's Uncle Richard, for example, detailed the hostile manner in which the Dus routinely treated their black customers and his own psychologically abusive experiences as their employee when interviewed by *Los Angeles Times* reporter Itabari Njeri.[192] Why was he not a witness against Soon Ja Du? The prosecution also had to make a case for Latasha's humanity and vulnerability that countered the defense's image of the black beast and/or brute. The ADA did call on Latasha's grandmother Ruth to speak at the sentencing hearing, but not as a witness who could have presented a fuller, more sympathetic picture of her murdered grandchild. The image of Latasha that emphasized her tragic hardships, admirable dreams, dedication to her young siblings, love of her grandmother, and personal accomplishments was a testimony that Denise Harlins and other members of the LHJC often took to public rallies and journalists. It was a testimony largely absent in the courtroom, because Carvajal called no trial witnesses to attest to these aspects of Latasha's life—not her friends, teachers, fellow church members, or family members. Not surprisingly, the Harlins family won the image war on the street, but Soon Ja Du's defense team won it in the courtroom. Even after the jury found Soon Ja Du guilty of voluntary manslaughter, Du's image victory in the courtroom tipped the scales of justice in her favor—at least in Judge Karlin's estimation.[193]

Indeed, Judge Karlin stood by her sentence of Du. Karlin never publicly repealed her decision in spite of the outcry, violence, and devastation directly linked to it. To the contrary, she has repeatedly defended it. On August 18, 1992, for example, Judge Karlin, in an appearance as guest speaker at the Koreatown Rotary Club, reiterated her belief that her sentencing was fair, and, not coincidentally, that she supported the Simi Valley verdict in the Rodney King incident. Like so many who had taken to the streets to declare "No justice, no peace" in late April 1992, spawning the deadliest and costliest race riot in United States history, Judge Joyce Karlin also understood that the question of justice in Latasha's "contested murder" linked this case to that of Rodney King.

FIGURE 7.1 "Roots of the Riots," Photograph by Kirk McKoy. Courtesy of the *Los Angeles Times*.

7

Whose Fire This Time?

Latasha Harlins . . . remember that name!*

Justice will not be served until those who are unaffected are as outraged as those who are.

—Benjamin Franklin

Every single person in the black community understood, or at least they believed they understood, what justice was in our courts when they saw a young black child being shot in the back of the head and the person being let off with a $500 fine and reimbursement to the family for the price of the funeral.

—Ira Reiner, Former LA District Attorney

Wilbur Thomas, a merchant in South Central Los Angeles, knew something was going to happen. In the meetings and protests following Judge Joyce Karlin's no-jail-time sentence of Soon Ja Du, there was a sense of an inevitable explosion looming. A merchant himself, Thomas must have been concerned that destruction might come to his sector of the South Central economy. "I don't know what it's going to lead to," he explained, "but a lot of people are fired up and they just can't seem to take it anymore."[1] He recalled being terribly upset— what could society expect after such a blatant miscarriage of justice? Five months later, Thomas and millions others had their answer.

Denise Harlins, the public face of the Latasha Harlins Justice Committee, indeed the public face of Latasha, recalled how frightening the actions were around her as the 1992 Los Angeles rebellion and riot exploded. She was on her way to the First African Methodist Episcopal Church (FAME) to give a speech that no doubt would link the injustice of Latasha's case with that of Rodney King's. Stopped along the way by young black men, she was certain she only was allowed to pass because of her race and gender. She was an eyewitness to the rapidly escalating violence and destruction. The "Rodney King issue and Latasha's issue were the reason rioters did what they did," Denise told a reporter ten years later. "People were going buck wild crazy."[2]

How did Denise know Latasha's "injustice" helped fuel the fires? She knew it because people went to her to tell her exactly why they acted. "It was a scary, scary time," Denise recalled. "I heard shooting and saw buildings burned to the ground. All the time, I heard people claim they were acting in Latasha's name."[3] Latasha's aunt became a touchstone for many—they wanted her to know they were acting to gain justice for Latasha. She never asked them to do so. She was committed to fighting the good fight. Unlike the politicians and community organizers, Denise noted, there was nothing in it for her except gaining justice for her loved one. She was fighting for Latasha—staging protest marches, organizing recall petitions, taking trips to the Justice Department, giving speeches, and courting the media. Denise was not going to burn and loot, and she did not want anyone else to do so either. But just as Harlins could not control what happened in Judge Karlin's courtroom the day she passed sentence on Soon Ja Du, Latasha's aunt could not control what happened on the streets of Los Angeles in late April 1992.

Denise Harlins, of course, was not rare in her assessment that the Los Angeles riots and rebellion of 1992 were not just about Rodney King but also about Latasha.[4] A *Los Angeles Times* reporter, after interviewing many Angelenos, noted coolly in an article written a week after the turmoil had begun to subside that "many of the people who burned and the people who watched the burning approvingly would remember three transcendent reasons: Rodney King, Latasha Harlins and Baby." As mentioned earlier, "Baby" was the dog whose Korean owner had been sentenced to jail time in Los Angeles after he was convicted of beating the cocker spaniel at about the same time that Judge Karlin had set Soon Ja Du free after she was convicted of killing

Latasha.[5] Historian Mike Davis believed that Latasha Harlins was a "kind of rallying cry," during the riots, explaining: "The name you heard most frequently on people's lips during the uprising was Latisha [*sic*] Harlins, the 15-year-old black girl killed by a Korean shop owner over a $ 1.79 bottle of orange juice." Sociologists Michael Omi and Howard Winant took Latasha's link to the uprising almost for granted, asserting that "the killing of 15-year-old Latasha Harlins by an L.A. Korean-American grocer in early 1991, and the subsequent handing down of a suspended sentence, served as an immediate prelude to the rioters' assaults on Korean merchants." Lou Cannon—political reporter, White House correspondent, and author of the most detailed monograph on the 1992 Los Angeles riots, added, "When the riots that some blacks called the Uprising erupted . . . the name of Latasha Harlins would be heard in Koreatown." Korean attorney and activist Angela Oh also noted of the uprising: "The disposition of the Latasha Harlins case was a major factor in the targeting of Koreans. Even today [1994] if people in South Central were asked to name one Korean, it would be Soon Ja Du."[6]

Korean and Korean American shopkeepers, reeling from the loss of so many of their businesses, searched for reasons why they had been targeted. The image of Du shooting Latasha, available because the Empire Liquor Market's antitheft video camera captured the event, was on a constant loop, along with the Rodney King beating video, on local and national TV news programs throughout the rebellion.[7] It was the Du video, many surmised, that led to their devastating victimization. Three years later, in 1995, another reporter spoke of the power that Latasha's memory invoked in that unforgettable late April when the second-largest city in America was forced to bring in the National Guard, US Marines, and the US Army to quell what seemed like an unending revolt. Miles Corwin of the *Los Angeles Times* explained that Latasha was a "cause célèbre." The *People v. Du*, Corwin assessed, not only caused tremendous difficulty between the African American and Korean/Korean-American communities but also "contributed to the rage that fueled the 1992 riots." Indeed, he noted, "Latasha's name was invoked by some rioters as they torched buildings in South-Central Los Angeles." Literary scholar and poet Nancy Schriffin concurred, asserting that she believed it was Latasha Harlins's "unpropitiated ghost—fallen before ripening"—that was the source of the riots in Los Angeles." Schriffin even dedicated part of her elegiac poem "Yahzreit" to Latasha and her connection to the riots.

> Los Angeles burning.
> Women, babies on their backs
> grab cans of food from shattered stores . . .
> Throat parched, unprepared to discuss Latasha Harlins,
> Her ghost beside me clutching Bible and bouquet,
> I move to the open doorway, listen
> For Your voice in the rumbling earth, gunshot."[8]

In the interim between 1992 and the rebellion's 15th year anniversary, the popular belief that Karlin's sentencing of Du was instrumental did not diminish. Writing for *Time* magazine in their anniversary coverage, Jesse Singal stated, "In many ways, the shooting death of 15-year-old Latasha Harlins . . . laid the foundation of anger and resentment that would eventually explode after the King verdict."[9] Even 20 years after her contested murder, people still remembered Latasha and the impact that the question of justice surrounding Karlin's sentencing of Du had on the "rage." The Los Angeles riots and rebellion ended in 54 deaths and 2,383 injured. Of those who lost their lives, 41 were killed by gunshot; three burned to death; six died in related car accidents; and four died after being beaten. More than 1,800 injured people flooded local hospitals. Many of the injuries were serious, including 198 gunshot wounds; 57 stab wounds; 17 burns; and more than 400 broken bones, concussions, and serious cuts.[10] The riots also resulted in horrific property loss—an estimated 3,600 fires, 1,100 destroyed buildings, 4,500 businesses looted, damaged, and/or destroyed (approximately 2,300 were Korean owned), and one billion dollars in total damage.[11] Add to these losses the discomfort and dismay of hundreds of thousands of local residents who lost electrical, water, and phone service; the closing of LAX; the loss of bus service to many parts of the city; and major freeway off-ramps closed; to say nothing of the deployment of the various armed services.[12] More than 12,000 persons were arrested.[13] Children were home because all local schools were closed, including some colleges.[14] Los Angeles—as in 1965—was in crisis.

Rodney King and the Question of Justice

Rodney Glen King was born on April 2, 1965, in Sacramento, California, the second child of Odessa and Ronald King, and one of four boys—Gailien, Rodney, Paul, and Juan. The family moved to Altadena when Rodney was a child. King's father, called "Kingfisher" because of his love of fishing, was a strict disciplinarian and a drinker. The combination did not bode well for Rodney who would bitterly recall the whippings his father gave him and his brothers after they had done something "inexcusable." When Mr. King beat him with an extension cord, Rodney remembered that he would scream, "almost passing out from the pain." The beatings were worse when Rodney's father drank—which was often. His mother only succeeded in keeping her husband from striking the boys in their faces; but could not diminish the number or intensity of the whippings her children endured. "The first person I ever hated," Rodney wrote in his autobiography, *The Riot Within*, "was my father."[15]

Like many of the people in their community, Rodney's parents worked hard, mostly as domestics and custodians. The couple cleaned houses in the day and Mr. King worked as a janitor at a medical facility at night. Not surprisingly, King's father believed that his boys should learn how to work early. He took them with him to help clean the medical center at night. Rodney was only eight when he started washing and buffering floors from 7 p.m. to 2 a.m. most nights. His work routine wreaked havoc on his ability to concentrate and succeed in school. Teachers, not knowing of Rodney's physical exhaustion, concluded that he had a learning difference and placed him in special education classes. Rodney recalled the experience as embarrassing and humiliating—one that led to peer teasing, bullying, and low self-esteem. Being labeled learning impaired meant that Rodney could not participate in team sports—an aspect of school life that he really enjoyed. When he finally was allowed to do so in high school, the experience helped his self-esteem recover some, but then he faced his coach's sexual harassment.[16] Those were only some of his early problems.

By the time that Rodney King was 11, he was drinking and on his way to becoming an alcoholic. Drinking, by his own account, made King feel relaxed, happy, in control, charming, and it distanced him emotionally from some of the hatred that he felt "all around" him. King's addiction to alcohol, he believed, was immediate. "I loved to drink from the start," he noted. It was the same addiction that Rodney attributed to his father's life ending at age 42. Rodney also began to smoke marijuana at about the same time he began drinking. But he was not a slacker. Just like his parents and his brothers, Rodney worked—cleaning, valet parking, flipping burgers at McDonald's, and even starting his own tree-trimming business. The financial independence that the money he earned gave him was a source of pride, but it also took him out of school. By the beginning of his high school senior year, Rodney's increasing problems with alcohol, his work schedule, and his frustration with not doing well academically pushed him out. He quit school and married his girlfriend. Within a few months, he was arrested for reckless driving. He also was arrested in July 1987 for domestic abuse, accused of beating his wife. King pled no contest and was given probation and a mandatory counseling regimen, which he did not follow.[17]

Rodney divorced and remarried—this time to a woman who had two sons by a previous marriage. King then had four children—two sons and two daughters. When he was 24, Rodney got into an argument with a shopkeeper in a convenience store in Monterey Park that ended with him being sentenced to two years in prison. The details of the incident that led to King's arrest remain contested by the defendant and his accuser, Tai Suck Baik. Both came to realize that language was a problem—Baik spoke little English and King could not communicate with the shopkeeper in Korean. According to Baik, Rodney tried to rob him—threatening to beat him with an iron rod if he did not cooperate. King disputed Baik's account, asserting that he tried to buy some gum with food stamps. When Baik seemed to refuse to accept the food stamps, the two started arguing. It was Baik, King recalled, who had the tire iron and struck him with it. Rodney claimed he had no weapon and could only deflect Baik's swing by throwing pies from a nearby rack at him. Baik finally caught King and tried to restrain him but was unable to do so. Rodney ran from the store and sped away. Baik, however, told the police that King stole $200 from his cash register before he managed to chase him from his store. When the police came to Rodney's residence ten days later, King told them he was guilty, purportedly because he was embarrassed by the police presence at his home. His lawyer later chastised Rodney for pleading guilty to a crime he did not commit, but by then it was too late. Out on parole after a year, Rodney King was looking forward to starting a new job. Unfortunately, he celebrated by drinking late into the night and then getting behind the wheel of a car with two friends. The rest is "history."[18]

Fifteen police officers, all white, confronted King and his two passengers that early morning on Foothill Boulevard in Lake Terrace. While they supposedly feared that Rodney was a dangerous man, high on PCP, blood tests later proved that King was indeed drunk (his blood alcohol was twice what it should have been), but he did not have any other drug in his system. As for his ability to inflict harm, King was not armed and did not have any weapons in his vehicle. Moreover, none of the policemen at the site seemed to have received any physical harm from their interaction with King. Rodney, on the other hand, sustained such a beating that he had to be hospitalized. The first hospital he was taken to sent him to a trauma center—his injuries were too extensive for them to handle. These injuries, in which the police seemed to have targeted Rodney's head and face, included at least nine skull fractures; a broken leg; a shattered eye socket and cheekbone; a concussion; injuries to both knees; and nerve damage that left his face partially paralyzed for the remainder of his life.[19] "I saw the blood come out of his face," CHP Officer Melanie Singer, who first reported King's speeding violation on the night he was beaten, testified at the Simi Valley trial of four police officers. "I heard the driver [King] scream. There is no doubt in my mind that he [Powell] hit Mr. King repeatedly in the face. I will never forget it to the day I die."[20]

Rodney King's family remembered watching the famous George Holliday videotape of Rodney's beating the next day and feeling sorry for the victim of what seemed liked an illegal police attack. The video took on an entirely different meaning when they realized it was Rodney. King's daughter, Lora King, who was only seven at the time, recalled that she hid in the bathroom crying while her mother "wailed" in front of the television. Visiting him in the hospital, King was hardly recognizable to the girl, and she worried he would die. Candice, Rodney King's eight year old, recounted the great sadness she endured and how her father's subsequent notoriety forced her paternal grandmother, "the glue of the family," to move some 60 miles away to escape public attention.[21]

The LAPD initially charged Rodney King with "felony evading," but later dropped that charge.[22] The Los Angeles Grand Jury indicted Los Angeles police Sergeant Stacey Koon and officers Lawrence Powell, Theodore Briseno, and Timothy Wind on March 14, 1991. They charged Powell, Briseno, and Wind with "assault by force likely to produce great bodily injury and a deadly weapon" and assault "under color of authority." They charged Koon as an accessory. Koon and Powell also faced charges of filing false police reports.[23] Four months later, the California Court of Appeals granted a change of venue for the trial to Simi Valley, a predominantly white community 35 miles from downtown Los Angeles and known to be a locale sympathetic to the LAPD.[24] When the jury for the case finally was impaneled, it was composed of ten whites, one Latino, and one Filipino-American.[25]

Even given the change of trial venue, the racial makeup of the jury, and Rodney King's past criminal record, most still believed that the Holliday video was incontrovertible evidence that the four police officers were guilty. Typically sedate political figures stepped forward to lead the outcry against the actions of Koon, Powell, Briseno, and Wind. Mayor Tom Bradley described the event as the "senseless and brutal beating of a helpless man." President George W. Bush spoke out boldly, noting of the videotaped beating, "It's sickening to see the beating that was rendered. There's no way in my view to explain it away. It was outrageous."[26] Even LAPD Chief of Police Daryl Gates had to admit that: "It was very, very extreme use of force—extreme for any police department in America. But for the LAPD, considered by many to be the finest, most professional police department in the world, it was more than extreme. It was impossible."[27]

What seemed really impossible to most persons was that Koon, Powell, Briseno, and Wind would be found not guilty—but that is precisely what happened on April 29, 1992.[28] Only the charge against Lawrence Powell was not settled, concluding in a hung jury. The federal government already had been investigating the possibility of civil rights violation charges once the criminal case in Los Angeles ended. With their Simi Valley acquittals, the Justice Department moved forward. Rodney King also pursued a number of civil suits—one against the City of Los Angeles and the others against Koon, Powell, Briseno, and Wind individually.

On August 4, 1992, the Justice Department did indict the four Los Angeles police officers for alleged violation of Rodney King's constitutional rights.[29] They charged Wind, Powell, and Briseno with using "unreasonable force" under color of law when they arrested him—a civil rights violation. Sergeant Koon was charged with allowing the other officers to use excessive force when it was his responsibility, as their supervisor, to make certain that King's civil rights were not violated.[30]

This time the case was heard in federal court in downtown Los Angeles. The jury also seemed to most people to be slightly more reflective of Los Angeles's racial diversity than the jury impaneled for the Simi Valley trial—nine whites, one Latino, and two blacks. There were a number of key differences in the presentation of the case against Koon, Powell, Bresino, and Wind as well. One of the most significant changes was that the prosecution called on Rodney King to testify. With King on the witness stand, he could counter the defenses's arguments that they beat him because he refused to be subdued and posed a great threat to them. King testified instead that it was the police officers who kept telling him to get up and to try to run away so that they would have an excuse to hit and taser him. "You better run. We're going to kill you. We're going to kill you, nigger, run!," King swore under oath they continuously yelled.[31] The prosecution also presented evidence that Lawrence Powell actually had, on his way to escorting King to the Los Angeles County-USC Medical Center, taken the beaten, bloodied, and broken King past his Foothill division police station to show off his "handiwork," a stop which Powell inadvertently omitted from his subsequent written report of the arrest.[32]

On April 17, 1993, the federal jury found Sergeant Stacey Koon and Officer Lawrence Powell guilty. Presiding Judge John G. Davies sentenced each to two and a half years in federal prison—the maximum sentence was ten years and a $250,000 fine. Both Officers Briseno and Wind were found not guilty. Many believed that the sentences were too light. Davies, however, explained that out of the 40-plus hits King received, only a few should be categorized as excessive use of force. The judge also spoke of the "humanity" of both Koon and Powell, making note of the prior military service of Koon, his success as a police officer, and his role as a father, while underscoring Powell's strong family support. The judge also suggested that Rodney King had provoked his beating.[33] "The incident would not [have] escalated to this point, indeed, it would not have occurred at all," the judge pronounced, "but for Mr. King's initial conduct."[34]

The Justice Department appealed Judge Davies's sentence, believing that it was too lenient. Two years later, the Ninth Circuit Court of Appeals concurred, and asked Judge Davies to amend his sentences. In 1996, the Supreme Court reversed the Court of Appeals's decision, but still asked Davies to lengthen the sentences. He did not. Stacey Koon and Lawrence Powell spent two years and two months in federal prison (October 1993 to December 1995) for their actions against King.[35]

Rodney King's civil suits against the city of Los Angeles, the four policemen, and their supervisor, Chief Daryl Gates, also wound their way through the courts. Judge John K. Davies, who presided over the federal case, also presided over these civil suits. The city accepted responsibility and decided on a payout of $3,816,535.45. Judge Davies ruled, however, that none of the officers involved in King's beating, or who supervised those involved, should be liable for King's injuries.[36]

Personally, Rodney King and Latasha Harlins did not seem to have much in common. Rodney was 25 years old in 1991; Latasha was only 15. King was born and raised in California; Latasha had migrated from East St. Louis when she was six. Rodney grew up with both of his parents, while Latasha spent only a few years with her parents before her mother's death and her father's abandonment. King had a few scrapes with the law, and actually was a convicted felon, before that fateful March night that the police stopped him. Moreover, Rodney was speeding that night and under the influence of alcohol. Latasha had a fight with Soon Ja Du after she was accused of shoplifting, but all evidence points to her not committing any crime. The money for the orange juice was in her hand. Indeed, she had never had any problems with law enforcement. Soon Ja testified that she believed that Latasha was going to kill her, but the girl was unarmed and eyewitness accounts noted that Latasha never verbalized a threat to Du. Rodney King survived his brutal beating by members of the LAPD. The morning that Soon Ja Du, a private citizen and proprietress, shot Latasha Harlins, she died. More than a year after his beating, the defendants in the King case were found not guilty by a Simi Valley jury. In a downtown Los Angeles courtroom, months before King's trial, Soon Ja Du was found guilty of killing Latasha. On the face of it then, it does not appear that King and Harlins had much in common beyond their race and, of course, the perception that it was indeed their race that had caused them both to be treated unjustly.

The question of justice for a black man and a black girl was the bottom line, but there was much to the backstory. The backstory bound Latasha and Rodney tightly and resonated deeply in the historical consciousness and reality of the black community across class, gender, and generational lines. Latasha was ten years younger than Rodney, but in the eyes of the black community, the two were both young—symbols of a community's savaged past and fragile future. As youth—one a female, the other a male; as members of the working class; and as citizens who had been victimized by persons believed to be more powerful, economically and socially, the black community viewed both Rodney and Latasha as victims whom the criminal justice system had not just failed to protect, but that had indeed contributed to their brutalization—the police in the case of King and the judge in the case of Harlins. The beating of King and the murder of Harlins no doubt resurrected the long, black memory of whippings, lynchings, dismemberment, rapes, and burnings—the "Emmett Till" lens of African American history—that indicted the criminal justice system as not just nonresponsive to black criminal victimization but, more often than not, as also part of that abuse. Harlins and King were linked arm and arm through this bloody history.

The Los Angeles uprising/riot/rebellion/rage/resistance of 1992 undoubtedly resulted from the sense that there were many community "injustices"—high unemployment and underemployment that led, in part, to competition across racial and ethnic lines for limited job opportunities; a lack of educational, health, and housing resources; a disproportionately large number of liquor stores as opposed to a small number of green or full-service grocers; systemic police brutality; and other social, economic, cultural, and political frustrations spoken to elsewhere in this book. Aspects of these events also smacked of a black nativist response to immigrant spatial and economic prominence, particularly the entrepreneurial presence of Korean business owners.[37] Blacks, however, were not the only participants, and Koreans were not the only targets. Koreans/Korean-Americans sustained tremendous property loss and damage (particularly the loss of stores that sold liquor), but so too did shops owned by Latinas/os and blacks. Reginald Denny was not the only person attacked at the corner of Florence and Normandie—he was not even the first. Other victims were Latino/a, black, Asian, and white.[38] One Korean American, Edward Song Lee, died in the uprising; but blacks constituted 44% of those killed in all related deaths; Latinos/as were 31% and whites were 22%.[39] The rebellion certainly was a multiracial and multi-ethnic one on many levels, with painful consequences for several ethnic and racial communities.[40]

Indeed, while blacks were 30% of the thousands arrested during the uprising, whites were 10%, and Latinos/as were 37%.[41] Some Asians of various ethnicities also were arrested for curfew violations and on weapons charges. The statistic regarding Latino/a participation is not surprising given that the population in Los Angeles County in 1990 was more Latino/a than black (11.2% black in the county, 37.8% Latino/a).[42] Given that Latinos/as outnumbered blacks by more than 3.5 to 1 in the total population, one easily understands the greater significance of black participation and what that meant for Korean businesses.

When one looks closely at the spatial location and movement of riot participants, for example, it is clear that, after targeting Korean-owned stores in their neighborhoods, South Central blacks moved on to target Koreatown. The two major areas of uprising activity were South Central/Compton and Koreatown. Population wise, South Central and Compton were predominantly black in 1990—60% and 54% respectively. Koreatown, however, was only 15% black that year, and 68% Hispanic.[43] When researchers looked at the participation of blacks and Latinos/as at these sites, there was a clear indication that those rioters who resided in Koreatown seemed to contain their activities to that location. Rioters from South Central and Compton, however, not only participated in the rebellion in their residential neighborhoods, but also spread north to Koreatown. Of those arrested in Koreatown for example—and keep in mind that those arrested were only a minority of the actual participants—35% were from South Central Los Angeles.[44] African Americans who lived in South Los Angeles attacked Korean-owned shops in South Central and Compton, but they also traveled up the connective thoroughfares of Vermont and Normandie Avenues to burn and loot Koreatown shops and, by extension, to harass and destroy the livelihoods of Korean shopkeepers.[45]

But it is not the case that blacks looted and burned Korean-owned shops only because of Latasha Harlins, and Latinos/as did so for other reasons.[46] As noted earlier, the rebellion developed for a number of reasons, not just the question of justice. Moreover, blacks and Latinos/as acted on overlapping concerns as well as motives that were distinct. Both groups, for example, were disproportionately affected by unemployment and underemployment. Both also shared the same urban spaces where Korean entrepreneurs operated their shops. Although more Latinos/as lived in Koreatown than blacks, and more blacks resided in South Central and Compton than Latinos/as at the time, both groups collectively made up the central client base for Korean-owned groceries, liquor stores, nail shops, dry cleaners, and gas stations in Koreatown and South Central.

Latinos/as who patronized these businesses, like blacks, complained of rude, disrespectful treatment at the hands of shop owners. Noted sociologists Lawrence Bobo, Camille Zubrinsky, James Johnson, and Melvin Oliver, who conducted a Los Angeles countywide social survey in 1992 that queried the feelings about racial and ethnic groups, found, for example, that Latinos/as "harbored the same grievances against Korean merchants and business owners as did blacks."[47] As with African Americans and Koreans—language, culture, and class differences often underlay much of this difficulty. So too did the sense that Koreans, as an immigrant group, seemed the more-welcome late twentieth-century immigrants and, as a result, were able to achieve economic success and social integration more easily than Spanish-speaking persons arriving from Central America. It would be wrong, however, to believe that the cause of Latasha Harlins—accused of shoplifting and then shot and killed by a Korean shopkeeper—did not garner sympathy in the Spanish-speaking community. Latino mothers and fathers were acutely aware of their own children's vulnerability in these shops. And while more Latinos/as found employment in Korean business and industrial establishments than blacks, these workers also complained of poor compensation and work conditions. Some, who fell in the category of undocumented laborers, felt particularly exploited. They were the cooks, dishwashers, custodians, stock handlers, seamstresses, and so forth who often worked long, uncomfortable hours for little pay and few, if any, benefits. More than a few Latinos/as residents in Koreatown also believed that they faced housing discrimination and abuse by Korean landlords. Korean shopkeepers and landlords, in their defense, would point to small profit margins, high rates of shoplifting, gang activity, and the inability of some to pay competitive rents as reasons for their cautious and some-times hostile, response to Latino/a customers, employees, and potential renters.[48]

Despite the complexity of reasons that led to the uprising, however, the two public icons of questioned justice that provided the spark and continued to fuel much of what occurred those last days of April and the first days of May 1992 were Rodney King and Latasha Harlins. The spec-ter of Latasha Harlins was a particularly powerful rallying point as blacks, Latinos/as, and others entered, looted, and destroyed Korean-owned businesses. As Pyong Gap Min asserts, violent hostilities between blacks and Koreans in the year after Latasha Harlins's death, as well as the brutal assault on Korean property during the uprising, were largely due to "the sentencing of Soon Ja Du, which was seen by many African Americans as unfair, biased, and too lenient for the shooting of an unarmed girl."[49] Political scientist Regina Freeer agrees, noting, "Many in the African American community connected this verdict in the case [*People v. Du*] with the verdict in the case of the officers tried for beating Rodney King. Together, the two came to represent vivid examples of the justice system's bias against African Americans."[50] This would not be the first time African Americans, or Americans more broadly defined, would have taken to the streets to protest the unjust treatment of vulner-able members of their community, defined as young, sometimes female, and always socially marginal.

Women, Youth, and the African American Race Riot

Race riots have had a long and ugly history in the United States. They also have been variously defined, with "race" serving as a wide and deep umbrella under which one typically finds "race," ethnicity, nativity, culture—especially religion and language—and class difference as es-sential variables that distinguish group actions that can include physical assault, property damage and loss, expulsion, disfranchisement, impris-onment, and even death. Such events, known as riots—but this is a ter-ribly contested term that participants and analysts have labeled variously as uprising, resistance, rebellion, or revolution[51]—can include a few people, hundreds, or even thousands.

Scores of race riots occurred in both the nineteenth and twentieth centuries in the United States, and blacks certainly were not always center stage as either victims or aggressors. Indeed, prior to the Civil War, it was more likely that immigrant groups like the Chinese, Mexicans, Irish, and Italians, rather than African Americans, would be the victims of group violence. Even after the Civil War, when emphasis on "controlling" the black physical, social, economic, and political presence led to appalling records of lynching and mob violence throughout the nation, nativism, xenophobia, and racism affected other groups profoundly, subjecting Catholics (especially those of Irish, Italian, and French Canadian descent), the Chinese and other Asian immigrants in the West, Jews and Italians in the East, and Native Americans throughout the nation to extralegal violence. These events occurred not infrequently with the tacit, if not outright, support of local, state, and/or national law enforcement, legislators, or the military.[52]

Just as with the Los Angeles "riot" of 1992, these events throughout history were the result of numerous concerns. But there always was one or a couple of events usually in rapid succession that set them off. There could be any number of types of sparks that led to the actual riots. One of the most consistent, however, was brutal or unjust treatment of a vulnerable, or innocent, member of the community, particularly a young person or female. Such events undermined community patriarchies, challenging the vitality and legitimacy of black manhood and the citizenship rights associated with that manhood. How, indeed, could men be men if they could not protect their women and youth? In the African American community, such sparks can be linked to a number of race riots in which blacks were the actors and not just the victims. G. Grant Williams, editor of the black newspaper *Philadelphia Tribune,* for example, advised his readers in the fall of 1917 when they were threatened with attacks on their homes to "stand your ground like men." To do so, in Williams's estimation, was to live not only as men but also as citizens: "Be quiet, be decent, maintain clean wholesome surroundings and if you are attacked defend yourselves like American citizens."[53] It was their right and presumption as male citizens, as men, Williams, and many others believed, to protect their women and youth against other citizens and even against the state if need be. This clearly was a theme in the African American community, slave and free, from the colonial era onward. In one of the earliest race riots in which blacks were involved, for example, in Detroit in 1863, black men shielded women and children from burning buildings and stones thrown by whites. As one of the victims, Lewis Pearce, recounted: "We then went there to defend the women and children. As soon as we left the shop they set it on fire."[54]

In the same year of the Philadelphia race riot (1917) that Grant Williams referred to, the quintessential icon of black manhood and citizenship—the black soldier—asserted his right to protect black womanhood in the face of police brutality. It was not long before a race riot was underway in Houston. When local white policemen Lee Sparks and Rufe Daniels illegally searched for an alleged gambler in the home of Mrs. Travers and did not find him, they turned their anger to the respected black woman and mother. Sparks and Daniels not only cursed, beat, and dragged Travers into the street in her under-clothes, but they decided to also send her to the local prison farm for 90 days because she was "one of those biggety nigger women."[55] Private Edwards of the 24th Infantry, stationed at nearby Camp Logan, was in the crowd and stepped forward to help a visibly humiliated, confused, and physically abused Mrs. Travers. The police retaliated by severely beating the black soldier and then arresting him along with Travers. Events quickly escalated between the police and white men in the town, on the one hand, and black soldiers located at the camp on the other. By nightfall, a full-scale riot was underway. As a result, 118 black soldiers, who had been ordered not to reenter Houston, were court-martialed, and 19 were sentenced to death (six of these death sentences later were commuted to life imprisonment by President Woodrow Wilson). Sixty-three others were given life sentences. The two white military officers who had participated were found not guilty. The local and federal government, as well as the police and the military, sent a message loud and clear—damn black womanhood and damn black manhood too if it meant questioning white authority and a white system of justice.[56] The lesson was not well learned. Although Mrs. Travers would not be the only female riot spark for African Americans, black youth also proved to be powerful triggers over the years. Indeed, the instances of race riot sparks flying from the abuse of black females and young people continued throughout the twentieth and into the twenty-first centuries.

When 17-year-old Eugene Williams, for example, drowned on July 27, 1919, in South Side Chicago after whites assaulted him with rocks, and then the Chicago police charged an innocent black man instead of the white man who actually had struck the boy, the Chicago Race Riot ensued. Thirty-eight persons (23 blacks, 15 whites) lost their lives in the late July-early August riot; thousands (mostly blacks) lost property, and 13 blacks were arrested (no whites).[57] In Harlem, in both 1935 and 1964, rumors that black youth had been killed (one by a white store clerk, and the other by a policeman) led to race rioting. In 1935, a Kresse Five and Ten Cent Store employee accused a 16-year-old black-Puerto Rican boy, Lino Rivera, of shoplifting a penknife worth ten cents. A small altercation occurred between the youth and the clerk, but rumors spread that the clerk had beaten the boy to death, and a riot erupted. Although Rivera was alive and well, a fact that finally was successfully circulated, rioters continued because another youth, 16-year-old Lloyd Hobbs, was shot to death by policeman John F. Mc Inerny early on in the rioting.[58] Twenty-nine years later, in July 1964, black rioters chanted "burn baby burn" for five days as they protested the death of 15-year-old James Powell, whom NYPD Lieutenant Thomas Gilligan shot and killed, allegedly for lunging at him with a knife—a knife that was not found in the subsequent investigation.[59] The black teen's death, one historian notes, was the "spark that set off the first riot in a major American city during the 1960s."[60]

Over on the West Coast, a similar trend was visible. The spark of the Watts riot of 1965, for example, was the arrest and perceived abuse, by white members of the California Highway Patrol and the LAPD, of a combination of black youth and women—21-year-old Marquette Frye, his brother Ronald, and his mother, Rena Price; as well as a young woman in the crowd whom spectators believed was pregnant. Frye was arrested for a DUI; his mother for interfering with the arrest—she jumped on the back of the arresting officer Lee Minikus; and a young woman for spitting on one of the policemen.[61] The crowd had seen a CHP officer hit Ronald in his forehead and then his stomach with his baton.[62] Those gathered at the site believed that Rena was rightfully upset because of the assault and arrest of her son and the impounding of her car. The crowd also believed that a LAPD officer on-site used excessive force to arrest a pregnant woman (she was not really pregnant but wearing a barber's smock). They were incensed by the physical abuse the police imposed for what they believed were petty crimes. Black onlookers also were upset that the police were arresting the woman in the smock, not only because they thought they were manhandling a pregnant woman, but also because those standing closest to her knew that she had not been the person who spit on the policeman. Injustice seemed to emerge from several scenarios in Watts that exceedingly hot summer day in August 1965.[63]

A year later on September 27, 1966, in the Bay View Hunter's Point area of San Francisco, another white policeman, while pursuing 16-year-old Matthew Johnson, a suspected car thief, fired a warning shot that struck the back of the unarmed boy's head. Matthew, who had not stolen a car, died on the streets of his neighborhood. The spectacle of his wrongful death at the hands of the police led to a riot.[64] One eyewitness recalled that soon after the shooting she saw a large group of men walking down the street, yelling: "We're not going to take it any more! That's it we're going to take care of these jokers [the police] once and for all!"[65] The witness, Cati Hawkins, noted that the men did not loot and burn because they were "thugs." "They did it out of the love for that child, Matthew Johnson. His killing was the catalyst for them going down to 3rd street and starting Uprising at that time."[66] That same year, the police in Roxbury, a predominantly black neighborhood in Boston, resorted to beating and threatening women and children participating in a sit-in at the local Department of Welfare. The women felt so threatened by the police who "dragged, kicked and pulled" them that some began throwing their children out of the windows to the waiting arms of onlookers below. Incensed by the treatment of these women and children, people began rioting.[67]

In the summer of 1968, a riot also occurred in Richmond, California. Again, the catalyst was abuse of a black youth. On June 25, the Richmond police shot and critically wounded Charles Mims, a 15-year-old boy suspected of car theft. "They killed that boy," was the shout that went through the black neighborhood as locals gathered, quickly assessed the situation, and began to stone and rock the police car. The riot that developed lasted another four days.[68]

And the list of these kinds of events—the image of young, vulnerable blacks being harmed, sometimes by the police, sometimes by other criminal justice personnel or actions—that sparked subsequent uprisings, goes on and on. One need only peruse the history of unrest in cities like Miami, which suffered a race riot in 1980 after five white policemen were acquitted of beating to death an unarmed black insurance salesman, Arthur McDuffie; and another similar event when a Hispanic police officer, Luis Alvarez, shot and killed Nevell Johnson, an African American youth.[69] Other cities with similar incidents derived from feelings of injustice for black victims, particularly youth, women, and others deemed especially vulnerable, include Tampa, Florida, in 1967 and 1986;[70] Newark, New Jersey, in 1967;[71] York, Pennsylvania, in 1969;[72] Crown Heights (Brooklyn), New York, in 1991;[73] St. Petersburg, Florida, in 1996;[74] Cincinnati, Ohio, in 2001;[75] Benton Harbor, Michigan, in 2003[76]; and Oakland, California, in 2009 and 2010.[77] Like Charles Mims, Nevell Johnson, Matthew Johnson, Oscar Grant, Mrs. Travers, and Lillie Mae Allen (killed before the York, Pennsylvania riot of 1969), Latasha Harlins and Rodney King were stirring examples of injustice. The result was the worst race riot in United States history.

Sparks Fly North, South, East, and West: The Beginning of the Los Angeles Riot/Rebellion/Civil Unrest/Uprising of 1992

If it wasn't for Latasha, there wouldn't have been an April 29th.

—Denise Harlins[78]

Judge Karlin should realize her decision is just as much an igniter of the Los Angeles riots as the acquittal of the four Los Angeles police officers. No remorse, no understanding, no compassion—those words describe Judge Karlin.[79]

—Mark Oliver, Los Angeles resident

The first 911 calls started to arrive at various police stations around the city soon after the Simi Valley jury began to pronounce the not guilty verdicts in the Rodney King beating case. Outside the courtroom, people congregated and verbal sparring erupted between those who agreed with the verdict and those who did not.[80] Downtown, close to Parker Center, the headquarters for the LAPD, protesters, many of them belonging to the Revolutionary Communist Party, began to gather.[81] In South Central, people began to act as well.

Many believe that the flashpoint was at Florence and Normandie. The harrowing video of Reginald Denny, a white truck driver, being pulled from his truck and brutally beaten has become a major symbol of the riots. The attack on Denny began at approximately 6:46 p.m. But before Denny's assault, several others had been beaten and robbed at that intersection—Larry Tarvin, Marisa Bejar and husband Francisco Aragon, Manuel Vaca, and Sylvia Castro were some of those attacked before Denny.[82] What most people also do not remember is that the first recorded attack—on property and person—occurred three blocks away from Denny, at approximately 4:00 p.m. at "Mr. Lee's," the Pay-Less Liquor and Deli, a local, Korean-owned grocery and liquor store.[83] There, several young black men entered Lee's store, grabbed bottles of beer and hit Mr. Lee's son, David, in the head with a bottle as he tried to stop them. "This is for Rodney King," one shouted.[84] This action—theft and assault on Korean property and person—was only the beginning. The conflation of the anger about Rodney King's verdict and anger at Korean entrepreneurs, as symbols of Soon Ja Du's murder of Latasha Harlins—both galling examples of black injustice—was fundamental. As Patricick Joyce notes in *No Fire Next Time: Black-Korean Conflicts and the Future of America's Cities*, "Rioters continued to invoke the name 'Rodney King' but they also spoke the name 'Latasha Harlins,'—the two had become intertwined via twin perceived failures of the justice system."[85] Black resident Pearl Bell decried at FAME on the evening of April 29: "There is just no justice for black people in Los Angeles—first Latasha Harlins and now Rodney King."[86]

For the next several hours, that site in South Central and the surrounding areas were the center of the events that became known as the Los Angeles riots. Still, quarrels, protests, looting, and fires also were beginning to break out in other parts of the city and surrounding areas—West Hollywood and Hollywood, Watts, Compton, Long Beach, downtown close to Parker Center, Pacoima, Inglewood, Culver City, Pomona, a community near Foothill Station where King was first arrested, even minimally in Westside communities like Westwood and Beverly Hills and, of course, in Koreatown.

As historian George Sanchez has aptly discerned, much of the violence in South Central, first particularly at the corner of Florence and Normandie, and in that general vicinity, was aimed at immigrants, or perceived immigrants—Latinos/as and Asian/Asian-Americans in particular.[87] In the couple of hours between the attack on David Lee and the beating of Reginald Denny, most of the victims were Latino/a. Altogether, of the 30 or so persons attacked at the corner of Florence and Normandie, only two were white—Reginald Denny and another white truck driver, Larry Tarvin, who was beaten and robbed only a few minutes before Denny.[88] As the rebellion developed, however, Koreans and their property became targets of protests and criminal intent. Indeed, after the Denny beating, three persons, mistaken as Korean, were beaten in the same intersection—Takao Hirato (whose first black rescuer also was beaten), Sai-Choi Choi, and Tam Tran.[89] Sanchez maintains that rioters began to shout out that first evening, "let the Mexican go," and "show the Koreans who rules."[90] But who was Korean? Many of those who meant to bring harm to Koreans could not differentiate a person from one Asian-descended ethnic group from another. "Suddenly I am scared to be Asian," Elaine Woo, the Chinese American sister of then City Councilman Mike Woo, admitted. "More specifically, I am afraid of being mistaken for Korean." When she spoke to her friends, many felt equally challenged by feelings they should not abandon Koreans in their moment of need, but also not wanting to suffer the wrath of angry protestors, rioters, and criminals. "Solidarity? Not when people who looked like us were getting shot or doing the shooting, we thought, with more than a little shame."[91]

By 6:00 p.m., on that same corner of Florence and Normandie, Korean-owned Tom's Liquor and Deli became the major focus of property assault and damage (before it mostly had been cars).[92] Another Korean liquor store soon went up in flames at Florence and Hoover. The owner's son, William, recalled, "My mother, my father and I witnessed it on live TV. I saw my father cry for the 1st time in my life."[93] And while Latinos/as hardly escaped victimization after that, as that first evening turned into night, many more Latinos/as were taking part in the protest and criminal activity rather than being the targets of it. "It was very specific to Koreans. Not to Chinese, not to Latinos. Not to African Americans. It was just really clear that it was specific toward Koreans," Angela Oh concluded.[94] Not surprisingly, Billy and Soon Ja Du's Empire Liquor Market was one of the first stores firebombed.[95]

As the rioters, who were comprised of an assortment of people—mostly young and male, some who were petty criminals and gang affiliated, and protestors—moved outward from those few blocks around Florence and Normandie, sites of ignition spread to other neighborhoods, other nearby urban centers south, west, and north, to cities as far away as Las Vegas, Oakland, San Francisco, Seattle, Pittsburg, Tampa, Washington, DC, Atlanta, New York City, and even Toronto, Canada.[96] By the dawn of April 30, Governor Pete Wilson had declared a state of emergency and requested the support of 2,000 National Guardsmen; at least 11 people had been killed; scores had been beaten; hundreds of shops had been looted; approximately three fires per minute were being reported; local bus service was suspended; curfews had been established in some areas; and the affected areas had moved north to Koreatown.[97] The preliminary battles in the form of protests, boycotts, and shootings (by blacks and Koreans) that had been going on between customers and shopkeepers since Latasha Harlins's death 13 months earlier were reaching a dramatic, almost apocalyptic, climax.

Sai-I-Gu (4-29)

I closed the store, and I was driving away, and I could already see a sea of fire. I couldn't think. Is this really happening? How could this be happening in America.

—Hyung Ko[98]

Approximately half the businesses destroyed during the Los Angeles riots/uprising belonged to Korean/Korean-Americans, and another one-third of those damaged were Korean owned. The rioters, protestors, and criminals did not have to actually go to Koreatown to wreak havoc on Korean businessmen and women. More Korean shops were located in South Central than in Koreatown. In 1990, Koreans owned 1,600 out of a total of 2,411, or two-thirds of all businesses in South Central. Not surprisingly then, Korean-owned stores in South Central were the most affected, surpassing more rates of damage, total destruction, and looting than in Koreatown and in the rest of the city as well.[99] A majority, 400 of 728, of liquor stores in South Central were looted, damaged, or completely destroyed with fire.[100] African Americans, who were the majority of those who participated in Korean property destruction in South Central, clearly meant to harm, if not literally "burn out," the Korean business presence in their communities. Sai-I-Gu was in South Central.[101]

Black businessmen and women realized that in order for their property to remain unharmed, they had to specify it was "black-owned." Edward Chang noted, for example, "You began to see 'This is a Black Owned Stored' signs everywhere to prevent rioters from attacking their stores."[102] Some Korean shop owners who were known to have employed blacks found themselves immune from attack or were protected by the employees who lived in the neighborhood. Sung-Sik Chris Kim stated with relief that her store was not harmed because she had all black employees and was herself just a tenant—the building was black owned.[103]

Large numbers of protestors/petty criminals/gang bangers/rioters arrived with the darkness, but some had started earlier in the evening. Dorothy Pirtle, who was 11 years old, recalled her great fear as she witnessed the looting, firebombing, and crowds running through the streets around her home shouting, "No justice, no peace!" A few warnings had gone out as anxious family members and friends, who had seen the verdicts announced on television, warned their loved ones to close up their shops early and come home. Other shopkeepers had heard the news themselves and knew they needed to flee. Jet Lee, a merchant in Compton, recalled that he notified his relatives who also were shopkeepers and told them to "get the hell out of there," which is precisely what he did. A few hours later, Mr. Lee discovered that his store was being looted. He called his employee, who lived across the street from the business and asked him for an update. "A couple of hours later he called me—it's on fire." Jin-Moo Chung, a grocer and swapmeet owner, was told by his friend to close his store. Chung did not do so because he wanted to try to protect the property of the others who sold out of his swapmeet. "I stayed there, to try to do everything I could."[104]

While family and friends desperately tried to reach loved ones who were merchants, employers, and employees in the affected areas, few knew of any organization or leader who could help them through this crisis. The only institution that offered immediate and sustained resources to the Korean community during this catastrophe was Radio Korea. By early that evening, personnel at the station had gone live to field emergency calls; to help facilitate communications between separated families; and to provide information on the location of the riot/rebellion hot spots, what had happened, and what to expect. Richard Choi, in particular, recalled that he left work at about 5:00 p.m. on April 29 and started home. When he realized that a "violent protest" had started, he went back to work at Radio Korea. By seven, he added, the station began to get calls with people in distress asking for help. "Before long, we thought, 'Let's just go live with the phone calls.' Because we . . . needed to let them know what was happening." Julie Carl, who was only nine at the time, recalled the chaos and despair. "For the first time in my life," she noted, "I heard middle-aged Korean men call Radio Korea and just cry." Richard Choi did not mince words when listeners called in: he told them to "flee." The first calls were from South Central and Compton, he added, but "as the night went on, everything started coming north."[105]

Radio Korea—that was just about it. The police were, from the accounts of many Koreans, of no help. Korean entrepreneurs soon came to believe that the same criminal justice system that blacks knew had failed them via Latasha and Rodney King, also failed to protect them (Koreans) from rioters and protestors. It was a shocking, brutal realization by Korean entrepreneurs, their families, and communities that they were left without protection—abandoned at their most vulnerable moment.

Story after story underscored shopkeepers's shock at the lack of protection from the police and the military. Jay Lee, who owned a furniture shop near Florence and Normandie, explained that looters broke into his store and began to steal and shoot. He had his wife, who was in another store, call the police to inform them that he and his employees were trapped by rioters. "We hid for three hours while people laughed and stole and rioted," he remembered. "The whole time, I kept thinking the police were coming."[106] But they did not come. Finally, someone set Mr. Lee's store on fire. He ran out of his shop, but he knew that two people were trapped inside the building. After finally finding a policeman, he explained the situation and asked for help, to no avail. "The officer didn't move." The next officer he encountered responded the same way. "I begged five officers to do something. But nothing. Had I been able to speak English better, I would have told them to have courage."[107]

Jay Kim, who was running for Congress at the time, recalled that the LAPD was "nowhere to be seen thanks to Police Chief Daryl Gates' 'let

Koreatown burn,' attitude. This was an unconscionable decision."[108] Bong Hwan Kim captured much of the dismay regarding the lack of police protection on that first night and next day when he noted: "I could never have anticipated that LAPD would just lose control like that. You assume that they're ready. But they had no idea."[109] Raphael Hong had hoped that the National Guard would help to secure his parents's property, the Inglewood Swapmeet, from harm or destruction. When his mother and father called him to ask what they should do, he reassured them that the National Guard was on its way to Los Angeles and that their property would be safe. "Don't worry about it," he told his mother. But the National Guard did not begin their patrols until 2 p.m. Thursday, almost a full day after the rioting/unrest had begun. Most of the Army and Marine forces remained in staging areas.[110] Raphael and his parents saw their swapmeet destroyed by fire on the local news Friday night. "My parents kind of went into shock," he explained. "They . . . lost everything. My father wanted to go to the store, and I said, 'No way. Don't get out of the house. Stay where you are. Don't even go near L.A.'"[111]

Despite the absence of a strong police presence, there were some heroic stories of police rescue and protection that emerged on that first night. Sergeant Lisa Phillips of the LAPD, for example, recalled that she and her partner, Dan Nee, rescued an Asian motorist who had been attacked. "A crowd had surrounded her car and started beating her," she noted. The crowd, which was in the hundreds, would not disperse even in the presence of police personnel. They had to aim their car at the crowd to get them to move back. Even then, two men refused to move. One was trying to break the woman's car window, and the other man was beating the woman with his fist. Officer Nee was able to get the woman out of the car. She was so beaten and bloody that both police officers believed the victim was dead. As Nee carried her to his patrol car, someone in the crowd hit him with a rock. The beaten woman fell from the officer's hands and "the crowd spontaneously burst into laughter."[112]

The LAPD's limited presence was not enough to convince Korean shopkeepers, who had heard via frantic phone calls and on Radio Korea of what had befallen their fellow entrepreneurs in South Central, Compton, and Inglewood, that anyone was about to help them. The truth was that the police did not get a handle on the situation early. In losing that opportunity, it would take a tremendous effort by the LAPD, the Sheriff's Department, the National Guard, and others to quell the rebellion. Los Angeles's city government and law enforcement had been caught with their pants down. "What struck me," Councilman Mike Woo confessed, "was how unprepared the city was."[113] Los Angeles County Supervisor Zev Yaroslavsky, who at the time of the uprising was a city councilman and part of Bradley's Westside coalition, reiterated Woo's concerns, noting that it never occurred to him that violence might erupt after the Simi Valley verdict was announced.[114]

No one had prepared for a spontaneous, quickly growing, moving, violent rebellion. LAPD Chief Daryl Gates went off to a fundraiser in the lush Westside community of Brentwood. The mayor was in a meeting with respondents to the Christopher Commission and then had gone over to the First African Methodist Episcopal Church to participate in a peace rally that he had helped plan. Bradley had not prepared for the awful event that the uprising would end up being, but he did fear that there would be a need to plead for calm if the verdicts were not guilty. Bradley and Gates, however, had not spoken to each other for a purported 13 months before the riot/rebellion took place. Their very public tug of war left city administrative and law enforcement agencies and personnel at loggerheads. While the city burned, the mayor and the chief of police maintained their crippling stand-off. Moreover, the later findings (October 1992) of the special commission created by the Los Angeles Board of Police Commissioners to "undertake an investigation to examine the Police Department's preparations in the event of a civil disturbance," found that the city was wholly unprepared to handle a civil disturbance of the magnitude that began on April 29.[115]

Few seemed to know what to do, and police in the precincts and on the streets were given mixed messages. Detective Ben Lee of the LAPD, for example, recalled the frustration that he and fellow officers felt when no one in the upper police administration would issue an order that first night to protect persons and property. They walked a tightrope because for them to become involved in any aspect of the riot/uprising would risk inflaming it even more. Still, many residents and entrepreneurs in various communities throughout Los Angeles, but particularly South Los Angeles, desperately needed and wanted their help. It was not just Koreans, after all, who were at risk and wanted police protection, but also Latinos/as, African Americans, and whites who lived, worked, owned property, or passed through these areas who did not want to be harmed. "I saw the flames, I saw people vandalizing the community . . . and I remember breaking down crying," Felicia Jones, an African American mother of three recalled.[116] By the time rioters and protestors reached Koreatown, some had vowed to protect their stores by any means necessary.

The Spectacle of Armed Korean Men: Was the Revolution Being Televised?

Koreatown was hit hard in this evolving and mobile storm of frustration, anger, protest, and crime.[117] The crowds moved on because the riot was not a static event and because Koreatown, symbolically, if not realistically, was the home of Korean entrepreneurs in the imagination of those who arrived there ready to loot and burn. Moving up and down Normandie, Vermont, and Western, rioters, protestors, and criminals left few Korean-owned shops or workspaces unscathed. At least 340 stores in Koreatown were attacked.[118] A list of property casualties read like a Korean business census: gas stations, nail salons, beauty supply and wig shops, liquor and deli stores, dry cleaners, gun shops, various manufacturing sites, clothing and toy shops, sporting goods businesses, drug stores, Radio Shacks, music and video shops, check-cashing establishments, photo shops, 99¢ stores, Payless shoe shops, Tae Kwon Do studios, and restaurants.[119] As the merchants, their families, and community tried to map a plan for protection, they turned again to the one institution that actively had assisted them through the first night of the chaos—Radio Korea. This time, the advice was not to flee—it was to stay, arm themselves, and protect person and property.[120]

Richard Choi had been convinced by shopkeepers who had come to the station to speak sorrowfully of their losses and the lack of state-sponsored protection, and to ask why they should abandon Koreatown rather than protect what they had worked for and created. Kee Whan Ha, who owned the Hannan Chain Supermarket on Olympic Boulevard, went on Radio Korea to encourage Koreans to arm themselves and stand their ground: "Don't go home. Protect your business. Your business is your life," he pleaded.[121] Some chose to do just that. Ha was among

FIGURE 7.2 "Looter with shopping cart," Photograph by Kirk McKoy. Courtesy of the *Los Angeles Times*.

those who took his own advice, mounting a vigorous armed defense of his property. So too did the owner of the California Market on Western and 4th, who shot his semiautomatic gun in the air to ward off marauding looters. Hyun Sik Song helped form the Korean American Young Adult Team, squads of ten men each who would be deployed when they were informed, usually through broadcasts on Radio Korea, that there was a need for protection.[122] Jong Min Kang helped to create the Korean Militia, which armed the defense squads.[123]

The spectacle of armed Korean shopkeepers dominated the news coverage of the events in Koreatown. The portrayal of armed Korean men, standing on rooftops and shooting their guns in the air or toward potential targets, was like nothing Los Angeles, or America for that matter, had seen. What had happened to the image of the sedate, hard-working, Christian model minority? That popular image was blown away, at least temporarily, by a new racialized image of the angry, out of control, violent, gun-toting Asian man. Largely taken out of context—these men were fighting for their livelihoods and their lives—the press used this new image to blame this faction of the victimized. Viewers were left to believe that Koreans got what they deserved—they were shooting without conscience or reason, just as Soon Ja Du had shot and killed Latasha Harlins. Peter Lee, who was a member of the Korean American Young Adult Team, recalled seeing, with disgust, a white reporter exclaiming in shock and horror: "Look at these Koreans. What are they doing? How could they do such a thing?"[124] Sophia Kim, a reporter for the *Korea Times* (English edition) also was incensed over the media's interpretation of Korean merchants's defense of Koreatown. She recalled an African American on Ted Koppel's *Nightline* blaming the racial tensions on trigger-happy Koreans.[125] Carl Rhyu, who had participated in the defense of Koreatown, asked rhetorically to those who criticized what he, and others, did: "If it was your own business and your own property, would you be willing to trust it to someone else? . . . When our shops were burning we called the police every five minutes, no response."[126] Still, there were those who spoke to the press in tones that suggested a kind of bravado that was unnerving. Richard Rhee, for example, offered a clear message of why he armed himself to protect his Koreatown business, stating, "Burn this down after 33 years? They don't know how hard I've worked. This is my market and I'm going to protect it." It was his other statement to the press, however, which caused pause: "It's just like war. I'll shoot and worry about the law later."[127]

The allusions to war were many. More than a few of the Korean men who armed themselves to protect their property wore military clothing. Jay Kim recalled that when he arrived in Koreatown, the men were wearing Marine uniforms and "Korean Marine bandanas."[128] Disturbing statements also continued to be broadcast. Doug Hee Ku, who helped protect Richard Rhee's California Market, for example, was quoted describing black and Latino looters as "like beasts . . . [t]hey are not men."[129] Portraying the enemy as completely different or alien, and, therefore, not warranting humane treatment, reminded some of typical imaging of a wartime enemy.[130] But both sides reimaged. When images of armed men, black and Latino on one side, Korean on the other, emerged, some could not help but see a developing race war.

The negative media image of violent Koreans was not helped by the two deaths that came by the friendly fire of those defending Korean property—Eddie Lee and a French Jewish security guard who worked at the Hannam Chain supermarket. "They were shooting to kill us. They didn't have the right to shoot to kill, even if we were looters. We weren't on their premises. We were about 30 yards away," James Kang, who was with Eddie Lee when he was shot and who was also shot, lamented. Ironically, Kang and Lee were members of the Korean American Young Adult Team who had armed themselves to help protect Korean properties from looters, but had been mistaken as looters themselves.[131]

The impression of Korean merchants protecting their property was compromised as well, as Sylvia Kim noted, by the repeated airing of the video of Soon Ja Du shooting Latasha Harlins in the back of her head. John Lee, who reported on the riots for the *Los Angeles Times,* believed that the manner in which the press depicted the Harlins shooting caused blacks to attack Koreans during the rebellion. "I do feel like the portrayal of how Latasha Harlins was killed and how the trial went down contributed to people's righteous indignation and fueled a lot of violence directed at Korean merchants," he remarked.[132] Kapson Yim Lee, a former editor of the *Korea Times* (English edition), was greatly disillusioned about the media's coverage of the riots, Koreans in general, and the Soon Ja Du shooting of Latasha Harlins in particular. Noting that "Du's case eventually led to a flash point of blacks' venting their frustrations about the Rodney King beating case on Koreans," largely because the media had portrayed Du's shooting of Latasha as a race issue, Lee underscored her belief that "it was not a racially motivated case."[133] Roy Hong, founder of the Korean Immigrant Workers Advocates, noted that the local and national news stations covering the riots/rebellion never ceased showing the videotape of the shooting. "Every hour they were showing Rodney King getting beaten, cops getting acquitted, and instantly they'd go to Soon Ja Du pulling the trigger on Latasha Harlins." Hong admitted that if he were young and black and viewing this news coverage, "I would want to go beat up some Korean guy right now."[134]

Many felt similarly. Interviewed by Michelle Jun in 1997, a Korean immigrant woman noted: "The Judge was wrong. She [Soon Ja] did not get any time . . . And I feel they were angry with Koreans. They think that she was set free and it was not fair." Still, Koreans "did not deserve that [the riots]."[135] Hyung Chung agreed. He was only eight years old and had lived in the United States for only three years when the uprising occurred. He was frightened, angry, and shocked by the violence that rocked the Koreatown he knew as home. It was only later that he learned of Latasha Harlins and her connection to the assault on Koreans. "I have never experienced a fear so dreadful as the one I had experienced as a child during the L.A. Riots," he offered on the occasion of the 20th anniversary of the rebellion. "I am still haunted by Latasha Harlins. I am unsure of how to honor her."[136]

Not everyone in Koreatown, however, had guns or used the ones that they did have. June Lim, who was 13 at the time and whose father owned a liquor store, recalled that her father took a moral stand and refused to use the gun that her uncle gave to him for protection. Jim-Moo-Chung refused to shoot his gun, even after looters shot him. He did not want to destroy another life.[137] Even those who felt forced to arm themselves and shoot, in the air, on the ground, or directly at persons, maintained that they only did so when attacked first. "I want to make it clear that we didn't open fire first," reported gun shop manager David Joo. At the time that Joo and others were being shot at, police were on the scene, but according to Joo, they "ran away in half a second. I never saw such a fast escape."[138]

Not all Korean shopkeepers armed themselves, nor did all Korean entrepreneurs believe that Judge Karlin's sentencing of Soon Ja Du was related to the assault on Koreans and Korean shopkeepers. Some, like Hung Chung, knew little, if anything, of the Latasha Harlins case at the time of the rebellion. Some solely associated the events to the acquittal of the LAPD officers in the Rodney King beating and Koreans being in the wrong place at the wrong time. Others believed that it was blacks lashing out as a result of economic differences. Some attributed it to black jealousy of Korean success. Carl Rhyu believed that "black people are jealous of the Koreans. They are lazy; we are working hard. They're not making money; we are making money."[139] Many saw Koreans as caught between whites and blacks, socioeconomically and spatially. As a result, Koreans became the scapegoat and safe target of racial frustration. "The riots opened the eyes of many Korean-Americans to how vulnerable Koreatown was, situated alongside Olympic Boulevard, a dividing line between white and black communities in downtown L.A.," former Congressman Jay Kim explained. Kim also believed that many of those who stole were possibly "illegal immigrants," who did not care about the Du case.[140] Others continued to insist that Koreans were targeted as a result of the TV media's portrayal of racial antagonism between blacks and Koreans.

Whether it was the actual details of *People v. Du*, especially the murder and light sentencing that caused protestors and rioters to attack Korean shops and their owners, or the recurring images of it in the media, the belief that a Korean shopkeeper had killed an unarmed black girl and was not sentenced time in prison for doing it was a tremendous spark on April 29 and over the next few days. Moreover, the media's role during the actual riots/rebellion was just a part of the public memory of Latasha Harlins. Recall that the case never was long out of sight, given the ongoing protests, the continual killings of blacks and Koreans in Korean shops in South Central (the death of Lee Arthur Mitchell, for example, and the shooting of nine-year-old Yuri Kang). Every new incident led to a discussion of Latasha's death and Karlin's sentencing of Du. Moreover, various machinations of the case had continued in the public eye over the year, even up to the time of the riots. The first recall attempt, alone, gave a continuous public face to, and airing of, the case. Members of the LHJC canvassed shopping centers, malls, parks, beaches, churches, schools, and even courthouses to gain signatures and to explain why they were battling to unseat Joyce Karlin. They came into contact with hundreds of thousands of people, garnering over 200,000 signatures between December 1991 and February 1992. Almost every month since November 1991, when Soon Ja Du was sentenced, therefore, some aspect of *People v. Du* was being publicly discussed. And of course, it was on April 21, 1992,—just eight days before the uprising began—that the California Court of Appeals announced that it was upholding Karlin's sentence of Du. *The People v. Du* had become a staple in local, vocal politics, in the months, weeks, and days before April 29, 1992.

"No Justice, No Peace" versus Peace

On Wednesday night, while some were rushing to the sites of looting and arson, others were gathering at the First African Methodist Episcopal Church. Between 6 and 8 p.m., a multiracial group of city political and religious leaders, along with 2,000 concerned citizens, came together for a peaceful rally.[141] The Reverend Cecil Murray and a number of other clergy had met several times with Mayor Tom Bradley to plan the event. "Chip" Murray recalled that "We didn't want any explosions in case the verdict was negative."[142] Reverend Murray had preached the prior Sunday about the necessity of people, whatever the Simi Valley verdict, to remain "cool."

"And if you're gonna burn something down," he advised, do not strike in your own community—turn your anger to votes to remove certain members of the state legislature or by standing up to Chief Daryl Gates and demanding his resignation.[143] Murray and a spate of other speakers the night of April 29, including Mayor Bradley, who was a member of FAME, and Denise Harlins, lamented the events of the day and pleaded for calm. The Reverend Clarence Eziokwu remembered that "even the gang representation was there. People don't realize how many community members were there [to prevent the riots]."[144] Some at the church even stopped rioters who were burning local buildings and then provided sanctuary for locals who already had lost their residences. Murray took it upon himself to provide a place for peaceful shelter and support for the next six months, leaving the church open 24 hours a day trying to bring "peace, harmony, and restoration."[145] But on that night, those who attended the meeting found little peace. Zev Yaroslavsky, who had been asked by the mayor to attend, recalled that when he left the meeting, like so many others, he found that his car had been destroyed by fire.[146]

Koreans Americans also made a concerted effort to usher in peace as soon as possible. On Friday, May 1, more than 1,000 held a peace rally in the heart of Koreatown at Wilshire and Western. That next day, 30,000 marched with white headbands signifying peace to Ardmore Park in Koreatown to offer a unified demonstration of support to those who had been victimized and to display a united effort of nonviolence.[147] The chants of "Peace" and "We want peace" seemed, Roy Hong, recalled, to be a direct counter to "No justice, no peace."[148] This remarkable event, the largest gathering of Korean Americans that had ever taken place in the United States, was a watershed moment of unity and ethnic identity formation in the Korean community across class and generational lines. The participants asked for peace, justice, and promised to rebuild what had been destroyed.[149] It was a bittersweet moment for all who had suffered through the uprising. Some chose to stay and rebuild; others gave up on that path to their American dream. And in South Central, many woke up to ugly reminders of the anger and frustration that had grown, once again, from the habitual sense of justice denied. Somewhere in their consciousness they realized that the community would limp back together, shops and homes would be rebuilt or replaced, deaths would be mourned, and that those arrested would settle their cases. Still, for the Harlins family, the sense of justice denied lingered on and on.

Epilogue: Justice?

I would like Judge Karlin and all those who voted for her to put themselves in the place of Latasha Harlins' family and ask yourself is this justice? . . . I say a black life is worth the same as a white life and you people out there better realize that fact!
—Mark Oliver, *Los Angeles Times*, June 14, 1992

When all was said and done, Koreatown looted and burned, the politicians had won or lost their elections, the press had written or recited their stories, and most of the protestors had put away their signs and stopped marching, the Harlins family had not gotten the justice they sought. Soon Ja Du did not spend another moment in jail, and Joyce Karlin retained her seat as a Superior Court judge. Latasha's sister and brother received a joint civil suit award of $300,000—that was it.[1] The justice the Harlins family questioned from almost the time that 15-year-old Latasha lost her life that Saturday morning at the Empire Market in South Central, had remained what it too frequently is for the poor, for blacks, and other people of color, for females, and for the young—a frustrating, painful reiteration of the inequalities in America society that touches, and often destroys, so many people's lives.

Even after the 1992 riots/rebellion/uprisings, the Latasha Harlins Justice Committee moved forward, but to no avail. They lost their effort to have Judge Karlin sanctioned for racism. They failed to have her defeated in the June 1992 election. Karlin went on to serve as a Superior Court judge for another five years. The city of Manhattan Beach later elected Joyce Karlin to their Council where she served as mayor for two terms. The LHJC did not succeed in their attempts to have the Justice Department indict Soon Ja Du for violation of Latasha's civil rights. The federal government never filed any charges against the convicted felon. The LHJC did manage to block Du's petition to visit Korea while on probation, but by 1997, Soon Ja Du was able to go wherever she pleased. Latasha's supporters lost, as well, their effort to buy the Empire Market and have it turned into a community center that would honor the fallen teen's memory. They could not afford the asking price of $680,000. The store was left empty for years, became a local eyesore frequented by "drug dealers, prostitutes and vagrants," and purportedly was foreclosed on by the California Korean Bank.[2] The Numero Uno grocery chain finally purchased and reopened it under their name in the late 1990s.[3] These were heartbreaking losses for Latasha's family and friends to bear. Still, Latasha's supporters were not the only ones who felt that justice had been denied them.

Korean/Korean-Americans believed that they too had suffered unreasonably—at the hands of the public, the media, and the criminal justice system. Many agreed that Soon Ja Du was guilty of a serious crime when she killed Latasha, but they also believed that she was scapegoated by the police who had been looking for someone to take the heat off of them after the videotaped beating of Rodney King surfaced a few days before Du's arrest. Korean shopkeepers lamented that they were left to negotiate their presence in the black and Latino/a communities while the media unfairly portrayed them as racist killers of black children, refusing to tell their side of the story that would underscore their violent victimization and losses through shoplifting. And then there were the boycotts, protests, and stores lost when organizations like the Brotherhood Crusade stepped in to demand respect for their black clientele. When these events culminated in the Los Angeles rebellion/riots of 1992, Korean Americans felt as if their world had exploded in their faces and no one—especially not the police—was there to protect them. Their race, their social status as immigrants, their economic class as shopkeepers, their political invisibility, many concluded, had robbed them too of equal protection under the law. How is it that the new model minority could be treated like any other racialized minority, they wondered? Like blacks in Houston in 1917? Tulsa, Oklahoma, in 1921? Or

Rosewood, Florida, in 1923? Or Latinos/as, blacks, and Filipinos in Los Angeles in 1943? Or even the Chinese at Calle de Negros in Los Angeles in 1871 and Rock Springs, Wyoming, in 1885? Or Hasidic Jews in Crown Heights in 1992?[4] How is it that the Korean/Korean-Americans became the target of so much destruction when Soon Ja Du was only one member of their community? How is it that the decisions of one judge, so far removed from Korean losses and the losses felt in the black community, could lead to all this pain, hardship, and destruction?

The personal and group histories of Soon Ja Du, Latasha Harlins, and Judge Joyce Karlin reveal some commonality as females and as members of minority races, ethnicities, and cultures. Their ancestral pasts at least indicate shared experiences of social, cultural, gendered, and racialized abuse, as well as inequality under the law. By 1991, however, the law was not just on Joyce Karlin's side; she was the law. When the *People v. Du* began on September 30, 1991, Judge Joyce Karlin clearly held a position of power vis-à-vis Soon Ja Du and Latasha Harlins. Her status in this hierarchy of females that the case exemplifies placed Joyce Karlin in a position to literally judge the actions of two other females, distinct from her in color, age, culture, education, and property. In the end, Judge Karlin's sentencing decision reflected what she perceived to be her differences from Latasha and the common ground—as a woman, wife, member of a model minority, and descendant of shopkeepers—she found with Du. And even she felt victimized—that she, and her career, had suffered as a result of what she labeled as an unwarranted attack by a "vocal minority" on her right to judicial discretion in sentencing the convicted felons who came before her.

This criticism of Judge Karlin's demeanor in the *People v. Du* did cost her. Although Karlin remained a Superior Court judge after sentencing Soon Ja Du, she spent the rest of her tenure on the bench in Juvenile Dependency Court—a clear indication that her star in the legal profession had been dimmed. Perhaps as time wore on, Karlin might have wondered if her own gender, inexperience, and even her race or ethnicity had played a part in creating the opportunity for her to preside over this extremely controversial case. She might have considered that these same variables might have influenced the manner in which the public, both those who supported her and those who opposed her, came to form their feelings about the decisions she made in the case and her suitability to serve as a Superior Court judge afterward.

While the Harlins family certainly believed they had lost most of their key battles for justice, they did not lose the fight to keep Latasha's injustice in the public's memory. Twenty years after the 1992 riots/uprising, people still remembered. Latasha Harlins is remembered in song; theater pieces; a Facebook page; Twitter; blogs; editorials; and in books and in articles in law, history, sociology, and anthropology journals. She is remembered in neighborhood chats. The day before the 20th anniversary of the Los Angeles explosion of 1992, I walked into a popular bookstore in Leimert Park—the black cultural center of South Los Angeles—to get a copy of Rodney King's new book, *The Riot Inside*. The man behind the counter pointed to a copy and then said quickly, and definitively, "As far as I am concerned, the riots were more about Latasha Harlins than Rodney King. I mean a black child walks into a store with the money to buy some orange juice, is shot in the back of the head by the store's owner, the jury finds her guilty, and the woman who shot her serves no jail time. Come on!"

Latasha is remembered every time a child of color is killed and their communities feel that justice is not rendered. She was remembered when Johannes Mehserle shot and killed Oscar Grant in an Oakland BART station. Convicted of involuntary manslaughter, Mehserle was sentenced to the minimum two years, but only served 11 months. Riots/protests occurred after his sentencing.[5] Latasha was remembered when George Zimmerman killed Trayvon Martin.[6] She especially was remembered when Brenda Hughes was killed.

On Thursday, November 21, 1996, Jo Won Kim shot and killed Brenda Hughes, the 17-year-old daughter of Salvadoran immigrants, while she was on her way to Franklin High School in Highland Park, a neighborhood in northeast Los Angeles. Hughes had sat in the car with a girlfriend, Teresa Cardona, while three male friends went into Henry's Market to buy cigarettes. While there, one placed a can of beer in his jacket. The store's owner, Jo Won Kim, demanded the beer be returned, and the young man handed it over. The store's security camera captured the incident. When the three young men left the shop, Kim, who mistakenly believed they had taken more than one can of beer, followed them with his pistol. As the car sped off, Kim shot multiple times into the vehicle, wounding one of the young men and killing Hughes, a popular high school senior, cheerleader, and softball player. Brenda, who was looking forward to college, had never even gotten out of the car to enter Kim's store that morning.[7]

The shopkeeper pled not guilty, relying on a defense quite similar to the one that Charles Lloyd and Richard Leonard had constructed for Soon Ja Du. Kim claimed that he did not know he was shooting into the car—just as Soon Ja Du testified she did not know she had shot Latasha. Kim pled that he was afraid for his life, just as Du testified that she believed Latasha was going to kill her. Kim explained that he had been plagued by gangbangers who shoplifted for years, just as the Dus contextualized Soon Ja's shooting of Latasha. Just as in the case of Latasha, however, police investigating Brenda's murder verified that the three young men in Kim's store that morning were not gang affiliated.[8] There were other similarities between the two cases. Both Soon Ja and Jon Won were close to 50, and they both had migrated from Korea in 1976. Kim's wife, Wha Sung Kim, who had been asleep in the store when the shooting occurred (Billy Du had been asleep right outside the Empire Market in his parked van when his wife shot Latasha), asserted that her husband "snapped" because constant shoplifting depleted their profits.[9] Like Du's attorney, Kim's counsel also tried to argue that the shopkeeper had a history of depression and his mental instability had caused him to shoot into the car.[10] Defense undoubtedly believed that if they could convince the judge that Kim suffered from a history of mental illness, as Du's attorneys convinced the judge of Soon Ja's tremendous emotional distress when they applied for bail, he might lower Kim's bail so that he could get out of jail. It is not surprising that Du's defense strategy served as a blueprint for Kim's. Tyson Park, who served as Jo Won Kim's attorney, had been Soon Ja Du's attorney before being replaced by Charles Lloyd and Richard Leonard. The other salient similarity was the immediate response by the family of the murdered girls: Brenda Hughes's mother and her entire family, like Latasha's relatives, were inconsolable—"Why did they have to take my baby from me," Mrs. Hughes cried repeatedly.[11]

As in the aftermath of Du's shooting of Latasha, vigils were held at Kim's store. Graffiti marked Henry's Market with a call for retribution: "Death to those who murder for $," read one message. Another sign poignantly, even poetically, asked Mr. Kim why he believed that any of his merchandise was worth the "life of a girl, an angel, a queen, a girlfriend, a friend, a customer, a stranger."[12] Some local residents, however, signed a petition attesting to Kim's strong character and supporting him. A friend watched the store in the following days because of rumors that it would be burned down in protest. That same friend, Willie Benavides, declared that the shooting "was a clear mistake. He thought his life was in danger, so he shot."[13] The police consulted with local leaders in an effort to keep the peace. Los Angeles City Councilman Richard Alatorre, the representative for Highland Park, quickly and publicly denounced Hughes's murder. "I am outraged that a store owner would respond with such violence in this situation," he told his constituents, but he was confident "that justice will be served."[14] The case was so similar to *People v. Du* that there was a real fear of civil unrest and violence. Why didn't it happen?

One of the principal reasons Brenda Hughes's distraught and angry community did not strike back was their quest for justice for their murdered child was answered. Unlike the case of the *People v. Du*, Mr. Kim's bail was set too high—$3.18 million—for him to afford to get out of jail once he was arrested the morning after Hughes's murder. Judge Glenette Blackwell also determined, after the preliminary hearing in March 1997, that Kim should stand trial for the murder of Hughes and the attempted murder of the other four persons who were in the car on the morning Kim shot into it.[15]

Faced with a possible life imprisonment if found guilty on all charges, Kim accepted a plea bargain on the day jury selection in his trial was set to begin. He subsequently was convicted of second-degree murder (the four attempted murder charges were dropped as part of the plea agreement). Superior Court Judge Robert J. Perry sentenced Jo Won Kim to 15 years to life in prison. Pat Dixon, who had served as the prosecutor on the case, believed the sentence of Kim had been both "logical and just."[16] The question of justice for Brenda Hughes had been settled. Her family could rest: justice, peace!

By the tenth anniversary of Latasha Harlins' death, Denise Harlins and the other members of the Justice Committee she had created, had found a way to move on with their lives, while vowing never to forget Latasha or the justice she was denied. Denise had to admit that after all the work she did to secure "justice," she was left feeling "tired and betrayed." She had decided to turn her love and energy into another family mission—raising three of her other nieces, who had been in foster care, as her own. They are, she noted with quiet pride, "beautiful girls, talented and smart and sharp."[17]

Appendix: Note on Sources and Further Reading

Contested Murder is not the first book to address the *People v. Du*. In 1997, Itabari Njeri published *Last Plantation: Color, Conflict, and Identity: Reflections of a New World Black*, an account of the Latasha Harlins-Du case that she links to a long essay on "colorism" and the changing place of race and color in contemporary U.S. society. As a journalist for the *Los Angeles Times*, Njeri was able to gain access to various members of the Harlins family, and their associates, for detailed interviews; accompany them to protests and rallies; and to be with them in the courtroom when the case was tried. Accounts of her interviews of the Harlins family are particularly revealing. Other works that somewhat engage this subject have focused particularly on the impact of this case on the 1992 Los Angeles riots/rebellion/uprising/unrest/ Sai-i-gu. Most of these authors agree that there was a particular link between Soon Ja Du's killing of Latasha Harlins and the light sentence Joyce Karlin gave to Du with the devastating destruction Korean/Korean-American shopkeepers faced in April 1992. The most significant of these discussions is found in Lou Cannon's *Official Negligence: How Rodney King and the Riots Changed Los Angeles and the LAPD* (1999). Cannon dedicates two chapters to this case and its connection to the riots/uprising. Legal scholar Neil Gotunda's 1993 article "Re-Producing the Model Minority Stereotype: Judge Joyce Karlin's Sentencing Colloquy in *People v. Soon Ja Du*," and his 1997 "Tales of Two Judges: Joyce Karlin in *People v. Soon Ja Du*; Lance Ito in *People v. O. J. Simpson*," also examines racial stereotyping in Judge Karlin's courtroom, albeit not from a gendered and/or generational perspective or one that views Karlin's racial/ethnic history as Jewish.

Works on the Los Angeles riots/rebellion of 1992 that speak to the devastation, various motivations and recovery efforts include: William Webster and Hubert Williams's, *The City in Crisis* (1992); Robert Gooding-Williams's edited *Reading Rodney King, Reading Urban Uprising* (1993); James K. Delk's *Fires and Furies: The L.A. Riots—What Really Happened* (1994); Mark Baldassare's edited *The Los Angeles Riots: Lessons for the Urban Future* (1994); Darnell Hunt's *Screening the Los Angeles 'Riots': Race, Seeing, and Resistance* (1996); The Staff of the *Los Angeles Times*, *Understanding the Riots: Los Angeles Before and After the Rodney King Case* (1996); Jervey Tervalon's *Geography of Rage: Remembering the Los Angeles Riots of 1992* (2002); and, Rodney King and Lawrence Spagnola's *The Riot Within: My Journey from Rebellion to Redemption* (2012).

Studies of the relationships among African Americans, Jewish Americans, and Korean Americans have formed a substantial historiography over the years and helped to frame my discussions of the connections between Judge Karlin, Soon Ja Du and Latasha Harlins. In trying to understand the historical trajectory of black-Jewish relations, I considered: Michael Lerner and Cornel West's *Jews and Blacks: A Dialogue on Race, Religion and Culture in America* (1996); Debra L. Schultz and Blanche Wiesen Cook's *Going South: Jewish Women in the Civil Rights Movement* (2001); Jennifer Lee's *Civility in the City: Blacks, Jews, and Koreans in Urban America* (2002); Edward Shapiro's *Crown Heights: Blacks, Jews and the 1991 Brooklyn Riot* (2006); Eric Sundquist's *Strangers in the Land: Blacks, Jews Post-Holocaust America* (2006); Eric Goldstein's *The Price of Whiteness: Jews, Race and American Identity* (2006); and particularly Cheryl Lynn Greenberg's *Troubling the Waters: Black Jewish Relations in the American Century* (2006). Other important scholarly works and autobiographies consulted include: Mary Antin's *The Promised Land* (1912); Neil C.

Sandburg's, *Jewish Life in Los Angeles* (1986); Susan Glenn's *Daughters of the Shtetl: Life and Labor in the Immigrant Generation* (1990); Sander Gilman's *The Jew's Body* (1991); Moshe Hartman and Harriet Hartman's *Gender Equality and American Jews* (1996); Beth Wenger's *New York Jews and the Great Depression: Uncertain Promise* (1996); Pamela S. Nadell's historical anthology *American Jewish Women's History: A Reader* (2003); Jonathan D. Sarna, et. al.'s edited work, *The Jews of Boston* (2005); Francis Dnkelspiel's *Towers of Gold: How One Jewish Immigrant Named Isaias Hellman Created California* (2008); and Haisa Diner's vital monograph *The Jews of the United States* (2009).

Other works of importance to this study because they contribute greatly to knowledge of the growing Korean presence in America and their experiences as a distinct ethnic/racial group in the last 50 years, especially their relationships with African Americans, include: Eui-Young Yu's *Black-Korean Encounter: Toward Understanding and Alliance: Dialogue Between Black and Korean Americans in the Aftermath of the 1992 Los Angeles Riot* (1994); Pyong Gap Min's *Caught in the Middle: Korean Communities in New York and Los Angeles* (1996); In-Jim Yoon's *On My Own: Korean Businesses and Race Relations in America* (1997); Keyoung Park's *The Korean American Dream: Immigrants and Small Business in New York City* (1997); Nancy Ablemann and John Lie's *Blue Dream: Korean Americans and the Los Angeles Riots* (1997); Kwang Chung Kim's edited collection *Koreans in the Hood: Conflict with African Americans* (1999); Edward Chang and Jeanette Diaz-Veizades's *Ethnic Peace in the American City* (1999); Eric Yamamoto's *Interracial Justice: Conflict and Reconciliation in Post-Civil Rights America* (2000); Patricia Wong Hall and Victor M. Hwang's edited collection *Anti-Asian Violence in North America: Asian-American and Asian Canadian Reflections on Hate, Healing and Resistance* (2001); Claire Jean Kim's *Bitter Fruit: The Politics of Black-Korean Conflict in New York City* (2003); Patrick Joyce's *No Fire Next Time: Black-Korean Conflict and the Future of America's Cities* (2003); Ilpyong J. Kim's edited *Korean-Americans: Past, Present and Future* (2004); Ji Yeon Yun's *Beyond the Shadow of Camptown: Korean Military Brides in America* (2004); and Min Hyoung Song's *Strange Future: Pessimism and the 1992 Los Angeles Riots* (2005). Useful as well when trying to unravel the historic relationships between blacks and Asian Americans within the law and the public imagination is Najia Aarim-Heriot's *Chinese Immigrants, African Americans, and Racial Anxiety in the United States, 1848–82*.

There is a growing body of fine literature on Asian Americans and Asian American women, in addition to that specifically about Korean/Korean-Americans cited above, that was especially useful for this particular pursuit. These works include: Amy Tachiki, Eddie Wong, and Franklin Odo's early edited work *Roots: An Asian American Reader* (1971); Bong Youn Choy's *Koreans in America* (1979); Mary Paik Lee's *Quiet Odyssey: A Pioneer Korean Woman in America* (edited by Sucheng Chan, 1990); Sucheng Chan's groundbreaking *Asian Americans: An Interpretive History* (1991); Keum-Young Chung Pang's *Korean Elderly Women in America: Everyday Life, Health, and Illness* (1991); Karin Aguilar-San Juan's edited *The State of Asian America: Activism and Resistance in the 1990s* (1994); Gary Okihiro's *Margins and Mainstreams: Asians in American History and Culture* (1994); Ronald Takaki's *Strangers from a Different Shore: A History of Asian Americans* (1998); Wayne Patterson's *The Korean Frontier in America: Immigration to Hawaii, 1896–1910* (1998); Young I. Song and Ailee Moon's edited collection *Korean American Women: From Tradition to Modern Feminism* (1998); Helen Zia's *Asian American Dreams: The Emergence of an American People* (2000); Frank Wu's essential *Yellow: Race in America Beyond Black and White* (2002); Sonia Shinn Sunoo's *Korean Picture Brides: A Collection of Oral Histories* (2002); *Asian/Pacific Islander American Women: A Historical Anthology* (2003), edited by Shirley Hune and Gail Nomura; Min Zhou and J. V. Gatewood's edited volume *Contemporary Asian America: A Multidisciplinary Reader* (2nd ed., 2007); Rosalind Chou and Joe R Feagin's collaboration *The Myth of the Model Minority: Asian Americans Facing Racism* (2008) and many fine articles found in *Amerasia Journal*, *Signs*, and *Women's Studies*.

The sources drawn on to discuss African Americans more generally and black females particularly are too numerous to include here, but are cited fully in the endnotes section for the book as they are referenced. Some of the most significant for the writing of this book include: A. Leon Higginbotham, Jr.'s *In the Matter of Color: Race and the American Legal Process: The Colonial Period* (1978); Kenneth Clark's classic *Dark Ghetto: Dilemmas of Social Power* (revised 1989); Gerald D. Jaynes and

Robin Williams, Jr.'s *A Common Destiny: Blacks and American Society* (1990); Andrew Hacker's *Two Nations: Black and White, Separate, Hostile, Unequal* (1992); Leslie Schwalm's *A Hard Fight for We: Women's Transition from Slavery to Freedom in South Carolina* (1997); Leon Litwack's *Trouble in Mind: Black Southerners in the Age of Jim Crow* (1998); Darlene Clark Hine and Kathleen Thompson's *A Shining Thread of Hope: The History of Black Women in America* (1998); Lawrence B. De Graaf, Kevin Mulroy and Quintard Taylor's reader *Seeking El Dorado: African Americans in California* (2001); Douglas Flamming's *Bound for Freedom: Black Los Angeles in Jim Crow America* (2005); RJ Smith's *The Great Black Way: L.A. in the 1940s and the Lost African American Renaissance* (2006); Josh Sides, *L.A. City Limits: African American Los Angeles From the Great Depression to the Present* (2006); Tricia Martineau Wagner's *African American Women of the Old West* (2007); Jacqueline Jones' *Labor of Love, Labor of Sorrow: Black Women, Work, and the Family, from Slavery to the Present* (rev. edition, 2009); Teresa Amott and Julie Matthaei's *Race, Gender and Work: A Multi-Cultural Economic History of Women in the United States* (Revised Edition, 2009); Teresa Danielle McGuire's *At the Dark End of the Street: Black Women, Rape, and Resistance—A New History of the Civil Rights Movement from Rosa Parks to the Rise of Black Power* (2010); and Isabel Wilkerson's *The Warmth of Other Suns: The Epic Story of America's Great Migration* (2010). I also relied on the *The Journal of African American History* for many articles that were extremely useful.

In writing *Contested Murder*, I benefited tremendously from a treasure trove of newspaper articles, private testimonies, biographies and autobiographies, and oral histories found in UCLA's Young Research Library. Stories from the *Los Angeles Times*, in particular, but as well the *Los Angeles Sentinel*, the *Korean Times* (English version), the *New York Times*, the *San Francisco Chronicle*, the *Chicago Tribune*, the *Philadelphia Enquirer*, and other nationally syndicated newspapers captured vital information, public attitudes, and a tremendous number of personal interviews that centered on various aspects of *People v. Du*.

Lastly, the world of historical research has changed tremendously since I began this work, and mostly for the better, through electronic archives, media sites, and online search engines. Many of the newspapers, magazines, obituaries, criminal records, court cases (originals and appeals), census records, population statistics, historic photographs, hate crime statistics, descriptions and data on race riots and rebellions, popular culture sources, and economic indices drawn on for this work were found online. Also available online was much of the genealogical and other information presented here for the Harlins, Du, and Karlin families, including birth, death, marriage, religious affiliation, travel, school, immigration, and military records, along with voting and residential patterns.

Notes

PREFACE

1. Official Court Reporter's Transcript of the Proceedings, Superior Court of the State of California for the County of Los Angeles, dept. no. 111, Hon. Joyce A. Karlin, Judge. *The People of the State of California, Plaintiff vs. Soon Ja Du, Defendant*, no. BA 037738 (hereafter referred to as *People v. Du*), 10,632 *passim*. Andrea Ford, "Korean Grocer Denies Pointing Gun at Girl," *Los Angeles Times* (hereafter *LAT*), Oct. 3, 1991, B1. Regarding Korean-black relations in contemporary Los Angeles, see, for example, Sumi Cho, "Korean Americans vs. African Americans: Conflict and Construction," in *Reading Rodney King, Reading Urban Uprising*, ed. Robert Gooding-Williams (New York: Routledge, 1993), 196–211. Also see in that text, Elaine Kim, "Home is Where the *Han* Is: A Korean-American Perspective on the Los Angeles Upheavals," 215–234; and the essays of Edward Chang, Ella Stewart, Jeff Chang, Larry Aubry, Eric Nakano, and Walter Lew in *Amerasia Journal* 19, no. 2 (1993): 1–54, 87–107, 149–56, 167–74.

2. King was arrested on March 3, 1991.

3. Courtroom described in Linda Deutsch, "Korean Grocer Gets Probation in Killing of Black Teen," *Daily News* (early edition), Nov. 17, 1991, A10.

4. Ibid.

5. *People v. Du*, vol. 4, Oct. 3, 1991, 618.

6. Ibid., 598.

7. See, for example, Cho, "Korean Americans vs. African Americans" in Gooding-Williams, *Reading Rodney King*; and Bill Boyarsky, "Echoes From Bitter Past in South L.A.," *LAT*, Mar. 27, 1991, http://articles.latimes.com/1991-03-27/local/me-975_1_south-l-a. Also see Kim, "Home is Where the *Han* Is," in Gooding-Williams, *Reading Rodney King*; and the essays of E. Chang, Stewart, J. Chang, Aubry, Nakano, and Lew in *Amerasia Journal*.

8. Tupac Shakur, "Hellrazor," http://www.lyricsmode.com/lyrics/t/tupac/#share; "Keep Ya Head Up," http://www.sing365.com/music/lyric.nsf/keep-ya-head-up-lyrics-2pac/c4ec4762b806b8824825686a000cd809; Ice Cube, "Black Korea," http://www.asklyrics.com/display/ice-cube/black-korea-lyrics.htm. Regarding controversy surrounding "Black Korea," see Mickey Hess, *Icons of Hip Hop: An Encyclopedia of the Movement, Music, And Culture*, vol. 2 (Westport, CT: Greenwood, 2007), 304.

9. "Tupac Shakur Songs," http://www.whosdatedwho.com/tpx_2376/tupac-shakur/songs.

10. "Legacy of the Riots: Charting the Hours of Chaos," *LAT*, April 29, 2002, http://articles.latimes.com/2002/apr/29/local/me-replay29.

11. Race, class, nativity, place of residence, age and religion are variables which pull at easy assumptions about the cultural identities of Latasha Harlins, Soon Ja Du, or Joyce Karlin. Latasha Harlins was African American, but her age (15 years) and her class (working poor), place of residence (South Central), and place of birth (East St. Louis) probably meant that her cultural traits, attitudes, and designs differed from those of an African American middle-aged, middle-class woman born and raised in suburbia, perhaps educated in private or parochial schools. The distinct cultural gulf between these two females might be almost as large as those between Soon Ja Du and Joyce Karlin. Likewise, Soon Ja Du's cultural identity and practices certainly were different from those of a Korean American girl of Latasha's age who attended an inner-city school. Joyce Karlin's Jewish American heritage, on the other hand, could place her in a disparately wide array of possible cultural attitudes, behaviors, and expectations. As one scholar of Jewish American women notes on the predicament of trying to write about "Jewish women" as a significant historical category, "just as the diversity of America's women precludes a single story, so too the diversity of America's Jewish women makes it difficult to construct a single, overarching narrative. Even ethnicity and religion, which would seem to bind Jewish women, are deeply variegated historical variables." In Karlin's case as well, the wealth of her family certainly had cultural ramifications that undoubtedly contributed to both her social distance and cultural difference from Harlins or Du, as well as most of the other women who came into her courtroom. Pamela S. Nadell, "On Their Own Terms: America's Jewish Women, 1954–2004 (Part Two: Recent American Jewish History, 1954–2004) *American Jewish History* 91, no. 4 (Sept. 2003): 390. The term social distance used here refers to that pioneered by Georg Simmel but lately reexamined by Philip Ethington in, for example, "The Intellectual Construction of 'Social Distance':Toward a Recovery of Georg Simmel's Social Geometry," *Cybergo*, modified June 21, 2007, http://www.cybergeo.eu/index227.html.

12. Pincus and Ehrich indicate, for example, that ethnic stereotypes of an earlier day were rooted in beliefs about the biological differences among people. Today, there is no longer a widespread or strongly held sense of biological inferiority. There is, rather, a sense of "cultural" difference. So, for example, minority groups are not rejected because they are seen as innately inferior, but because their "lifestyle" is unacceptable. F. L. Pincus, and H. J. Ehrich, introduction to their *Race and Ethnic Conflict*, 2nd ed. (Boulder, CO: Westview, 1999), 1–7.

13. The racial makeup of Compton in 1990 was 55% black, 1.8 % white, .5% Asian, .5% Pacific Islander, 1.3% Native American, and 42% Hispanic. "Racial/Ethnic

Composition of Cities by Percentages, Los Angeles County, 1990 Census," *Los Angeles Almanac,* http://www.laalmanac.com/population/po38_1990.htm.

14. Section 1 of the Fourteenth Amendment reads: "All persons born or naturalized in the United States and subject to the jurisdiction thereof, are citizens of the United States and of the State wherein they reside. No State shall make or enforce any law which shall abridge the privileges or immunities of citizens of the United States; nor shall any State deprive any person of life, liberty, or property, without due process of law; nor deny to any person within its jurisdiction the equal protection of the laws." Information Institute, Cornell Law School, http://topics.law.cornell.edu/constitution/amendmentxiv.

15. Chart 1, "Minority Proportion of the Incarcerated Population by State," Feb. 22, 2002, and Table 2b, "Rates of Incarceration Among 100,000 Women (18–64)," Human Rights Watch Press Backgrounder, found at: http://www.hrw.org/backgrounder/usa/race/pdf/chart1.pdf.

16. The District of Columbia had the largest percentage, overall, of black and Latino incarceration—95% of its incarcerated population. Ibid.

17. Joe Hicks is quoted in Penelope McMillarn, "'I'll Never Quit': The Slaying of Latasha Harlins Impels Her Aunt on A Crusade," *LAT,* Jan. 3, 1993, http://articles.latimes.com/1993-01-01/local/me-2961_1_harlins-family.

CHAPTER 1

1. Dr. Riley's testimony is drawn from the official autopsy of Latasha Harlins, performed on March 18, 1991, Official Court Reporter's Transcript of the Proceedings, Superior Court of the State of California for the County of Los Angeles, dept. no. 111, Hon. Joyce A. Karlin, Judge. *The People of the State of California, Plaintiff vs. Soon Ja Du, Defendant,* no. BA 037738 (hereafter referred to as *People v. Du*), 10,632, in the author's possession, 135.

2. The age range for Latasha Harlins indicated in this statistic is 14–17 years. Ninety-four percent of African American homicide victims, however, are killed by African Americans. Most female homicides are committed by men. As such, Harlins's death at the hands of Du was quite unusual. James Alan Fox and Marianne W. Zawitz, US Dept. of Justice, Bureau of Justice Statistics, *Homicide Trends in the United States* (Washington, DC: US Dept. of Justice, BJS, 2010), under "Trends by Race" and "Trends by Gender," http://bjs.ojp.usdoj.gov/content/pub/pdf/htius.pdf.

3. Ibid., under "Trends by Race" and "Victim/Offender Relationship." Interracial homicides have increased since the 1990s. A similar report from 1999 showed only three out of ten homicides were interracial when the victim and offender were strangers. Ibid., US, 3.

4. Latasha's sister is referred to as "Veronica" in Itibari Njeri's work; however, several articles from the *Los Angeles Times* refer to her as Christina. See Njeri, *The Last Plantation: Color, Conflict, and Identity: Reflections of a New World Black* (Boston: Houghton Mifflin, 1997), 63; Jesse Katz and John H. Lee, "Conflict Brings Tragic End to Similar Dreams of Life," *LAT,* Apr. 8, 1991, A19; Penelope McMillan, "'I'll Never Quit': The Slaying of Latasha Harlins Impels her Aunt on a Crusade," *LAT,* Jan. 1, 1993, http://articles.latimes.com/1993-01-01/local/me-2961_1_harlins-family.

5. "Order to Show Cause and Temporary Restraining Order" (Domestic Violence/Uniform Parentage)," *Crystal Harlins v. Sylvester Acoff* (Mun. Ct. L.A. County, Aug. 7, 1984, no. D112275) (hereafter cited as *Harlins v. Acoff*).

6. *People v. Du*, Oct. 1, 1991, 142.

7. JonSandy Campbell in discussion with the author, Oct. 1, 2004. Author met JonSandy through her enrollment at UCLA.

8. Ibid.

9. *People v. Superior Court (Du)* (1992) 5 Cal. App. 4th 822 (7 Cal. Rptr. 2d 177); "Karlin Did Not Abuse Discretion," *Korea Times*, May 4, 1992, 6.

10. US Department of Commerce, Bureau of the Census, *Tenth Census of the United States, 1880, Horn Lake, DeSoto, Mississippi*; Roll: *646*; Family History Film: *1254646*; Page: *454A*; Enumeration District: *053*; Image: *0542*. http://www.ancestry.com.

11. In the 1920 federal census is Luella Hallins (later Lula Thomas) living with her father, Squire Hallins (46) in Beat 2 in Sunflower, Mississippi. She is 16 in 1920. Her mother's name is Cora (39), and she has the following siblings: Rosie Lee (19), B. W. Hallins (18), Marie Hallins (12), Inell Hallins (10), and Benjamin Hallins is two-and-three-quarters years old. US Dept. of Commerce, Bureau of the Census, *Fourteenth Census of the United States: 1920–Population: Mississippi*, roll T625_894, Sunflower, Sunflower County, Mississippi, Beat 2, e.d. 118, 12B, family no. 286, household of Squire Hallins, line 94, image 652, http://www.ancestry.com/.

Sunflower, Mississippi, was an extremely small, rural community, famous only for the people who left. One of Ruth's parents' contemporaries would have been Willie Best, who was among the most prolific black actors of the 1930s and 1940s. Best appeared in more than 124 films and was a regular on the CBS comedy *My Little Margie*.

12. At the age of 38, Ed was the head of a household that consisted of his wife Lula, who was also 38; their two sons Ed and Ben, ages 15 and 13, respectively; and Lula's son by another man, Ernest Hallins, who was 18 at the time. Ed and his parents were born in Alabama. Lula and her parents were born in Mississippi. Ernest had been born in Mississippi. They were all listed as farm hands. US Dept. of Commerce, Bureau of the Census, *Fifteenth Census of the United States: 1930–Population: Alabama*, roll 46, Bethany, Pickens County, Alabama, e.d. 27, 9B, family no. 157, household of Ed Thomas, line 61, image 504, http://www.ancestry.com/.

13. Teresa Saunders, "WWII Comes to Life in at Aliceville POW Museum," *ALFA Friends and Family: Alabama Farmers Federation Publication* (Winter 2006), http://www.alfafarmers.org/friendsnfamily/friendsnfamilyStory.phtml?id=4103.

14. Bureau of the Census, *1930–Population: Alabama*, 9B.

15. Njeri, *Last Plantation*, 74.

16. Leon Litwack, *Trouble in Mind: Black Southerners in the Age of Jim Crow* (New York: Alfred A. Knopf, 1998), 52–325 *passim*.

17. Ibid., 13–5, 218–70 *passim*; Darlene Clark Hine and Kathleen Thompson, *A Shining Thread of Hope: The History of Black Women in America* (New York: Broadway Books, 1998), 193; Michael W. Fitzgerald, "Reconstruction in Alabama," *Encyclopedia of Alabama*, July 28, 2011, http://encyclopediaofalabama.org/face/Article.jsp?id=h-1631.

18. Virginia Van der Veer Hamilton, *Alabama: A History* (New York: W.W. Norton, 1984), 44–7.

19. "The Lynching Calendar: African Americans Who Died in Racial Violence in the United States, 1865–1965," http://www.autopsis.org/foot/lynchplaces1.html.

20. M. Watt Espy and John Ortiz Smykla, "Executions in the US, 1608–2002: The ESPY File, Executions By State," Death Penalty Information Center, 1–20 *passim*, Mar. 2011, http://www.deathpenaltyinfo.org/documents/ESPYstate.pdf; Bgill, "Female Hangings, 1632 to 1900," Fold 3 (blog), May 12, 2007, last modified Oct. 13, 2011, http://www.fold3.com/page/821_female_hangings_1632_to_1900/; Laura James, "Women and the Death Penalty in Alabama—Part One: The Rare Victorian Hanging," *CLEWS: Historic True Crime* (blog), Nov. 15, 2005, http://www.laura-james.com/clews/2005/11/women_and_the_d_1.html.

21. Espy and Smykla, "Executions in the US," 1–20 *passim*; Bgill, "Female Hangings"; James, "Women and the Death Penalty."

22. Transcript testimony of Amelia Robinson of Tuskegee, Alabama quoted in "Remembering Jim Crow: A Documentary by American RadioWorks," from a broadcast by Deborah Amos on NPR's *Morning Edition* (Feb. 27, 2002), American RadioWorks, Oct. 2001, http://americanradioworks.publicradio.org/features/remembering/transcript.html.

23. "Thirty Years of Lynching in the United States, 1889–1918" (New York: NAACP, April 1919), cited in Henritta Vinton Davis, "Black Women Who Were Lynched in America," Henrietta Vinton Davis's weblog, Aug. 1, 2008, http://henrietavintondavis.wordpress.com/2008/08/01/black-women-who-were-lynched-in-america/.

24. "NAACP Papers, part 7: The Anti-Lynching Campaign, 1912–1955," series B: Anti-Lynching Legislative and Publicity Files, 1916–1955 [June or July 1922?], Library of Congress (microfilm, reel 3, frames 570–3), quoted in "The Anti-Lynching Crusaders: The Lynching of Women," *Digital History*, Sept. 8, 2008, http://www.digitalhistory.uh.edu/learning_history/lynching/anti_lynching1.cfm.

25. Ida B. Wells, *Southern Horror and Other Writings: The Anti-Lynching Campaign of Ida B. Wells, 1892–1900*, ed. Jacqueline Jones Royster (Boston: Bedford/St. Martins, 1997), esp. 127–30.

26. Hamilton, *Alabama*, 47, 88–9; Dan T. Carter, *Scottsboro: A Tragedy of the American South* (Baton Rouge: Louisiana State University Press, 1969); Leon F. Litwack, "Hellhounds," in *Without Sanctuary: Lynching Photography in America*, ed. James Allen, Hilton Als, Jon Lewis, and Leon F. Litwack (Santa Fe, NM: Twin Palms, 2000), 12; Espy and Smykla, "Executions in the US," 1–20 *passim*.

27. Wells, *Southern Horrors*, 31, 129–30.

28. Danielle L. McGuire, *At the Dark End of the Street: Black Women, Rape, and Resistance—A New History of the Civil Rights Movement from Rosa Parks to the Rise of Black Power* (New York: Knopf, 2010), 3–7.

29. Chocolatesmoothie, "Rape of Black Women in the Jim Crow Era: Why Is It Left Out of History?" The Dawn Ali Network (blog), March 9, 2011, http://www.dawnali.com/lovinmysistas/index.php?topic=2629.0.

30. Eugene Gordon, "Alabama Authorities Ignore White Gang's Rape of Negro Mother," *Worker* (New York), Nov. 19, 1944, 10, http://2.bp.blogspot.com/KLQtXd-ocwHo/TWBjmISEBcI/AAAAAAAAAEs/bqvsWsWfFsc/s1600/alabama-authorities-ignore-rape-of-negro-mother.jpg.

31. Black Republicans were threatened with reenslavement and some were auctioned off for $2 per month as a result of the election riot of 1874 in Eufaula, Alabama. US Congress, House, *House Select Committee on the Memphis Riots*, 39th Congress, 1st sess., 101, July 25, 1866 (Reprint, New York: Arno Press, 1969); Regarding the Eufaula riot, see Mary Ellen Curtin, *Black Prisoners and Their World, Alabama, 1865–1900*, (Charlottesville: University Press of Virginia, 2000), 55–6; Regarding race riots in general, see Paul Mitchell, *Race Riots in Black and White* (Englewood Cliffs, NJ: Prentice Hall, 1970).

32. "Race Riot in Alabama," *New York Times*, Oct. 20, 1902.

33. "Denies Gordo Race Riot," *New York Times*, December 12, 1907; "Alabama Mob Would Wipe Out Entire Negro Population," *New Orleans Picayune*, December 11, 1907, accessed August 12, 2011, http://cgi.ebay.com/1907-newspaper-Gordo-AL-ABAMA-Race-Riot-KILL-ALL-NEGROES-/370482748707#ht_2851wt_698 (site discontinued).

34. "Rural Section Scene of Racial Strife," *Memphis Evening Appeal*, July 8, 1930. Emelle is located in Sumter County on the southern border of Pickens County. Pickens County houses both Gordo and Aliceville, the home town of Ruth Harlins. Emelle is known not for the race riot which occurred there in 1930, however, but for being the site of the largest hazardous waste landfill in the Unites States. Sumter County's population is 75% black, which corroborates a significant number of studies that link race and poverty to environmental hazards. "More Minorities Live around Emelle Site Study Finds Disproportionate Number of Minorities around Several of Nation's Biggest Toxic Facilities," *Mobile Register* (Alabama), Aug. 26, 1994, 1.

35. Jacqueline Jones, *Labor of Love, Labor of Sorrow: Black Women, Work and the Family, from Slavery to the Present*, (New York: Basic Books, 1985), 96–8; Litwack, *Trouble in Mind*, 52–325 passim; Darlene Clark Hine and Kathleen Thompson, *A Shining Thread of Hope: The History of Black Women in America* (New York: Broadway Books, 1998), 167–71; National Education Association, http://www.brown-vboard.net/resources/pdf/ms_02b.pdf.

36. That same year, less than 33% of employed white women were domestics; about 33% were in industry; 10% were professionals; 7% in clerical; and 4% in sales. See Teresa L. Amott and Julie A. Matthaei, *Race, Gender and Work: A Multicultual Economic History of Women in the United States* (Boston: South End Press, 1991), 157–8.

37. Amott and Matthaei, *Race, Gender and Work*, 158.

38. During the decade she left, the state's overall population increased from 2.83 to 3.06 million, but its black population declined by 0.4%. William Warren Rogers, Robert David Ward, Leah Rawls Atkins, and Wayne Flynt, *Alabama: The History of a Deep South State* (Tuscaloosa, Alabama: University of Alabama Press, 1994), 518.

39. Quoted in: Jesse Katz and John H. Lee, "Conflict Brings Tragic End," *LAT*, Apr. 8, 1991, A19.

40. Brenda Stevenson, "Abolition," in *Black Women in America: An Historical Encyclopedia*, ed. Darlene Clark Hine, vol. 1 (New York: Carlson, 1993), 1–2.

41. Regarding the black women's club movement see, for example, Deborah Gray White, *Too Heavy a Load: Black Women In Defense of Themselves, 1894–1994* (New York: W.W Norton, 1999).

42. Shirley Ann Wilson Moore, "'Your Life Is Really Not Just Your Own:' African American Women in Twentieth-Century California," in *Seeking El Dorado: African Americans in California*, eds. Lawrence B. De Graaf, Kevin Mulroy, and Quintard Taylor (Los Angeles: Autry Museum of Western Heritage, 2001), 219; Hine and Thompson, *A Shining Thread of Hope*, 180–2.

43. Hine and Thompson, *A Shining Thread of Hope*, 192–205, 217–33; Lawrence B. De Graaf and Quintard Taylor, "African Americans in California History, California in African American History," in De Graaf, Mulroy, and Taylor, *Seeking El Dorado*, 18.

44. Njeri, *Last Plantation*, 83.

45. With regard to the attitudes that socioeconomically poor, urban blacks hold about the police, and their distinction from whites of similar socioeconomic status, see, for example, Richard Scaglion and Richard G. Condon, "The Structure of Black and White Attitudes Towards the Police," *Human Organization* 39, no. 3 (Fall 1980): 280–83.

46. Kenneth Clark, *Dark Ghetto: Dilemmas of Social Power*, 2nd ed. (Middletown, CT: Wesleyan University Press, 1989), 63–110 *passim*; William Julius Wilson, *The Truly Disadvantaged: The Inner City, the Underclass, and Public Policy* (Chicago: University of Chicago Press, 1987).

47. Njeri, *Last Plantation*, 75.

48. Jones, *Labor of Love, Labor of Sorrow*, 156–60.

49. Illinoistown became East St. Louis in 1859 when it was officially laid out, surveyed, and plotted. Barb Baugher, Diane Timlin, and Mark Child, "History of East St. Louis," East St. Louis Social History Project, University of Illinois at Urbana-Champaign, last modified Oct. 29, 1995, http://www.eslarp.uiuc.edu/la/la437-f95/reports/History/timeline.html.

50. Ibid.

51. Tara Fasol, "Notorious Gangster Charlier Birger Hanged 80 Years Ago," *The Southern*, http://thesouthern.com/news/local/article_3e055ed8-033d-556c-bb05-36b8a195e240.html; Bill Monson, "The Sheltons, Downstate Gangsters," *Zephyr* (Galesburg, IL), http://www.thezephyr.com/monson/sheltons.htm.

52. Malcolm McLaughlin, *Power, Community, and Racial Killing in East St. Louis* (New York: Palgrave MacMillan, 2005), 45–55.

53. Dennis R. Judd and Robert E. Mendelson, *The Politics of Urban Planning* (Urbana: University of Illinois Press, 1973), xii, 4–5.

54. Baugher, Timlin, and Child, "History of East St. Louis."

55. Tabitha C. Wang, "East St. Louis Race Riot: July 2, 1917," Black Past.com, http://www.blackpast.com/?q=aah/east-st-louis-race-riot-july-2-1917.

56. Ibid.

57. Bill Nunes, "Race Riot at East St. Louis—1917," East St. Louis Social History Project, University of Illinois at Urbana-Champaign, Oct. 29, 1995, http://www.eslarp.uiuc.edu/ibex/archive/nunes/esl%20history/race_riot.htm; McLaughlin, *Power, Community and Racial Killing*, 7–124; Also see: Elliott M. Rudwick, *Race Riot at East St. Louis, July 2, 1917* (New York: World, 1964).

58. Nunes, "Race Riot at East St. Louis."

59. Ibid. See also "Brutal 1917 East St. Louis White-on-Black Race-Riot Disaster: Worst in American History," Biot Report #414, March 20,2007, Suburban Emergency Management Project, http://www.semp.us/publications/biot_reader. php?BiotID=414.

60. McLaughlin, *Power, Community, and Racial Killing*, 29–63 passim.

61. Ibid., 157.

62. Ibid.

63. Ibid., 158.

64. Ibid.

65. Melvin Oliver, James Johnson, and Walter Farrell, "Anatomy of a Rebellion: A Political-Economic Analysis," in *Reading Rodney King, Reading Urban Uprising*, ed. Robert Gooding-Williams (New York: Routledge, 1993), 119, table 9.1.

66. The second-largest city with a population of more than 50,000 persons. Baugher, Timlin, and Child, "History of East St. Louis"; Nunes, "Race Riot at East St. Louis."

67. Ibid.

68. Judd and Mendelson, *The Politics of Urban Planning*, 18.

69. Typically, about 107 men for every 100 women migrated. In 1940, 550 more black women than men lived in East St. Louis. US Dept. of Commerce, Bureau of the Census, *Fifteenth Census of the United States: 1930*, vol. 3, pt. 1 (Washington, DC: GPO, 1932), 610, 619, 629; US Dept. of Commerce, Bureau of the Census, *Sixteenth Census of the United States: 1940*, vol. 2, pt. 2 (Washington, DC: GPO, 1942).

70. Less than 1% of black women worked in sales and clerical positions and slightly more than 2% were in management/administration. Their professional ranks had improved some since 1900, but only slightly—3.4% were designated professionals (up from 1.2%, but again these primarily were teachers). In 1939, 4.3% of employed black women in the United States were professionals, but still less than 1% were proprietors, managers, officials, or craftsmen. Seventy percent still worked in domestic and other kinds of service, 16% were farmworkers and only 6.2% were factory operatives. In 1949, service still accounted for 61% of black women's work. They had gained increase representation in factories by almost 8% and clerical sales 3%. A precipitous 10% decline in farm labor resulted largely from southern outmigration. Gerald David Jaynes, and Robin M. Williams, Jr., eds., *A Common Destiny: Blacks and American Society* (Washington DC: National Academy Press, 1989), 273, table 6-1; Jones, *Labor of Love*, 261–2.

71. In 1949, the year that Ruth Harlins came to St. Louis, southern black women's annual earnings were 17% less compared with southern women than when compared with white women in other regions of the nations. By 1959, factory work had not increased to more than 14% and farm labor was still at 1949 levels. By 1984, black women's earnings nationally were 97% that of white women, 78% that of black men, and 53% that of white men, everywhere except in the South were they were still only 83% of that of white women. Ibid.

72. Jaynes and Williams, *A Common Destiny*, 273, table 6.1, 296–8, quote on 297; Jones, *Labor of Love*, 261–2.

TABLE 1.1 National Occupation Distribution of African American Women, 1900–1990

Occupation	1900	1920	1930	1940	1950	1960	1970	1980	1990
Agriculture	44.2*		24.7*	1	9.4	3.6	1.4	.6	
Manufacture	2.6*	7.0+	5.5+	6.2	14.9	14.1	17.6	14.9	
External Household Service	43.5*		53.5*	60	42	35.2	17.5	6.5	
Wholesale and Retail Trades				4.2	10.3	10.1	12.2	14.3	
Clerical and Sales				1.4	5.4	10.8	23.4	32.4	
Professional and Technical	1.2*		3.4*	4.4	6.4	6.5	11.6	16.2	
Managerial, Administrative And Official	0.5*		1.2*	.7	1.4	1.8	1.9	3.7	
Public Administration				.6	2.2	3.8	5.9	8.0	
Other Service				10.5	19.1	21.4	25.7	24.3	

Sources: Unless otherwise designated, the data for this table is drawn from: Jaynes and Williams, *A Common Destiny*, 273, table 6-1. All data signaled by (*) have been taken from: Teresa L. Amott and Julie A. Matthaei, *Race, Gender and Work*, 158, table 6.1. All data signaled by (+) have been taken from: Jacqueline Jones, *Labor of Love, Labor of Sorrow*, 201, 208, 237.

73. "Sumner High School, the First School West of the Mississippi for Blacks, Established in 1875 (among Graduates are Grace Bumbry, Arthur Ashe and Tina Turner)," in "Travel Advisory; Black History in St. Louis" *New York Times*, May 10, 1992, Travel section.

74. Njeri, *Last Plantation*, 92.

75. Ibid., 7, 88.

76. Ibid., 90.

77. Ibid., 7, 88.

78. *The People of the State of California v. Cora Mae Anderson*, official transcript (Mun. Ct. L.A. County, January 15, 1986, Super. Ct. L.A. County, Nov. 30, 1985, no. 85-15065), 3–38, (hereafter cited as *People v. Anderson*); Denise Harlins, in discussion with the author, July 16, 1993.

79. Njeri, *Last Plantation*, 74.

80. Ibid., 58–9.

81. See Jaynes and Williams, *A Common Destiny*, 519.

82. Lee Rainwater, *Behind Ghetto Walls: Black Family Life in a Federal Slum* (Chicago: Aldine, 1970), 48–61, quote on 51.

83. Ibid.

84. G. Louis Heath, "Corrupt East St. Louis: Laboratory for Black Revolution," HieroGraphics Online, last modified November 24, 2004, http://hierographics.org/CorruptEastStLouis.htm, first published in *Progressive* 34, no.10 (Oct. 1970).

85. Ibid.

86. Hine and Thompson, *A Shining Thread of Hope*, 174–7; Louie Robinson, "Death Threatens Western Town," *Ebony*, June 1967, 60–6, http://www.ebony.com/archives.

87. R.J. Smith, *The Great Black Way: L.A. in the 1940s and the Lost African American Renaissance* (New York: Public Affairs, 2006), 40–1.

88. Moore, "'Your Life Is Really Not just Your Own,'" 213.

89. Jack D. Forbes, "The Early African Heritage of California," in De Graaf, Mulroy, and Quintard, *Seeking El Dorado*, 73, 90n1; also see Marne L. Campbell, "African American Women, Wealth Accumulation, and Social Welfare Activism in 19th Century Los Angeles," *Journal of African American History*, vol. 94, no. 4 (Fall 2012), 376–400.

90. Forbes, "The Early African Heritage," 79.

91. Ibid., 79–81. Forbes has a detailed discussion of "racial hybridization and the attempts to "whiten" or racially reclassify early California families, not only in Los Angeles, but also in Santa Barbara, San Jose, Monterey, and San Francisco. As the population in these villages increased, reclassification efforts diminished the recorded number of African-descended residents. This effort was initiated by the persons themselves and supported by authorities who allowed people to do so. Even so, the colonial government would not allow African-descended persons to move completely out of their "racial status," and its implied social, political, and occupational status. Still, racially mixed persons of partial African descent were able to become prominent, serving as mayors, with high military commissions, and successful business people. See ibid., 80–7.

92. Ibid., 89. For a discussion of black Los Angeles during the mid-twentieth century, see Josh Sides, *L.A. City Limits: African American Los Angeles from the Great Depression to the Present* (Berkeley: University of California Press, 2003), *passim*; Douglas Flamming, *Bound for Freedom: Black Los Angeles in Jim Crow America* (Berkeley: University of California Press, 2005), *passim*; and Smith, *The Great Black Way, passim*.

93. By 1900, black women were 48% of black population in California. Willi Coleman, "African American Women and Community Development in California," in De Graaf, Mulroy, and Quintard, *Seeking El Dorado*, 103, table 1.

94. Christopher Clayton Smith, "Los Angeles: A Tradition of Violence" (senior honors thesis, UCLA, Department of History, 2011), 36.

95. William Deverell, *Whitewashed Adobe: The Rise of Los Angeles and the Remaking of Its Mexican Past* (Berkeley: University of California Press, 2005), 14.

96. Smith, "Los Angeles," 39.

97. See, for example, Kaitlin Boyd's, "Constructing Criminals: Black Angeleno Women, the LAPD, and the Sex Trade, 1928–1938," M.A. Thesis, Program in

Afro-American Studies, UCLA, July 2012, 22–23. Boyd presents throughout her thesis compelling evidence regarding the criminalization of black women in early twentieth-century Los Angeles.

98. De Graaf and Taylor, "African Americans in California History," 15.

99. San Francisco, which had for the second half of the nineteenth century the largest number of black residents (1910), only had 1,642. In 1960, California had a total of 883,861 African American residents; Los Angeles had 334,916. Ibid., 19, 33.

100. Among the female population in Langston, Oklahoma, 95% were literate. Hine and Thompson, *A Shining Thread of Hope*, 174–7.

101. Moore, "'Your Life Is Really Not Just Your Own,'" 215–6; Hine and Thompson, *A Shining Thread of Hope*, 180–2.

102. Hine and Thompson, *A Shining Thread of Hope*, 192–205, 217–33; De Graaf and Taylor, "African Americans in California History," 18.

103. Njeri, *Last Plantation*, 92–3; DeGraff and Taylor, "African Americans in California History," 8.

104. Los Angeles in 1980 had a population of 2,966,850. It was the third-largest US city after New York and Chicago. Blacks were only 12.6% of LA County's population that year. Whites were 67.9%, Asian and Pacific Islanders were 5.8%, and Latinos were 27.6%. Alejandra Lopez, "Demographics of California Counties: A Comparison of 1980, 1990, and 2000 Census Data," in *CCSRE Race and Ethnicity in California: Demographics Report Series*, series advisors Matthew Snipp and Al Camarillo (Stanford, CA: Center for Comparative Studies in Race and Ethnicity, Stanford University, 2002), http://ccsre.stanford.edu/reports/report_9.pdf; U.S. Dept. of Commerce, Bureau of the Census, "Table 21. Population of the 100 Largest Urban Places: 1980," US Census Bureau: People and Households, last modified June 15, 1998, http://www.census.gov/population/www/documentation/twps0027/tab21.txt. See also "Demographics of the City of Los Angeles, 2000," The Religion-In-The-Americas Database, http://www.prolades.com/glama/la5c007/demographics_2000.htm.

105. Black females represented only 2.3% of Los Angeles in 1980. Census data show 268,147 black women resided in Los Angeles (city), out of a total population of 2,966,850. General Population Characteristics: California 6-89 (table 25) entire population.

106. Moore, "'Your Life Is Really Not Just Your Own,'" 223–4.

107. In 1984, for example, the earning capacity of black women nationally was 97% that of white women; up from 41%, 45 years earlier. Still, black women like those in the Harlins family who had perhaps fewer skills and certainly less education than some others, felt the financial gains less. Jaynes and Williams, *A Common Destiny*, 273, table 6.1, 296–8.

108. "Doris Davis Running Hard and Fast," *LAT*, Sept. 23, 1973, pt. 10, 1; "Black Americans in Congress, U. S. House of Rep., *History, Art and Archives*, Member Profiles, http://history.house.gov/Exhibitions-and-Publications/BAIC/Black-Americans-in-Congress/.

109. Sides, *L.A. City Limits*, 61–3.

110. Georges Sabagh and Mehdi Bozorgmehr, "Population Change: Immigration and Ethnic Transformation," in *Ethnic Los Angeles*, ed. Roger Waldinger and Mehdi Bozorgmehr (New York: Russell Sage, 1996), 87–9.

111. Ibid., 79, quoting the title of a book by David Rieff.

112. "City of Los Angeles Population by Community & Race 1990 Census," *Los Angeles Almanac*, http://www.laalmanac.com/LA/la00a.htm (site updated, 1990 Census data no longer available). See "Los Angeles: Population Profile," http://www.city.data.com/us-cities/The West/Los-Angeles-Population-Profile.html.

113. According to Ong, blacks were 13.4% of the impoverished in Los Angeles in 1989. Paul Ong, "Poverty and Employment Issues in the Inner Urban Core," in *South Central Los Angeles: Anatomy of an Urban Crisis*, ed. Allen J. Scott and E. Richard Brown, Working Paper Series, Ralph and Goldy Lewis Center for Regional Policy Studies, UCLA School of Public Affairs, Los Angeles, June 1, 1993, 2, http://escholarship.org/uc/item/4149t7pm.

114. Ibid., 7. According to Ong:

> The core is enormous, covering 105 square miles. It cuts across city boundaries, taking in parts of the City of Los Angeles, Inglewood, and Compton, and the unincorporated area of East Los Angeles. Within Los Angeles City, the core includes parts or all of the communities of Hollywood, Koreatown, Pico-Union, Adams, and South Central. The total population, according to the 1990 census, is over 1.6 million, and if this area was a city, it would rank fifth nationally, slightly behind Houston but ahead of Philadelphia. The core houses only 18.4 percent of the County's total population, but houses 38.0 percent of the County's poor. Not surprisingly, it is also the area where the violence of the 1992 riots/rebellion was concentrated.

115. Ibid., 3, table 1. The media wage gap between employed white and black men, for example, had shrunk to 31% by 1989. The median wage gap between employed white and black women had shrunk to 9%. The median wage gap between white and nonwhite Hispanic male and workers was 54 %and 50% respectively. Ibid., 5.

116. Njeri, *Last Plantation*, 66.

117. McMillan, "I'll Never Quit."

118. Gary Webb, "'Crack' Plague's Roots Are in Nicaragua War: Colombia-Bay Area Drug Pipeline Helped Finance CIA-Backed Contras '80s Effort to Assist Guerrillas Left Legacy of Drugs, Gangs in Black L.A.," *San Jose Mercury News*, Aug. 18, 1996, A1; Gary Webb, "Odd Trio Created Mass Market for 'Crack' L.A. Dealer Might Get Life," *San Jose Mercury News*, Aug. 19, 1996, A1; Gary Webb, "War on Drugs' Unequal Impact on U.S. Blacks: Contra Case Illustrates the Discrepancy, Nicaraguan Goes Free," *San Jose Mercury News*, Aug. 20, 1996, A1; Michael R. Bromwich, CIA, *Executive Summary: Contra-Crack Cocaine Controversy*, U.S Dept. of Justice Office of the Inspector General Special Report (December 1997), 1–7, http://www.justice.gov/oig/special/9712/exec.htm; US Congress, House of Representatives, California Representative Maxine Waters, "Congressional Black Caucus Seminar Draws 2,000," news release, Sept. 13, 1996, http://www.house.gov/waters/pr913cb.htm (site discontinued); http://newsmine.org/content.php.01=cabal-elite/cia-drug-mafia/cia-connection-la-crack-trade.txt.

119. Webb, "'Crack' Plague's Roots Are in Nicaragua War," A1; Webb, "Odd Trio Created Mass Market for 'Crack,'" A1; Webb, "'War on Drugs' Unequal Impact on U.S. Blacks," A1; Bromwich, *Executive Summary*, 1–7; US Congress, "Congressional Black Caucus Seminar Draws 2,000."

120. Webb, "'Crack' Plague's Roots Are in Nicaragua War," A1.

121. Webb, "Odd Trio Created Mass Market for 'Crack,'" A1.

122. Katz and Lee, "Conflict Brings Tragic End," A19; *Harlins v. Acoff.*

123. Harlins, discussion, July 16, 1993.

124. Katz and Lee, "Conflict Brings Tragic End," A19.

125. Njeri, *Last Plantation*, 69. Crystal Harlins's autopsy report notes that at the time of her death cocaine was in her body. Vester Harlins was arrested in Los Angeles County for the possession and sale of cocaine base. Autopsy report, Crystal Harlins, *People v. Anderson*; *People v. Sylvester A. Acoff* (Super. Ct. L.A. County, n.d., No. LAA3131504701), 1. (hereafter cited *People v. Acoff*).

126. Autopsy report, Crystal Harlins, *People v. Anderson.*

127. *Harlins v. Acoff.*

128. Quotes from ibid.

129. Ibid.

130. Njeri, *Last Plantation*, 69.

131. Lucy Salcido Carter, Lois A. Weithorn, and Richard E. Behrman, "Domestic Violence and Children: Analysis and Recommendations," *Domestic Violence and Children* 9, no. 3 (Winter 1999): 6–7; "The Affects of Domestic Violence on Children," Alabama Coalition Against Domestic Violence, http://www.acadv.org/children.html.

132. Carter, Weithorn, and Behrman, "Domestic Violence and Children," 6–7.

133. Ibid.

134. Violence Policy Center, "When Men Murder Women: An Analysis of 1998 Homicide Data. Females Murdered By Males in a Single Victim/Single Offender Incident. Part Two: Black Women," Oct. 2000, http://www.vpc.org/studies/dv3two. htm. Although the analysis of this data is drawn from a national study in 1998, its findings replicate data provided by the Department of Justice for the time period when Crystal Harlins was stalked and beaten by Vester Acoff. Although murder rates declined after 1999 for blacks and whites, male and female, male offenders of female victims, both black and white, remained the majority of homicide cases where these women were murdered. Moreover, so too did the disproportionately large murder rate of black females by intimates compared with the murder rate of white females by intimates. A similar study in 1998 by the Violence Policy Center involving Hispanic women in the five states which reported their ethnicity indicated that these women had a murder rate by intimates slightly higher than that of white women, but much less than black women. The study concluded that in 1998 the overall female homicide rate for Hispanic females is 2.89 per 100,000, with the white and black female homicide rates at 2.09 and 8.84 per 100,000, respectively. Violence Policy Center, "When Men Murder Women: An Analysis of 1998 Homicide Data. Females Murdered By Males in a Single Victim/Single Offender Incident. Part Three: Hispanic Women," Oct. 2000, http://www.vpc.org/studies/dv3three.htm. See also Fox and Zawitz, *Homicide Trends in the United States*, under "Intimate Homicide."

135. Black female "girlfriends" were most likely killed of all female victims by an "intimate." There is no evidence that Crystal Harlins and Vester Acoff ever married. Fox and Zawitz, *Homicide Trends in the United States*, under "Intimate Homicide."

136. Dorie Klein, "The Dark Side of Marriage: Battered Wives and the Domination of Women," in *Judge, Lawyer, Victim, Theif: Women, Gender Roles, and Criminal Justice*, ed. Nicole Hahn Rafter and Elizabeth Anne Stanko (Boston: Northeastern University Press, 1982), 89.

137. Quoted in Marchel'le Barber, "Why Some Men Batter, and Why Some Women Take It," *Ebony*, Oct. 1990, 56.

138. Quoted in ibid., 56.

139. Ibid., 58.

140. Ibid., 54–8; Rev. Arlington Pryor, "Domestic Violence: When Love Becomes Hurtful!" Black Women's Health.com, http://www.blackwomenshealth.com/blog/domestic-violence-when-love-becomes-hurtful/.

141. Klein, "The Dark Side of Marriage," 85.

142. Barber, "Why Some Men Batter, and Why Some Women Take It," 1.

143. Klein, "The Dark Side of Marriage," 87.

144. Ibid., 88; Barber, "Why Some Men Batter, and Why Some Women Take It," 1.

145. Autopsy Report, Crystal Harlins, *People v. Anderson*.

146. Center on Addiction and the Family, "Effects of Parental Substance Abuse on Children and Families," Phoenix House, http://www.coaf.org/professionals/effects%20.htm; Marina Barnard and Neil McKeganey, "The Impact of Parental Problem Drug Use on Children: What Is the Problem and What Can Be Done to Help?" *Addiction* 99, no. 5 (May 2004): 552–9, http://www.ncbi.nlm.nih.gov/pubmed/15078229.

147. Ibid.

148. "Savannah: Fourteen Philadelphia, Pennsylvania," in *Sugar in the Raw: Voices of Young Black Girls in America*, ed. Rebecca Carroll (New York: Three Rivers Press, 1996), 76.

149. *Harlins v. Acoff.*

150. *People v. Anderson*, 3–38.

151. With regard to the impact of cocaine use by female homicide victims, a study conducted in New York City for 1990–1991 indicates, for example, that "72 percent of African-American women ages 25 to 34 had been using cocaine before they died compared with 38 percent of white men and 44 percent of African-American men" and 59% of white women in that same age group. Cocaine was found in the bodies of 31% of New York homicide victims during this time frame. Also of importance with regard to Crystal Harlins's murder, the New York study found that firearms were used in "about three-fourths" of all the murders committed. Neil Swan, "31% of New York Murder Victims Had Cocaine in Their Bodies," *NIDA Notes* 10, no. 2 (Mar.–Apr. 1995), 1–2, http://archives.drugabuse.gov/NIDA_Notes/NNVol10N2/Homicide.html; Fox and Zawitz, *Homicide Trends in the United States*, under "Trends by Race" and "Weapons Used."

152. *People v. Anderson*, 3–38.

153. Njeri, *Last Plantation*, 61.

154. *People v. Anderson*, 1–2.

155. Ibid., 1–9, quote of Ruth Harlins, 6.

156. Quoted in Njeri, *Last Plantation*, 69.

157. Ibid., 71.

158. Campbell, discussion.

159. Njeri, *Last Plantation*, 58–9.

160. Quote from ibid., 61.

161. Ibid., 86.

162. "Latisha," in Carroll, *Sugar in the Raw*, 49.

163. Njeri, *Last Plantation*, 69.

164. Illinois State Prison System, Index of Defendants in Criminal Cases: Sylvester Acoff.

165. Bret Hart Middle School Honor Roll Annual Luncheon Programs, 6th Grade, 7th Grade, 1988, 1989, Bret Hart Middle School Library.

166. Katz and Lee, "Conflict Brings Tragic End," A19.

167. Njeri, *Last Plantation*, 92–3.

168. "Latisha," in Carroll, *Sugar in the Raw*, 51.

169. Quoted in Njeri, *Last Plantation*, 76.

170. Ibid., 77–8.

171. Ibid., 80.

172. Ibid., 78, 80.

173. Campbell, discussion.

174. Katz and Lee, "Conflict Brings Tragic End," A1, A18–A19, quote from A19.

175. Quoted in Njeri, *Last Plantation*, 79.

176. Campbell, discussion.

177. Katz and Lee, "Conflict Brings Tragic End," A19.

178. If Foster was sexually involved with Latasha when she was 14 and/or 15 years old, he could have been arrested for statutory rape or rape in the third degree (sex with a minor under the age of 16). Criminal and civil penalties could have applied. Noy S. Davis and Jennifer Twombly, *State Legislators' Handbook for Statutory Rape Issues* (Washington, DC: American Bar Association, Center on Children and the Law, 2000), 2–4, 10–1.

179. Intelius.com search lists Gerald Foster 1114 92nd Street W with a birth date of January 1, 1959. Latasha's birth date was January 1, 1976.

180. "How to Protect Your Child From Sexual Predators and Other Dangers," *Ebony*, Aug. 2002, 116.

181. Of course, there are some exceptions. Black females, especially victims of rape and sexual abuse, have mounted their own publicity and resistance campaigns that are just now beginning to get more widespread attention in the community. See, for example, the website, Dancing in the Darkness, at http://www.dancinginthedarkness.com, which includes the detailed narratives of more than 650 survivors. Early pioneers in the movement include Maya Angelou who writes of her rape in her much lauded *I Know Why the Caged Bird Sings* (reprinted, New York: Random House, 2002).

182. Campbell, discussion.

183. Ibid.

184. "Latisha," in Carroll, *Sugar in the Raw*, 45–6; ibid., 51.

185. Quoted in Njeri, *Last Plantation*, 143. Information drawn from Njeri. Marcolette Wideman may be an alias name being used by Njeri.

186. Ibid., 146.

187. Ibid.

188. Ibid., 143.

189. With regard to the alleged relationship between Latasha Harlins and Jerry Foster, the following California legal codes would apply under Penal Code section 261.5: (a) Unlawful sexual intercourse is an act of sexual intercourse accomplished with a person who is not the spouse of the perpetrator, if the person is a minor . . . (d) Any person 21 years of age or older who engages in an act of unlawful sexual intercourse with a minor who is under 16 years of age is guilty of either a misdemeanor or a felony, and shall be punished by imprisonment in a county jail not exceeding one year, or by imprisonment in the state prison for two, three, or four years; (e) (1) Notwithstanding any other provision of this section, an adult who engages in an act of sexual intercourse with a minor in violation of this section may be liable for civil penalties in the following amounts: . . . and (e) (1) (D) An adult over the age of 21 years who engages in an act of unlawful sexual intercourse with a minor under 16 years of age is liable for a civil penalty not to exceed twenty-five thousand dollars ($25,000). Cal. Pen. Code, § 261.5, subds. (a)-(e) (1) (D).

190. A very good discussion of turn of the twentieth-century laws, court actions, and societal responses to age-of-consent issues, particularly in California, can be found in Mary Odem, *Delinquent Daughters: Protecting and Policing Adolescent Female Sexuality in the United States, 1885–1920* (Chapel Hill: University of North Carolina Press, 1995).

191. Ibid., 79–81.

192. The author refers here to the light sentence the defendant received after being found guilty of killing Latasha's mother in 1986; *People v. Anderson*, 3–38.

193. Njeri, *Last Plantation*, 141–3.

CHAPTER 2

1. *The People of the State of California v. Soon Ja Du* (Cal. Super. Ct. L.A. County, Dept. 111, 1991, no. BA037738), vol. 3, Oct. 2, 1991, 322.

2. *People v. Du*, vol. 1, Sept. 30, 1991, 10–62 *passim*; Andrea Ford, "Korean Grocer Denies Pointing Gun at Girl," *LAT*, Oct. 3, 1991, B1; Regarding Korean-black relations in contemporary Los Angeles see, for example, Sumi Cho, "Korean Americans vs. African Americans: Conflict and Construction," in *Reading Rodney King, Reading Urban Uprising*, ed. Robert Gooding-Williams (New York: Routledge, 1993), 196–211. See also Elaine Kim, "Home is Where the *Han* Is: A Korean-American Perspective on the Los Angeles Upheavals," in Gooding-Williams, *Reading Rodney King,* 215–234; Edward Chang, "From Chicago to Los Angeles: Changing the Site of Race Relations," *Amerasia Journal* 19, no. 2 (1993): 1–3; Edward Chang, "Jewish and Korean Merchants in African American Neighborhoods: A Comparative Perspective," *Amerasia Journal* 19, no. 2 (1993): 5–21; Ella Stewart, "Communication between African Americans and Korean Americans: Before and After the Los Angeles Riots," 23–53; Jeff Chang, "Race, Class, Conflict and Empowerment: On Ice Cube's 'Black Korea,'" *Amerasia Journal* 19, no. 2 (1993): 87–107; Larry Aubry, "Black-Korean American Relations: An Insider's Viewpoint," *Amerasia Journal* 19, no. 2 (1993): 149–156; Erich Nakano, "Building Common Ground—The Liquor Store Controversy," *Amerasia Journal* 19, no. 2 (1993): 167–170; and Walter Lew, "Black Korea," *Amerasia Journal* 19, no. 2 (1993): 171–4.

3. Ford, "Korean Grocer Denies Pointing Gun at Girl," B1.

4. Njeri, *Last Plantation*, 94, 106.

5. *People v. Du*, vol. 3, Oct. 2, 1991, 320.

6. Hamish McDonald, "South Korea Owns Up to Brutal Past," *Sydney Morning Herald*, Nov. 15, 2008, http://www.smh.com.au/news/world/south-korea-owns-up-to-brutal-past/2008/11/14/1226318928410.html. See also Charles J. Hanley, Jae-Soon Chang, and Randy Herschaft, "Mass Killings in Korea: Commission Probes Hidden History of 1950," Associated Press, 2008, http://hosted.ap.org/specials/interactives/_international/korea_masskillings/index.html?SITE=A.

7. Ibid., A18–9.

8. The economy of the Republic of Korea was increasing 8% annually from the early years of the 1960s and continued to do so during the next few decades. Jong Wha-Lee, "Economic Growth and Human Development in the Republic of Korea, 1945–1992," Occasional Paper 24 Series, Human Development Reports, 1, http://hdr.undp.org/en/reports/global/hdr1997/papers/jong-wha_lee.pdf.

9. *People v. Du*, vol. 2, Oct. 1, 1991, 216–7.

10. Others argue that Korean women participated more in their home country's work force. Park also includes statistics that indicate women were 41% of the South Korean labor force in 1989. Kyeyoung Park, *The Korean American Dream: Immigrants and Small Business in New York City* (Ithaca: Cornell University Press, 1997), 114–6.

11. Katz and Lee, "Conflict Brings Tragic End," A18.

12. Park, *Korean American Dream*, 126–8.

13. Katz and Lee, "Conflict Brings Tragic End," A18.

14. Ibid.

15. Young I. Song, "A Korean-Centered Perspective on Korean American Women Today," in *Korean American Women: From Tradition to Modern Feminism*, ed. Young I. Song and Ailee Moon (Westport, CT: Praeger, 1998), 3.

16. Elaine Kim, "The Social Reality of Korean American Women: Toward Crashing with the Confucian Ideology," in Song and Moon, *Korean American Women*, 24.

17. Keum-Young Chung Pang, *Korean Elderly Women in America: Everyday Life, Health, and Illness* (New York: AMS Press, 1991), 102–3; quote on 103.

18. Kim, "Social Reality of Korean American Women," 27.

19. Lisa Park, "A Letter to My Sister," in *Contemporary Asian America: A Multidisciplinary Reader*, ed. Min Zhou and J. V. Gatewood, 2nd ed. (New York: New York University Press, 2007), 426.

20. Ji-Yeon Yun, *Beyond the Shadow of Camptown: Korean Military Brides in America*, Kindle ed. (New York: New York University Press, 2004), under "American Fever."

21. Kim, "Social Reality of Korean American Women," 27; Pang, *Korean Elderly Women in America*, 63.

22. Elaine H. Kim, "'At Least You're Not Black': Asian Americans in U.S. Race Relations," in "Crossing Lines: Revisioning U.S. Race Relations," ed. Anthony M. Platt, Elaine Kim, and Susan Roberta Katz, special issue, *Social Justice* 25, no. 3 (Fall 1998): 3–12.

23. Kim, "Social Reality of Korean American Women," 27; Pang, *Korean Elderly Women in America*, 63.

24. KAGRO (Korean American Grocers Association) statistic, quoted in Katz and Lee, "Conflict Brings Tragic End," A18.

25. Edna Bonacich, "The Social Costs of Immigrant Entrepreneurship," *Amerasia Journal* 14, no. 1 (1989): 119–28; Glenn Omatsu, "The 'Four Prisons' and the Movements of Liberation: Asian American Activism from the 1960s to the 1990s," in Zhou and Gatewood, *Contemporary Asian America*, 78.

26. Katz and Lee, "Conflict Brings Tragic End," A18.

27. Dexter H. Kim, "1, 867 KA Storeowners Suffer Heaviest Toll: Damages Estimated at $347 Million," *Korea Times*, May 11, 1992, 1, 8.

28. Compton had slightly more Asian/Asian-American residents in 1990 (114). Njeri, *Last Plantation*, 116-17.

29. Andrea Ford, "Videotape Shows Teen Being Shot After Fight," *LAT*, Oct. 1, 1991, B1.

30. Song, "Korean-Centered Perspective," 4.

31. Katz and Lee, "Conflict Brings Tragic End," A18.

32. Pang, *Korean Elderly Women*, 87.

33. Katz and Lee, "Conflict Brings Tragic End," A18.

34. Mr. Kim is quoted in Kyeyoung Park, "Use and Abuse of Race and Culture: Black-Korean Tension in America," *American Anthropologist* 98, no. 3 (Sept. 1996): 495. Soon Ja Du's surname precedes her given name in this context due to Korean cultural convention.

35. *People v. Du*, vol. 2, Oct. 1, 1991, 219–21.

36. Katz and Lee, "Conflict Brings Tragic End," A18; *People v. Du*, vol. 2, Oct. 1, 1991, 218, 295–6.

37. Katz and Lee, "Conflict Brings Tragic End," A18.

38. *People v. Du*, vol. 2, Oct. 1, 1991, 156.

39. Jack Leonard and Andrew Blankstein, "Chester Turner, Serial Killer on Death Row, is Charged with Four More Murders," *LAT*, Feb. 2, 2001, http://articles.latimes.com/2011/feb/02/local/la-me-serial-killer-20110202; "Serial Killer: Chester Dwayne Turner," Homicide Report, *LAT*, n.d. http://projects.latimes.com/homicide/list/chester-dewayne-turner/.

40. "Map: Grim Sleeper Killings, 1985–2007," Homicide Report, *LAT*, July 7, 2010, http://projects.latimes.com/homicide/list/grim-sleeper-killings/.

41. Katz and Lee, "Conflict Brings Tragic End," A18.

42. Ibid.

43. Njeri, *Last Plantation*, 95.

44. Ibid.

45. Patrick Joyce, *No Fire Next Time: Black-Korean Conflicts and the Future of American Cities* (Ithaca: Cornell University Press, 2003), 23–4.

46. *People v. Du*, vol. 1, Sept. 30, 1991, 74.

47. Katz and Lee, "Conflict Brings Tragic End," A18.

48. Joyce, *No Fire Next Time*, 24.

49. Njeri, *Last Plantation*, 95.

50. Quote from a resident in the neighborhood where Latasha Harlins lived and where the Empire Liquor Market was located, found in Nancy Abelmann and Jon Lie, *Blue Dreams: Korean Americans and the Los Angeles Riots* (Cambridge: Harvard University Press, 1995), 158.

51. Katz and Lee, "Conflict Brings Tragic End," A18.

52. Ibid.

53. *People v. Du*, vol. 2, Oct. 1, 1991, 224–5.

54. Richard Fruto, "Soon Ja Du's Two Tormentors Prison Bound," *Korea Times*, Sept. 15, 1991, 1.

55. Pyong Gap Min, *Caught in the Middle: Korean Communities in New York and Los Angeles* (Berkeley: University of California Press, 1996), 121.

56. Yun, *Beyond the Shadow of Camptown*, under "Prodigal Daughters, Filial Daughters."

57. Kim, "At Least You're Not Black," 4.

58. "Blackface in White & Yellow," YouTube video, posted by "BlackTruthForever," Aug. 15, 2009, http://www.youtube.com/watch?vv=vo5LKHMV3i4&feature=related.

59. Olalekan Waheed Temidire, "The Bubble Sisters and Racism in Korea," Allhiphop.com editorial, Mar. 19, 2003, http://allhiphop.com/2003/03/19/the-bubble-sisters-and-racism-in-korea/. See also Editorial, "Bubble of Ignorance," Chosunilbo, Feb. 26, 2003, http://english.chosun.com/.

60. Ibid.

61. "Hines Ward Speaks out About Lingering Korean Racism," Chosunilbo, May 15, 2006, http://english.chosun.com/site/data/html_dir/2006/05/15/2006051561019.html.

62. Yun, *Beyond the Shadow of Camptown*, under "Prodigal Daughters, Filial Daughters."

63. 1992 New York City Survey, quoted in Min, *Caught in the Middle*, Table 12, 121.

64. Report of Patricia Dwyer, quoted in Njeri, *Last Plantation*, 250.

65. Min, *Caught in the Middle*, 123–4.

66. Janet Clayton, "Tenuous New Alliances Forged to Ease New Korean-Black Tensions," *LAT*, (home edition), July 20, 1987, 1.

67. Min, *Caught in the Middle*, 121–5.

68. Frank Wu, *Yellow: Race in America Beyond Black and White* (New York: Basic Books, 2002), 31.

69. Ying Ma, "Black Racism," *United for a Multicultural Japan (UMJ)* Newsletter 2 no. 30, n.d., http://www.tabunka.org/newsletter/black_racism.html.

70. Wu, *Yellow*, 7–8.

71. Althea Yip, "Remembering Vincent Chin: Fifteen Years Later, a Murder in Detroit Remains a Turning Point in the APA Movement," *Asian Week: The Voice of Asian America* 18, no. 43 (June 13, 1997), http://asianweek.com/061397/feature.html; Christine Ho, "The Model Minority Awakened: The Murder of Vincent Chin—Part I" USAsians.net, 2003 http://us_asians.tripod.com/articles-vincentchin.html.

72. Yip, "Remembering Vincent Chin"; Ho, "The Model Minority Awakened—Part 1."

73. Helen Zia, *Asian American Dreams: The Emergence of an American People* (New York: Farrr, Strauss, and Giroux, 2000), 61.

74. Yip, "Remembering Vincent Chin"; Sucheng Chan, *Asian Americans: An Interpretive History* (New York: Twayne, 1991), 176–8.

75. Ebens also was found liable in a civil suit for $1.5 million. Rather than pay it, he divested all his assets and left the state. Chan, *Asian Americans*, 178; Yip, "Remembering Vincent Chin."

76. Quoted in Park, *Korean American Dream*, 142.

77. Yu, *Yellow*, 12–3; Committee of 100, *American Attitudes Toward Chinese Americans and Asian Americans* (New York: Committee of 100, 2001), "Summary of Findings," 18–9, http://www.committee100.org/publications/survey/C100survey. pdf.

78. Rosalind Chou and Joe R. Feagin, *The Myth of the Model Minority: Asian Americans Facing Racism* (Boulder: Paradigm, 2008), 75, 91–6.

79. Wu, *Yellow*, 30–1.

80. Quoted in Victor M. Hwang, "The Interrelationship between Anti-Asian Violence and Asian America," in *Anti-Asian Violence in North America: Asian-American and Asian Canadian Reflections on Hate, Healing and Resistance*, ed. Patricia Wong Hall and Victor M. Hwang (New York: Rowman and Littlefield, 2001), 46.

81. Ibid., 47.

82. Julie Chao, "Hate Crimes Against Asians Rise: Victims Often Feel Powerless, Blame Themselves; Some Suffer Flashbacks," *San Francisco Examiner*, Oct. 26, 1997, http://www.sfgate.com/cgi-bin/article.cgi?f=/e/a/1997/10/26/METRO12135.dtl.

83. Hwang, "The Interrelationship between Anti-Asian Violence and Asian America," 54.

84. For discussions of the modern history of black-Korean relations, see, for example, Park, *The Korean American Dream*, and Min, *Caught in the Middle*.

85. Courtland Milloy, "Increasing Self-Respect," *Washington Post*, Oct. 7, 1986, B3; Linda Wheeler, "Ill Will Over Good Hope Carry-Out in SE," *Washington Post*, Oct. 26, 1986, B1, C1; Karlyn Barker, "Blacks Demand Ouster of Asian Carryout Business," *Washington Post*, Sept. 30, 1986, B 2. Blacks in the neighborhood seem to have believed that the businessowner, Hung Chan Cheung, was Korean; but he was Chinese.

86. Jake Doherty, "Black-Korean Alliance Says Talks Not Enough: Disbands," *LAT*, Dec. 4, 1992, 1–2, http://articles.latimes.com/1992-12-24/news/mn-3564_1_ black-korean-alliance.

87. For a comprehensive list and discussion of these events see Joyce, *No Fire Next Time*, esp.12–16.

88. Ibid., 123. Young Kim also implemented most of these changes within a week after signing the agreement.

89. Ibid., 123–4. Black business owners were particularly involved in the protest that endured for more than a week.

90. "Merchants, Blacks Reach Agreement," *LAT*, Dec. 3, 1989, http://articles. latimes.com/1989-12-03/local/me-270_1_black-community.

91. Joyce, *No Fire Next Time*, 125. When the altercation between the black customer and the Korean owner occurred, police were called to the scene but refused to arrest the owner. An eyewitness then wrote a letter to city officials describing what had happened and City Attorney Kenneth Hahn charged the owner with misdemeanor assault.

92. Chou and Feagin, *Myth of the Model Minority*, x.

93. Wu, *Yellow*, 40–1, 49.

94. Quoted in Ki-Taek Chun, "The Myth of Asian American Success and Its Educational Ramifications," in *The Asian American Educational Experience*, ed. Don T. Nakanishi and Tina Yamano Nishida (New York: Routledge, 1994), 96.

95. John H. Kim, ed. "A Brief History of Korean Americans," National Association of Korean Americans, 2003, http://www.naka.org/resources/history.asp.

96. Ibid.

97. The Chinese exclusion act did not apply to migration to Hawaii until 1889, when the United States officially annexed the islands. Teresa L. Amott and Julie A. Matthaei, *Race, Gender and Work: A Multicultural Economic History of Women in the United States* (Boston: South End Press, 1991), 204.

98. Kim, "A Brief History of Korean Americans."

99. Sonia Shinn Sunoo, ed., *Korean Picture Brides: A Collection of Oral Histories* (Bloomington, IN: Xlibris, 2002), 172–7.

100. Amott and Matthaei, *Race, Gender and Work*, 95.

101. David M. Reimers, "The Korean-American Immigrant Experience," paper presented at The Legacy of Korea: Fiftieth Anniversary Conference (University of Missouri, Kansas City, MO, Oct. 25–27, 2001), http://www.trumanlibrary.org/korea/leffler.htm (site discontinued).

102. The most respected general histories of the African American experience include John Hope Franklin and Evelyn Brooks Higginbotham, *From Slavery to Freedom: A History of African Americans* 9th ed., (New York: McGraw-Hill, 2011); and Darlene Clark Hine, William Hine, and Stanley Harrold, *African Americans: A Concise History* (Upper Saddle River, NJ: Prentice Hall, 2003).

103. Amott and Matthaei, *Race, Gender and Work*, 193–249 *passim*.

104. William Speer, *The Oldest and the Newest Empire: China and the United States* (Cincinnati: National, 1870), 588–601, Internet Archive, http://archive.org/details/cu31924067561559.

105. Amott and Matthaei, *Race, Gender and Work*, 203.

106. Min, *Caught in the Middle*, 27. Other works also have explored Korean immigration. They include Alice Yun Chai, "Freed from the Elders but Locked into Labor: Korean Immigrant Women in Hawaii," *Women's Studies* 13, no. 3 (1987): 223–34; Bong-Youn Choy, *Koreans in America* (Chicago: Neilson Press, 1979); Kingsley K. Lyu, "Korean Nationalist Activities in Hawaii and the Continental United States, 1900–1945, Part I: 1900–1919," *Amerasia Journal* 4, no.1 (1977): 23–90; Wayne Patterson, *The Korean Frontier in America: Immigration to Hawaii, 1896–1910* (Honolulu: University of Hawaii Press, 1988); Linda Shin, "Koreans in America, 1903–1945," in *Roots: An Asian American Reader*, ed. Amy Tachiki, Eddie Wong, and Franklin Odo (Los Angeles: Asian American Studies Center, UCLA, 1971), 201–6.

107. Ryan Ige, "Immigrants," Pacific University's Portal on Korea, Nov. 27, 2003, http://mcel.pacificu.edu/korea/culture/immigrants.php.

108. Sunoo, *Korean Picture Brides*, 208.

109. Ibid.

110. Sunoo, *Korean Picture Bride*, 79–80.

111. Ige, "Immigrants."

112. *New York Tribute* editorial, quoted in Amott and Matthaei, *Race, Gender and Work*, 195. The Chinese Exclusion Act barred Chinese women from immigrating, even the wives of US residents except merchants. Sunoo, *Korean Picture Bride*, 204.

113. Chan, *Asian Americans*, 54–5.

114. Sunoo, *Korean Picture Brides*, 80.

115. Reimers, "Korean-American Immigrant Experience."

116. Amott and Matthaei, *Race, Gender and Work*, 195.

117. Min, *Caught in the Middle*, 27–8.

118. Chan, *Asian Americans*, 120–1.

119. Smith, *The Great Black Way*, 140–1.

120. The Gallup poll is quoted in Chan, *Asian Americans*, 121.

121. *Chinese Exclusion Repeal Act of 1943* (ch. 344, Dec. 17, 1943), *U.S. Statutes at Large 57* (1943), 600–1.

122. Chan, *Asian Americans*, 121.

123. George C. Mitchell, *Matthew B. Ridgway: Soldier, Statesman, Scholar, Citizen* (reprint, Mechanicsburg, PA: Stackpole Books, 2002), 44.

124. Reimers, "The Korean American Immigrant Experience."

125. Min, *Caught in the Middle*, 28.

126. In-Jin Yoon, *On My Own: Korean Businesses and Race Relations in America* (Chicago: University of Chicago Press, 1997), 58–9; Reimers, "The Korean American Immigrant Experience."

127. Min, *Caught in the Middle*, 34. California has attracted large percentages of other Asian ethnic groups. In 1990, 50% of Filipino Americans, 46% Vietnamese Americans, 43% of Chinese Americans resided in the state. Japanese Americans, as well as Chinese Americans and Filipino Americans, all outnumbered Koreans in Los Angeles County in 1990. But Korean Americans still were more concentrated in Los Angeles County than any other Asian ethnic group—60% as compared with 42% Japanese, 35% Chinese, 30% Filipino. Min argues that many Koreans migrated to Southern California (Los Angeles and Orange Counties) because of a number of conditions, including Koreatown's development as a cultural, social, and commercial center; quality of colleges and universities; warm weather; and the presence of other Asian groups. Ibid., 34; for the statistics, see ibid., 34–5.

128. Melvin L. Oliver, James H. Johnson Jr., and Walter C. Farrell Jr., "Anatomy of a Rebellion: A Political-Economic Analysis," in Gooding-Williams, *Reading Rodney King*, 119.

129. Pyong Gap Min and Young I. Song, "Demographic Characteristics and Trends of Post-1965 Korean Immigrant Women and Men," in Moon and Song, *Korean-American Women*, 50–2.

130. Aileen Moon, "Demographic and Socioeconomic Characteristics of Korean American Women and Men" in Song and Moon, *Korean American Women*, 39.

131. By 2000, the numbers of blacks in Los Angeles County had declined by 6%, while the numbers of API had increased by 25%. Data from the US Census, cited in "Race/Ethnic Composition Los Angeles County, 1990–2010: Population-All Races," *Los Angeles Almanac*, http://www.laalmanac.com/population/po13.htm.

132. Moon, "Demographic and Socioeconomic Characteristics," 36.

133. Min, *Caught in the Middle,* 33.

134. Jaynes and Williams, *A Common Destiny,* 134–5.

135. Kwang Chung Kim and Shin Kim, "The Multiracial Nature of Los Angeles Unrest in 1992," in *Koreans in the Hood: Conflict with African Americans,* ed. Kwang Chung Kim (Baltimore: Johns Hopkins University Press, 1999), 28.

136. In Jin Yoon, *On My Own: Korean Businesses and Race Relations in America* (Chicago: University of Chicago Press, 1997), 125, table 3.5.

137. Occupational data cited in Ilpyong J. Kim, "A Century of Korean Immigration to the United States: 1903–2003," in *Korean-Americans: Past, Present and Future,* ed. Ilpyong J. Kim (Elizabeth, NJ: Hollym, 2004), 32, table 7.

138. Economists note that the per capita income in the United States can vary according to the method of calculation. The various calculations for 1987 are $18, 841 and $20, 049. I have chosen to use the more conservative of these estimates. Bulent Temel, "GDP Per Capita: An Accurate or a Bum Steer?" About.com, economics.about.com/library/weekly/aa043004a.htm. Also see: Min and Song, "Demographic Characteristics and Trends," 53.

139. Min, *Caught in the Middle,* 28, 35.

140. Ibid., 35–36; Eui-Young Yu, "Koreatown, Los Angeles: Emergence of a New Inner-City Ethnic Community," *Bulletin of Population and Development Studies* 14 (1985): 29–44.

141. Min, *Caught in the Middle,* 40. See also Illsoo Kim, *New Urban Immigrants: The Korean Community in New York* (Princeton: Princeton University Press, 1981).

142. Approximately 25% of Koreans in Southern California are members of Catholic institutions. Min, *Caught in the Middle,* 40.

143. Ibid., 41.

144. The majority of Koreans are Buddhists. The United States has an especially large number of Christians who immigrated. Ibid., 40.

145. Yoon, *On My Own,* 45.

146. Min, *Caught in the Middle,* 42.

147. Katz and Lee, "Conflict Brings Tragic End," A19.

148. Min, *Caught in the Middle,* 40–5. Min writes in detail about the kind of support that Korean Christian churches, alumni associations, and media provided the Korean community in Los Angeles. He also compares this support network with similar institutions of support in New York. He is correct in his analysis, although he does not present a gendered analysis of these institutions.

149. Ibid., 43.

150. Ibid.

151. Yoon, *On My Own,* 42–5.

152. Ibid., 142–5.

153. Ibid.

154. Sumi K.Cho, "Korean Americans vs. African Americans: Conflict and Construction," in Gooding-Williams, *Reading Rodney King,* 200.

155. Yoon, *On My Own,* 145.

156. Cho, "Korean Americans vs. African Americans," 200.

157. Min, *Caught in the Middle,* 43–4.

158. Joyce, *No Fire Next Time*, 24.

159. Ivan Light and Elizabeth Roach, "Self-Employment: Mobility Ladder or Economic Lifeboat?" in *Ethnic Los Angeles*, ed. Roger Waldinger and Mehdi Bozorgmehr (New York: Russell Sage, 1996), 200–1.

160. Yoon, *On My Own*, 20–1. Pakistani's were ranked 28th; Asian Indians, 31st; Chinese, 50th; Thai, 55th; Japanese, 59th; Vietnamese, 73rd; Cambodians, 78th; Hawaiians, 84th; Filipino, 90th; Laotians, 96th; Guamanians, 97th; Samoans, 98th; and Malaysians, 99th.

161. Ibid. Yoon also documents the developing trend by conducting the same survey for 1980. During that year, Koreans ranked 8th in self-employment rates following, in order: Palestinians, Jordanians, Iraqis, Russians, Israelis, Iranians, and Lebanese. African Americans were ranked 92nd that year. The national average was 9.0. Ibid., 18–9.

162. The major exception were those of Guyanese descent, ranked no. 22 with an average family income of $48,910. Guyana, located on the northern coast of South America, is populated by people of African, French, Dutch, British, and Amerindian descent. Ibid., 22.

163. James H. Johnson and Melvin L. Oliver, "Economic Restructuring and Black Male Joblessness: A Reassessment," in *Urban Labor Market and Job Opportunity*, ed. George Peterson and Wayne Vroman (Washington, DC: Urban Institute, 1992), 130–47; US Census, *Statistical Abstract of the United States: 1999*, "Unemployment Rate by Race and Hispanic Origin, 1980–1998," 412, http://www.census.gov/prod/99pubs/99statab/sec13.pdf; and Oliver, Johnson, and Farrell, "Anatomy of a Rebellion," 122.

164. Yoon, *On My Own*, 22.

165. Moon, "Demographic and Socioeconomic Characteristics," 43, table 4.2.

166. Korean American women's marital status continued: 3.9% divorced, 1.2% separated, 43.1% never married, 5.3% widowed. Moon, "Demographic and Socioeconomic Characteristics," 42, table 4.2.

167. Ibid.

168. Peter Schmidt, "Gap Between White, Black Dropout Rates Has Virtually Closed," *Education Week*, Mar. 1, 1995, www.edweek.org/ew/articles/1995/03/01/23census.h14.html.

169. Moon, "Demographic and Socioeconomic Characteristics," 37.

170. Information regarding the assimilation and use of English among API immigrants, drawn from David E. Lopez, "Language: Diversity and Assimilation," in Waldinger and Bozorgmehr, *Ethnic Los Angeles*, 157–8.

171. Moon, "Demographic and Socioeconomic Characteristics," 42, table 4.2.

172. William Wilbanks, "Murdered Women and Women Who Murder: A Critique of the Literature," in *Judge, Lawyer, Victim, Thief: Women, Gender Roles, and Criminal Justice*, ed. Nicole Hahn Rafter and Elizabeth A. Stanko (Boston: Northeastern University Press, 1982), 167.

173. While stereotypes of API women, Latinas, and black females tend to be singular "types" that deny significant variables such as socioeconomic status. Those of white women, tend to be more varied and consider class, and sometimes cultural origins (Jewish, Italian, Irish, British, French, etc.). For discussions of female

stereotypes in US society, see Amanda Diekman, Alice Eagly, Antonio Mladinic, Maria Cristina Ferreira, "Dynamic Stereotypes about Women and Men in Latin America and the United States," *Journal of Cross Cultural Psychology* 36, no. 2 (Mar. 2005): 209–26.

174. Wilbanks, "Murdered Women and Women Who Murder," 167.

CHAPTER 3

1. Quotation and other information regarding the police contact of the Harlins family after her death found in Itabari Njeri, *The Last Plantation: Color, Conflict, and Identity: Reflections of a New World Black* (Boston: Houghton Mifflin, 1997), 60–61.

2. Campbell, discussion, Oct. 1, 2004.

3. Danny Bakewell, in discussion with the author, Nov. 30, 2004; Yussef Simmons, in discussion with the author, Nov. 16, 2004 and Nov. 30, 2004.

4. Bakewell, discussion; Simmons, discussions.

5. 102 Cong. Rec. E1300 (May 7, 1992) (statement of Hon. Dymally), Library of Congress: Thomas, http://thomas.loc.gov/home/thomas.php.

6. Bakewell, discussion; Itabari Njeri, "Swapping Lessons: In Black-Korean Conflict, Both Sides Gain a Better Understanding," *LAT*, Jan. 11, 1990, E1, E10.

7. Marsha Mitchell, "Teenager's Slaying Heightens Black-Korean Tensions," *Los Angeles Sentinel*, Mar. 28, 1991, A1.

8. Newspaper owner Charlotta Bass, for one, used her newspaper, the *California Eagle*, to mount such a campaign in the 1930s in Los Angeles, particularly in the Central Avenue community. She had been inspired to do so by similar action taken by the owners of the *Chicago Defender* and the *Chicago Whip*. See, for example, "Charlotta Bass, Her Story," Charlotta Bass and the California Eagle, Southern California Library for Social Studies and Research, under "Business Person," http://www.socallib.org/bass/story/activist.html; Cheryl Lynn Greenberg, *"Or Does It Explode?": Black Harlem in The Great Depression* (New York: Oxford University Press, 1991), 114–139; Steven J. Gold, "Immigrant Entrepreneurs and Customers Throughout the Twentieth Century," in *Not Just Black And White: Historical And Contemporary Perspectives on Immigration, Race and Ethnicity in the United States*, ed. Nancy Foner and George M. Fredrickson (New York: Russell Sage, 2004), 323–4.

9. Mitchell, "Teenager's Slaying Heightens Black-Korean Tensions," A1.

10. Editorial, "A Time for Reason and Calm," *Los Angeles Sentinel*, Mar. 28, 1991, A6.

11. Marsha Mitchell, "Bakewell: Taking Our Community Back—Economically," *Los Angeles Sentinel*, Apr. 4, 1991, A1.

12. Ibid.

13. Bakewell, discussion; Mitchell, "Bakewell," A1.

14. Claire Jean Kim, *Bitter Fruit: The Politics of Black-Korean Conflict in New York City* (New Haven: Yale University Press, 2000), 109–55; Pyong Gap Min, *Caught in the Middle: Korean Communities in New York and Los Angeles* (Berkeley: University of California Press, 1996), 148–52; Njeri, "Swapping Lessons," E1, E10; Chang and Yu, "Chronology," xiii–vi.

15. Mitchell, "Teenager's Slaying Heightens Black-Korean Tensions," A16.

16. Edward Chang, "Jewish and Korean Merchants in African-American Neighborhoods: A Comparative Perspective," *Amerasia Journal* 19, no. 2 (Spring 1993): 7.

17. Mitchell, "Teenager's Slaying Heightens Black-Korean Tensions," A16.

18. Ibid.

19. Ibid.

20. The other communities focused on were: Gardena/South Bay and Monterey Park/West San Gabriel Valley. Marsha Mitchell, "Asians Start Program in Interethnic Relations," *Los Angeles Sentinel*, Apr. 18, 1991, A3.

21. Bill Boyarsky, "Echoes from Bitter Past in South L.A.," *LAT*, Mar. 27, 1991, http://articles.latimes.com/1991-03-27/local/me-975_1_south-l-a.

22. Marsha Mitchell, "Council of Multicultural Publications Formed," *Los Angeles Sentinel*, Apr. 18, 1991, A3.

23. "A Time for Reason and Calm," *Los Angeles Sentinel*, Mar. 28, 1991, A6.

24. Larry Aubry, "Urban Perspective," *Korea Times*, Apr. 17, 1991.

25. Jarrette Fellows Jr., "In Wake of Teen Killing: Koreans, Blacks Try to Bridge Cultural Gap," *Los Angeles Sentinel*, Apr. 11, 1991, A1.

26. Richard Reyes Fruto, "Soul-to-Seoul Healing: Biggest Black KA Meeting in L.A. History Held in Watts," *Korea Times*, Apr. 17, 1991, 1, 5.

27. John Dart, "Korean Immigrants, Blacks Use Churches as Bridge to Ease Tensions," *LAT*, Nov. 9, 1985, B4.

28. Marsha Mitchell, "Police Keep Watch at Scene of Teen Killing," *Los Angeles Sentinel*, Apr. 11, 1991, A3.

29. Sophia Kyung Kim, "Watts Story: Good Neighbor Grocer Chung Lee Nurses Broken Heart," *Korea Times*, Apr. 17, 1991, 1, 4, quotes from 1.

30. Denise Harlins, in discussion with the author, July 23, 1993.

31. Marsha Mitchell, "The Harlins Family: After the Tragedy and the Verdict (Part One)," *Los Angeles Sentinel*, Dec. 5, 1991, A3. Denise Harlins represented the Harlins family in the interview. Brother David represented the LHJC.

32. Denise Harlins, in discussion with the author, July 23, 1993.

33. Marsha Mitchell, "Vigil Held for Slain Teenager," *Los Angeles Sentinel*, May 16, 1991, A3.

34. "Father of Girl Killed by Store Owner Files Suit," *Los Angeles Sentinel*, May 2, 1991, A1.

35. Njeri, *Last Plantation*, 65.

36. "Merchant Kills Robber During Hold-Up Attempt," *LAT*, June 6, 1991, B2.

37. Marsha Mitchell, "Black Man Killed by Korean Merchant; No Charges Filed," *Los Angeles Sentinel*, June 13, 1991, A1; Rick Holguin and John Lee, "Boycott of Store Where Man Was Killed Is Urged," *LAT*, June 18, 1991, B1.

38. Mitchell, "Black Man Killed by Korean Merchant," A1.

39. Holguin and Lee, "Boycott of Store Where Man Was Killed," B1.

40. Ibid., B8.

41. Ibid., B1.

42. The police reported that the incendiary device caused no damages. "Molotov Cocktail Tossed onto Boycotted Store," *LAT*, June 19, 1991, http://articles.latimes.com/1991-06-19/local/me-817_1_molotov-cocktail.

43. Mitchell, "Black Man Killed by Korean Merchant," A7.

44. "Merchant Kills Robber During Hold-Up Attempt," B2; Holguin and Lee, "Boycott of Store Where Man Was Killed," B8.

45. Holguin and Lee, "Boycott of Store Where Man Was Killed," B8.

46. Dennis Schatzman, "Selective Buying Campaign Begins Saturday Morning," *Los Angeles Sentinel*, Sept. 12, 1991, A1.

47. Ibid.

48. Ibid., A18.

49. Frank Clifford and Sheryl Stolberg, "Blacks and Koreans, with Bradley's Aid, Make Truce," *LAT*, Oct. 4, 1991, A1.

50. Ibid.

51. Sheryl Stolberg and Frank Clifford, "Black-Korean Truce Termed 'Very Fragile,'" *LAT*, Oct. 5, 1991, http://articles.latimes.com/1991-10-05/local/me-3230_1_city-officials.

52. The exact terns were: (1) Park's store would be closed for a minimum of 30 days and the boycott suspended for a maximum of four months; (2) KAGRO would negotiate the sale of John's Liquor store; (3) the African American Honor Committee would have the first opportunity to purchase the store; (4) the store was to be sold without its liquor license; (5) the Honor Committee and KAGRO would work together to found a "dispute resolution center" that would try to mediate disputes before a boycott begins; (6) the Brotherhood Crusade would donate $25,000 for the Center; (7) the two factions also would draft a "code of ethics" that would police the actions and attitudes of merchants; (8) they would establish a jobs program encouraging Korean merchants to hire black youth; and (9) local banks would provide sensitivity training to would-be merchants before lending them money to open new stores. Clifford and Stolberg, "Blacks and Koreans," A15.

53. Ibid.

54. Ibid.

55. Clifford and Stolberg, "Black-Korean Truce."

CHAPTER 4

1. Itabari Njeri, *The Last Plantation: Color, Conflict and Identity: Reflections of a New World Black* (Boston: Houghton Mifflin, 1997), 99.

2. Andrea Ford and John H. Lee, "Racial Tensions Blamed in Girl's Death," *LAT*, Mar. 20, 1991 B1; Kay Hwangbo, "Karlin Supports King Verdict," *Korea Times*, Aug. 24, 1992, 1.

3. Njeri, *Last Plantation*, 101.

4. John Lee, "Grocer Sells Brooklyn Store That Was Target of a Boycott," *LAT*, May 30, 1991, http://articles.latimes.com/1991-05-30/news/mn-3770_1_boycott-organizers.

5. Njeri, *Last Plantation*, 100.

6. Richard Leonard in discussion with the author, June 3, 2003.

7. Anna La Jeunesse, "Judge Lois Anderson Smaltz, Los Angeles County Superior Court Profile," *Daily Journal* (2002–2003).

8. Njeri, *Last Plantation*, 102–103.

9. Leonard, discussion, June 3, 2003.

10. Ibid.; Richard Leonard, in discussion with the author, Sept. 21, 2004.

11. Marsha Mitchell, "Family to Hold Vigil for Slain Teenager," *Los Angeles Sentinel*, May 9, 1991, A21; Richard Fruto, "Peacemakers Do the Right Thing," *Korea Times*, Apr. 3, 1991, 1, 12.

12. Njeri, *Last Plantation*, 100.

13. Leonard, discussion, Sept. 21, 2004.

14. Njeri, *Last Plantation*, 117.

15. Richard Fruto, "Son's Cry before Du Conviction: 'My Mother Is a Scapegoat,'" *Korea Times*, Oct. 21, 1991, 1; Njeri, *Last Plantation*, 241.

16. Leonard, discussion, Sept. 21, 2004.

17. *The People of the State of California v. Soon Ja Du* (Cal. Super. Ct. L.A. County, Dept. 111, 1991, no. BA037738), vol. 1, Sept. 30, 1991, A1–A2.

18. Ibid., A2.

19. Ibid., A4–A5.

20. Ibid., A2.

21. Ibid., A7–A9.

22. Ibid., A12–A15.

23. Ibid., 4–5.

24. Ibid., 5.

25. Ibid., 6–7.

26. *People v. Du*, vol. 4, Oct. 3, 1991, 400. Detective Johnson testified that Latasha Harlins had $2.00 in cash when her body was found. There is no indication of how much, if any, change she had.

27. *People v. Du*, vol. 1, Sept. 30, 1991, 7, 32–35. There had been some discrepancies in Ismail Ali's description of the argument between Du and Harlins. Under direct and cross-examination, he stated that only Du had used the word "bitch" in reference to Harlins, but the defense attorney hoped to challenge Ali's credibility as a witness by having his sister establish that both Du and Harlins had used profanity and that Harlins had used the profane language first.

28. Ibid., 32–35.

29. Andrea Ford, "Videotape Shows Teen Being Shot After Fight," *LAT*, Oct. 1, 1991; Andrea Ford and Tracy Wilkinson, "Grocer Is Convicted in Teen Killing," *LAT*, Oct. 12, 1991; Andrea Ford, "911, TV Tapes Tell Different Tales in Killing of Teen-Ager," *LAT*, Oct. 2, 1991, http://articles.latimes.com/1991-10-02/local/me-3102_1_black-girl; Katz and Lee, "Conflict Brings Tragic End," A19; Marsha Mitchell, "Teenager Shot, Killed in Dispute Over Orange Juice," *Los Angeles Sentinel*, Mar. 21–27, 1991, A1.

30. *People v. Du*, vol. 1, Sept. 30, 1991, 41.

31. Ibid., 35.

32. Ibid., 53.

33. Ibid., 53.

34. Ibid., 16.

35. Ibid., 91–2.

36. Ibid., 94–5.

37. Ibid., 75–6.

38. Ibid., 87.

39. Ibid., 100.
40. Ibid., 102.
41. Ibid., 105.
42. Ibid., 106.
43. *People v. Du*, vol. 2, Oct. 1, 1991, 194–5.
44. Ibid., 189–191.
45. Ibid., 200–3.
46. Ibid.
47. Ibid., 203–4.
48. Ibid., 204–5.
49. Ibid., 210–2.
50. Ibid., 223.
51. Ibid., 224.
52. Ibid., 225.
53. Ibid., 227–8.
54. Ibid., 244–5.
55. Ibid., 246–7.
56. Ibid., 249–58.
57. *People v. Du*, vol. 3, Oct. 2, 1991, 288.; vol. 2, Oct. 1, 1991, 241.
58. *People v. Du*, vol. 3, Oct. 2, 1991, 288.
59. Ibid., 276–8.
60. Ibid., 275–82.
61. Quoted in Njeri, *Last Plantation*, 106.
62. *People v. Du*, vol. 3, Oct. 2, 1991, 297–303 *passim*.
63. Ibid., 296–300.

> KARLIN: Counsel, why don't you define "burglary" so there is no
> confusion.
> LEONARD: Just so there's no confusion, burglary is when somebody
> comes into your place and takes something from your place when you
> are not present. Usually it's during the closing of store hours . . . Do
> you understand that?
> JOSEPH DU: Yes. (298).

And again:

> KARLIN: Counsel, perhaps you might define "shoplifting."
> LEONARD: I was just going to do so, your honor. Let me tell you the
> difference between a burglary and shoplifting. Burglary normally
> happens when the store is closed, usually at night, and nobody is
> there. Somebody breaks into the store, takes something from the store
> and then leaves. Shoplifting is when you are working in the store,
> somebody comes in, takes an item without paying, and then leaves the
> store. Do you understand the difference now between the two?
> JOSEPH DU: Yes. (298–299).

64. *People v. Du*, vol. 2, Oct. 1, 1991, 223.

65. *People v. Du*, vol. 3, Oct. 2, 1991, 303.

66. Ibid., 310–2.

67. Ibid.

68. Ibid., 313–8.

69. Ibid., 350–1.

70. Ibid., 321.

71. Ibid., 323.

72. Ibid., 322.

73. Ibid., 327—328.

74. Ibid., 327.

75. Ibid., 330; 330–1.

76. Ibid., 334–7.

77. Ibid., 334, 341.

78. Ibid., 345–6.

79. Ibid., 347.

80. Ibid., 347–8.

81. Ibid., 369.

82. Ibid., 373–7.

83. Ibid., 381–2.

84. *People v. Du*, vol. 4, Oct. 3, 1991, 387–8.

85. In her instructions to the jury, Karlin defined second-degree murder as "the unlawful killing of a human being with malice aforethought when there is manifested an intention unlawfully to kill a human being. Murder of the second degree is also the unlawful killing of a human being when the killing resulted from an intentional act, the natural consequences of the act are dangerous to human life, and the act was deliberately performed with knowledge of the danger to and with conscious disregard for human life." She defined voluntary manslaughter as

> the unlawful killing of a human being without malice aforethought. Every person who unlawfully kills another human being without malice afore-thought but with an intent to kill is guilty of voluntary manslaughter. There is no malice aforethought if the killing occurred upon a sudden quarrel or heat of passion or in the honest but unreasonable belief in the necessity to de-fend oneself against imminent peril to life or great bodily injury. To reduce an intentional felonious homicide from the offense of murder to manslaughter upon the ground of sudden quarrel or heat of passion, the provocation must be of such character and degree as naturally would excite and arouse such passion, and the assailant must act under the influence of that sudden quarrel or heat of passion. . . . The question to—to be answered is whether or not, at the time of the killing, the reason of the accused was obscured or disturbed by passion to such an extent a would cause the ordinarily reasonable person of average disposition to act rashly and without deliberation and reflection and from such passion rather than from judgment.

Involuntary manslaughter is "every person who unlawfully kills a human being without malice aforethought and without an intent to kill is guilty of the crime." Ibid., 389, 418–33.

86. Ibid., 437.

87. Ibid., 458–9.

88. Ibid., 461.

89. Cora Mann quoted in Jocelyn M. Pollock, *Criminal Women* (Cincinnati: Anderson, 1999), 28.

90. *People v. Du*, vol. 4, Oct. 3, 1991, 482–5.

91. Ibid., 489–90.

92. Ibid., 489.

93. Ibid., 503–4.

94. Ibid., 518.

95. Ibid., 517.

96. Ibid., 512.

97. Ibid., 513.

98. Charisse Jones, "Deliberations in Trial of Grocer Interrupted for Ruling on Dispute," *LAT*, Oct. 10, 1991, B3.

99. *People v. Du*, vol. 4, Oct. 3, 1991, 579–80.

100. Ibid., 582–5.

CHAPTER 5

1. Joyce Ann Karlin's (JK) travel information found in Records of the Immigration and Naturalization Service, *Passenger and Crew Lists of Vessels Arriving at New York, New York, 1897–1957*, ancestry .com: roll T715_8158, flight of JK to Idlewild, NY from Maiquetia, Venezuela, June 7, 1952, p. 59, line 1; roll T715_8421, flight of JK from Paris, France to New York, NY, Feb.17, 1954, p. 339, line 19; roll T715_8887, flight of JK from Frankfurt, Germany to New York, New NY, June 20, 1957, p. 350, line 6.

2. Herman Rosenthal and S. Janovsky, s.v. "Chernigov," JewishEncyclopedia.com, 1906, http://www.jewishencyclopedia.com/articles/14534-tschernigoff. Louis Karlan indicates on his WWI registration that he was born in Chernigov. I assume he meant the city Chernigov, the capital of the district so named. He may have, however, meant the district itself. If so, then the concentration of Jewish residents was much lower. Only 5% of people living in the province were Jewish (114,630 out of 2.3 million residents). United States Selective Service System, World War I Selective Service System, *Draft Registration Cards, 1917–1918*, roll 1685005, Roxbury, Suffolk County, MA, draft board 16, Sept. 11, 1918, http://www.ancestry.com/.

3. Gerald Surh, "Ekaterinoslav City in 1905: Workers, Jews, and Violence," *International Labor and Working Class History* 64 (Fall 2003): 139–66; Herman Rosenthal, "Kiev," JewishEncyclopedia.com, 1906, http://www.jewishencyclopedia.com/articles/9314-kiev.

4. Jonathan D. Sarna, "A Great Awakening: The Transformation That Shaped Twentieth-Century American Judaism," in *American Jewish Women's History*, ed. Pamela S. Nadell (New York: New York University Press, 2003), 46–51.

5. NARA, *Crew Lists of Vessels Arriving at Boston, Massachusetts, 1917–1943*, serial T938, roll 91, transportation of Elia Kurlansky from Liverpool, England to Boston, MA, Mar. 2, 1906, line 11, http://www.ancestry.com/.

6. NARA, *Crew Lists of Vessels Arriving at Boston, Massachusetts, 1917–1943*, serial T938, roll 218, transportation of Mones Karlinsky from Liverpool, England to Boston, MA, May 14, 1914, line 2, http://www.ancestry.com/.

7. Bureau of the Census, *Thirteenth Census of the United States, 1910*, roll T624_616, Boston, Suffolk County, MA, e.d. 1945, page 7B, family no. 135, household of Morris Karlin, line 90, image 979, http://www.ancestry.com/; NARA, *Crew Lists of Vessels Arriving at Boston, Massachusetts, 1891–1943*, serial T938, roll 98, http://www.ancestry.com, *Boston Passenger and Crew Lists, 1820–1943*. Provo, UT, USA: http://www.ancestry.com, 2006.

8. Bureau of the Census, *Thirteenth Census, 1910*, roll T624_616, Suffolk County, Boston, MA, e.d. 1945, p. 7B, family no. 135, household of Morris Karlin, line 90, image 979, http://www.ancestry.com/.

9. States Bureau of the Census, *Twelfth Census of the United States, 1900*, roll T623_1088, Manhattan, New York, New York, e.d. 170, p. 7B, family no. 135, household of Morris Karlan, line 93, microfilm 1241081, http://www.ancestry.com/.

10. Bureau of the Census, *Fourteenth Census of the United States, 1920*, roll, T625_735, Boston, Suffolk County, MA, ward 13, e.d. 350, p.18B, family no. 398, household of Louis Karlin, line 86, image 842, http://www.ancestry.com/.

11. Ibid.

12. Ibid.

13. William A. Braverman, "The Emergence of a Unified Community, 1880–1917," in *The Jews of Boston*, ed. Jonathan D. Sarna, Ellen Smith, and Scott-Martin Kosofsky (New Haven: Yale University Press, 2005), 69.

14. Gerald H. Gamm, "In Search of Suburbs: Boston's Jewish Districts, 1843–1994" in Sarna, Smith, and Kosofsky, *Jews of Boston*, 149–50; David Kaufman, "Temples in the American Athens: A History of the Synagogues of Boston," in Sarna, Smith, and Kosofsky, *Jews of Boston*, 188.

15. The Jewish population in Boston at mid-nineteenth century who were foreign born was 44% from northeastern Germany (Prussia, Poland, Posen, and Russia); 19% from southwestern Germany (Bavaria, Baden, and Saxony); and 27% from unspecified areas in Germany. Ellen Smith, "'Israelites In Boston,' 1840–1880" in Sarna, Smith, and Kosofsky, *Jews of Boston*, 48.

16. Braverman, "Emergence of a Unified Community," 69.

17. Ibid., 66. The reform movement already had taken hold in Boston by the time the Karlinskys arrived. According to David Kaufman, Jewish rabbis from Germany who were university trained began to usher in the changes as early as 1868. Other contributing factors included a slight "Protestantization," that lent itself to shorter services, acquiring buildings that had been Christian churches and calling them temples, the use of choirs and organs in services; an Americanization of the immigrant community and the influence of youth. Kaufman, "Temples in the American Athens," 180–1.

18. Quoted in Braverman, "Emergence of a Unified Community," 74.

19. Mary Antin, *The Promised Land* (Boston and New York: Houghton Mifflin, 1912), under "Tarnished Laurels."

20. Ibid., under "Dover Street."

21. Braverman, "Emergence of a Unified Community," 74–5.

22. Gamm, "In Search of Suburbs," 42.

23. Antin, *The Promised Land*, under "Miracles."

24. "Aspiration, Acculturation and Impact: Immigration to the United States, 1789–1930," Harvard University Library Open Collections Program, http://ocp.hul.harvard.edu/immigration/timeline.html.

25. Letter from Prescott F. Hall, secretary of the Immigration Restriction League to Sir, circa 1898–1907, "Series I, Correspondence to and from the IRL," Immigration Restriction League Records, 1893–1921 (US), MS Am 2245, folder 1046, sequence 4, Houghton Library, Harvard University, Cambridge, MA, nrs.harvard.edu/urn-3:FHCL.Hough:hou00163.

26. Hasia Diner, *The Jews of the United States* (Berkeley: University of California Press, 2009), 174; Letter from the Immigration Restriction League to the Immigration Protection League, Jan. 25, 1898, "Series I, Correspondence to and from the IRL," sequence 1–3.

27. Diner, *Jews of the United States*, 173.

28. George Kibbe Turner, "Daughters of the Poor: A Plain Story of the Development of New York City as a Leading Center of the White Slave Trade of the World, Under Tammany Hall," *McClure's* 34 (Nov. 1909): 45–61 *passim*, Brock University, Mead Project, http://www.brocku.ca/MeadProject/Turner/Turner_1909b.html.

29. Diner, *Jews of the United States*, 174.

30. A picture of there neighborhood circa 1930 can be found at the Los Angeles Public Library Digital Catalog. Downtown neighborhood near Karlin residence, c. 1930 (Temple Block).

31. Bureau of the Census, *Fifteenth Census of the United States, 1930*, roll 139, Los Angeles, CA, Los Angeles County, e.d.159, p. 20A, family no. 316, household of Joseph Karlin, line 16, image 430.0, FHL microfilm 2339874, http://www.ancestry.com/.

32. Data taken from Bureau of the Census in "General Population by City: Los Angeles County, 1850–1900," *Los Angeles Almanac*, http://www.laalmanac.com/population/po25.htm; Nancy Holden, "The Early Jewish Presence in Los Angeles, 1845–1945," *Roots-Key* (newsletter of the Jewish Genealogical Society of Los Angeles) 23 no. 2 and 3 (Summer/Fall 2003).

33. Horace Bell, *On the Old West Coast: Being Further Reminiscences of a Ranger* (New York: William Morrow, 1930), 10.

34. Neil C. Sandberg, *Jewish Life in Los Angeles: A Window to Tomorrow* (Lanham, MD: University Press of America, 1986), 27–8.

35. Jack D. Forbes, "The Early African Heritage of California," in *Seeking El Dorado: African Americans in California*, ed. Lawrence B. De Graaf, Kevin Mulroy, and Quintard Taylor (Los Angeles: Autry Museum of Western Heritage, 2001), 83–5.

36. Sandberg, *Jewish Life in Los Angeles*, 27.

37. Judy Kahn Gorman, "Peter M. Kahn, 1878–1952," *Roots-Key* 23, no. 2 and 3 (Summer/Fall 2003), http://home.earthlink.net/~nholdeneditor/PeterMKahn.htm.

38. Francis Dnkelspiel, *Towers of Gold: How One Jewish Immigrant Named Isaias Hellman Created California* (New York: St. Martin's Press, 2008), 98–123 *passim*, 333.

39. Ibid., 120–2. Data drawn from the American Jewish Yearbook 1908, the American Jewish Yearbook 1919, and the 1920 Los Angeles City Directory in "Jewish Institutions in Los Angeles: 1908 and 1920," "Research Documents," http://home.earthlink.net/~nholdeneditor/Contents.htm.

40. Diner, *Jews of the United States*, 210.

41. Ibid., 210–1.

42. US Holocaust Memorial Museum, "Charles E. Coughlin," *Holocaust Encyclopedia*, May 11, 2012, http://www.ushmm.org/wlc/en/article.php?ModuleId=10005516.

43. Diner, *Jews of the United States*, 211–2; "1935: Steps Toward Destruction," *Holocaust Chronicle*, 2009, 88, http://www.holocaustchronicle.org/staticpages/89.html.

44. City of Anaheim, "Anaheim Police Department History: 1920," 2012, City of Anaheim, http://www.anaheim.net/articlenew2222.asp?id=667.

45. For example, activities of the Klan in Denver in the 1930s and 1940s where both Jewish and Catholic opponents to the political power of Klan leaders or sympathizers were pistol-whipped, kidnapped, and received death threats. See Robert A. Goldberg, "Denver: Queen City of the Colorado Realm," in *The Invisible Empire in the West: Toward a New Historical Appraisal of the Ku Klux Klan in the 1920s*, ed. Shawn Lay (Urbana: University of Illinois Press, 2004), 48, 56.

46. Carlos Larralde and Griswold del Castillo, "San Diego's Ku Klux Klan, 1920–1980," *Journal of San Diego History* 46, no. 2 and 3 (Spring/Summer 2000), http://www.sandiegohistory.org/journal/2000-2/klan.htm.

47. State of California, "Great Register of Voters," 1936, roll 40, Los Angeles, Los Angeles County, CA, precinct no. 1865, "Karlin, Joseph, 26½ Thornton Av, Salesman, D," image 676, California State Library, Sacramento, CA, http://www.ancestry.com/.

48. State of California, "Great Register of Voters," 1946, roll 66, Santa Monica, Los Angeles County, California, precinct no. 88, "Karlin, Joseph, 136 Hill St, D," image 216, California State Library, Sacramento, CA, http://www.ancestry.com/.

49. The children moved out later that decade, so that by 1954, Joseph and Sadie, still Democrats, were living alone at 3749 Redwood Avenue in Venice. Joseph Karlin(sky) died in Los Angeles in August 1969 or February 1962. Social Security Administration, "Social Security Death Index, Master File," "Joseph Karlin," born: May 21, 1896, last residence: Los Angeles 90034, death: Aug. 1969; State of California, "Great Register of Voters," 1954, roll 98, Los Angeles, Los Angeles County, CA, precinct no. 3828, "Karlin, Joseph, 3749 Redwood Av, D," image 844, California State Library, Sacramento, CA, http://www.ancestry.com/; Bureau of the Census, *Fifteenth Census of the United States, 1930*, roll 233, Denver, Denver, CO, ed. 33, 19A, family no. 207, household of Solomon Siletzsky, line 47, image 931.0, FHL microfilm 2339968, http://www.ancestry.com/.

50. Regarding the OSS, see Patrick K. O'Donnell, *Operatives, Spies and Saboteurs: The Unknown Story of WW II's OSS* (New York: Citadel Press, 2004), *passim*.

51. "Karlin's Capers," *Hollywood Reporter*, July 26, 1994, 2, Myron Karlin File, Academy of Motion Picture Arts and Sciences, Margaret Herrick Library, Beverly Hills, CA (hereafter, MHL); Cynthia Dizikes, "Veterans Sacrifice Honored in Song and Speech," *Easy Reader News*, Nov. 17, 2005, http://archive.easyreadernews.com/story.php?StoryID=20027770&IssuePath=.

52. "Karlin's Capers," 2; Dizikes, "Veterans Sacrifice Honored"; "Biography of Myron Karlin," Marquis Who's Who, Feb. 9, 2011, http://search.marquiswhoswho.com/.

53. Sandberg, *Jewish Life in Los Angeles*, 37; see also Neal Gabler, *An Empire of Their Own: How the Jews Invented Hollywood* (New York: Doubleday,1988), esp. 3; and Otto Friedrich, *City of Nets: A Portrait of Hollywood in the 1940's* (New York: Harper and Row, 1986), *passim*.

54. "Biography of Myron Karlin."

55. Harry, Sam, Albert, and Jack Warner migrated from Poland, which was then part of the Russian Empire, and lived in Baltimore, Youngstown (OH), Pittsburg, and elsewhere before coming to Hollywood. Gabler, *Empire of Their Own*, 3, 123–9.

56. "Myron Karlin," *Hollywood Reporter*, Jan. 8, 1985, 2, Myron Karlin File, MHL.

57. "Karlin Knighted," *Variety*, June 13, 1984, 3, Myron Karlin File, MHL.

58. "Executives," *New York Times*, Jan. 9, 1985, D2; "WB's Karlin, France's Lang Huddle on the Merging of Art and Commerciality," *Variety*, June 8, 1983, 2, Myron Karlin File, MHL.

The name Motion Picture Export Association of American was changed to the Motion Picture Association of America in 1985. "The Motion Picture Association of America (MPAA) and its international counterpart, the Motion Picture Association (MPA) serve as the voice and advocate of the American Motion picture, home video and television industries." See "About Us," Motion Picture Association of America, 2011, http://www.mpaa.org.

59. Will Tusher, "MPEAA's Karlin Honored With '86 Jerusalem Award," *Variety*, Jan. 14, 1986, Myron Karlin File, MHL.

60. Ibid.

61. Martin Berg, "Judicial Profile: Judge Joyce A. Karlin, Los Angeles Superior Court," *Los Angeles Daily Journal*, Feb. 9, 1993, 1399–1400.

62. Michael Ebner, "Lake Forest, Il," Encyclopedia of Chicago, online edition. http://www.enclopedia.chicagohistory.org/pages/709.html.

63. Ibid.

64. Deerfield, IL, US School Yearbooks Database, http://www.ancestry.com.

65. Earl W. Hayter, *Education in Transition: The History of Northern Illinois University* (DeKalb: Northern Illinois University Press, 1974), 442–74.

66. Kathy Morris Wolf, "Karlin, Joyce Ann," *California Courts and Judges*, 8th ed. (Los Angeles: James, 1996), under "GQ."

67. Ibid.

68. Pamela Susan Nadell, "On Their Own Terms: American Jewish Women, 1854–2000," in "Part Two: Recent American Jewish History, 1954–2004," Special Issue: The 350th Anniversary of the Jewish People in America, *American Jewish History* 91 no. 3–4, (Sept./Dec. 2003): 397.

69. In 1910, they constituted approximately 19% of the New York City population. Moshe Hartman and Harriet Hartman, *Gender Equality and American Jews* (Albany: State University of New York Press, 1996), 9, 23–38, statistics from 28.

70. From a study conducted on Jewish women aged 3–39. Nadell, "On Their Own Terms," 396.

71. By 1990, more than 50% of Jewish women nationally had a BA degree, and more than 25% had a graduate or professional degree. Hartman and Hartman, *Gender Equality and American Jews*, 33–5. This data applies to Jews and other whites 25 years and older in 1990.

72. Source: http://www.census.gov/population/www/socdemo/education/phct41.html.

U.S. Census Bureau, *Decennial Census of Population, 1940 to 2000*, April 6, 2006, in Half-Century Of Learning: Historical Census Statistics On Educational Attainment in the United States, 1940 to 2000," United States Census Bureau, See

TABLE 5.1 Percent of the Population 25 Years and Over with a Bachelor's Degree or Higher by Sex, Race, and Hispanic Origin, for the United States: 1940 to 2000.

Sex, race and Hispanic origin	1940	1950	1960	1970	1980	1990	2000
Both Sexes							
White	4.9	6.6	8.1	11.3	17.1	21.5	26.1
Black	1.3	2.2	3.5	4.4	8.4	11.4	14.3
Asian and Pacific Islander	4.0	7.5	11.3	20.4	32.9	36.6	44.1
American Indian and Alaska Native	0.8	1.3	1.9	3.8	7.7	9.3	11.5
Hispanic (of any race)	(NA)	(NA)	(NA)	(NA)	7.6	9.2	10.4
White non-Hispanic	(NA)	(NA)	(NA)	(NA)	17.4	22.0	27.0
Male							
White	5.9	7.9	10.3	14.4	21.3	25.0	28.2
Black	1.4	2.1	3.5	4.2	8.4	11.0	13.1
Asian and Pacific Islander	4.2	7.8	13.1	23.5	39.8	41.9	48.2
American Indian and Alaska Native	0.9	1.4	2.2	4.5	9.2	10.1	11.4
Hispanic (of any race)	(NA)	(NA)	(NA)	(NA)	9.4	10.0	10.2
White non-Hispanic	(NA)	(NA)	(NA)	(NA)	21.7	25.6	29.3
Female							
White	4.0	5.4	6.0	8.4	13.3	18.4	24.1
Black	1.2	2.4	3.6	4.6	8.3	11.7	15.2
Asian and Pacific Islander	3.1	7.0	9.0	17.3	27.0	31.8	40.4
American Indian and Alaska Native	0.7	1.3	1.7	3.1	6.3	8.6	11.6
Hispanic (of any race)	(NA)	(NA)	(NA)	(NA)	6.0	8.3	10.7
White non-Hispanic	(NA)	(NA)	(NA)	(NA)	13.6	18.8	24.8

Source: U.S. Census Bureau, Decennial Census of Population, 1940 to 2000, April 6, 2006, in Half-Century Of Learning: Historical Census Statistics On Educational Attainment in the United States, 1940 to 2000," United States Census Bureau http://www.census.gov/hhes/socdemo/education/data/census/half-century/index.html.

the reproduction of the Census Bureau's table of the percent of the population with a BA or higher. (Table 5.1)

73. Sucheng Chan, *Asian Americans: An Interpretive History* (New York: Twayne, 1991), 54–9.

74. Diner, *Jews of the United States*, 209.

75. Jerome Karabel, *The Chosen: The Hidden History of Admission and Exclusion at Harvard, Yale and Princeton* (New York: Houghton, Mifflin, Harcourt, 2005), 78.

76. Charles Jaret, "Troubled by Newcomers: Anti-Immigrant Attitudes and Action During Two Eras of Mass Immigration to the United States," *Journal of American Ethnic History* 18, no. 3 (Spring 1999): 16–21; Charles Hirschmann, "Immigration and the American Century," *Demography* 42, no. 4 (Nov. 2005): 601–2.

77. Karabel, *Chosen*, 79.

78. Ibid., 76–110 *passim*.

79. Diner, *Jews of the United States*, 209. Quotes taken from Marcia Synott, "Numerus Clausus (United States)," in *Antisemitism: A Historical Encyclopedia of Prejudice and Persecution*, vol. 1, ed. Richard S. Levy (Santa Barbara, CA: ABC-CLIO, 2005), 514–5.

80. Diner, *Jews of the United States*, 209.

81. Barnard, however, did not establish a Jewish quota. Quote is from Helen Lefkowitz Horowitz, *Alma Mater: Design and Experience in the Women's Colleges from Their Nineteenth Century Beginnings to the 1930s* (Amherst: University of Massachusetts Press, 1993), 259.

82. Barron H. Lerner, "In a Time of Quotas, a Quiet Pose in Defiance," *New York Times*, May 26, 2009, D5.

83. Beth Wenger, *New York Jews and the Great Depression: Uncertain Promise* (New Haven: Yale University Press, 1996), 23.

84. Susan Glenn, *Daughters of the Shtetl: Life and Labor in the Immigrant Generation* (Ithaca: Cornell University Press, 1990), 67. Glenn notes that data from the US Immigration Commission indicated that "only 8 percent of Russian wives were working, compared with 11 percent of Poles, 17 percent of southern Italians, 20 percent of Germans, 25 percent of Bohemians, and 68 percent of Blacks." Ibid.

85. Ibid., 67.

86. Nadell, "On Their Own Terms," 396.

87. By 1990, more than 50% of Jewish women nationally had a BA degree, and more than 25% had a graduate or professional degree, and it showed in the kind of work they performed. Ibid., 397. The Jewish female occupational sample that Nadell constructs indicates that 7.8% were teachers, 7.6% were clerical workers, 7.3% were secretaries, 7.0% were sales clerks, 6.8% were in managerial positions, 1.8% were office managers, 4.8% were bookkeepers, 1.8% were accountants, 3.2% were social workers, 2.4% were registered nurses, and 2% were real estate agents. Ibid.

88. Ibid.

89. Percentages and other data derived from statistics provided by Terence C. Halliday, "Six Score Years and Ten: Demographic Transitions in the American Legal Profession, 1850–1980," *Law and Society Review* 20, no. 1 (1986): 62 n. 53–78, table 1. See also Barbara Curran, "American Lawyers in the 1980s: A Profession in Transition," *Law and Society Review* 20, no. 1 (1986): 19–52.

90. This was a phenomenon driven by social, cultural, and political successes of the civil rights and women's rights movements, coupled with changes in the national economy and the overall legal profession. This gendered change occurred at the same time, for example, that the number of lawyers, in general, was increasing greatly and not only women were beginning to have a substantial presence, but racial minorities as well. Between 1970 and 1980, lawyers in the population at large increased from 1 in 572 to 1 in 418. Halliday, "Six Score Years and Ten," 62; Curran, "American Lawyers in the 1980s," 20, table, 25.

91. Curran, "American Lawyers in the 1980s," 20, table, 25.

92. Women in this cohort were underrepresented overall in private firms, but overrepresented in government agencies, legal aid, federal, state and local judiciaries, state and local governments and private associations—69% vs. 56%. Most males in private firms in the cohort were partners and females were most likely to be associates. Ibid., 27, 31, 33, 35, 42, 45, 49.

93. Halliday, "Six Score Years and Ten," 77, appendix. Midwest included Ohio, Indiana, Michigan, Illinois, Wisconsin, Minnesota, Iowa and Missouri. Pacific included California, Oregon, Washington, Alaska and Hawaii. Statistics are for 1970. They shift slightly up for the Pacific in 1980 to 15.6% and lower in the Midwest to 20.3%. Ibid.

94. Indeed, most experts agree that when senior partners in a law firm contemplated a "model" for a law partner, it was not a female. As such, they concluded: "Women associates are required to embody standards that are an exaggerated form of a partnership ideal, and these standards are imposed uniquely on women." Curran, "American Lawyers in the 1980s," 48, table 30. For a discussion of gender bias in the legal profession, see ibid., 45–51. Discussion on senior partners's views regarding model partners is found in Fiona M. Kay and John Hagan, "Raising the Bar: The Gender Stratification of Law-Firm Capital," *American Sociological Review* 63, no. 5 (Oct. 1998): 735–41, quote from 741.

95. David N. Laband and Bernard F. Lentz, "Is There Sex Discrimination in the Legal Profession: Further Evidence on Tangible and Intangible Margins," *Journal of Human Resources* 28, no. 2 (Spring 1993): 230–58. Stephen J. Spurr and Glenn T. Sueyoshi, "Turnover and Promotion of Lawyers: An Inquiry into Gender Differences," *Journal of Human Resources* 29, no. 3 (Summer 1994): 813–42, find, for example, when examining promotion of lawyers in 2 cohorts (1969–1973 and 1980–1983) that men were more likely, particularly in the first cohort, to be promoted to partner than females and that females were more likely to leave the firm as a result of not being promoted. While the rate of promotion of females increased in the second cohort, the male promotion rate was still greater. See also Edith Elisabeth Flynn, "Women as Criminal Justice Professionals: A Challenge to Change Tradition," in Rafter and Stanko, *Judge, Lawyer, Victim, Thief*, 318–319 and 305–40 *passim*. There is also evidence, however, that male judges treated female attorneys at trial somewhat preferentially, perhaps to appear as a gentleman. Phyllis Jo Baunach and Nicole Hahn Rafter, "Sex-Role Operations: Strategies for Women Working in the Criminal Justice System," in Rafter and Stanko, *Judge, Lawyer, Victim, Thief*, 346–7.

96. Berg, "Judicial Profile," 1399–1400; Kay and Hagan, "Raising the Bar," 728–43.

97. "Marriage Announcement: Babst-Karlin," *LAT*, May 29, 1977, G4; California Dept. of Health Services, Center for Health Statistics, *California Marriage Index, 1960–1985*, Joyce A. Karlin (26), Joel M. Babst (29), May 1, 1977, Los Angeles, CA, http://www.ancestry.com.

98. California Dept. of Health Services, Center for Health Statistics, *California Divorce Index, 1966–1984*, Joel M. Babst, Joyce A. Babst, Apr. 30, 1984, Los Angeles, CA, http://www.ancestry.com.

99. Florida Dept. of Health, *Florida Marriage Index, 1927–2001*, vol. 5704, certificate 092873, Joel Mark Babst, Sept. 16, 1984, Miami, Dade County, FL, http://www.ancestry.com.

100. Wolf, "Karlin, Joyce Ann," under "GQ."

101. Ibid., Berg, "Judicial Profile," 1400.

102. Wolf, "Karlin, Joyce Ann," under "GQ".

103. Berg, "Judicial Profile," 1400; Wolf, "Joyce Ann Karlin," under "GQ."

104. Lou Cannon, *Official Negligence: How Rodney King and the Riots Changed Los Angeles and the LAPD* (Boulder, CO: Westview Press, 1999), 169.

105. Njeri, *Last Plantation*, 155.

106. "Judicial Selection in the States: California," American Judicature Society (AJS), 2012, http://www.judicialselection.us/judicial_selection/index.cfm?state=CA.

107. Lavine also had worked in Washington for the US Justice Dept. He too began in Compton where he heard civil, criminal, and family law cases. Rebecca Kuzins, "Judicial Profile, Judge Richard Lavine," *Los Angeles Daily Journal*, August 14, 1984.

108. Women made up 18% during 1989–1990 and 17.79% during 1991–1992. Marie T. Hough and Nancy L. Wookfolk, eds., *The American Bench: Judges of the Nation*, 5th ed. (Sacramento: Forster-Long, 1990), 225; Marie Hough, Nancy Jellison, James Hoffman, eds., *The American Bench: Judges of the Nation*, 6th ed. (Sacramento: Forster-Long, 1992), 216–7.

109. Flynn, "Women as Criminal Justice Professionals," 318. Flynn notes that in 1977, only one woman had been appointed to the US Supreme Court; women held only ten federal judgeships out of 583; nine women were on the highest state appellate courts; and lower courts had 5.8% female judges. Ibid.

110. Beverly Blair Cook, "Moral Authority and Gender Difference: Georgia Bullock and the Los Angeles Women's Court," *Judicature* 77, no. 3 (Nov.–Dec. 1993): 144–55.

111. Ibid., 145–7, quote from 147.

112. Ibid.

113. Ibid.

114. Ibid., 145.

115. Ibid., 145–7, quote from 152–3.

116. Ibid., 145–7, quote from 153.

117. Joyce S. Sterling, "The Impact of Gender Bias on Judging: Survey of Attitudes Toward Women Judges," *Colorado Lawyer* 22 (Feb. 1993): 257.

118. Dick Goldberg, "Judicial Profile: Judge William F. Fahey, Los Angeles County Superior Court" *Los Angeles Daily Journal*, Sept. 10, 1999.

119. Ibid.

120. Ibid.

121. Deborah Bogen, Mark Thompson, and Elizabeth Smith, "Fahey, William F.," in *California Courts and Judges* (Costa Mesa, CA: James, 2000), 299.

122. Cannon, *Official Negligence*, 149.

123. Goldberg, "Judicial Profile."

124. Ibid.

125. Readers will recall that Lois Anderson-Smaltz was one of the presiding judges assigned to Soon Ja Du's trial before the venue was changed from Compton to downtown Los Angeles. She was the last judge to preside over the case before it was appointed to Joyce Karlin.

126. Ibid.

127. Ibid.

128. Ibid.

129. Ibid.

130. Ibid.

131. Bogen, Thompson, and Smith, "Fahey, William F.," 299–300.

132. Indeed, in one profile article on Judge Fahey found in *California Courts and Judges* the author concluded: "Most interviewees [defense attorneys and prosecutors] were critical of Judge Fahey's judicial demeanor." Some interviewesd characterized his "temperament/demeanor." Ibid.

133. Ibid.

134. Ibid.

135. Njeri, *Last Plantation*, 116–7; http://www.usbeacon.com/housing/California/Manhattan Beach-1990.htm. (site updated; information from 1990 no longer available).

136. Diner, *Jews of the United States*, 26.

137. Ibid., 25–6.

138. Cheryl Lynn Greenberg, *Troubling the Waters: Black Jewish Relations in the American Century* (Princeton: Princeton University Press, 2006), 6.

139. See, for example, discussions of Jewish "diversity" and the internal conflicts associated with it in Sander Gilman, *The Jew's Body* (New York: Routledge, 1991), 169–93; and Greenberg, *Troubling the Waters*, 30–4.

140. See, for example, Eric L. Goldstein, *The Price of Whiteness: Jews, Race, and American Identity* (Princeton: Princeton University Press, 2006), chs. 1–4.

141. Greenberg, *Troubling the Waters*, 6.

142. Najia Aarim-Heriot, *Chinese Immigrants, African Americans, and Racial Anxiety in the United States, 1848–82* (Urbana: University of Illinois Press, 2003), 19.

143. Wu, *Yellow*, 47.

144. Quoted in Natsu Taylor Saito, "Model Minority, Yellow Peril: Functions of 'Foreignness' in the Construction of Asian American Legal Identity," *Asian Law Journal* 4 (May 1997): 72–3.

145. For example, see ibid., 71–96.

146. Gary Brecin, "*The Wasp*: Stinging Editorials and Political Cartoons," *Bancroftiana* (newsletter), 121, Fall 2002, http://bancroft.berkeley.edu/events/bancroftiana/121/wasp.html.

147. The *Ram's Horn* billed itself as "an interdenominational social gospel magazine," published in Chicago in the 1890s and early 1900s. Most of its cartoons, including the one in figure 5.5, were drawn by Frank Beard. "The Rush of the Immigrants," US

163. Greenberg, *Troubling the Waters*, 42.

164. Ibid., 42, 94, 164.

165. Debra L. Schultz, *Going South: Jewish in the Civil Rights Movement* (New York: New York University Press, 2001), *passim*, quote on 37.

166. Ibid., 37–39.

167. Ibid., 3.

168. Ibid., 31–90 *passim*.

169. Quoted in ibid., 42.

170. Quoted in ibid., 40–1.

171. Greenberg, *Troubling the Waters*, 46.

172. Ibid., 226–7.

173. Beverly Horsburgh, "Jewish Women, Black Women: Guarding Against the Oppression of Surrogacy," *Berkeley Women's Law Journal* 8 (1993): 30.

174. A three-day race riot occurred in Crown Heights (Brooklyn), New York in August 1991. Blacks became enraged when Josef Lisch ran a red light, crashed into a building, causing part of the edifice to break off and fall on seven-year-old Gavin Cato, killing him. Lisch was a Hasidic Jew, trying to stay within the motorcade of his rabbi when the accident occurred. Cato, who was the son of Guyanese immigrant parents, did not receive medical attention quickly, although Lisch did. Local blacks (many immigrants from the Caribbean) were incensed and attacked Jewish residents, pedestrians, and onlookers. One such pedestrian was Yankel Rosenbaum, a graduate student from Israel, who was killed by Limerick Nelson. Jeffrey Goldberg, "The Hard Truth About the Crown Heights Riots," *Atlantic*, Aug. 11, 2011, http://www.theatlantic.com/national/archive/2011/08/the-hard-truth-about-the-crown-heights-riots/243448/; Andy Soltis, "Furor over Sharpton Speaking at Crown Heights Riot-Anniversary Forum," *New York Post*, Aug. 18, 2011, http://www.nypost.com/p/news/local/brooklyn/crown_hts_fury_38tR1JfphLH4X9An8W8VYL. For a detailed analysis of this riot and its aftermath, see Edward Shapiro, *Crown Heights: Blacks, Jews and the 1991 Brooklyn Riot* (Lebanon, NH: Brandeis University Press, 2006).

175. Diner, *Jews of the United States*, 274–6; Greenberg, *Troubling the Waters*, 225.

176. Greenberg, *Troubling the Waters*, 224–5.

177. Ibid., 125.

178. Ibid., 237; Judith Rosenbaum, "Introductory Essay(s): Tensions in Black Jewish Relations," Jewish Women's Archive, 2012, http://jwa.org/teach/livingthelegacy/tensions-in-black-jewish-relations; Nancy McLean, *Freedom Is Not Enough: The Opening of the American Workplace* (Cambridge: Harvard University Press, 2008), 186.

179. Ralph J. Sonenshein, "Los Angeles Coalition Politics," in *The Los Angeles Riots: Lessons for the Urban Future*, ed. Mark Baldassare (Boulder, CO: Westview Press, 1994), 49; Patrick Joyce, *No Fire Next Time*, 128.

180. Glenn Omatsu, "'Four Prisons' and the Movements of Liberation: Asian American Identity through Performing Blackness, 1969–1972," *Contemporary Asian America: A Multidisciplinary Reader*, 2nd ed., ed. Min Zhou and J.V. Gatewood (New York: New York University Press, 2007), 57.

181. Ibid., 57.

182. Denize Springer, "Campus Commemorates 1968 Student-Led Strike," *San Francisco State News*, Sept. 22, 2008, http://www.sfsu.edu/~news/2008/fall/8.html; Omatsu, "'Four Prisons' and the Movements of Liberation," 59–62.

183. Laura Pulido, *Black, Brown, Yellow and Left: Radical Activism in Los Angeles* (Berkeley: University of California Press, 2006), 157–61.

184. Edward Chang, "Building Minority Coalitions: A Case Study of Koreans and African Americans," *Korea Journal of Population and Development* 21, no. 1 (July 1992): 37–56; Doherty, "Black-Korean Alliance," 1–2; Joyce, *No Fire Next Time*, 10–133.

185. Quoted in Min, *Caught in the Middle*, 180. For a general discussion of Jewish and Korean business relations, see ibid., 183. See also Jennifer Lee, *Civility in the City: Blacks, Jews, and Koreans in Urban America* (Cambridge: Harvard University Press, 2002), 20–47.

186. Min, *Caught in the Middle*, 180–1.

187. See, for example, Chang, "Jewish and Korean Merchants," 5–21.

188. Rabbi Douglas Kahn, "Jews and Emerging Minorities: Jewish-Asian Relations," *Journal of Jewish Communal Service* 68, no. 3 (1992): 227.

189. Ibid., 227–8.

190. Tim Alper, "Why South Koreans Are in Love with Judaism," *Jewish Chronicle Online*, May 12, 2011, http://www.thejc.com/lifestyle/lifestyle-features/48771/why-south-koreans-are-love-judaism.

191. Ted Belman, "Talmud Study Now Mandatory in South Korea," trans. by "The Muqata" from YNET, *Israpunit* (blog), Mar. 27, 2011, http://www.israpundit.com/archives/34782.

192. Song Oh, "Asians: The New Shiksas?" *JewishJournal.com*, Apr. 17, 2003, http://www.jewishjournal.com/singles/article/Asians_the_new_shiksas_20030418/.

193. Amadu Jacky Kaba, "The Family and Political Unity between Blacks and Jews in the United States," *International Journal of Humanities and Social Science* 1, no. 21, special issue (Dec. 2011), 168–9.

194. Quoted in Christopher Stringer and Robin McKie, *African Exodus: The Origins of Modern Humanity* (New York: Holt Paperbacks 1998), 190.

195. Clarence Page, "Black Immigrants, an Invisible 'Model Minority,'" Real Clear Politics, Mar. 19, 2007, http://www.realclearpolitics.com/articles/2007/03/black_immigrants_an_invisible.html.

196. John R. Logan, "America's Newcomers," Lewis Mumford Center for Comparative Urban and Regional Research, University at Albany, June 18, 2003, 14, http://mumford1.dyndns.org/cen2000/NewComersReport/NewComer01.htm.

197. The Leadership Conference on Civil Rights and Human Rights, "Cause for Concern: Hate Crimes in America," (Washington, DC: LCCRHR, 2001), http://www.civilrights.org/publications/reports/cause_for_concern/. Looking specifically at 1995, this report indicates that blacks overall are the most targeted for hate crimes. Jews are targeted the most for religion, and Hispanics are targeted the most for ethnicity or national origin. These statistics still held in 2009, with African Americans being the targets of 34% of all hate crimes in the United States; Jews were the second most likely targets. Hate crimes against API actually declined since the

earlier report to 2.5% while those against Arabic Americans increased. Leadership Conference on Civil Rights Education Fund, "Confronting the New Faces of Hate: Hate Crimes in America, 2009" (Washington, DC: LCCRHR, 2009), under "Hate Crimes against African Americans," http://www.civilrights.org/publications/hate-crimes/. Regarding API victimization, see National Asian Pacific American Legal Consortium, "Backlash Final Report: 2001 Audit Against Asian Pacific Americans," 9th Annual Report (Washington, DC: NAPALC, 2001), http://www.advancingequality.org/files/2001_Audit.pdf.

198. "Latest Hate Crime Statistics: Reported Incidents, Number of Victims Decrease," FBI, Nov. 22, 2010, http://www.fbi.gov/news/stories/2010/november/hate_112210/hate_112210.

199. "The Hate Crimes Statistics Act (HCSA)," Anti-Defamation League, http://www.adl.org/issue_government/hate_crime_statistics_act.asp.

200. K. Connie Kang, "40% of Koreans in Poll Ponder Leaving: Riots: Survey of Business Owners Finds Deep Concern. Blacks also Voice Fears but Fewer Want to Relocate," *LAT*, Mar. 19, 1993, 1–2, http://articles.latimes.com/1993-03-19/local/me-12656_1_african-american-business-owners. The article presented some of the data of Nadine Koch and H. Eric Schockman.

201. Findings from Byron Jackson's 1988 research, "Los Angeles Racial Group Consciousness and Political Behavior Survey," compiled in Edward T. Chang, "New Urban Crisis: Korean-African American Relations," in *Koreans in the Hood: Conflict with African Americans*, ed. Kwnag Chung Kim (Baltimore: Johns Hopkins University Press, 1999), 44–6.

202. Tom W. Rice, "Jewish Attitudes Toward Blacks and Race Relations," American Jewish Committee (AJC), 1990, http://www.bjpa.org/Publications/details.cfm?PublicationID=3035; Murray Dubin, "Jews Tolerant Towards Blacks, Study Shows," *Inquirer* (Philadelphia), May 18, 1990, http://articles.philly.com/1990-05-18/news/25886187_1_school-integration-blacks-jewish-attitudes.

CHAPTER 6

1. Richard Leonard, in discussion with the author, Oct. 21, 2004.

2. *The People of the State of California v. Soon Ja Du* (Cal. Super. Ct. L.A. County, Dept. 111, 1991, no. BA037738), vol. 4, Nov. 15, 1991, 596.

3. Al Martinez, "A Ghost That Won't Go Away," *LAT*, Jan. 16, 1992, B2.

4. *People v. Du*, vol. 4, Nov. 15, 1991, 589.

5. Ibid., 594, 606.

6. Ibid., 606–7.

7. Ibid., 607.

8. Ibid.

9. Ibid., 607–8.

10. Marsha Mitchell, "Reiner Blackballs Karlin," *Los Angeles Sentinel*, Nov. 21–27, 1991, A1, A21.

11. *People v. Du*, vol. 4, Nov. 15, 1991, 602.

12. Ibid., 596.

13. Ibid., 593.

14. Ibid., 595.

15. Ibid., 595.

16. Ibid., 591, 593, 595.

17. Report of Patricia Dwyer quoted in Njeri, *Last Plantation*, 250.

18. *People v. Du*, vol. 4, Nov. 15, 1991, 616.

19. Ibid., 601.

20. Ibid.

21. Ibid., 616.

22. Ibid., 621.

23. Ibid., 614–5.

24. Ibid., 610.

25. Ibid., 622.

26. Ibid.

27. Ibid., 611–2.

28. Ibid., 605–613 *passim,* quote from 612–3.

29. Ibid., 613.

30. Ibid., 624–6.

31. Ibid., 630–1.

32. "Probation Given to Shopkeeper Who Killed Girl," *San Francisco Chronicle*, Nov. 16, 1991, A19.

33. *People v. Du*, vol. 4, Nov. 15, 1991, 624.

34. Ibid., 625.

35. Ibid., 626.

36. Ibid., 627.

37. Ibid., 628–9.

38. Ibid., 629.

39. Ibid., 622.

40. Ibid., 623–4.

41. Quotes from Denise and Ruth Harlins and Gina Rae taken from Andrew Okun and James R. Martin, "Du Convicted: Korean Grocer Faces 16 Years," *Los Angeles Sentinel*, Oct. 17, 1991, A1, A12.

42. Ibid., A12.

43. Marsha Mitchell, "Homicidal Week: At Least 40 Die in Southland Spree," *Los Angeles Sentinel*, Oct. 24, 1991, A1. See also Mitchell, "Activists Denounce the Shooting," A1.

44. Ibid.

45. Mitchell, "Activists Denounce the Shooting," A17.

46. Ibid., A1.

47. Caption under photograph in "Violence Condemned," *LAT*, Oct. 24, 1991, B2.

48. Ibid.

49. Mitchell, "The Harlins Family: After the Tragedy and the Verdict, Part One," *Los Angeles Sentinel, Dec.* 5, 1991, A3.

50. Denise Harlins represented the Harlins family in the interview. Brother David represented the LHJC. Marsha Mitchell, "The Harlins Family," A3. "Anniversary: The Harlins Tragedy" *Los Angeles Sentinel*, Mar. 19, 1992, A1. (Denise and

brother David spokesmen). "Interview: The Latasha Harlins Justice Committee," *Los Angeles Sentinel*, Mar. 26, 1992, A1, A11–12.

51. Richard Reyes Fruto, "Angry Blacks Say Mayor Siding with Koreans," *Korea Times*, Sept. 15, 1991, 3.

52. Hugo Martin, "Korean Shopkeeper Killed in Robbery," *LAT*, Oct. 30, 1991, B3.

53. K. W. Lee, "An American Passage: Latasha Becomes Part of Our Collective Conscience," *Korea Times*, Nov. 25, 1991, 1, 6.

54. Philip Sneiderman, "Puppy Love: Abused Cocker Spaniels is Deluged by Well Wishers," *LAT*, July 14, 1991, http://articles.latimes.com/1991-07-14/local/me-3605_1_cocker-spaniel.

55. Herschel David Hunt, "What's Black Life Worth," *Los Angeles Sentinel*, Dec. 5, 1991, A6.

56. "Judges Sentence Draws Fire," *LAT,* Nov. 25, 1991, B4.

57. Jeff Meyer, "Many at Meeting Express Outrage at Probation for Grocer in Killing," *Los Angeles Daily News*, Nov. 17, 1991, A8.

58. Ibid.

59. Ibid.

60. Quoted in Cannon, *Official Negligence*, 171.

61. Meyer, "Many at Meeting Express Outrage," A8.

62. Associated Press, "L.A. Blacks Protest Sentence," *San Francisco Examiner*, Nov. 25, 1991, B1.

63. Martinez, "A Ghost That Won't Go Away," B2.

64. Associated Press, "L.A. Blacks Protest Sentence," B1.

65. Gerald Faris and Ashley Dunn, "Anti-Karlin Protesters Enter Courthouse," *LAT*, Nov. 23, 1991, B1.

66. Ibid.

67. Marsha Mitchell, "Community Pushes Reiner to Appeal Du Sentence," *Los Angeles Sentinel*, Nov. 28, 1991, A17.

68. Faris and Dunn, "Anti-Karlin Protesters," B12.

69. Marsha Mitchell, "Community Pushes Reiner," A17.

70. Danny Bakewell, in discussion with the author, Aug. 29, 2003; Karen Nikos, "Judge Faces Protests in Grocer Case," *Los Angles Daily News*, Nov. 20, 1991, A4.

71. Danny Bakewell, discussion; Nikos, "Judge Faces Protests," A4.

72. Mitchell, "Karlin Being Judged," A20.

73. Linda Deutsch, "Korean Grocer Gets Probation," *Los Angeles Daily News* (early edition), Nov. 17, 1994, A10.

74. Reiner was referring to the use of a procedural rule in criminal cases that allowed both the prosecuting and the defending attorney to each reject one judge before a trail begins. Mitchell, "Karlin Being Judged," A20. See also Mitchell, "Reiner Blackballs Karlin," A1, A21; Andrea Ford, "Angry Groups Vow to Drive Judge in Grocer Case from the Bench," *LAT*, Nov. 20, 1991, B3.

Reiner eventually had to withdraw his threat to "blackball" Karlin under heavy criticism from local bar associations, jurists, and private citizens, not the least of whom were African American civil rights leaders who believed repeated usage of the rule would backfire on black defendants. Superior Court Presiding Judge

Ricardo Torres, for example, accused Reiner of trying to use the Du case to bolster his political support in the black community to help his ailing reelection campaign. "She has an excellent reputation, she's a law-and-order type no question," Torres offered in Karlin's support. Sacramento Judge and California Judges Association President, Michael Mellman, agreed as did all 18 members of the judge executive committee of the Los Angeles Superior Court. Mitchell, "Reiner Blackballs Karlin," A1, A21; Ford, "Angry Groups Vow," B3.

75. Dean E. Murphy, "Reiner to Seek New Sentence in Girl's Trial," *LAT*, Nov. 17, 1991, B1.

76. Laurie Levenson, "Reiner is Out of Bounds," *LAT*, Nov. 22, 1991, B7.

77. Karen Nikos, "'Miscarraige of Justice' Claimed: Reiner Blasts Judge's Probation Sentence for Korean Grocer in Slaying," *Los Angeles Daily News*, Nov. 19, 1991, A4.

78. Quoted in Mitchell, "Community Pushes Reiner," A1.

79. Levenson, "Reiner is Out of Bounds," B7.

80. Murphy, "Reiner to Seek New Sentence," B1.

81. Mitchell, "Karlin Being Judged," A20; Sheryl Stolberg, "Reiner Backs off from Plan to Block Karlin," *LAT*, Nov. 26, 1991, B1–4; Dean E. Murphy, "Prospects for Successful Appeal of Grocer's Sentence Seen as Slim," *LAT*, Nov. 26, 1991, B1–4.

82. Henry Weinstein, "Appeal Panel Hears Lawyers' Debate on Sentence by Karlin's Court," *LAT*, Mar. 5, 1992, B3.

83. Quoted in Cannon, *Official Negligence*, 169.

84. Murphy, "Reiner to Seek New Sentence," B1.

85. Elaine Kim, "Between Black and White: An Interview with Bong Hwan Kim," *The State of Asian America: Activism and Resistance in the 1990s*, ed. Karin Aguilar-San Juan (Boston: South End Press, 1994), 84.

86. Marcia Choo, in discussion with the author, June 6, 2012.

87. Quoted in Kim, "Between Black and White," 86.

88. Marsha Mitchell, "Teenager's Slaying Heightens Black-Korean Tensions," *Los Angeles Sentinel*, Mar. 28, 1991, A16.

89. Ibid.

90. Althea Yip, "Remembering Vincent Chin: Fifteen Years Later, a Murder in Detroit Remains a Turning Point in the APA Movement," *Asian Week: The Voice of Asian America* 18, no. 43 (June 13, 1997), http://asianweek.com/061397/feature.html; Christine Ho, "The Model Minority Awakened: The Murder of Vincent Chin," USA-sians.net, 2003, "Part 1," http://us_asians.tripod.com/articles-vincentchin.html.

91. Quoted in Yip, "Remembering Vincent Chin."

92. Marsha Mitchell, "The Harlins Family," A3.

93. "Restraint on Protests at Judge's Home Lifted," *LAT*, Jan. 17, 1992, B2.

94. Marc Lacey and Nancy Forrest, "Council Rejects Law Barring Picketing of Private Homes," *LAT*, Jan. 23, 1992, B3.

95. "Karlin's Husband Ran Over Protester's Foot, Group Says," *LAT*, Mar. 12, 1992, B2.

96. Denise Harlins, in discussion with the author, July 16, 1993; Denise Harlins, in discussion with the author, Nov. 17, 1993; Members of LHJC, in discussion with

the author, July 15, 1993; Members of LHJC protest, July 15, 1993; Eric Malnic, "Presiding Judge and Jurist in Case of Korean Grocer Receive Recall Papers," *LAT*, Jan. 2, 1992, B2.

97. Sheryl Stolberg, "Man Shot by Merchant in Fear of Robber," *LAT*, Nov. 23, 1991, B1.

98. Ibid.

99. Ibid.

100. Ibid.

101. "Minority Groups Say Hate Crimes Escalating Against Asians," *Los Angeles Sentinel*, Dec. 26, 1991, A3, A14.

102. Jesse Katz, "Fatal Shooting in Holdup Stirs Sorrow, Not Surprise," *LAT*, Dec. 16, 1991, B1.

103. Seth Mydans, "Hawthorne Journal; Two Views of Protest at Korean Shop," *New York Times*, Dec. 24, 1991, 1–2, http://www.nytimes.com/1991/12/24/us/hawthorne-journal-two-views-of-protest-at-korean-shop.html; "Korean Grocer to be Charged in Attack on Girl," *LAT*, Dec. 19, 1991, B2.

104. Murphy, "Reiner to Seek New Sentence," B1.

105. Howard Johnson, a local attorney also ran for DA that year, but he made no public statements on the case or the sentence. Roger Grace, "Political Career of Ira K. Reiner Takes a Nosedive," Metropolitan News Company, Mar. 5, 2010, http://www.metnews.com/articles/2010/perspectives031510.htm.

106. Kenneth J. Garcia, "Tanenbaum Begins Effort to Unseat Reiner," *LAT*, Apr. 21, 1991, J1.

107. Grace, "Political Career of Ira K. Reiner."

108. Sheryl Stolberg, "Reiner Uses Karlin Issue Against Foes," *LAT*, Apr. 17, 1992, B1.

109. Ibid.

110. Reiner had not just failed to successfully prosecute LA police officers for the beating of Rodney King and was unsuccessful in appealing Du's sentence; other important losses included failing to gain convictions in the John Landis case and the MacMartin preschool molestation case. Grace, "Political Career of Ira K. Reiner"; Seth Mydans, "Los Angeles Prosecutor Bows Out of the Spotlight," *New York Times*, Sept. 19, 1992, 1–2, http://www.nytimes.com/1992/09/19/us/los-angeles-prosecutor-bows-out-of-the-spotlight.html.

111. Henry Weinstein, "Appeal Panel Hears Lawyers' Debate," *LAT*, Mar. 5, 1992, B3; "Donald Etra: Los Angeles Criminal Defense Lawyer," Law Offices of Donald Etra, 2011, http://www.donaldetra.com/.

112. Weinstein, "Appeal Panel Hears Lawyers' Debate," B3; Justice Margaret Grignon graduated first in her class from Loyola Law School in 1974; Karlin graduated three years earlier. Justice Grignon's resume found in "Hon. Margaret M. Grignon: California Court of Appeal, Second District, Retired," Alternative Resolution Centers, 2007, http://arc4adr.com/honmargaretmgrignon.html.

113. Weinstein, "Appeal Panel Hears Lawyers' Debate," *LAT*, Mar. 5, 1992, B3.

114. All quotes from Ibid.

115. *The People v. The Superior Court of Los Angeles County (Soon Ja Du)* 5 Cal. App. 4th 822; 7 Cal. Rptr. 2d 177; *People v. Superior Court (Du)* 1992 Cal. App. LEXIS 525; 92 Cal. Daily Op. Service 3464; 92 Daily Journal DAR 5313, http://www.lexis-nexis.com/hottopics/lnacademic.

116. K. W. Lee, "Karlin Did Not Abuse Discretion: Appeal's Court Releases Opinion Upholding Du Sentencing," *Korea Times*, May 4, 1992, 6; Sheryl Stolberg, "Karlin Remains on Criminal Bench," *LAT*, Nov. 28, 1991, B1, B6; Tracy Wilkinson and Frank Clifford, "Korean Grocer Who Killed Black Teen Gets Probation," *LAT*, Nov. 16, 1991, A26; Denise Harlins, "Latasha Harlins Justice Committee Forges Ahead Despite Setbacks," organizational statement, n.d.

117. *People v. Superior Court (Du)*.

118. Ibid.

119. Ibid.

120. Ibid.

121. Ibid.

122. Martinez, "A Ghost That Won't Go Away," *LAT* B2; "Local News in Brief," *LAT, Dec.* 27, 1991, B1.

123. "Drive Seeks to Recall Judge in Slaying Case," *New York Times*, Jan. 2, 1992, http://www.nytimes.com/1992/01/02/us/drive-seeks-to-recall-judge-in-slaying-case.html?src=pm.

124. "Local News in Brief," B1.

125. Martinez, "A Ghost That Won't Go Away," B2.

126. Edward Chang and Jeannette Diaz-Veizades, *Ethnic Peace in the American City: Building Community in Los Angeles and Beyond* (New York: New York University Press, 1999), 77.

127. Martinez, "A Ghost That Won't Go Away," B2.

128. Ibid.

129. Ibid.

130. Ibid.

131. At least one person took note of the change in Judge Karlin's appearance from an earlier time in her career. Vincent Caballero, of Pomona, wrote to the *Los Angeles Times* in March 1992 with a loaded query: If Latasha Harlins, like Judge Karlin, had the benefit of a consulting firm to shape her image, would the outcome of the Du trial had been different? "Perhaps if Latasha's hairstyle were modified to project the image of a true victim," he mused, "she would have gained more respect as a human being." Vincent Caballero, "Judge Karlin Fights Back (Opinion)," *LAT*, Mar. 8, 1992, M4.

132. Sheryl Stolberg, "Judge Karlin's Race Is Closely Watched Series," *LAT*, May 27, 1992, B1; Todd S. Purdum, "Rose Bird, Once California's Chief Justice, Is Dead at 63," *New York Times*, Dec. 6, 1999, http://www.nytimes.com/1999/12/06/us/rose-bird-once-california-s-chief-justice-is-dead-at-63.html?pagewanted=all&src=pm.

133. Kay Hwangbo "Karlin Supports King Verdict," *Korea Times*, Aug. 24, 1992, 1; Njeri, *Last Plantation*, 258–60; Joel Kotkin, "Ten Years After: The Jews Remain," JewishJournal.com, Apr. 25, 2002, http://www.jewishjournal.com/los_angeles/article/ten_years_after_the_jews_remain_20020426/; Rob Eshman, "Honoring Marlene," JewishJournal.com, Apr. 25, 2002, http://www.jewishjournal.com/rob_eshman/article/honoring_marlene_20020426/.

134. Stolberg, "Judge Karlin's Race," B1.

135. Ibid.

136. Ibid.

137. Hector Tobar, "Judge Who Gave Probation in '91 Killing Quits," *LAT*, Feb. 11, 1997, B1; Denise Harlins quote from Njeri, *Last Plantation*, 20.

138. Stolberg, "Judge Karlin's Race," B1.

139. Ibid.

140. Ibid.

141. Cerrell also noted that they opted to use the media to their advantage because the budget his firm negotiated for their work was low, only $150,000. Joseph Cerrell, "L.A. Law (Joyce A. Karlin's Campaign for Judicial Position in Los Angeles, California) (24 Winning Ideas)," *Campaigns and Elections,* Jan. 1993, http://www.lexisnexis.com/hottopics/lnacademic.

142. Joyce Ann Karlin, "Judge Karlin's Reelection," *LAT,* June 1, 1992, M4.

143. Sheryl Stolberg, Fredrick M. Muir, and Hector Tobar, "Local Elections: Judge Karlin's Win Baffles Black Leaders," *LAT,* June 4, 1992, B1.

144. Richard Reyes Fruto, "Karlin Wins Election," *Korea Times,* June 8, 1992, 1, 7.

145. Stolberg, Muir, and Tobar, "Judge Karlin's Win Baffles," B1.

146. Ibid.

147. Ibid.

148. Walter Kennedy, "Judge Karlin's Reelection (Opinion)," *LAT,* June 14, 1992, M4.

149. Roxanna H. Fransconi, "Judge Karlin's Reelection (Opinion)," *LAT,* June 14, 1992, M4.

150. Mark Oliver, "Judge Karlin's Reelection (Opinion)," *LAT,* June 14, 1992, M4.

151. Brenda Bankhead, "Judge Karlin's Reelection (Opinion)," *LAT* June 14, 1992, M4.

152. Stolberg, Muir, and Tobar, "Judge Karlin's Win Baffles," B1.

153. "U.S. Looks into Korean Slaying of Black," *New York Times,* Nov. 26, 1992, http://www.nytimes.com/1992/11/26/us/us-looks-into-korean-grocer-s-slaying-of-black.html?src=pm.

154. Erin J. Aubry, "New Effort to Recall Judge Karlin Begins," *LAT* (Crenshaw), July 4, 1993, 11.

155. "Judge in Furor is Reassigned," *New York Times,* Jan. 25, 1992, http://www.nytimes.com/1992/01/25/us/judge-in-furor-is-reassigned.html?src=pm.

156. Aubry, "New Effort to Recall," 11.

157. "Korean Grocer Settles Suit in Girl's Slaying," *New York Times,* July 9, 1992, http://www.nytimes.com/1992/07/09/us/korean-grocer-settles-suit-in-girl-s-slaying.html?src=pm.

158. Miles Corwin, "As Public Memories Fade, a Private Mission Endures" *LAT,* Nov. 18, 1995, B1.

159. Ice Cube, "Black Korea" AskLyrics.com, 2011, http://www.asklyrics.com/display/ice-cube/black-korea-lyrics.htm. Regarding controversy surrounding "Black Korea," see Mickey Hess, *Icons of Hip Hop: An Encyclopedia of the Movement, Music, and Culture,* vol. 2 (Westport, CT: Greenwood Press, 2007), 304; Anthony Choe, "Ice Cube's 'Black Korea': Racially-Charged Rap," *Yisei Magazine* 5, no. 2 (Spring 1992), http://www.hcs.harvard.edu/~yisei/issues/spring_92/ys92_6.html.

160. Tupac, "Hellrazor," Lyrics Mode, 2012, http://www.lyricsmode.com/lyrics/t/tupac/hellrazor.html; "Tupac Keep Yo Head Up," Lyrics Mode, 2012, http://www.lyricsmode.com/lyrics/t/tupac/keep_your_head_up.html; Ice Cube, "Black Korea."

161. "Keep Ya Head Up-2Pac," Billboards.com, 2012, http://www.billboard.com/#/song/2pac/keep-ya-head-up/2035548.

162. "Tupac, "Hellrazor."

163. Ibid.

164. Tupac, "I Wonder If Heaven Got a Ghetto," AZLyrics.com, 2012, http://www.azlyrics.com/lyrics/2pac/iwonderifheavengotaghetto.html.

165. For example, Tupac Shakur, "The Best of 2Pac-Part 2: Life" (Interscope Records, Amaru Entertainment, Inc., 2007) CD, only contains "Keep Ya Head Up."

166. Anna Deavere Smith, *Twilight: Los Angeles, 1992* (New York: Dramatists Play Service, 2003).

167. "Latasha Harlins' Memorial Page," Myspace, http://www.myspace.com/132895327; "The Media Portrayals of LA Riots, 20 Years Later," Tumblr (blog), http://www.tumblr.com/tagged/latasha+harlins; "Latasha Harlins," Facebook, http://www.facebook.com/pages/Latasha-Harlins/115989025115022. Information on Trayvon Martin death found in Matt Gutman and Laura Effron, "Trayvon Martin Case: Timeline of Events," ABC News, May 8, 2012, http://abcnews.go.com/blogs/headlines/2012/05/trayvon-martin-case-timeline-of-events/.

168. LaVerne71, "Do You Guys Remember Latasha Harlins," Lipstick Alley (blog), July 20, 2011, http://www.lipstickalley.com/f50/do-you-guys-remember-latasha-harlins-317783/#post7797863.

169. I refer here, of course, to the legal theory known as "intersectionality," pioneered by legal scholar Kimberle Crenshaw and others that takes into account the "intersection" of multiple categories of identity (typically social variables, but sometimes as well biological, intellectual, cultural, etc.) that are associated with one person and that has varying influence, but influence nonetheless, on how that person is treated in the justice system. See for example, Kimberle Crenshaw, "Demarginalizing the Intersection of Race and Sex: A Black Feminist Critique of Antidiscrimination Doctrine, Feminist Theory and Antiracist Politics," *University of Chicago Legal Forum* (189): 139–67; Jennifer C. Nash, "Re-thinking Intersectionality" *Feminist Review* 89, (2008): 1–15; Leslie McCall, "The Complexity of Intersectionality," *University of Chicago Press* 30, no. 3 (Spring 2005): 1771–800.

170. *People v. Du*, vol. 4, Nov. 15, 1991, 623–4.

171. Karlin also defended her reasons for her sentencing of Du in the *LAT*. See Joyce Karlin, "'Great Provocation and Duress.' The Judge in the Du Manslaughter Trial Explains her Reasons for Imposing Probation Rather than Prison Time," *LAT*, Nov. 22, 1991, B7.

172. *People v. Du*, vol. 4, Nov. 15, 1991, 624–9 *passim*.

173. "Interview: Judge Joyce Karlin, Part II," *Los Angeles Sentinel*, Mar. 12, 1991, A2.

174. *People v. Du*, vol. 4, Nov. 15, 1991, 627.

175. See, for example, K. Sue Jewell, *From Mammy to Miss America and Beyond: Cultural Images and the Shaping of US Social Policy* (New York: Routledge Press, 1993). Jewell argues in a general manner, for example, that with regard to the legal justice system, "The rights of women, in general, and African American women in particular, are less likely to be protected than those of any other group in society, because African American women occupy the lowest position on this [social] hierarchy." Ibid., 123.

176. *People v. Du*, vol. 2, Oct. 1, 1991, 141–7.

177. "Social control theory" as applied to sentencing decisions takes into consideration biases that may occur in court outcomes and sentencing with regard to race, gender, and other socially important variables. The basic premise is that sentencing is related to the assessment of a defendant's social behavior as the "likelihood of 'respectable' or law-abiding behavior is increased . . . the application of formal social control is decreased." Karlin describes Du as law-abiding, therefore not requiring incarceration. Family, in particular, influences treatment before the court. This is particularly so in the assessment of females. Kathleen Daly notes, for example, that "familied women are least likely subject to criminal justice controls and sanctions . . . of all familial groups, familial women benefit most by the importance the court places on the maintenance and protection of family life." Indeed, Karlin references Du's family commitment and obligations in her sentencing statement. Kathleen Daly, "Discrimination in the Criminal Courts: Family, Gender, and the Problem of Equal Treatment," *Social Forces* 6, no. 1 (Sept. 1987): 153, 168. Regarding sentencing and gender roles, see also Gayle S. Bickle and Ruth D. Petersen, "The Impact of Gender-Based Family Roles on Criminal Sentencing," *Social Problems* 38, no. 3 (Aug. 1991): 372–94. Bickle and Petersen conclude that, although other factors also are important, their study "underscores the importance of marital status and the presence of dependents . . . providing caretaker support for dependents," all criteria that Judge Karlin used in her analysis of the victimization of Du and Harlins and which influenced her sentencing. Regarding treatment of juveniles in the court system as a result of social environment variables, see Dale Dannefer and Russell K. Schutt, "Race and Juvenile Justice Processing in Court and Police Agencies," *American Journal of Sociology* 87, no. 5 (Mar. 1992): 1113–32.

178. *People v. Du*, vol. 2, Oct. 1, 1991, 141–2.

179. Ibid., 146–7.

180. *People v. Du*, vol. 4, Oct. 3, 1991, 541–2.

181. For thoughtful discussions of black youth, especially males, in the criminal justice system and how they are portrayed in the media, see Darnell F. Hawkins and Nolan E. Jones, "Black Adolescents and the Criminal Justice System," in *Black Adolescents*, ed. Reginald L. Jones (Berkeley: Cobb and Henry, 1989), 403–25. See also, Jewell Garrett Holliday, "Black Adolescents and Youth: An Update on an Endangered Species," in Jones, *Black Adolescents*, 3–27; D. Huizinga and D. Elliott, *Juvenile Offenders' Prevalence, Offender Incidence, and Arrest Rates by Race* (Boulder: Institute of Behavioral Sciences, 1985); B. Krisberg, I. Schwartz, G. Fishman, Z. Eiskovits, and E. Guttman, *The Incarceration of Minority Youth* (Minneapolis: Humphrey Institute of Public Affairs, 1986); Coramae Richey Mann, *Female Crime and Delinquency* (Tuscaloosa: University of Alabama Press, 1984); Mann, *Unequal Justice: A Question of Color* (Bloomington: Indiana University Press, 1993); Concetta C. Culliver, ed., *Female Criminality: The State of the Art* (New York: Garland, 1993); and Jewelle Taylor Gibbs, Ann F. Brunswick, Michael E. Connor, Richard Dembo, Tome E. Larson, Rodney J. Reed, Barbara Solomon, eds., *Young, Black, and Male in America: An Endangered Species* (Westport, CT: Auburn House, 1988).

182. *People v. Du*, vol. 3, Oct. 2, 1991, 320–79 *passim*, especially 325, 328–31. For popular depictions of Asian immigrants as the model minority, and their comparison to blacks, see, for example, CBS, *Sixty Minutes*, "The Model Minority," Feb. 1,

1987; "Asian Americans: The Drive to Excel," *Newsweek on Campus*, Apr. 1984, 4–15; "America's Super Minority," *Fortune*, Nov. 26, 1986; William Raspberry, "Beyond Racism," *Washington Post*, Nov. 19, 1984. See also Ronald Takaki, *A Different Mirror: A History of Multicultural America* (Boston: Little, Brown, 1993), 414–17; Ronald Takaki, "Comparisons Between Blacks and Asian Americans Unfair," *Seattle Post-Intelligencer*, Mar. 21, 1985.

183. Regarding racialized gender stereotyping of Asian Americans and African Americans, there is a vast and growing literature, both produced by scholars of various social science disciplines and by journalists. A sample of this outpouring includes Patricia Hill Collins, *Black Feminist Thought: Knowledge, Consciousness, and the Politics of Empowerment* (London: Harper Collins, 1990), esp. 67–90; Joseph White and James H. Cones III, *Black Man Emerging: Facing the Past and Seizing a Future in America* (New York: Routledge Press, 1999), 67–90; Deborah White, *Ar'n't I a Woman?: Female Slaves in the Plantation South* (New York: Norton, 1984); Angela Davis, "The Legacy of Slavery: Standards for a New Womanhood" in *Women, Race and Class* (New York: Random House, 1981); Michele Wallace, *Black Macho and the Myth of the Superwoman* (New York: Dial Press, 1978); Mary Helen Washington, introduction to *Black Eyed Susans: Classic Stories by and about Black Women* (Garden City: Anchor, 1980); Valerie Matsumoto, "Desperately Seeking 'Deirdre': Gender Roles, Multicultural Relations, and Nisei Women Writers of the 1930s," *Frontiers* 12, no. 1 (1991): 19–32; Eun Sik Yang, "Korean Women of America: From Subordination to Partnership, 1903–1930," *Amerasia Journal* 11, no. 1 (1984): 1–28; Ki-Taek Chun, "The Myth of Asian American Success and Its Educational Ramifications" in *The Asian American Educational Experience: Source Book for Teachers and Students*, ed. Don T. Nakanishi and Tina Yamano Nishida (New York: Routledge Press, 1995), 95–112; Bob H. Suzuki, "Education and Socialization of Asian Americans: A Revisionist Analysis of the 'Model Minority' Thesis," in Nakanishi and Nishida, *Asian American Educational Experience*, 113–32; Russell Endo, "Japanese Americans: The 'Model Minority' Perspective," in *The Social Reality of Ethnic America*, ed. Rudolph Gomez, Clement Cottingham, Russell Endo, and Kathleen Jackson (Lexington, MA: D. C. Heath, 1974), 189–213; Elaine Kim, "'Such Opposite Creatures': Men and Women in Asian American Literature," *Michigan Quarterly Review* 29 (Oct. 1990): 68–93; E. H. Kim, "The Myth of Asian American Success," *Asian American Review* 2 (1975): 122–49; "Japanese Outdo Horatio Alger," *LAT*, Oct. 17, 1977, A1; "Success Story: Outwhiting the Whites," *Newsweek*, June 21, 1971, 24–5; "Success Story of One Minority Group in U.S.," *U.S. News and World Report*, Dec. 26, 1966, 73–6; Yoko Yoshikawa, "The Heat Is on Miss Saigon Coalition: Organizing Across Race and Sexuality," in *The State of Asian America: Activism and Resistance in the Nineties*, ed. Karin Aguilar-San Juan (Boston: South End Press, 1994), 275–94; See also in that same volume, Sonia Shah, "Presenting the Blue Goddess: Toward a National Pan-Asian Feminist Agenda," 147–157.

184. *People v. Du*, vol. 4, Oct. 3, 1991, 629.

185. Neil Gotanda, "Re-Producing the Model Minority Stereotype: Judge Joyce Karlin's Sentencing Colloquy in *People v. Soon Ja Du*," in *Reviewing Asian America: Locating Diversity*, ed. Wendy L. Ng, Soo-Young Chin, James S. Moy, and

Gary Y. Okihiro (Pullman: Washington State University Press, 1995), ch. 7; Neil Gotanda, "Tales of Two Judges: Joyce Karlin in *People v. Soon Ja Du*; Lance Ito in *People v. O. J. Simpson*," in *The House That Race Built: Original Essays by Toni Morrison, Angela Y. Davis, Cornel West, and Others on Black Americans and Politics in America Today*, ed. Wahneema Lubiano (New York: Random House, 2010), Kindle edition, ch. 4.

186. Cynthia Lee, *Murder and the Reasonable Man: Passion and Fear in the Criminal Courtroom* (New York: New York University Press, 2003), 138–46, quote from 139.

187. Ibid., 144.

188. *People v. Du*, vol. 3, Oct. 2, 1991, 322–3.

189. *People v. Du*, vol. 4, Oct. 3, 1991, 629.

190. Ibid., 630.

191. Elizabeth Anne Stanko, "Would You Believe This Woman? Prosecutorial Screening for 'Credible' Witnesses and a Problem of Justice," in Rafter and Stanko, *Judge, Lawyer, Victim, Thief*, 78.

192. Njeri, *Last Plantation*, 94–6.

193. Cynthia Lee also discusses this aspect of the case, indicating that this case is one example in which the judge "relied upon positive stereotypes about Korean Americans and negative stereotypes about African Americans in deciding Du's sentence." Lee, *Mirror and the Reasonable Man*, 161. Lee is drawing on the analysis of law scholar Neil Gotanda in "Re-Producing the Model Minority Stereotype," in Ng, Chin, Moy, and Okihiro, *Reviewing Asian America*.

CHAPTER 7

* Epigraphs: One of the first three website comments given at the end of the online version. See Rebecca Trouson and Joel Rubin, "Many Say L.A. Is Safer 20 Years After 1992 Riots, Poll Finds," *LAT*, Apr. 11, 2012, http://www.latimes.com/news/local/la-me-riot-survey-20120412,0,4231065.story. Reiner is quoted in Lou Cannon, *Official Negligence: How Rodney King and the Riots Changed Los Angeles and the LAPD* (Boulder, CO: Westview Press, 1999), 172.

1. Jeff Meyer, "Many at Meeting Express Outrage at Probation for Grocer in Killing," *Los Angeles Daily News*, November 17, 1991, A8.

2. Denise Harlins quoted in "Of Riots and Rebellions," *Vibe Magazine*, Apr. 2002, 124.

3. Ibid.

4. Michael Omi and Howard Winant, "The Los Angeles 'Race Riot,' and Contemporary U.S. Politics," in *Reading Rodney King, Reading Urban Uprising* agree that the case "served as an immediate prelude to rioters' assaults on Korean merchants." Sumi Cho in that same volume noted that Du's killing of Harlins and Karlin's sentencing of Du "forced this reckoning" of the riots. Regina Freer in her article "Black-Korean Conflict" (1994) agrees. While Freer is careful to discern the various economic issues at hand as well, she asserts that the Soon Ja Du shooting of Latasha "came to symbolize the long-standing animosity between black patrons and Korean merchants . . . the African American community viewed this shooting

History: Pre-Columbian to the Millennium, 2012, http://www.ushistory.org/us/38c.asp. Beneath the cartoon at the time of publication was an explanation which read: "DURING four hundred and more years this continent has been the melting pot for the population of the Eastern hemisphere. For three-fourths of that time the yearly infusions of raw metal was so slight that it was not hard to compound them with the native stock and preserve the high character of American citizenship. But when alien immigration pours its stream of half a million yearly, as has been frequently done during the last decade, and when that stream is polluted with the moral sewage of the old world, including its poverty, drunkenness, infidelity and disease, it is well to put up the bars and save America, at least until she can purify the atmosphere of contagion which foreign invasion has already brought." Ironically, Beard uses a quote by a Jewish religious figure, Jeremiah, as his caption. "Multimedia Histories Section: The Stranger at Our Gate," Ohio State University, Department of History, 2012, http://ehistory.osu.edu/osu/mmh/Rams_horn/content/StrangerAtOurGate.cfm

148. Gilman, *Jew's Body*, 171.

149. Ibid., 172.

150. Ibid., 99. Gilman notes that Jews are considered this way in nineteenth-century "racial science."

151. Robert Knox, *The Races of Men: A Fragment* (Philadelphia: Lea and Blanchard, 1850), 133, quoted in Gilman, *Jew's Body*, 172.

152. Peter F. Langman, "Including Jews in Multiculturalism," in *Readings for Diversity and Social Justice: An Anthology on Racism, Antisemitism, Sexism, Heterosexism, Ableism and Classism*, ed. Marianne Adams, Warren J. Blumenfeld, Rosie Castaneda, Heather W. Hackman, Madeline L. Peters, and Ximena Zuniga (New York: Routledge, 2000), 171.

153. Gilman, *Jew's Body*, 174.

154. Langman, "Including Jews In Multiculturalism," 171; ibid., 172.

155. Langman notes, for example, that Jews were believed to be an "alien race" that would either "not assimilate, or would intermarry and thus pollute the racial purity of America." Ibid., 171.

156. Krystyn R. Moon, "Finding *A Trip to Coontown*," *African American Review* 44, nos. 1–2, (Spring/Summer 2011): 7.

157. Bob Cole, "The Wedding of the Chinee and the Coon: Comic Song and Chorus" (New York: Howley, Haviland, c. 1897), in "Frances G. Spencer Collection of American Sheet Music," Baylor University, 5, http://digitalcollections.baylor.edu/cdm/ref/collection/fa-spnc/id/19236.

158. Greenberg, *Troubling the Waters*, 46.

159. "Ethan Michaeli, 'The Holocaust and the *Defender*: Two Generations of Jewish Reporters at a Black Newspaper,'" in "Calendar of Events," UC Santa Cruz Center for Jewish Studies, Dec. 2, 2012, http://cjs.ucsc.edu/events/ethan-michaeli-upcoming-talk/.

160. Greenberg, *Troubling the Waters*, 41. See also Eric Sundquist, *Strangers in the Land Blacks, Jews, Post-Holocaust America* (Cambridge: Harvard University Press, 2009), chpts. 1, 3, and 5.

161. Greenberg, *Troubling the Waters*, 41.

162. Rosalyn Terborg-Penn, "Survival Strategies Among African American Female Workers: A Continuing Process," in *Women, Work, and Protest: A Century of U.S. Women's Labor History*, ed. Ruth Milkman (New York: Routledge, 1985), 151.

as the last straw in the context of a history of abuse of the black community." Pyong Gap Min, in his groundbreaking study *Caught in the Middle: Korean Communities in New York and Los Angeles* (1996), explained, "When the news of Du's five-year probation was released, many Koreans considered it a victory for their community. Probably none of them suspected that a court decision favoring a Korean defendant would contribute to the victimization of Korean stores in riots five months later." Likewise, scholars who contributed to Kwam Chung Kim's edited collection *Koreans in the Hood: Conflict with African Americans* (1999), Soon Ja Du's shooting of Latasha Harlins is noted as one of the important sources of black hostility and violence toward Koreans in Los Angeles in 1991 and 1992 by Edward Chang, Keyoung Park, Inchul Choi, and Shin Kim. Although Chang, Park, and Choi understood, as did Lee, Ablemann and Lie, the importance of the media in associating a public image of black-Korean tension with Latasha Harlins, they also understood her death to be a "flash point." Eric Yamamoto cites the case as one of the very important justice grievances between Korean Americans and blacks. Angelo N. Ancheta, in *Race, Rights, and the Asian American Experience* (1998), also noted that Latasha's death and Karlin's light sentencing of Du was especially important in the targeting of Korean businesses during the rebellion. "The shooting death of black teenager Latasha Harlins by Korean store owner Soon Ja Du," Ancheta explained, "was a key incident that pre-dated the rioting against Korean stores. After Mrs. Du received a light sentence for the shooting, tensions ran even higher. The rioting . . . was seen not only as a response to the verdict in the Rodney King beating case, but as an expression of pent-up anger and resentment against Korean merchants." Lou Cannon, in his massive work, *Official Negligence: How Rodney King and the Riots Changed Los Angeles and the LAPD* (1999) dedicated two chapters to *People v. Du*, noting, "The granting of probation to Soon Ja Du ignited a fire in South Central that was fueled by decades of neglect, indifference, and injustice." Patrick D. Joyce, writing 11 years after the 1992 rebellion, in *No Fire Next Time: Black-Korean Conflicts and the Future of America's Cities*, was clear in his conclusion: the murder of Latasha by Du and Karlin's light sentence "led the city down the path to the riots." The majority of scholars of the Korean American experience have concluded that there was a vital connection between the Latasha Harlins case and Sai-i-gu, but not all are convinced. Nancy Abelmann and John Lie in *Blue Dreams: Korean Americans and the Los Angeles Riots* (1995), for example, assert that the Koreans they interviewed found no connection between Du-Karlin-Harlins and the assault on Korean shops. The authors concluded from their research that "there is no clear-cut ethnic polarization" between Koreans and blacks, that indeed the notion of a "black-Korean conflict" is not useful when analyzing the Los Angeles rebellion/riot. Both Ablemann and Lie, as well as Jennifer Lee in *Civility in the City: Blacks, Jews and Koreans in Urban America* (2002), refer to the concept of "black-Korean conflict" as "quickly popularized and exploited by the media," although Lee did concede that "frictions increased on March 16, 1991, when in the South Central district of Los Angeles, Korean storeowner Soon Ja Du shot and killed an African American teenager, Latasha Harlins, over an allegedly stolen bottle of orange juice." Lee's work is about the day-to-day relations of merchants and customers; the work does not explore conflict but rather "social order, routine and civility," examining in particular the ways in which merchants try to "manage tensions and smooth out incidents before they escalate into racially charged anger." Race, she adds however, "is never absent," and, in extreme cases, "race is mobilized in violent ways, becoming the source of protest motivations that lead to boycotts and fire-bombings." The Los Angeles riot, Lee, concluded was an example of this kind of "extreme."

Michael Omi and Howard Winant, "The Los Angeles 'Race Riot,' and Contemporary U.S. Politics," in *Reading Rodney King, Reading Urban Uprising*, ed. Robert Gooding-Williams, (New York: Routledge Press, 1993), 107; Sumi Choi, "Korean Americans vs. African Americans: Conflict and Construction," ibid, 209; Regina Freer, "Black-Korean Conflict," in *The Los Angeles Riots: Lessons for the Urban Future*, ed. Mark Baldassare (Boulder, CO: Westview Press, 1994), 188; Pyong Gap *Caught in the Middle: Korean Communities in New York and Los Angeles* (Oakland: University of California Press, 1996), 86; Edward Chang, "New Urban Crisis: Korean-African Relations," in *Koreans in the Hood: Conflict with African Americans*, ed. Kwang Chung Kim (Baltimore: Johns Hopkins University Press,1999), 39; Keyoung Park, "Use and Abuse of Race and Culture: Black-Korean Tension in America," in ibid., 60; Inchul Choi, "Contemplating Black-Korean Conflict in Chicago," in ibid., 157; and Inchol Choi and Shin Kim, "Portrait of a Community Program: The African American and Korean American Community Meditation Project," in ibid., 178; Eric Yamamoto, "Critical Race Praxis: Race Theory and Political Lawyering Practice in Post-Civil Rights America," *Michigan Law Review* 95, no. 4 (Feb. 1997): 825 n. 24; Angelo N. Ancheta, *Race, Rights, and the Asian American Experience* (New Brunswick, NJ: Rutgers University Press, 1998), 166; Lou Cannon, *Official Negligence: How Rodney King and the Riots Changed Los Angeles and the LAPD* (Boulder, CO: Westview Press, 1999), 173; and Patrick Joyce, *No Fire Next Time: Black-Korean Conflict and the Future of America's Cities* (Ithaca: Cornell University Press, 2003), 143; Nancy Ablemann and John Lie, *Blue Dream: Korean Americans and the Los Angeles Riots* (Cambridge: Harvard University Press, 1997), ch. 6, quote from 158; Jennifer Lee, *Civility in the City: Blacks, Jews, and Koreans in Urban America* (Cambridge: Harvard University Press, 2006), 1–2, including quotes. See also King-Kok Cheung, "(Mis)interpretations and (In)justice: The 1992 Los Angeles 'Riots' and 'Black-Korean Conflict,'" *MELUS* 30, no. 3 (Fall 2005):3–40.

5. "Understanding the Riot, Part 1: The Path to Fury: Chapter 5: 'At last they *see* we're not lying to them.'" *LAT*, May 11, 1992. http://articles.latimes.com/1992-05-11/news/ss-1361_1_los-angeles-police/3.

6. Mike Davis, "The Rebellion that Rocked a Superpower," *Socialist Review* (London) 152 (June 1992): 8; Omi and Winant, "The Los Angeles 'Race Riot,'" in Gooding-Williams, *Reading Rodney King*, 107; Cannon, *Official Negligence*, 72. Angela Oh quoted in Cannon, *Official Negligence*, 172.

7. Elaine Kim, "Home Is Where the 'Han' Is: A Korean American Perspective on the Los Angeles Upheaval," *Social Justice* 20, no.1/2 (Spring/Summer 1993): 1–21.

8. The poem's name means the anniversary of the death of someone important in a person's life. Ariela Pelaia, "How to Light Yahzreit (Memorial)

Candles," in "Religion and Spirituality: Judaism," About.com, http://judaism. about.com/od/judaismbasics/a/How-To-Light-Yahrzeit-Memorial-Candles. htm. Nancy Shiffrin's poem appears by courtesy of the author. "Yahrzeit," will appear in Shiffrin's upcoming collection *The Vast Unknowing* (Concord, MA: Infinity, 2013), 106–7.

9. Jesse Singal, "Key Figures: Soon Ja Du," in "The L.A. Riots: 15 Years After Rodney King," *Time*, Apr. 27, 2007, 12, http://www.time.com/time/specials/2007/ la_riot/article/0,28804,1614117_1614084_1614514,00.html.

10. Michael Meyers, Tracy Thomas, and Helene Webb, "Path of Destruction," *LAT*, May 10, 1992, 1–2, http://articles.latimes.com/1992-05-10/news/mn-2534_1_ los-angeles-county.

11. Mark L. Kean, a Democrat in the House of Representatives (Virginia), the first Korean to serve in this capacity, lived in Los Angeles in April 1992. He did not hesitate to recall Latasha's death and Karlin's sentence as major precipitating events when he chastised Marion Berry for the recent verbal attacks toward Korean entrepreneurs working in predominantly black neighborhoods in Washington, DC. See Mike DeBonis, "Lessons from Marion Barry's Anti-Asian Comments," District of DeBonis (blog), *Washington Post*, Apr. 6, 2012, http://www.washingtonpost.com/blogs/mike-debonis/post/lessons-from-marion-barrys-anti-asian-comments/2012/04/06/gIQAzS33zS_blog.html; Kwang Chung Kim and Shin Kim, "The Multiracial Nature of Los Angeles Unrest in 1992," in *Koreans in the Hood: Conflict with African Americans*, ed. Kwang Chung Kim (Baltimore: Johns Hopkins University Press, 1999), 25–6; Meyers, Thomas, and Webb, "Path of Destruction," 1–2.

12. Meyers, Thomas, and Webb, "Path of Destruction," 1–2.

13. "Charting the Hours of Chaos," in "Legacy of the Riots: 1992–2002," *LAT*, Apr. 29, 2002, 1–4, http://articles.latimes.com/2002/apr/29/local/me-replay29.

14. Ibid.

15. Rodney King and Lawrence Spagnola, *The Riot Within: My Journey from Rebellion to Redemption* (New York: HarperOne, 2012), 1–7; ibid., 9–10 quote on p. 10; ibid., 16.

16. Ibid., 9–13.

17. Ibid., 24–31; Douglas O. Linder, "Famous American Trials: Los Angeles Police Officers' (Rodney King Beating) Trials," University of Missouri, Kansas City, School of Law, 2001, under "The Arrest Record of Rodney King," http://law2.umkc. edu/faculty/projects/ftrials/lapd/lapd.html.

18. For a detailed description of the Rodney King-LAPD beating incident, see Cannon, *Official Negligence*, 20–45.

19. Linder, "Rodney King Beating Trials," under "A Trial Account."

20. Quoted in Linder "Rodney King Beating Trials," under "In Their Own Words."

21. Gretchen Voss, "Rodney King's Daughters: The World Watched as Their Father Was Beaten," *Glamour*, Mar. 21, 2012, 1–4, http://www.glamour.com/magazine/2011/02/rodney-kings-daughters-the-world-watched-as-their-father-was-beaten.

22. Linder, "Rodney King Beating Trials," under "Police Reports."

23. "Hate-Motivated Violence: The Rodney King Case and Possible Implications for Canada," the Nizkor Project, 1991–2011, http://www.nizkor.org/hweb/orgs/canadian/canada/justice/hate-motivated-violence/hmv-006-00.html.

24. Ibid.

25. Linder, "Rodney King Beating Trials," under "A Trial Account," under "Chronology."

26. Bradley quoted in Richard Pearson, "Tom Bradley Dies at 80," *Washington Post*, Sept. 30, 1998, B6. President Bush quoted in Christopher Reed, "A Vicious Assault on a Black Motorist by a Group of White Los Angeles Policemen has Turned into a National Issue," *Guardian*, Mar. 22, 2012, http://www.guardian.co.uk./2012/mar/22/archive-1991-president-bush-sickened-rodney-king.

27. Quoted in Linder, "Rodney King Beating Trials," under "In Their Own Words." Despite Chief Daryl Gates's sense that the LAPD did not typically use excessive force, the Christopher Commission found that the use of excessive force, particularly when handling racial minorities, was a systemic problem in the LAPD. *Report of the Independent Commission of the Los Angeles Police Department* (Los Angeles: Independent Commission of the LAPD, 1991), xii.

28. See detailed discussion of the criminal trial regarding the LAPD beating of Rodney King in Cannon, *Official Negligence*, 174–262.

29. King and Spagnola, *Riot Within*, 90–1.

30. "Hate-Motivated Violence."

31. King and Spagnola, *Riot Within*, 102.

32. Ibid., 97.

33. Ibid., 104.

34. Quoted in Tracey L. Meares, "Exploring Departures Based on the Victim's Wrongful Conduct: *U.S. v. Koon*," *Federal Sentencing Reporter* 7, no. 4, Criminal Law Defenses at Sentencing (Jan.-Feb. 1995): 201–2.

35. Linder, "Rodney King Beating Trials," under "A Trial Account"; Meares, "Exploring Departures," 201–4, 213.

36. King and Spagnola, *Riot Within*, 119, 121, 125.

37. George J. Sanchez, "Face the Nation: Race, Immigration, and the Rise of Nativism in Late Twentieth Century America," in "Immigrant Adaptation and Native-Born Responses in the Making of Americans," special issue, *International Migration Review* 31 no. 4 (Winter 1997): 1010–1. Sanchez argues that indeed the Los Angeles uprising of 1992 manifest itself first as a racialized nativist event, in which mostly immigrants were targets of robbery and assault.

38. Ibid.

39. Sarah Ardalani, Thomas Suh Lauder, Maloy Moore, and Ken Schwencke, "The Los Angeles Riots: 20 Years Later, Death During the Riots," *LAT*, Apr. 25, 2012, http://spreadsheets.latimes.com/la-riots-deaths/.

40. Regarding the multiracial attributes of the rebellion/riot, see Kim and Kim, "Multiracial Nature," 17–36.

41. Joan Petersilia and Alan Abrahamse, "A Profile of Those Arrested," in Baldassare, *Los Angeles Riots*, 140–3.

42. Given Place Media, "Racial/Ethnic Composition: Los Angeles County, 1990–2010 Census," *Los Angeles Almanac*, 2012, http://www.laalmanac.com/population/po13.htm. The 1990 Census did not allow persons to identify with more than one race.

43. Albert Bergensen and Max Herman, "Immigration, Race, and Riot: The 1992 Los Angeles Uprising," *American Sociological Review* 63, no. 1 (Feb. 1998): 43; For statistics on percentage of Latinos/as living in Koreatown in 1990, see Abelman and Lie, *Blue Dreams*, 105.

44. Bergensen and Herman, "Immigration, Race, and Riot," 51.

45. Ibid.; Paul Watts, "Revisiting the 1992 Los Angeles Riots: An Analysis of Geographic Perspectives" (master's thesis, Louisiana State University, 2003), 32–3.

46. Latinos is a broad category that includes Mexican, Mexican American, and Central American persons (principally from Mexico, Honduras, Guatemala, El Salvador, Nicaragua, and Costa Rica). Scholars have been careful to underscore the class differences in those who participated in the rebellion. For blacks, as well as Latinos, most of those arrested (our only clear indication of participants) were working poor or unemployed. Mexican Americans typically had greater access to wealth, education, health care, housing, and political participation than newer immigrants from Mexico or other parts of Central America. Of the 3,500 Latinos/as arrested during the rebellion 1,200 were undocumented.

47. Lawrence Bobo, Camille L. Zubrinsky, James H. Johnson Jr., and Melvin L. Oliver, "Public Opinion Before and After a Spring of Discontent," in Baldassare, *Los Angeles Riots*, 121.

48. Ibid., 121–4; Melvin Oliver, James H. Johnson Jr., and Walter C. Farrell Jr., "Anatomy of a Rebellion: A Political-Economic Analysis," in Gooding-Williams, *Reading Rodney King*, 118–22, 131–2, and 140 n. 34 where the authors discuss the findings from a Spanish-speaking focus group interviewed soon after the uprising. These findings underscore the complaints of Spanish-speaking Angelenos regarding their interactions with Korean shopkeepers, landlords, and employers.

49. Min, *Caught in the Middle*, 89–91. Min also discusses the differences in motives of African Americans and Latino/as. See ibid., 91.

50. Regina Marie Freer, "From Conflict to Convergence: Interracial Relations in the Liquor Store Controversy in South Central Los Angeles" (PhD diss., University of Michigan, 1999), 88.

51. Some discussion of the appropriate title for events of April 29 through May 4, 1992 can be found at Watts, "Revisiting the 1992 Los Angeles Riots," 4; James H. Johnson, Cloyzelle K. Jones, Walter Farrell, Melvin Oliver, "The Los Angeles Rebellion, 1992: A Preliminary Assessment From Ground Zero," (working paper, UCLA Center for the Study of Urban Poverty, Los Angeles, CA, 1992), iii; A. T. Callincoes, "Meaning of Los Angeles Riots," *Economic and Political Weekly* 27, no. 30 (July 25, 1992): 1603–6.

52. See, for example, Roger Daniels, *Coming to America*, 2nd ed. (New York: Harper Perennial, 2002), 265–84; Susan Olzak, "Labor Unrest, Immigration, and Ethnic Conflict in Urban America, 1880–1914," *American Journal of Sociology* 94, no. 6 (May 1989): 1303–33; Wallace S. Hutcheon Jr., "The Louisville Riots of August, 1855," *Register of the Kentucky Historical Society* 69 (1971): 150–72; "Riot on Ward's Island: Terrific Battle Between German and Irish Immigrants," *New York Times*, Mar. 6, 1868, http://query.nytimes.com/gst/abstract.html?res=F00E10F73D541B749 3C4A91788D85F4C8684F9; Russell S. Gilmore, "Orange Riots" in *The Encyclopedia of New York City*, ed. Kenneth T. Jackson (New Haven: Yale University Press, 1995), 866; "Riot in Buffalo: Strike of Irish and German Stevedores, the Police Force

Overpowered Final Arrest of the Ringleaders," *New York Times*, Aug.13, 1862, http://www.nytimes.com/1862/08/13/news/riot-buffalo-strike-irish-german-stevedores-police-force-overpowered-final.html; Richard Gambino, *Vendetta: The True Story of the Largest Lynching In U.S. History* (Toronto: Doubleday, 1977); Priscilla Long, "White and Indian Hop Pickers Attack Chinese in Squak (Issaquah) on September 7, 1885," Free Online Encyclopedia of Washington State History, July 1, 2000, http://www.historylink.org/index.cfm?DisplayPage=output.cfm&File_Id=2746; Robert C. Kennedy, "On This Day: On March 27, 1886, Harper's Weekly Featured a Cartoon About Anti-Chinese Violence," *New York Times*, Mar. 27, 2001, http://www.nytimes.com/learning/general/onthisday/harp/0327.html; Sucheng Chan, *Asian Americans: An Interpretive History* (New York: Twayne, 1991), 48–54; Benjamin Madley, "California's Yuki Indians: Defining Genocide in American Indian History," *Western Historical Quarterly* 39, no. 3 (Aug. 2008): 303–32.

53. Quoted in Vincent P. Franklin, "The Philadelphia Race Riot of 1918," *Pennsylvania Magazine of History and Biography* 99, no. 3 (July 1975): 338.

54. Firsthand accounts are found at "A Thrilling Narrative From the Lips of the Sufferers of the Late Detroit Riot, Mar. 6, 1863, with the Hair breadth Escapes of Men, Women and Children, and Destruction of Colored Men's Property, Not Less Than $15,000" (electronic edition) in "Documenting the American South," Apex Data Services, Academic Affairs Library, University of North Carolina, Chapel Hill, 2001 (first published in Detroit, MI, by the author, 1863), http://docsouth.unc.edu/neh/detroit/detroit.html.

55. Martha Gruening, "Houston: An N.A.A.C.P. Investigation," *Crisis* 15 (Nov. 1917), 14–9, quote from 15.

56. Robert V. Haynes, "Houston Riot of 1917," in *Handbook of Texas Online*, Texas State Historical Association, http://www.tshaonline.org/handbook/online/articles/jch04; Robert V. Haynes, "The Houston Mutiny and Riot of 1917," *Southwestern Historical Quarterly* 76, no. 4 (Apr. 1973): 418–39; Edgar A. Schuler, "The Houston Race Riot, 1917," *Journal of Negro History* 29, no. 3 (July 1944): 300–38.

57. "Indict 17 Negro Rioters: Grand Jury Begins Work in Chicago—10,000 on Guard," *New York Times*, Aug. 5, 1919; Walter White, "N.A.A.C.P.—Chicago and Its Eight Reasons," *Crisis* 18 (October 1919): 293–7; "A Crowd of Howling Negroes," *Chicago Daily Tribune*, July 28, 1919; "28 Dead, 500 Hurt In Three-Day Race Riots in Chicago," *New York Times*, July 30, 1919.

58. Nicole A. Plummer, "Harlem Riots of 1935," in *Encyclopedia of African American History, 1896 to the Present: From the Age of Segregation to the Twenty-first Century*, vol. 1, ed. Paul Finkleman (New York: Oxford University Press, 2009), 375–7; Jay Maeder, "Race War: March-April 1935, Chapter 109," *New York Daily News*, June 11, 2000, http://articles.nydailynews.com.

59. Dalea Bean, "Harlem Riot of 1964," in Finkleman, *Encyclopedia of African American History*, 377–8.

60. Daniel J. Monti, "Patterns of Conflict Preceding the 1964 Riots: Harlem and Bedford-Stuyvesant," *Journal of Conflict Resolution* 23, no. 1 (Mar. 1979): 51.

61. Anthony Oberschall, "The Los Angeles Riot of August 1965," *Social Problems* 15, no. 3 (Winter 1968): 333–4. Oberschall notes that "The Frye arrest on the evening of August 11 provided a spark which ignited the accumulated frustrations of the South Los Angeles population." Ibid., 333.

62. Paul Watts, "Revisiting the 1992 Los Angeles Riots," 8.

63. Valerie Reitman and Mitchell Landsberg, "Watts Riots, 40 Years Later," *LAT*, Aug. 11, 2005. See also the McCone Commission, "Violence in the City: An End or a Beginning," University of Southern California, n.d., especially under "144 Hours in August 1965," http://www.usc.edu/libraries/archives/cityinstress/mccone/contents.html.

64. Anthony Daniel Perez, Kimberly M. Berg, and Daniel J. Myers, "Police and Riots, 1967–1969," *Journal of Black Studies* 34, no. 2 (Nov. 2003): 167; Kelsey Finch, "Trouble in Paradise: Postwar History of San Francisco's Hunters Point Neighborhood" (unpublished honors thesis, Stanford University, 2008), 48.

65. Perez, Berg, and. Myers, "Police and Riots," 167; Jasmine Sydullah, "A Point of Resistance: The Hunter's Point Uprising of 1966," *Poor*, June 25, 2010, http://www.poormagazine.org/node/2875.

66. Quoted in Sydullah, "A Point of Resistance."

67. Perez, Berg and Myers, "Police and Riots," 168-9.

68. Quote and discussion found in Robert E. Kapsis, "Deliquency and Riot Patterns in Black Residential Areas," *Social Problems* 23, no. 5 (June 1976): 571.

69. Gladys Knight, "Miami (Florida) Riot of 1982," 418–20, and Gladys Knight, "Miami (Florida) Riot of 1980," 414–8, both in *Encyclopedia of American Race Riots*, vol. 1, ed. Walter Rucker and James N. Upton (Westport, CT: Greenwood Press, 2006).

70. In 1976, the Tampa police shot and killed unarmed 19-year-old Martin Chambers. In 1987, the Tampa police killed, via choke hold, Melvin Eugene Hair, who was mentally incapacitated. Nicole Hutcheson, "40 Years of Seeking Justice," *Tampa Bay Times* (South Pinellas edition), July 26, 2007; Jeffrey Good and David Plott, "Disturbance Sears East Tampa," *Tampa Bay Times*, Feb. 20, 1987.

71. Two Newark policemen arrested John Weerd Smith, a taxi driver, beating him gravely during the arrest. Max Herman, "Ethnic Succession and Urban Unrest in Newark and Detroit During the Summer of 1967" (Newark: Cornwall Center Publication Series, 2002), 2.

72. Riots broke out in York, Pennsylvania related to concerns that black youth and women were being brutalized by members of white gangs. Seventeen-year-old Taka Nii Sweeney was shot; so too was Lillie May Allen. Allen, who was from Aiken, South Carolina, was visiting her sister. She jumped out of a stalled car to ask the armed white gang members not to shoot at the car, but instead they shot more than 100 rounds into the car, killing Allen. After the first two incidents, and before gangs killed Allen, a white policeman, Henry C. Schaad, was killed by a black protestor. "1969 York Riots: The Murders of Lillie Allen and Henry C. Schaad," *York Daily Record/York Sunday News*, Feb. 12, 2010, http://www.ydr.com/blackhistory/ci_14392482.

73. A three-day race riot occurred in Crown Heights (Brooklyn), New York in August 1991. Jeffrey Goldberg, "The Hard Truth About the Crown Heights Riots," *Atlantic*, August 11, 2011, http://www.theatlantic.com/national/archive/2011/08/the-hard-truth-about-the-crown-heights-riots/243448/; Andy Soltis, "Furor over Sharpton Speaking at Crown Heights Riot-Anniversary Forum," *New York Post*, Aug. 18, 2011, http://www.nypost.com/p/news/local/crown_hts_fury_38tR1JfphLH4X9An8W8VYL. For a detailed analysis of this riot and its

aftermath, see Edward Shapiro, *Crown Heights: Blacks, Jews and the 1991 Brooklyn Riot* (Lebanon, NH: Brandeis University Press, 2006).

74. A race riot began in St. Petersburg, Florida on October 24, 1996, after the death of 18-year-old Tyrone Lewis, an African American male, whom local police pulled over because they suspected him of car theft (although the car was not stolen). Officer James Knight shot and killed unarmed Lewis. "Riot Erupts in St. Petersburg, Florida, after White Cop Shoots and Kills Black Motorist," *Jet*, Nov. 11, 1996, http://findarticles.com/p/articles/mi_m1355/is_n26_v90/ai_18851764/.

75. A four-day riot occurred in Cincinnati, Ohio (the largest since the 1992 Los Angeles rebellion) when white police officer Steven Roach shot and killed 19-year-old, African American Timothy Thomas during an on-foot pursuit on April 17, 2001. Thomas was not armed. John Larson, "Behind the Death of Timothy Thomas Shooting of 19-year-old Brings to Light Pattern of Ticketing that Raises Questions of Racial Profiling," *Dateline NBC*, Apr. 10, 2004, http://www.msnbc.msn.com/id/4703574/ns/dateline_nbc-dateline_specials/t/behind-death-timothy-thomas/#.T631WphuBFI. Thomas was only one of 15 black males killed at the hands of the Cincinnati police between 1995 and 2001; Paul Gottbrath, "Suit Kicks Off Battle over Racial Profiling," *Cincinnati Post* (online edition), Mar. 14, 2001, http://web.archive.org/web/20061020200910/http://www.cincypost.com/2001/mar/14/suit031401.html.

76. A two-day riot occurred in Benton Harbor, Michigan, after Terrance Shurn, who was being chased by a police officer, crashed his motorcycle and died. Shurn was African American and the police officer was biracial. "Racist Cop Brutality Sparks Outrage in Michigan Town," *Militant* 67, no. 23 (July 7, 2003), http://www.themilitant.com/2003/6723/index.shtml; Jerry Goldberg, "Why Benton Harbor Exploded," *Worker's World*, July 3, 2003, http://www.hartford-hwp.com/archives/45a/556.html.

77. Two riots occurred in Oakland, California, concerning the shooting and death of African American Oscar Grant. One riot occurred soon after the shooting. Another occurred when BART police officer Johannes Mehserle was found guilty of involuntary manslaughter, rather than second-degree murder or voluntary manslaughter in the death of Oscar Grant. Mehserle shot and killed unarmed, 22-year-old Oscar Grant in the back while he was seated on the ground on January 1, 2009. Grant's death was videotaped by several onlookers. "Mehserle Verdict Protest Turns Ugly; 78 People Arrested," KTUV.com, Aug. 26, 2010; http://www.ktvu.com/news/news/mehserle-verdict-protest-turns-ugly-78-people-arre/nK5Km/; Philip Matier and Andrew Ross, "BART 'N-word' Bombshell Waiting to Go Off," *San Francisco Chronicle*, June 29, 2009, http://www.sfgate.com/cgi-bin/article.cgi?f=/c/a/2009/06/28/BA4E18EMPH.DTL&tsp; Demian Bulwa, "Grant Took Picture of Mehserle, Prosecutor Says," *San Francisco Chronicle*, June 10, 2010, http://www.sfgate.com/cgi-bin/article.cgi?f=/c/a/2010/06/09/BAD21DSRGI.DTL; "Over 150 Arrested in California Race Riot After Minimal Jail Sentence Given to White Officer Who Killed Unarmed Black Man," *Mail Online*, November 6, 2010, http://www.dailymail.co.uk/news/article-1327214/Johannes-Mehserle-riots-Over-150-arrested-California-sentencing-white-officer-killed-unarmed-black-man-Oscar-Grant.html.

78. Denise Harlins, in discussion with the author, Nov. 17, 1993.

79. Mark Oliver, "Judge Karlin's Reelection (Opinion)," *LAT*, June 14, 1992, http://articles.latimes.com/1992-06-14/opinion/op-1035_1_judge-karlin-s-reelection-latasha-harlins-black-life.

80. "Charting the Hours of Chaos," *LAT*, Apr. 29, 2002, in *Los Angeles Fire Department Historical Archive*, http://www.lafire.com/famous_fires/1992-0429_LA-Riots/LATimes-2002-0429-0501/2002-0429_latimes_ChartingTheHoursofChaos.htm.

81. Bob Sipchen, "Fueled by the Flames: Revolutionary Communist Party Sees L.A. Riots as an Opening to be Seized," *LAT*, Sept. 11, 1992, http://articles.latimes.com/1992-09-11/local/me-154_1_revolutionary-communist-party.

82. Watts, "Revisiting the 1992 Los Angeles Riots," 16; Sanchez, "Face the Nation," 1010.

83. "Charting the Hours of Chaos," in "Legacy of the Riots, 1992–2002," *LAT*, Apr. 29, 2002, http://articles.latimes.com/2002/apr/29/local/me-replay29.

84. Quote in David Whitman, "The Untold Story of the LA Riot," *U.S. News and World Report*, May 23, 1993, http://222.usnews.com/usnews/news/articles/930531/archive_015229_4.htm.

85. Patrick Joyce, *No Fire Next Time: Black-Korean Conflicts and the Future of America's Cities* (Ithaca: Cornell University Press, 2003), 149.

86. Quoted in Cannon, *Official Negligence,* 261.

87. Sanchez, "Face the Nation," 1010–1.

88. Ibid., 1011.

89. Ibid.; Whitman, "Untold Story of t he L.A. Riot."

90. Quoted in Sanchez, "Face the Nation," 1011.

91. Elaine Woo, "Asian Identity Crisis Fades to Worries of Everyday Life," *LAT*, Apr. 28, 2012, http://articles.latimes.com/2012/apr/28/local/la-me-riot-four-voices-woo-20120428.

92. Whitman, "Untold Story of the L.A. Riots."

93. William, "From Oppressor to Partner," *LAT*, Apr., 22, 2012, http://www.latimes.com/news/local/la-riotstories-shello,4690087.html story#story_68.

94. Eugene Yi, "L.A. Riots in Our Own Words," *KoreAm*, Apr. 2012, http://iamkoream.com/april-issue-la-riots-in-our-own-words/.

95. Robert Greene, "Forgotten Flashpoint: A Week After Rodney King," *LAT*, Apr. 27, 2012, http://www.articles.latimes.com/2012/apr/27/news/la-ol-riot-latasha-harlins-20120421.

96. Las Vegas: Dirk Johnson, "After the Riots, Mob Violence Continues in Las Vegas," *New York Times*, May 19, 1992, http://www.nytimes.com/1992/05/19/us/after-the-riots-mob-violence-continues-in-las-vegas.html. Oakland: "L.A. Riots," *South Central History*, n.d., http://www.southcentralhistory.com/la-riots.php. San Francisco: Paul Fusco, "USA. San Francisco, CA. Rodney King Riot Arrests," Magnum Photos, http://www.magnumphotos.com/Catalogue/Paul-Fusco/1992/USA-San-Francisco-CA-Rodney-King-riots-arrests-NN19627.html. Seattle: Sally MacDonald, "Family Shop that Survived War and Fire Rises from Ashes of Riots, *Seattle Times*, Mar. 1, 1993 http://community.seattletimes.nwsource.com/archive/?date=19930301&slug=1688184; "Rice Best Candidate in Race for

Governor," *Seattle Times*, Aug. 25, 1996, http://community.seattletimes.nwsource.
com/archive/?date=19960825&slug=2345756. Pittsburgh: George Church, "The
Fire This Time," *Time*, June 24, 2001, http://www.time.com/time/magazine/ar-
ticle/0,9171,1101920511-159620,00.html. Tampa and Washington, DC: Meyers,
Thomas, and Webb, "Path of Destruction." Atlanta: Church, "Fire This Time."
New York City: Min, *Caught in the Middle*, 93–4;Toronto: Shawn Micallaef,
"1992 Yonge Street Riots," *Spacing Toronto*," Jan. 13, 2009, http://spacingtoronto.
ca/2009/01/13/1992-yonge-street-riot/.

97. "Charting the Hours of Chaos," under "Wednesday, Apr. 29, 1992," and
"Thursday, Apr. 30, 1992."

98. Quote from Hyung Ko, in Yi, "L.A. Riots in Our Own Words," under
"I. Protect Our Town."

99. Figures from Joyce, *No Fire Next Time*, 149–50.

100. Freer, "From Conflict to Convergence," 88.

101. South Central had the most physical and monetary damage due to the
riots/uprising; since most of this damage and loss was sustained by Korean shopkeepers in Los Angeles, they were more affected than actual shopkeepers in Koreatown. Joyce, *No Fire Next Time*, 150; Min, *Caught in the Middle*, 91.

102. Yi, "L.A. Riots in Our Own Words." The following paragraphs rely heavily
on Yi, "L.A. Riots in Our Own Words."

103. Ibid.

104. All quotes from ibid.

105. All quotes from ibid.

106. Ibid.

107. Ibid.

108. Jay Kim, "Opinion," *Korea Times*, Sept. 30, 2010, http://www.koreatimes.
co.kr/www/news/opinon/2012/05/306_73767.html.

109. Yi, "L.A. Riots in Our Own Words."

110. "Charting the Hours of Chaos."

111. Yi, "L.A. Riots in Our Own Words."

112. Ibid.

113. Ibid.

114. Zev Yaroslavsky Comments, in "Why History Matters: The 20th Anniversary of the Los Angeles Riots," Symposium of the Autry National Center and the
Department of History, UCLA, June 6, 2012.

115. William Webster and Hubert Webster, *The City in Crisis: A Report by the
Special Advisor to the Board of Police Commissioners on the Civil Disorder in Los
Angeles, October 21, 1992* (Los Angeles: Office of the Special Advisor to the Board of
Police Commissioners, 1992), 1; Cannon, *Official Negligence*, 265.

116. Paige Brettingen, "L.A. Riots: 20 Years Later, Still Trying to Heal," *Neon
Tommy* (online publication for the Annenberg School of Communication & Journal-
ism, USC Annenberg), Apr. 24, 2012, http:///www.neontommy.com/news/2012/04/
la-riots-20-years-later-still-trying-heal.

117. The header is a reference to the late black poet Gil Scot Heron's song, "The
Revolution Will Not Be Televised," Internet Archives, Mar. 10, 2001, http://archive.
org/details/TheRevolutionWillNotBeTelevised.

118. Min, *Caught in the Middle,* 90.

119. Adrian Glick Kudler, "Mapping the LA Riots From Rodney King to Koreatown," *Curbed Los Angeles,* Apr. 30, 2012, http://la.curbed.com/archives/2012/04/mapping_the_la_riots_from_rodney_king_to_koreatown.php.

120. Yi, "L.A. Riots in Our Own Words."

121. Ibid.

122. Ibid.

123. Dominique DiPrima and Jasmyne Cannick, "The Front Page Radio Show Transcript," KJLH-FM, Apr. 26, 2012, http://www.eurweb.com/2012/04/the-state-of-korean-and-black-relations-post-latasha-harlins-and-the-92-civil-unrest/.

124. Yi, "L.A. Riots in Our Own Words."

125. Ibid.

126. Quoted in Seth Mydans, "Riot in Los Angeles: Pocket of Tension; A Target of Rioters, Koreatown is Bitter, Armed and Determined," *New York Times,* May 3, 1992, http://www.nytimes.com/1992/05/03/us/riot-los-angles-pocket-tension-target-rioters-koreatown-bitter-armed-determined.html?pagewanted=all.

127. Quoted in Ashley Dunn, "King Case Aftermath: A City in Crisis," *LAT,* May 2, 1992, http://articles.latimes.com/1992-05-02/news/mn-1281_1_police-car.

128. Kim, "Opinion."

129. Quoted in Dunn, "King Case Aftermath: A City in Crisis," *LAT,* May 2, 1992.

130. See, for example, Ervin Staub, "The Psychology of Perpetrators and Bystanders," *Political Psychology* 6, no. 1 (Mar. 1985): 61–85, in which the author argues that "one way to subvert such feeling [responsibility for the life and welfare of others] is to exclude certain people from the realm of humanity, to define them on various bases as subhuman, or as representing danger to oneself, to one's way of life and values. At the extreme, a complete reversal of morality may take place, so that the murder of some human beings becomes what's morally good, a service to humanity." Ibid., 77.

131. Yi, "L.A. Riots in Our Own Words."

132. Quoted in Dennis Romero, "L.A. Riots: LAPD Tried to Displace its Racism Problem and 'Put it On a Korean Merchant,'" *Los Angeles Weekly,* Apr. 26, 2012, http://blogs.laweekly.com/informer/2012/04/la_riots_korean_los_angeles_times_john_lee.php?.

133. Kapson Yim Lee, "15 Years After LA Riots (Opinion)," *Korea Times,* Apr. 27, 2007, http://www.koreatimes.co.kr/www/news/opinon/2012/05/197_1938.html.

134. Yi, "L.A. Riots in Our Own Words."

135. Korean female, Los Angeles, woman, interviewed by Michelle Jun, Nov. 20, 1997, Los Angeles, CA (transcript in author's possession).

136. Hyun Chung, "Remembering the Riots," *LAT,* Apr. 29, 2012, http://www.latimes.com/news/local/la-riotstories-shell,0,4690087.htmlstory#story_74.

137. Ibid.

138. Quoted in Mydans, "Pocket of Tension."

139. Quoted in ibid.

140. Kim, "Opinion."

141. "Charting the Hours of Chaos."

142. Quoted in Catherine Green, "L.A. Riots: Rev. Cecil Murray Sees Progress in Inclusive Society," *Neon Tommy*, Apr. 24, 2012, http://www.neontommy.com/news/2012/04/la-riots-rev-cecil-murray-sees-progress-inclusive-society.

143. Quoted in Cannon, *Official Negligence*, 253.

144. Quoted in Brettingen, "20 Years Later."

145. Quoted in Green, "Rev. Cecil Murray Sees Progress."

146. Yaroslavsky, "Why History Matters."

147. "Charting the Hours of Chaos."

148. Roy Hong, in Yi, "L.A. Riots in Our Own Words," under "II. Rallying Together."

149. Min, *Caught in the Middle*, 155.

EPILOGUE

1. Rodney King received $3.8 million for being beaten, more than 10 times what Latasha's heirs received after she was murdered. Andrea Ford, "Settlement Awarded to Harlins' Siblings but Not Father," *LAT*, July 29, 1992, http://articles.latimes.com/1992-07-29/local/me-4609 1 latasha-harlins.

2. Elston Carr, "'Chaos' at Shuttered Store, Residents Say," *LAT*, May 23, 1993, http://articles.latimes.com/1993-05-23/news/ci-39030_1_area-residents.

3. Ron-Gong Lin II, "Request Stirs Memories of Time of Rage," *LAT*, Jan. 28, 2005, http://articles.latimes.com/2005/jan/28/local/me-liquor28.

4. See chapter 7 for a discussion of the Houston race riot/massacre; James S. Hirsch, *Riot and Remembrance: The Tulsa Race War and Its Legacy* (Boston: Houghton Mifflin, 2002); Thomas R. Dye, "Rosewood, Florida: The Destruction of an African American Community," *The Historian* 58, no. 3 (Spring 1996): 605–22; Eduardo O. Pagan, *Murder at the Sleepy Lagoon: Zoot Suits, Race, and Riot in Wartime L.A.* (Chapel Hill: University of North Carolina Press, 2006); Scott Zesch, "Chinese Los Angeles in 1870–1871: The Makings of a Massacre," *Southern California Quarterly*, 90 (Summer 2008): 109–58; Craig Storti, *The Incident at Bitter Creek: The Story of the Rock Springs Chinese Massacre* (Ames: Iowa State University Press, 1990); Edward Shapiro, *Crown Heights: Blacks, Jews and the 1991 Brooklyn Riot* (Lebanon, NH: Brandeis University Press, 2006).

5. Steven Luo, "Judge Orders Mehserle's Release from Jail," *California Beat*, June 10, 2011, http://www.californiabeat.org/2011/06/10/news-alert-judge-orders-mehserles-release-from-jail.

6. "More Evidence to Be Released in Trayvon Martin Case, Judge Rules," *CNN Justice*, June 13, 2012, http://articles.cnn.com/2012-06-13/justice/justice_florida-teen-shooting_1_judge-rules-law-enforcement-witnesses?_s=PM:JUSTICE.

7. Ken Ellingwood and K. Connie Kang, "A Student, a Shopkeeper and a Moment of Tragedy," *LAT*, Nov. 23, 1996, http://articles.latimes.com/1996-11-23/news/mn-2089_1_franklin-high-school.

8. "Friends Mourn Slain Girl," *Los Angeles Daily News*, Nov. 23, 1996, http://www.thefreelibrary.com/FRIENDS+MOURN+SLAIN+GIRL.a084033167.

9. Maki Becker and Abigail Goldman, "Grocer Pleads Not Guilty in Slaying," *LAT*, Nov. 26, 1996, http://articles.latimes.com/1996-11-26/local/me-3189_1_grocer-pleads.

10. Eric Malnic, "Lawyer Mentions 2 Possible Defense Plans for Grocer," *LAT*, Dec. 5, 1996, http://articles.latimes.com/1996-12-05/local/me-5889_1_defense-attorney.

11. Maria Hughes quoted in Jeanette DeSantis, "Girl's Family Drowning in Pain: Youngest Remembered for High Spirits, Big Plans," *Los Angeles Daily News*, Nov. 24, 1996, http://www.thefreelibrary.com/GIRL'S+FAMILY+DROWNING+IN +PAIN+YOU. . . 11/17/2010.

12. Quotes taken from James Rainey, "Slain Teenager's Funeral Brings a Call for Peace," *LAT*, Nov. 30, 1996, http://articles.latimes.com/1996-11-30/local/me-4362_1_franklin-high-school.

13. Willie Benavides quoted in Becker and Goldman, "Grocer Pleads Not Guilty in Slaying."

14. Richard Alatorre quoted in Gordon, "Friends Mourn Slain Girl."

15. "Grocer Ordered Tried in Slaying of Girl 17," *LAT*, Mar. 13, 1997.

16. Greg Krikorian, "Guilty Plea Entered by Grocer in Girl's Death," *LAT*, Aug. 5, 1997, http://articles.latimes.com/1997/aug/05/local/me-19659.

17. Denise Harlins quoted in "Of Riots and Rebellions," *Vibe*, Apr., 2002, 124–5.

Index